Praise for *Regulating Emotions*

"Interdisciplinarity is a concept often claimed in scientific research but rarely fulfilled. This excellent volume shows that an interdisciplinary approach enriches each discipline's understanding of how emotions and their expressions are controlled on a bio-psychological as well a socio-cultural level." *Sighard Neckel, University of Vienna*

"Emotional regulation is ubiquitous, pervasive and elemental involving biological, psychological, cultural and behavioural processes. It is fundamental for individual and collective life. *Regulating Emotions* is an invaluable guide—comprehensive, profound and highly original." *Jack Barbalet, University of Leicester*

"This is a state-of-the-art book on how social and cultural processes can be utilized to regulate the most basic biological and psychological aspects of human emotion. Its multidisciplinary perspective is unique and should be of great interest to anyone interested in how human emotions become regulated or dysregulated." *Douglas Hollan, UCLA*

"An exciting state-of-the-art book, interdisciplinary in its scope, informative and challenging in its contributions, and at the heart of conceptual construction fitting together the building blocks of emotion regulation and its significance for human well-being. Working my way through this intriguing reader gave me stimulating insights into how culture and social necessities may co-construct emotion regulation—and dysregulation." *Manfred Holodynski, University of Münster*

New Perspectives in Cognitive Psychology

New Perspectives in Cognitive Psychology is a series of works that explore the latest research, current issues, and hot topics in cognitive psychology. With a balance of research, applications, and theoretical interpretations, each book will educate and ignite research and ideas on important topics.

Memory and Emotion: Interdisciplinary Perspectives
Edited by Bob Uttl, Nobuo Ohta, and Amy L. Siegenthaler

Involuntary Memory
Edited by John H. Mace

Regulating Emotions: Culture, Social Necessity, and Biological Inheritance
Edited by Marie Vandekerckhove, Christian von Scheve, Sven Ismer, Susanne Jung, and Stefanie Kronast

REGULATING EMOTIONS

Culture, Social Necessity, and Biological Inheritance

EDITED BY **Marie Vandekerckhove**
Christian von Scheve
Sven Ismer
Susanne Jung
Stefanie Kronast

Blackwell
Publishing

BLACKWELL PUBLISHING
350 Main Street, Malden, MA 02148-5020, USA
9600 Garsington Road, Oxford OX4 2DQ, UK
550 Swanston Street, Carlton, Victoria 3053, Australia

The right of Marie Vandekerckhove, Christian von Scheve, Sven Ismer, Susanne Jung, and Stefanie Kronast to be identified as the Authors of the Editorial Material in this Work has been asserted in accordance with the UK Copyright, Designs, and Patents Act 1988.

First published 2008 by Blackwell Publishing Ltd

1   2008

Library of Congress Cataloging-in-Publication Data

Regulating emotions : culture, social necessity, and biological inheritance / edited by Marie Vandekerckhove . . . [et al.].
     p.   cm. — (New perspectives in cognitive psychology; 3)
   Includes bibliographical references and index.
   ISBN 978-1-4051-5863-3 (hardcover : alk. paper)
   1. Emotions. I. Vandekerckhove, Marie.

   BF531.R445 2008
   152.4—dc22
                          2007030478

A catalogue record for this title is available from the British Library.

Set in Univers and 10/12.5 pt Sabon
by The Running Head Limited, Cambridge, www.therunninghead.com
Printed and bound in Singapore
by Fabulous Printers Pte Ltd

The publisher's policy is to use permanent paper from mills that operate a sustainable forestry policy, and which has been manufactured from pulp processed using acid-free and elementary chlorine-free practices. Furthermore, the publisher ensures that the text paper and cover board used have met acceptable environmental accreditation standards.

For further information on
Blackwell Publishing, visit our website:
www.blackwellpublishing.com

CONTENTS

NOTES ON EDITORS AND CONTRIBUTORS

Charlotte Bloch, Department of Sociology, University of Copenhagen, Denmark

Silvia A. Bunge, Department of Psychology and Helen Wills Neuorscience Institute, University of California, Berkeley, USA

David S. Chun, Department of Psychology, University of California, Davis, USA

Pamela M. Cole, Department of Psychology, Pennsylvania State University, USA

Tracy A. Dennis, Department of Psychology, Hunter College, City University of New York, USA

Nancy Eisenberg, Department of Psychology, Arizona State University, Tempe, USA

Leslie Greenberg, Department of Psychology, York University, Toronto, Canada

James J. Gross, Department of Psychology, Stanford University, USA

Sarah E. Hall, Department of Psychology, Pennsylvania State University, USA

Claire Hofer, Department of Psychology, Arizona State University, Tempe, USA

Sven Ismer, Department of Movement Science, University of Hamburg, Germany

Susanne Jung, independent consultant

Arvid Kappas, School of Humanities and Social Sciences, Jacobs University Bremen, Germany

Stefanie Kronast, independent consultant

Sarah E. Martin, Department of Psychiatry and Human Behavior, E. P. Bradley Hospital, Warren Alpert Medical School of Brown University, USA

Iris B. Mauss, Department of Psychology, University of Denver, USA

Mario Mikulincer, School of Psychology, Interdisciplinary Center, Herzliya, Israel

Aurore Neumann, Department of Psychology, Catholic University of Louvain at Louvain-la-Neuve, Belgium

Martin Peper, Department of Psychology, University of Marburg, Germany

Pierre Philippot, Department of Psychology, Catholic University of Louvain at Louvain-la-Neuve, Belgium

Poul Poder, Department of Sociology, University of Copenhagen, Denmark

Fred Rothbaum, Department of Child Development, Tufts University, Medford, USA

Maria von Salisch, Department of Psychology, Leuphana University Lüneburg, Germany

Christian von Scheve, Institute of Sociology, University of Vienna, Austria

Phillip R. Shaver, Department of Psychology, University of California, Davis, USA

Gisela Trommsdorff, Department of Psychology, University of Konstanz, Germany

Marie Vandekerckhove, Department of Cognitive and Biological Psychology, University of Brussels, Belgium, and Department of Internal Medicine and Centre of Psychosomatics, University Hospital Ghent, Belgium

Roland Vauth, Psychiatric Outpatient Department, University Hospital Basel, Switzerland

Nathalie Vrielynck, Department of Psychology, Catholic University of Louvain at Louvain-la-Neuve, Belgium

Unni Wikan, Department of Social Anthropology, University of Oslo, Norway

FOREWORD

The Research Group "Emotions as Bio-Cultural Processes" that was in residence at the Center for Interdisciplinary Research (ZiF) at the University of Bielefeld from 2004 to 2005 had been set up to explore the interactions between the biological and the socially coded, culture-specific aspects of emotions. All five editors of the present book have been Junior Fellows of this Research Group. The young scientists, who, with only one exception, entered this one-year residence as postgraduate students at the beginning of their dissertation plans and projects, brought a breath of fresh air with them in many ways. They did not just brighten up our academic lives with unconventional leisure-time pursuits, but, with the courage and freshness—but also the tenacity—of youth, they kept on introducing complex and demanding topics into our discussions.

The regulation of emotions and their socio-cultural as well as bio-psychological preconditions—an issue that has attracted increasing attention in recent years—are such complex and many-layered subject areas. The individual disciplines are approaching them with mostly extremely heterogeneous approaches, concepts, and terminologies. At first glance, this plurality of definitions and models makes emotion regulation appear to be a very vague and shapeless field of research. As the heads of the research group on "Emotions as Bio-Cultural Processes," we had initially been strongly tempted to put the topic of emotion regulation aside—and avoid making the interdisciplinary dialogue on emotions even more complicated than it already is. Nonetheless, the Junior Fellows were not deterred by our temptation and enthusiastically organized a workshop on "Regulating Emotions: Social Necessity and Biological Inheritance" in December 2004 at the ZiF.

Several renowned emotion researchers attended this successful event, and the Junior Fellows decided to collect revised versions of the papers presented together with further articles and to publish them in a book. Their goal was not only to present new studies on emotion regulation but also, and above all, to facilitate the dialogue between the disciplines.

With their characteristic zeal, our five Junior Fellows got down to work on the present book, and the outcome passed through the review process of a most renowned publishing house—something they can justifiably feel proud of! Marie Vandekerckhove, Christian von Scheve, Sven Ismer, Susanne Jung, and Stefanie Kronast present an up-to-date, fascinating, and coherent book that makes a major contribution to the field of emotion regulation research and in particular to the work of the Research Group "Emotions as Bio-Cultural Processes."

This is a good opportunity for us to express our warm thanks to them —not just for organizing the workshop and producing this book, but also for their total commitment during the year we did research together in Bielefeld. They were a pleasure to work with.

Birgitt Röttger-Rössler and Hans J. Markowitsch
Halle / Bielefeld, April 2007

ACKNOWLEDGMENTS

We would like to express our sincere thanks to the organizers of the Research Group on "Emotions as Bio-Cultural Processes" at the University of Bielefeld's Center for Interdisciplinary Research (ZiF), Hans J. Markowitsch and Birgitt Röttger-Rössler, for giving us the opportunity to participate in this intellectually challenging and also highly sociable endeavor. The year we spent as fellows at the ZiF in Bielefeld has given us an insight in and understanding of emotions that is unique in its extraordinarily wide interdisciplinary scope and its profound disciplinary foundations. This of course would not have been possible without the contribution of all the group's members, whom we would equally like to thank: Michael Casimir, Irene Daum, Eva-Maria Engelen, Susanne Erk, Manfred Holodynski, Gerald Hüther, William Jankowiak, Margot Lyon, Sighard Neckel, Bradd Shore, Achim Stephan, and Harald Welzer.

Also, we would like to thank the research group for granting us the opportunity to organize the group's international workshop on "Regulating Emotions: Social Necessity and Biological Inheritance" from which the chapters in this volume have emerged. Furthermore, we thank the whole staff at the ZiF, in particular the group's research assistant Henrik Bollermann, who have contributed invaluably not only to organizing this particular workshop but also to making our time at the ZiF most enjoyable and successful. Thank you!

Last but not least we owe thanks to our executive editor at Wiley-Blackwell, Christine Cardone, for her encouragement and confidence in this project from the beginning on. We also thank our project editor Sarah Coleman, whose support and advice throughout the critical stages have always been most helpful.

Marie Vandekerckhove, Christian von Scheve, Sven Ismer,
Susanne Jung, and Stefanie Kronast

Regulating Emotions: Culture, Social Necessity, and Biological Inheritance

Marie Vandekerckhove, Christian von Scheve, Sven Ismer, Susanne Jung, and Stefanie Kronast

What seems so compelling about the regulation of emotions to researchers in many different disciplines is that within this theme, questions concerning the alleged antipodes nature and nurture or biology and culture are conflating in most obvious ways. We suspect that this is precisely the reason why emotion regulation has recently attracted such exceptional attention in a scientific environment that is characterized by a growing interest in bridging disciplinary boundaries. Without a doubt, the topic of emotion regulation has experienced a boom at the beginning of the 21st century, with many important contributions coming from academic disciplines as diverse as psychology, neuroscience, anthropology, psychotherapy, and sociology—not to mention the more popular writings and counseling literature.

Research on emotions in the past 20 years has increasingly portrayed emotions as highly functional phenomena of crucial evolutionary significance and biological grounding—in individual as well as in social and cultural terms. Clearly, this has not always been the case. From the Greek philosophers to the Scottish moralists, emotions have often been considered as disturbing and irritating occurrences in human life, in particular in domains requiring calm analysis, deep thinking, or polite manners. However, in other areas emotions have never ceased to be "that certain something," more or less legitimately serving as most compulsive means and ends of human action.

Although emotions are ubiquitous in human affairs, it seems not too bold to claim that what has separated "man" from "animal" in many societies and cultures till today is the potential and the ability to keep one's emotions *under control*. That is, to hide them from and adapt them to these affairs, not to forget oneself when faced with indignity, to keep calm even after 20 minutes on the telephone service line, or to be courteous at another boring dinner party. This social necessity to keep emotions under control seems to arise, for one thing, from emotions' compelling nature to direct peoples' actions, either as an urging feeling to act ("action tendency") or as a strong motive in itself (e.g., getting relief from one's anger) (Baumeister, Vohs, DeWall, & Zhang, 2007; Frijda, 1986; Loewenstein & Lerner, 2003).

If this is true, then there must be something about emotions and emotional behavior that is potentially dangerous or at least undesirable from a social or societal point of view. This, in turn, would mean that emotions' evolutionary founded "wisdom of the ages" (Lazarus, 1991, p. 820) is not as timeless as it seems, and, indeed, emotions and emotion-based actions are notoriously suspected to undermine the "wisdom" of social order and cultural integrity and to promote deviant behavior—they are thus supposed to be kept at bay in many different contexts and for many different reasons (see Gross, Richards, & John, 2006). The same can be said from an individual point of view: because emotions frequently occur outside of conscious awareness (Barrett, Ochsner, & Gross, 2007; Winkielman & Berridge, 2004) and are—at least in part—equally involuntarily expressed to others (Kappas, 1997; Russell, Bachorowski, & Fernandez Dols, 2003) they may well foil consciously pursued individual goals, for example in a poker game, in concentrating on a difficult math exam, or when trying to conceal a lie (Ekman, 2004).

Changing environmental demands change the contingencies of our emotions. Not all emotional reactions are always adaptive and beneficial, and this seems even more true for modern societies. Emotions are, so to speak, evolutionary relics that may well go over the top in a number of situations. They seem to "happen to us" and to have us in their grip; they let us do things that we often enough come to regret at later times. But emotions are not reflexes—they are more like an alarm bell that prompts for action or further investigation of the cause of the alarm. Thus, they are also subject to potential change and revision: the ability to regulate emotions allows people to keep them in line with prevailing environmental conditions and socio-cultural demands.

This might lead to the impression that the social and individual functions ascribed to emotions are somewhat restricted to primeval environments and ancestral challenges, that they are a mere biological inheritance, rigid and increasingly useless in human affairs. But nothing could be more misleading. Research on emotions has continuously emphasized that they are indispensable components of many intraindividual functions, for example, cognitive, physiological, phenomenological, or behavioral (Levenson, 1999). They are equally important in social encounters by contributing to the formation or disruption of social relationships, the emergence of social bonds, and the coordination of social action and interaction (Frank, 1988; Frijda & Mesquita, 1994; Keltner & Haidt, 1999). Moreover, recent research indicates that they are also involved in most complex societal functions, such as the enforcement and maintenance of social norms and social order (Fehr & Fischbacher, 2004; Thoits, 2004). Thus, the question seems to be legitimate whether "emotions [are] *ever* to be regulated?" (Gross, 1999, p. 552).

How is it, then, that emotions are still considered somewhat awkward at times—despite these well known individual and social functions? If all emotions and emotion eliciting conditions were the same in all cultures and societies, then there probably would be not much fuzz about emotion regulation in cultural context. But research on emotions has not only revealed different functions of emotions with respect to their biological foundations, but at the same time continuously highlighted their variability, flexibility, and adaptability—in particular with respect to these functions (e.g., decoupling stimulus from response and accentuating behavioral options rather than directly causing behavior, see Scherer, 1994, and Baumeister et al., 2007) but also in view of their elicitation and experience (see Mesquita & Markus, 2004, and Turner & Stets, 2006, for an overview). What is considered disgusting in one culture may be highly appreciated in another, what is considered embarrassing at work may be highly welcome in family life, and what evokes shame in one culture may elicit pride in another one.

The debate on whether emotions are evolutionary hard-wired reactions to environmental challenges or outcomes of social and cultural practices is almost as old as research on emotions. Whatever the ultimate answer to this question might be, the fact seems to be that there is considerable cultural and intrasocietal variability in the eliciting conditions of emotions, their experience, and expression, in particular in view of self-conscious or "higher social" emotions such as shame, guilt, embarrassment, and pride (Mesquita & Karasawa, 2004; Tangney & Fischer, 1995).

One path to answering the above stated question might therefore be found in the assumption that social and cultural representations of emotions have evolved in many different ways, whereas their underlying biological architecture—the affect system—has largely remained unchanged and thus universal, and that emotion regulation serves to adapt and fine-tune this system to the respective socio-cultural contexts (cf. Ochsner & Gross, 2007; Mesquita & Albert, 2007). In line with this reasoning is a definition of emotion regulation as "the process by which individuals influence which emotions they have, when they have them, and how they experience and express these emotions" (Gross, 1998, p. 275).

And this is—roughly speaking—the path this volume is following. It seems almost clear to us that in view of more or less disparately evolved socio-cultural systems, the causes, occasions, techniques, and goals of emotion regulation also differ between and even within the distinct social and cultural contexts. However, this is only one side of the coin. The other side is that intercultural differences in emotions in turn beg the question of how these variations are brought about and implemented in a specific socio-cultural environment. A number of articles in the present volume suggest that emotion regulation *as such* is a crucial factor in bringing about intercultural and intrasocietal differences in emotions. In adopting the idea that culture and society are fundamentally shaping and thereby "regulating" emotions, one-factor models of emotion regulation are providing answers to these questions in conceptualizing emotion regulation as a process that is not limited to an actual emotion episode, but rather extends to ontogenetic development and socio-cultural evolution (Campos, Frankel, & Camras, 2004). According to this view, emotions are already regulated *prior* to their actual elicitation in that they (and their social representations) are simply more salient, more despised, more sought after or more avoided in one culture than in another (cf. Mesquita & Leu, in press).

There is a further intriguing aspect to the one-factor view: If we had to constantly and consciously monitor our emotions in view of their appropriateness and social adequacy, we would soon run out of cognitive resources in everyday life. Therefore, not only do different cultures and social environments set the stage for the regulation of emotion and provide corresponding goals, but they also actively and purposefully engage in regulative developmental processes through social institutions, for example, socialization practices, the corroboration of social and individual goals, belief systems, habits and rituals, knowledge, or specific norms, rules, and codes of conduct. They entail what in this volume is dubbed "automatic emotion regulation."

It was precisely this twofold relationship between an evolutionary and biologically rooted affect system on the one hand, and highly differentiated social and cultural concepts and representations of emotions on the other hand that had motivated us as editors to marshal this interdisciplinary overview on the regulation of emotion. The incentive for this volume goes back to a workshop at the Center for Interdisciplinary Research (ZiF) at Bielefeld University in 2004 that was hosted by the center's research group on "Emotions as Bio-Cultural Processes." The year long work of this research group had mainly concentrated on identifying linkages between biological and socio-cultural determinants of emotions (cf. Röttger-Rössler & Markowitsch, in press). It soon turned out that the many facets of emotion regulation are a major factor in finding this linkage—from the point of view of almost all the disciplines involved in the group: psychology, neuroscience, philosophy, anthropology, sociology, and psychiatry.

However, the vivid discussions at the workshop have made it clear that the distinct disciplines have considerable difficulties in mutually communicating their concepts and approaches—if only on a semantic level in many cases. For example, when psychologists talk about "emotion regulation" (e.g., Gross & Thompson, 2007), sociologists are used to discuss "emotion work" and "emotion management" (Hochschild, 1979; cf. Grandey, 2000); and when anthropologists refer to an emotional "ethos," sociologists advance "social norms" and psychologists bring forward "representations" (cf. Mesquita & Leu, in press).

Thus, the aim of this volume ultimately is to bring together the different disciplines involved in research on emotion regulation and to harbor an interdisciplinary dialogue that sharpens each discipline's understanding and awareness of the respective paradigms. This dialogue is facilitated by the main thread of the book, namely the question of how social and cultural aspects of emotion regulation interact with regulatory processes on the biological and psychological level. The contributors thereby deal with the evolutionary assumptions implied by the volume's title and at the same time highlight the role of social and cultural requirements in the adaptive regulation of emotion. Put in a nutshell: the articles in this collection revolve around the basic question whether emotion "is ever not regulated" (Gross, 1999, p. 565).

The volume is divided into four parts. The contributions in Part I discuss conceptual and foundational issues of a bio-cultural perspective on emotion regulation. The chapters in Part II illustrate the role of culture and social interaction in the development of emotion regulation. The chapters in Part III assess the consequences of potential conflicts between social and individual expectations, emotions, and emotion regulation from a psychopathological perspective. Finally, the contributions in Part IV highlight the socio-cultural environment as affecting and being affected by emotion regulation.

The first part of the volume is introduced by Arvid Kappas who vividly argues that emotion and emotion-control are part and parcel of the same processes. According to Kappas, any scientifically viable theory of emotion also has to be a theory of emotion-control, being able to predict for a particular person in a particular event and context how he/she will react, e.g., with regard to expressive behavior. Kappas criticizes current theories for failing in this respect by merely invoking concepts such as display rules, feeling rules, unknown social intentions, or idiosyncratic appraisals as straw men. He goes on to show that as long as the display rules, feeling rules, etc. are not included in the boundaries of the emotion theories, it will not be possible to make any predictions that could be tested in the real world.

Iris Mauss, Silvia Bunge, and James Gross in their chapter are concerned with the question of how socio-cultural contexts affect individuals' emotion regulation. Their analysis rests upon the fact that most prior research on emotion regulation has focused on deliberate rather than automatic forms of emotion regulation. From a socio-cultural point of view, they argue, this is particularly unfortunate, since they suspect socio-cultural factors to have a pervasive effect on emotion regulation through automatic processes. Mauss, Bunge, and Gross start their argument by distinguishing two types of emotion regulation: response-focused (which takes place after an emotion is initiated) and antecedent-focused (which takes place before an emotion is fully initiated) emotion regulation. They subsequently review how socio-cultural contexts engender response- and antecedent-focused automatic emotion regulation and how these two types of regulation in turn affect individuals' emotional responding and well-being. They suggest that automatic emotion regulation is shaped by cultural contexts providing the individual with implicit norms and automatized practices that can be either situationally or emotionally cued. Importantly, they find that antecedent-focused automatic regulation seems to be relatively adaptive while response-focused automatic regulation seems to be relatively maladaptive.

Claire Hofer and Nancy Eisenberg in their contribution review research relevant to understanding the biological, that is, genetic and molecular, bases of emotion regulation and the relations of emotion-related regulation to socialization and developmental outcomes in several cultures. In doing so, they give a concise overview of the biological makeup of effortful control and self-regulation on the one hand, and the different environmental influences on emotion regulation, in particular socialization conditions, on the other hand. In addition, Hofer and Eisenberg focus primarily, albeit not solely, on individual differences in measures of dispositional emotion-related self-regulation. Although they conclude in calling for more efforts to be made to better measure emotion regulation and related constructs, Hofer and Eisenberg emphasize that, although there are differences among socialization beliefs and practices across cultures, there is also some degree of universality in the processes involved in the influence of socialization on emotion-related regulation.

Leading in the second part of this volume that shifts attention from individual to interactional and developmental processes in emotion regulation, Gisela Trommsdorff and Fred Rothbaum seek to understand cultural differences in emotional regulation by examining differences in the development of the self. They assume that emotion regulation is related to a person's self-construal and to his/her goals and in their comprehensive review integrate evidence on culture-specific construals of the self as well as on cultural differences in goal orientation. The processes and outcomes of emotion regulation, they argue, should strongly depend upon these different conceptions of self and goals. To corroborate their argument, they consider extensive evidence of cultural differences in child-rearing conditions and socialization practices. Trommsdorff and Rothbaum clearly show that common assumptions and findings from Western research on emotion regulation that are often treated as universal are not quite so and that a thorough understanding of emotion regulation can only rest on a culture-informed theory.

Phillip Shaver, Mario Mikulincer, and David Chun, in their chapter, marshal an attachment theoretical approach to emotion regulation. Attachment theory (Bowlby, 1982) provides an understanding of the developmental origins of individual differences in emotion regulation, in particular within close relationships. Originally based on studies concerned with human infants' emotional bonding with their mothers, attachment theory has more recently moved towards analyzing emotional attachments in adults and also to individual differences in emotion regulation associated with different patterns of attachment styles. Shaver, Mikulincer, and Chun outline attachment theory, review psychological and neuropsychological research on attachment-related individual differences in emotion regulation, and show how security-related regulation processes foster mental health and prosocial behavior. The theoretical model they develop suggests that attachment security and the ability to regulate emotion is closely associated with a variety of prosocial feelings and caregiving behaviors: Secure attachments make it easier to focus and meet others' social needs, whereas insecure attachments interfere with empathic perceptions of others' needs and thus decrease the likelihood of effective prosocial behavior.

Maria von Salisch in her contribution gives a detailed overview of the developmental influences on the regulation of emotion, the socialization of emotion regulation, and the development of interindividual differences. Her analysis is based on a process model of emotion generation and develops around four main themes that comprise the better part of developmental research on emotion regulation: the fundamental changes in emotional development in childhood and adolescence; the multidimensional development of emotion regulation; the shift from interpersonal to intrapersonal emotion regulation; and the differential development of emotion regulation. Her analysis of the available evidence culminates in an original transactional model of emotional development that puts the four themes of emotion regulation under one overarching and integrative perspective.

The chapters in Part III of this volume focus on potential problems and difficulties arising from the social expectations and individual needs related to emotion regulation. They highlight probable consequences of mismatches between socio-cultural expectations and individual emotions and outline clinical and psychopathological implications. In doing so, Pamela Cole, Tracy Dennis, Sarah Martin, and Sarah Hall take on the developmental theme of the previous part and investigate the interplay of emotion regulation and the early development of psychological competence and psychopathology. Because they assume emotional processes to be inherently regulatory, Cole, Dennis, Martin, and Hall first discuss conceptual challenges of defining and measuring emotion and distinguishing emotion regulation from emotion in regard to both typical and atypical development in early childhood. They describe four specific dimensions of emotion regulation that are pertinent to psychopathological risk and can be inferred from behavioral observations. Referring to a clinical case example of a young child with a major depressive disorder, they present testable predictions about how children at risk for depression can be distinguished from typically developing children on the basis of behavioral observations. Concluding, they provide a set of concepts and suggest methods of measurement that can be used to test hypotheses about individual differences in emotion regulation.

Pierre Philippot, Aurore Neumann, and Nathalie Vrielynck investigate a dimension of emotional information processing that they deem relevant for emotion regulation in general and for psychopathology in particular: the specificity versus generality at which emotional information is processed. Specificity in this model refers to the activation of detailed and precise information about specific emotional experiences well circumscribed in episodes lasting less than a day. Generality in turn refers to the activation of generic information about emotion, for example, features that tend to be repeatedly experienced during a given emotion or abstract information about more extended periods of time. Philippot, Neumann, and Vrielynck start with a review of research showing that several emotional disorders are characterized by an overgenerality bias in emotional information processing. Subsequently, they question the validity of naïve theories sustaining this bias by referring to a cognitive model of emotion regulation that is based on multilevel theories of emotion. They then examine the regulatory consequences of processing emotional information at a specific or overgeneral level and finally outline implications for psychopathology and clinical intervention.

Martin Peper and Roland Vauth in their chapter then review the difficulties in defining and assessing socio-emotional competencies that comprise diverse functional domains related to emotion regulation, for example, awareness of one's own emotions, perception of emotions in others, and coping and management skills. Peper and Vauth first inspect the basic constructs and functional components of emotions and discuss the structure and typical definitions of socio-emotional abilities. They give a concise overview of the assessment of emotion regulation by means of psychometric tests and critically review the methodological difficulties involved. Taking schizophrenia as an exemplary clinical application, Peper and Vauth describe typical deficits of emotional processing in these patients and present a rehabilitation program that is based on an original neuropsychological working model of emotion regulation and focuses on the training of high-level socio-emotional skills.

Leslie Greenberg and Marie Vandekerckhove even more shift attention from emotional self-regulation to the regulation of emotions by another person by investigating in detail how emotion regulation and its disorders can be approached from a psychotherapeutic perspective. In combining affective neuroscience and one-factor models of emotion regulation they explore the role of the client–therapist relationship in the treatment of emotion related disorders. Based on the emotion-focused therapy approach originally developed by Greenberg (2002), they assign a dual role to emotion regulation in therapeutic relationships: First, the relationship is therapeutic in and of itself by serving an emotion regulation function which is internalized over time. Second, the relationship functions as a means to an end. The client–therapist relationship, they argue, should offer an optimal environment for facilitating specific modes of emotional processing because emotions are much more likely to be approached, tolerated, and accepted in the context of a safe relationship. Greenberg and Vandekerckhove articulate a number of principles of emotion assessment and emotional change in therapy by referring to different aspects of emotion generation and regulation. They conclude by presenting evidence and techniques on how maladaptive emotions can be transformed into more adaptive emotions in a therapeutic setting.

The chapters in Part IV of the present volume highlight the sociocultural context as the primary object of inquiry, both as an immediate and "one-factor" cause for emotion regulation, and as an object that is equally affected by regulated emotions. Unni Wikan in her illuminating essay describes cases of honor killings in northern Europe in order to illustrate the consequences of emotions that are regulated in ways that differ from those prevailing in most Western cultures. By giving a detailed description of a prominent case of honor killing in Denmark, Wikan gives an insight in how the mechanisms underlying these acts are tied to the regulation of emotion. She draws on her long-term empirical research on honor and shame in the Middle East and thereby sheds light on what honor "is" and how it needs to be understood to combat rising violence, in particular against women. Wikan, in her chapter, explores the intrapersonal and interpersonal mechanisms involved and illustrates how honor is at once a matter of pride and oppression.

Poul Poder makes explicit how a specific social environment—in this case a particular organization—shapes the interpretation of feelings and thus their regulation. Taking anger as an example, Poder illustrates how certain types of emotional experiences are silenced rather than welcomed in a specific environment. He presents evidence from a case study on processes of organizational restructuring and shows how employees and executives handle anger in quite different ways. Poder in particular illustrates how anger is not acknowledged in the relationship between management and employees. The chapter explains how anger can be viewed as integral to morality and that this approach can be considered an alternative to the predominant research on the regulation of anger. Poder outlines how emotion regulation can be understood as a phenomenon facilitated by specific "politics of expression." According to this view, the regulation of anger is linked to issues of culture and social structure, and is thus not simply a question of particularly ill-tempered personalities.

In a similar vein, Charlotte Bloch discusses the issue of how moods are regulated by emotional cultures. In her contribution she presents evidence on how "flow" and "stress" experiences as specific mood states are interpreted and handled in different contexts of everyday life in modern Western societies. Bloch explicates the way in which emotional cultures play an active, but often overlooked role in people's everyday interpretations and evaluations of pleasant and unpleasant moods; with the term "emotional cultures", she refers to different spheres of everyday life that are found in many modern Western societies. In her study, she investigates different strategies of handling flow and stress in work-life, family-life, and leisure-time. Bloch concludes that emotional cultures act as interpretive filters which not only shape and mediate, but also actively disturb or suppress specific moods.

We are confident that we have been able to assemble a volume that on the one hand reflects the lively debates and the extraordinary atmosphere at the workshop out of which many contributions originated and informs the different disciplines about neighboring paradigms, approaches, and findings in research on emotion regulation. On the other hand, we believe that we have managed to solicit additional contributions that fit this interdisciplinary exchange and further contribute to an understanding of emotion regulation across disciplinary boundaries. In sum, we hope that this volume is an important contribution to the field of emotion regulation research and will stimulate further theorizing and empirical research across many disciplines.

REFERENCES

Barrett, L. F., Ochsner, K. N., & Gross, J. J. (2007). On the automaticity of emotion. In J. A. Bargh (Ed.), *Social psychology and the unconscious: The automaticity of higher mental processes* (pp. 173–217). New York: Psychology Press.

Baumeister, R. F., Vohs, K. D., DeWall, C. N., & Zhang, L. (2007). How emotion shapes behavior: Feedback, anticipation, and reflection, rather than direct causation. *Personality and Social Psychology Review, 11*, 167–203.

Bowlby, J. (1982). *Attachment and loss: Vol. 1. Attachment* (2nd ed.). New York: Basic Books. (Original ed. 1969).

Campos, J. J., Frankel, C. B., & Camras, L. (2004). On the nature of emotion regulation. *Child Development, 75*, 377–394.

Ekman, P. (2004). *Emotions revealed*. London: Orion.

Fehr, E., & Fischbacher, U. (2004). Third-party punishment and social norms. *Evolution and Human Behavior, 25*, 63–87.

Frank, R. H. (1988). *Passions within reason*. New York: Norton.

Frijda, N. H. (1986). *The emotions*. Cambridge: Cambridge University Press.

Frijda, N. H., & Mesquita, B. (1994). The social roles and functions of emotions. In S. Kitayama & H. R. Markus (Eds.), *Emotion and culture* (pp. 51–88). Washington, DC: American Psychological Association.

Grandey, A. A. (2000). Emotion regulation in the workplace: A new way to conceptualize emotional labor. *Journal of Occupational Health Psychology, 5*, 95–110.

Greenberg, L. S. (2002). *Emotion-focused therapy: Coaching clients to work through feelings*. Washington, DC: American Psychological Association.

Gross, J. J. (1998). The emerging field of emotion regulation: An integrative review. *Review of General Psychology, 2*, 271–299.

Gross, J. J. (1999). Emotion regulation: Past, present, future. *Cognition and Emotion, 13*, 551–573.

Gross, J. J., Richards, J. M., & John, O. P. (2006). Emotion regulation in everyday life. In D. K. Snyder, J. A. Simpson, & J. N. Hughes (Eds.), *Emotion regulation in couples and families: Pathways to dysfunction and health* (pp. 13–35). Washington, DC: American Psychological Association.

Gross, J. J., & Thompson, R. A. (2007). Emotion regulation. Conceptual foundations. In J. J. Gross (Ed.), *Handbook of emotion regulation* (pp. 3–24). New York: Guilford.

Hochschild, A. R. (1979). Emotion work, feeling rules, and social structure. *American Journal of Sociology, 85*, 551–575.

Kappas, A. (1997). The fascination with faces: Are they windows to our soul? *Journal of Nonverbal Behavior, 21*, 157–161.

Keltner, D., & Haidt, J. (1999). Social functions of emotion at four levels of analysis. *Cognition and Emotion, 13*, 505–521.

Lazarus, R. S. (1991). Progress on a cognitive-motivational-relational theory of emotion. *American Psychologist, 46*, 819–834.

Levenson, R. W. (1999). The intrapersonal functions of emotion. *Cognition and Emotion, 13*, 481–504.

Loewenstein, G., & Lerner, J. S. (2003). The role of affect in decision making. In R. J. Davidson, K. R. Scherer, & H. H. Goldsmith (Eds.), *Handbook of affective sciences* (pp. 619–642). New York: Oxford University Press.

Mesquita, B., & Albert, D. (2007). The cultural regulation of emotions. In J. J. Gross (Ed.), *Handbook of emotion regulation* (pp. 486–503). New York: Guilford.

Mesquita, B., & Karasawa, M. (2004). Self-conscious emotions as dynamic cultural processes. *Psychological Inquiry, 15*, 161–166.

Mesquita, B., & Leu, J. (in press). The cultural psychology of emotion. In S. Kitayama & D. Cohen (Eds.), *The handbook of cultural psychology*. New York: Guilford.

Mesquita, B., & Markus, H. R. (2004). Culture and emotion: Models of agency as sources of cultural variation in emotion. In A. S. R. Manstead, N. H. Frijda, & A. Fischer (Eds.), *Feelings and emotions: The Amsterdam Symposium* (pp. 341–358). New York: Cambridge University Press.

Ochsner, K. N., & Gross, J. J. (2007). The neural architecture of emotion regulation. In J. J. Gross (Ed.), *Handbook of emotion regulation* (pp. 87–109). New York: Guilford.

Röttger-Rössler, B., & Markowitsch, H. J. (Eds.) (in press). *Emotions as biocultural processes*. New York: Springer.

Russell, J. A., Bachorowski, J.-A., & Fernandez-Dols, J.-M. (2003). Facial and vocal expressions of emotion. *Annual Review of Psychology, 54*, 329–349.

Scherer, K. R. (1994). Emotion serves to decouple stimulus and response. In P. Ekman & R. J. Davidson (Eds.), *The nature of emotion: Fundamental questions* (pp. 127–130). New York: Oxford University Press.

Tangney, J. P., & Fischer, K. P. (Eds.) (1995). *Self-conscious emotions. The psychology of shame, guilt, embarrassment, and pride*. New York: Guilford.

Thoits, P. A. (2004). Emotion norms, emotion work and social order. In A. S. R. Manstead, N. H. Frijda, & A. Fischer (Eds.), *Feelings and emotions: The Amsterdam Symposium* (pp. 359–378). New York: Cambridge University Press.

Turner, J. H., & Stets, J. E. (2006). Sociological theories of human emotions. *Annual Review of Sociology, 32*, 25–52.

Winkielman, P., & Berridge, K. C. (2004). Unconscious emotion. *Current Directions in Psychological Science, 13*, 120–123.

PART I

Emotion and Regulation: Between Culture and Biology

1

Pssssst! Dr. Jekyll and Mr. Hyde are Actually the Same Person! A Tale of Regulation and Emotion

Arvid Kappas

Emotions serve many functions, including regulatory functions, for the individual and for others. At the same time emotions are themselves subject to regulation both by the individual and by others. In fact, it is possible to look at emotions as intrapersonal and interpersonal processes at the same time. Thus, the complexity of nested levels of regulatory feed-forward and feedback loops calls for a dynamic systems approach to emotions. To make matters slightly more challenging, it becomes increasingly evident that different emotional components, such as central and peripheral physiological responses, thoughts and feelings, expressive and other behaviors are all subject to modulation by various processes, some of them intentional and some not, some of them culturally shaped and some not, some occurring in social situations and others not, and we are aware of some of them, and of some we are not. Arguably, automatic and conscious appraisals are causal antecedents to most emotional phenomena and yet, they too are subject to different levels of control, further complicating a clear separation of cause and effect when it comes to emotions.

One of the main theses I will make in this chapter is that emotion and emotion-control are part and parcel of the same processes and any scientifically viable theory of emotion must also be a theory of emotion-control. In an ideal scenario, a theory should be able to predict for a particular person, for a particular event, in a particular context, how s/he will react for example with regard to their expressive behavior. In practice, all current theories fail in this regard and invoke concepts such as display rules, feeling rules, unknown social intentions, or perhaps idiosyncratic appraisals as the reason for such a failure. But as long as the display rules, feeling rules, etc. are not included in the domain boundaries covered within the emotion theories, it is not possible to make any predictions that could be tested in the real world. I will point out some of the critical issues in current theories of emotion and emotion-control and discuss potential directions to address these issues.

 ## CAN A CAR SIT IN ITS OWN DRIVER'S SEAT? A CURIOUS CASE OF RECURSION

Subjectively, emotions appear to do something to us. That is, *emotions* can be perceived as an entity separable from the self, the *me*. While on the one hand we typically understand emotions as something arising within us, they appear, on the other hand, to take on a mind of their own and act upon us. We feel "gripped," "seized," and "overcome" (Averill, 1994, p. 265). The fact that the bus driver closed the door right in front of me made *me* angry. The anger is *me*. But when we are *in the grasp of anger*, we might interpret our being driven to "bad deeds of passion" as a consequence of our "animal nature" (Averill, 2006, p. 4) and "incompatible with intelligent judgment" (Lazarus & Lazarus, 1994, p. 198)—as if the anger was a separate entity *doing things with me*. Surely, the persistent threat of an internal tug-of-war with such powerful forces poses a threat to an idealized rational mind. Thus, it is not surprising that controlling passions, or in other terms, *the regulation of emotions*, has been a much-discussed topic in western philosophy (for an interesting view on regulating emotions in a Buddhist context see Ekman, Davidson, Ricard, & Wallace, 2005) going back thousands of years to the philosophers of ancient Greece (Gross, 1998a; Lazarus & Lazarus, 1994; see also Solomon, 2000). Damasio (2000) summarizes that "philosophy, notwithstanding David Hume and the tradition that originates with him, has not trusted emotion and has largely relegated it to the dismissible realms of animal and flesh" (p. 38). In psychology, emotion regulation is a very current topic as the present volume attests.

But if it is not *us*, who then is in the driver's seat of emotions? Arguably, emotions are an integral part of an individual. Thus, on closer thought, it appears confusing that an individual could be his or her own victim. A car cannot be in its own driver's seat without wondering who drives the car in the driver's seat—an example of what Dennett refers to as the homunculus fallacy (Dennett, 1991; see also Kappas, 2001). In contrast, some theorists (e.g., Averill, 2006; see also Cornelius, 1996; Solomon, 2006) suggest that the concept of emotions as something that is passively experienced is a consequence of subjective experience but basically erroneous. In fact, the view of *emotions as passions* denies the fact that the actor in emotions is indeed the individual him- or herself. Thus, according to Averill or Solomon, emotions can or should be conceived of as actions rather than passions.

The most common way of dealing with the subjective reality of passions is to conceive of an individual as a fragmented entity and, in consequence, limit the concept of *self* to our conscious experience—the "voice in our head." Buck (1988) refers to this self as "a system of linguistically structured rules about behavior that are built up from experience in the individual's particular physical, social, and bodily environment" (p. 487). Other mental or physical processes might then not be part of that self, but happen to be contained within the body of the individual and exert certain influences on the self. These forces might be conceived of as motivations, drives, or instincts by psychologists or biologists—they might be referred to as "id" by psychoanalysts, "mental illness," "madness," or "evil spirits" depending on the cultural context, or, these days, we might talk about "automaticity" (see Bargh & Williams, 2006). Frijda (1986) argues forcefully that

> the emotion system should be viewed as a system governed by dual, reciprocal control. Dual control is rather usual in biological systems. It is found in movement control by the simultaneous action of antagonistic muscles, in autonomic response in the interplay of sympathetic and parasympathetic activity, in hormonal response, to name a few instances. Evidently, dual control permits finer tuning than does single-graded excitation. (p. 405)

The implicit or explicit consequence of most of the models alluded to is to consider an active and autonomous self that must exert executive power to regulate emotions either before they arise (by approaching or avoiding certain situations) or to control different components of emotions while they occur (for example cognitive or expressive regulation mechanisms; see also Gross, 1998a; Gross & Thompson, 2007; Mauss, Bunge, & Gross, this volume; Philippot, Neumann, & Vrielynck, this volume). However, this is not the framework I will be using in this chapter. Instead, I argue that emotions are *integrated* with other dynamic mental and physiological processes that are largely self-regulating at different levels (bodily systems, the mind, social interaction, culture). To avoid confusions regarding the frequently used term "self-regulation" I will refer to the tendency of emotions to regain homeostasis as *implicit regulation of emotion*. Conscious efforts to regulate emotions are but one added facet to this multilayered regulatory system (see also Baumeister, Vohs, DeWall, & Zhang, 2007). By excluding implicit regulatory processes from emotion-regulation theory (Gross & Thompson, 2007) and research (by focusing on situations of questionable ecological validity) progress in understanding emotion (regulation) is limited.

Gross and Thompson (2007) argue that

> on its own, the phrase 'emotion regulation' is crucially ambiguous, as it might refer equally well to how emotions regulate something else, such as thoughts, physiology, or behavior (regulation *by* emotions) or to how emotions are

themselves regulated (regulation *of* emotions). However, if a primary function of emotions is to coordinate response systems (Levenson, 1999), the first
sense of emotion regulation is coextensive with emotion. For this reason we
prefer the second usage, in which emotion regulation refers to the heterogeneous set of processes by which emotions are themselves regulated. (p. 7)

This line of reasoning has an intuitive appeal. Surely, if everything related
to emotions is part of regulation then the value of the term *emotion regulation* might appear questionable. And yet, there is a problem in trying
to dissect a stage in a nested multiple-level feedback system and cut out a
fragment of cause–effect relationships[1] (cf. Forrester, 1971).

EMOTIONS AS REGULATORS

When discussing the notion of the regulation of emotion, it is necessary
to consider that emotions are primarily regulatory processes themselves.
Whereas emotions were frequently considered by some as an animalistic
part of human nature that needs to be suppressed to avoid interference
with rational thought and action, the post-Darwinian consensus considers emotions foremost as *functional* for the individual in the here-and-
now, as well as for the species in the long run. Whereas some theorists
place the emphasis more on the here-and-now (e.g., Averill, 1994), others
have focused more on the significance of having evolved emotional mechanisms that enhance fitness even if not all emotional episodes appear
functional (see Cosmides & Tooby, 2000). It would appear that both
types of functions cannot be denied. "Emotions are curious adaptations
that are part and parcel of the machinery with which organisms regulate
survival" (Damasio, 2000, p. 54).

Evolution has provided increasingly complex means of facilitating survival including the adaptation to events in the environment. Slow changes
in environmental conditions shift the advantageousness of morphologi-
cal structures (e.g., in dealing with hot or cold temperatures) and certain
behavioral patterns (e.g., in dealing with the prevalence of prey or pred-
ators). However, there is also the need to respond to environmental challenges at a micro-scale. Reflexes are highly functional and successful in
reacting to well-specified and stereotypical challenges. Hence, reflexes of
different complexity can be found in very simple organisms, such as the
flatworm or the sea slug *Aplysia* (e.g., Peretz, Jacklet, & Lukowi, 1976).
In fact, reflex-like behaviors can even be found in plants without the implication of a nervous system, such as the Venus flytrap (Forterre, Skotheim,
Dumais, & Mahadevan, 2005). Humans, in contrast, exhibit a variety of

reflexes of differing complexity underlining the ongoing functionality of a hard-wired adaptational system to environmental and internal challenges. But going beyond reflexes, the general plasticity of our cortex provides profound flexibility in adapting hard-wired mechanisms to the demands of specific cultural contexts, just as the very existence of certain brain-networks places boundaries on this flexibility (see Panksepp, 1998).

The problem with reflexes is, of course, their rigidity and inflexibility with regard to both the conditions eliciting them as well as the resulting behavior. Humans still depend on reflexes to survive but have evolved a variety of mechanisms and strategies to provide further flexibility. Adaptation can be provided much faster and more effectively by learning during the lifetime of an individual. An even higher degree of plasticity is provided by reasoning via symbolic thought (e.g., Slovic & Peters, 2006). Interestingly, some psychologists appear to have no difficulties studying motivation, emotion, or cognition, as if these constructs were natural kinds and separable. However, on a functional level, all three concepts are clearly interrelated solutions to the demand for behavioral flexibility in complex environments and they are all embodied in a complex and highly interconnected brain (e.g., Buck, 2000). In fact, it is perhaps more appropriate to talk of *brains* in the plural. This is not only to make the argument that a brain is truly not just a general purpose processing device, such as a computer, but instead a connected network of structures with different properties (e.g., Panksepp, 1998). Instead, I want to make the argument that humans as a social species have a variety of ways of dealing with environmental challenges and they include interaction, social structures, and at least in some, culture. It would be wrong to limit a consideration of emotion and emotion regulation to single brains when affect can be and is concurrently processed, distributed over more than one individual. This is particularly evident in certain infant caregiver interactions (see Kappas & Descôteaux, 2003; Cole, Dennis, Martin, & Hall, this volume; von Salisch, this volume) but occurs in many other situations as well. Averill (1992) remarked that "one of the most striking peculiarities about most social-psychological theories of emotion is that they are basically nonsocial" (p. 15). In fact, unfortunately, most theories of emotion and emotion regulation do not consider dyadic or higher-order interactions as levels of analysis in their own right. I will later return to emotion regulation as an operating characteristic of interaction.

Consider a simple case of human adaptation. By accident you put your hand on a hot stove plate. Moving the hand away is reflexive and does not require learning.[2] However, it is a fact that the experience of pain is highly emotionally charged and leads to learning—and thus, avoiding this experience in the future (see Baumeister et al., 2007). Scherer (e.g., 1984) argued that one function of emotions is to decouple stimulus and response. He proposed that

> emotion has evolved as a relevance detection and response preparation system in species in which organisms can perceive and evaluate a wide range of environmental stimuli and events (even those that are irrelevant for survival) and have an extensive repertoire of behavioral response alternatives at their disposal. (Scherer, 1994, p. 128)

In other words, when we see the stove plate again we are alerted by bodily and subjective reactions. In terms of Arnold (1960), who is considered the founder of appraisal theory, the hot plate is now perceived (appraised) as *bad for me*. This is not a cold cognition—it is *charged*. There is an *action tendency* to avoid the object and the motivational force and subjective affective experience varies for example with the distance to it. And yet, if we want to, we can touch the plate again. This is the meaning of Scherer's notion of decoupling—emotions guide, they push, they pull, but with few exceptions they do not force us. Baumeister et al. (2007) similarly argue in the context of their feedback theory that the main impact of an emotion is *not to cause behavior directly*, but to stimulate cognition to deal with an event or situation.

Considering an example, such as that of the hot plate, it becomes obvious that emotions have an important regulatory function. What is regulated here and who regulates? The organism's behavior is regulated. Emotion is one of the mechanisms/features the organism in question possesses as a regulator. In procedural terms, memory representations of a particular object (the hot plate) and a particular event (touching the hot plate) have been associated with a negative valence in the initial encounter. The activation of these representations when seeing and recognizing the hot plate likely causes a change in the activation of what Panksepp (e.g., 1998) calls the FEAR circuit,[3] including cortical and subcortical *interactions*, that in turn results in various changes in sympathetic and parasympathetic autonomic activation, endocrine activity (particularly hypothalamic-pituitary-adrenal axis, HPA), expressive behavior, cognitive activity (see also Fenske & Raymond, 2006), and subjective experience (note that subjective experience is not necessary for an emotion to be present—see Winkielman and Berridge, 2004). In addition, conceptual processing most likely triggers a causal attribution of this activation to the proximity of the *dreaded* object.

Note that emotion is *a* regulator, not *the only* regulator. Gray (2004) suggested an *integration* between emotions and cognitive control using a metaphor of integration in a baseball team:

> If subprocesses of emotion . . . and of cognitive control . . . can influence each other selectively, rather than only in a diffuse, global, or nonspecific manner, emotion and cognitive control are integrated. That is, the existence of selective interactions implies something interesting about the underlying mental architecture: Although the two systems may be largely separable or distinct, they are also inseparable, in a strong sense. They intertwine so closely that at times it is impossible to discern which is doing what, and yet both are clearly contributing to the overall function. (p. 46)

Thus, it is not emotion in the sense of an independent entity that regulates behavior, but the interaction of emotion and cognition in the sense of integration that Gray alludes to in the quote above. This is not the same image as the dual control in the Frijda quote above. In this sense reacting in a particular way might appear an emergent property of various contributions of the brain—not necessarily the consequence of a tug of war between emotion and its control.

☐ IMPLICIT REGULATION OF EMOTIONS

So what happens when the hot plate is avoided for a few minutes or re-encountered? Habituation to the presence of the hot plate will cause the activation of the FEAR circuit to decay (also Frijda, 1986). Autonomous activation will return to its previous state. Homeostasis will be regained. So who or what regulated the emotion here? The basic structure of emotion is self-regulating at multiple levels. Firstly, habituation causes a dynamic change in the eliciting condition, the appraisal process in the case of a simple threat-stimulus like that in the hot-plate example. Secondly, the central and peripheral activation decays not only because of habituation to the eliciting situation, but because reactions decay naturally due to a variety of feedback mechanisms (for example in the context of HPA axis responses to stress, see Kudielka & Kirschbaum, 2005; on opponent process theory, Mauro, 1992; see also Berridge, 2004).[4]

How do we regulate hunger? A particularly successful strategy is eating. How do we regulate thirst? We drink. Basic motivations bias us to change the state of our body by changing the goal-state of the organism. As the term motivation here is a proxy for need-state we can reformulate the previous sentence as: Need states change goal states. In humans, this involves changes in cognition. For example, attentional processes render food-relevant stimuli more salient when hungry (Morris & Dolan, 2001). It also involves changes in emotion. For example, food-stimuli are seen as more self-relevant (cf. Arnold, 1960) and as more pleasant (see Lozano, Crites, & Aikman, 1999; Ferguson & Bargh, 2004). The motivation-emotion-cognition complex increases the likelihood that we find and ingest food to regulate hunger. Must we eat when we are hungry? Of course not. We can postpone eating because we are in a meeting. We can refuse to eat because we are involved in a hunger strike, or because we rather chose to give the last bit of food to our starving offspring.

While Scherer (e.g., 1994) asserted that emotions decouple stimulus and response, the same is true for motivation and certainly for cognition. What motivations do is to bias our behavior in a particular fashion. In most cases, following the motivational bias will self-regulate the motivational state. In other words, motivation is typically auto-regulating specific need-states. Thus, research on motivation has typically focused on how need-states influence behavior and not as much on how motivations are regulated by the individual, social, or cultural structures. Of course, the latter has been of interest in a variety of contexts ranging from Freud's reflections on defense mechanisms such as sublimation or repression on to delay of gratification (e.g., Mischel, Shoda, & Peake, 1988)—a concept that is gaining interest in the context of emotional intelligence (Goleman, 1995). Why is it that emotions are not seen primarily as integrated processes (with cognition and motivation) with the potential to bias behavior, but instead as being called forth and having to be controlled?

Coming back to the hunger example—is this not an exemplary case of a two-factor process, such as that alluded to in the Frijda quote above? It appears that when we are hungry we eat. We stop eating when we are not hungry. If we do not eat, despite being hungry it is the control of hunger that intervenes. But, in fact, the relationship of hunger and eating is much more complicated in humans. Berridge comments on Dethier's use of the term "hunger" in explaining the eating behavior of flies (1967, as cited in Berridge, 2004):

> Basically, a fly has two eating reflexes. An excitatory one makes it eat whenever it lands on food, and an inhibitory one stops eating when the fly stomach becomes full. If the inhibitory reflex was removed by cutting a sensory nerve from the fly gut, Dethier [1967] found that the fly would continue to eat until it burst its tiny stomach. This pair of opposing reflexes can be viewed as controlling the fly's eating drive, but although that intervening variable may be causally elegant, it is almost appallingly simple both neurally and psychologically. If that is all that hunger is, then, the brains of mammals, like us, seem to contain a lot of unnecessary neurons and limbic circuits. (p. 187)

In fact the starting and stopping of eating in humans is regulated by a complicated heterarchy[5] of factors internal and external to the organism. It cannot be understood simply by a "drive to eat" and "the control of that drive." Some of these factors appear to be related to establishing balance—

homeostasis, but others not. When trying to identify a control hierarchy of motivational processes based on the neural architecture of the circuits involved, one is bound to fail. "Looking at a forebrain limbic wiring diagram, one is struck by the looping swirls of complexity, not just a near linear top-down hierarchy"(Berridge, 2004, p. 204).

Are there auto-regulatory features in emotions? For instance, how might we regulate anger? As Averill showed (1982) we do not actually aggress frequently when angry, but we do, as Darwin (1872) already pointed out, typically express a readiness to engage in confrontation. Similarly, various bodily changes occur that are associated with the current situational demands, as well as with anger specific reactions (e.g., Stemmler, 2004). Anger biases our behavior in a particular fashion—it increases the probability of certain types of behaviors and it facilitates these. Given that most situations involving anger involve social interaction, a cascade of events typically follows that will often, but not always, lead to a situational change that causes anger to subside. For example, the person who just cut into the line at the supermarket when being frowned at might apologize and get to the back of the line. Particularly Lazarus included this problem-focused coping as an integral part of emotion—not a separate process following elicitation of emotion (e.g., Lazarus & Lazarus, 1994; consider also the discussion of emotional behavior as a mode of coping in Frijda, 1986). In this example there was no violent exchange, but the facial activity communicated dissatisfaction—possibly a statement that social norms were violated.

What happened here? One could either say that anger was *controlled*, because there was no outright violence, or that a level of response was shown that was targeted at achieving optimally the social motivation to call the perpetrator to order. The former way of characterizing the episode uses terminology of *controlling impulses*, the latter a *social feedback system to implicitly regulate interaction*. Gross and Thompson (2007, p. 6) refer to these processes as the *recursive aspect* of emotions. One could restate what happened as "a little bit of anger prevented more anger." The termination of the offending behavior, a consequence of an emotional display, accompanied by some subjective experience of anger causes anger to subside. Note, that different contexts, in different cultures, might require minimal displays of anger—if any display at all—for everybody to know that a violation has occurred (cf. Trommsdorff & Rothbaum, this volume). It might not be necessary to control expression in this case, if no expression is required (see Fridlund, 1994, for the relationship of social motivation and expression; also Hess, Banse, & Kappas, 1995; Parkinson, 2005). Here narratives and scripts may be internalized to a point where the process of implicit regulation may be a consequence of external conditions. In this case multiple goals coexist, such as a goal to create or maintain harmony that cannot be separated from the current situation. In such a case no effort might be required not to express emotions.

Just as motivations bias cognition, emotions bias cognition in support of the function of a specific emotion (e.g., Philippot, Baeyens, Douilliez, & Francart, 2004; Philippot et al., this volume). Just as in the case of need states, emotions need not unconditionally lead to specific behaviors. Importantly, but not exclusively, volition can intervene at various points in the cascade of events and change ongoing or anticipated processes and events (Baumeister et al., 2007). In fact, much of the literature on emotion regulation (cf. Gross, 1998a) focuses on such volitional control. However, before going into more detail with regard to the regulation of emotions I wanted to highlight in this section that (a) emotions are themselves regulatory processes, a fact that is often overlooked or neglected and (b) emotional, cognitive, and motivational components are always intricately interwoven at all stages of episodes that are considered emotional. In the following, a more detailed analysis will follow on the regulation of (the regulatory process of) emotions.

REGULATING EMOTIONS: THE CASE OF FACIAL FEEDBACK

Emotions cannot be regulated *directly* by volitional efforts. Instead, indirect means are used, such as changing cognitions to affect appraisal processes, or components of the emotional response, such as expressive behavior, are regulated to feed back to the emotional state:

> The resistance of emotion to direct control is, in short, a puzzle to self-regulation researchers. Why did the human self-regulatory capacity evolve so as to be able to exert direct control over actions and thoughts, but not emotions? The answer, we think is that you cannot control your emotions because the purpose of emotions is to control you.
>
> Emotions are a feedback system for facilitating behavioral learning and control. If they were themselves controllable, they would lose that crucial function. (Baumeister et al., 2007, p. 175)

The notion that the relationship between emotional states and expressive behavior is a two-way street was already outlined by Darwin (1872). He asserted that the inhibition of an expression will dampen concurrent subjective experience and inversely, that the amplification of an expression will equally amplify subjective experience. Darwin went so far as to suggest that posing an expression might elicit emotional experiences. These ideas were amplified by James's theory, as for James the feeling was a function of the perception of emotional responses—including expression. Since then, the idea that expression influences subjective experience and physiological activity has been tested in a variety of paradigms. In the context of facial activity this notion has been referred to as the *Facial Feedback Hypothesis*.

Since the 1970s, there have been several demonstrations of facial feedback effects. While some studies failed to show feedback effects, and others were criticized on methodological grounds, there is increasing evidence that the facial feedback is a real phenomenon (for recent reviews see Capella, 1993; McIntosh, 1996).

For example Lanzetta, Cartwright-Smith, and Kleck (1976) instructed their subjects to conceal or to exaggerate their expressive reaction to electrical shocks. This early study is particularly interesting as it demonstrated not only changes in reported pain intensity but corresponding physiological changes as well. In this case, phasic skin conductance changes, indicative of sympathetic autonomic activation decreased in the inhibition condition and increased in the exaggeration condition. This result is a strong argument against the notion that self-reports of emotion in feedback studies are due to experimental demand effects.

Similarly, Hess, Kappas, McHugo, Lanzetta, and Kleck (1992) used physiological measures as well as a behavioral dependent variable that was intended to counter alternative explanations of the findings based on demand effects. In this study, participants were to self-generate four different emotional states (anger, happiness, sadness, peacefulness) or to self-generate the states while expressing the emotions strongly, as if to communicating how they felt. In addition they were just asked to pose each of the four states. When participants felt, in the first two conditions, that they experienced the target emotion they were supposed to press a hand-held button. The results demonstrated clearly that the instruction to generate an emotion and express it clearly led to increases in self-report, increases in physiological responses, and a much shorter latency to press the button. In other words, expressing an emotion strongly facilitates getting into this state.

A particularly elegant study was conducted by Strack, Martin, and Stepper (1988). They asked their participants in an elaborate cover story to hold a pen in their mouth while performing several tasks. In one case, the participants were to hold the pen with their lips, in the other condition with their teeth. Unobtrusively, this makes smiling almost impossible for the first group, but not for the second. In one of the tasks, the participants had to evaluate how funny a set of cartoons was. Those participants who could not smile rated the cartoons as less funny. There is widespread agreement that the results of this study, which are consistent with the facial feedback hypothesis, cannot be explained by demand effects (cf. Soussignan,

2002, for an extended replication). Similar paradigms have also been successfully employed to demonstrate feedback effects involving expressions other than smiling such as the furrowing of the brow (Larsen, Kasimatis, & Frey, 1992), or changes in posture induced by different chairs (Stepper & Strack, 1993; see also Riskind & Gotay, 1982; Wilson & Peper, 2004).

There is also empirical evidence that producing specific facial expressions leads to changes in subjective experience and physiological responses concordant with these expressions (Ekman, Levenson, & Friesen, 1983; Levenson, Ekman, & Friesen, 1990). In these studies participants were asked to move specific muscles using a "Directed Facial Action Task." However, this paradigm has been criticized because it is vulnerable to demand effects and there might be physiological changes induced by the different difficulty of certain movements (Boiten, 1996; but see response by Levenson & Ekman, 2002).

Recently, the voluntary use of regulating emotions indirectly via a suppression of expressive behavior has become a topic of interest in the emotion regulation literature. Gross and his colleagues have repeatedly demonstrated that suppressing emotions via expressive regulation does not lead to a reduction of physiological activity, but instead to an increase (e.g., Gross, 1998b; Gross & Levenson, 1993, 1997; Harris, 2001; see Gross & Thompson, 2007). Furthermore there appear to be costs to this strategy as regards cognitive resources (e.g., Richards & Gross, 1999, 2000; cf. Richards, 2004) and even long-term effects that impact on social relations (Butler et al., 2003).

How can the findings of Gross and his colleagues that suppressing facial responses increases physiological responses to emotional stimuli be reconciled with findings in the context of the Facial Feedback Hypothesis that appear to show the opposite pattern? First of all, not all emotions are equal (Kappas, 1989; Gross & Levenson, 1993)—while Gross and Levenson (1993) and Gross (1998b), for example, used disgusting films, the pattern was less clear for amusing films (Gross & Levenson, 1997). In fact, Kappas (1989, study 2) demonstrated that participants who were asked to control their emotions in response to happy and disgusting films differed with regard to the strategies they reported after the fact. While there was some evidence for expressive regulation for the amusing films (which in study 1 had been shown to be an effective technique to reduce the experience of amusement; Kappas, McHugo, & Lanzetta, 1989), there was little evidence for spontaneous expressive control to disgusting stimuli (which in study 1 was not an effective strategy to reduce subjective experience in disgust; Kappas et al., 1989). Perhaps, despite similar instructions, the paradigm of Gross and colleagues was perceived as being more stressful than that in other studies (e.g., Lanzetta et al., 1976). A clue to this can be found in the observation of Gross and Levenson (1993; 1997) that skin conductance increased after the instructions but *before* the stimuli were actually shown! A conclusive answer as to the differences with regard to the findings in these studies cannot be given at the present. However, what should be emphasized is that there is no indication that the inhibition of facial responses would ever lead to an *increase* in subjective experience. Thus, positive subjective experience can be dampened by facial inhibition and there is evidence for negative expressions in some cases (e.g., Lanzetta et al., 1976).

Perhaps, there is a difference between spontaneous and overlearned regulation of facial behavior in real situations and the laboratory situation. What if there are situations in real life that lead to facial regulation without requiring effort? This is of course difficult to test, but there is empirical evidence that points towards a decoupling of facial behavior and facial experience as a function of social context. For example, Hess et al. (1995) demonstrated that there was coherence between the intensity of funny films and facial activity when friends watched these together. This was not the case when watching films in the explicit or implicit presence of strangers. Thus, possibly, there is a decoupling of expression and experience in certain social situations. But could such effects be automatic and independent of effortful processing? A first clue comes from a recent study of Kappas and Küster (2006). Here a priming task was used to activate the concepts of "us" and "them." Smiling behavior toward a subsequent funny film was modulated in that those participants who had been primed to a "them" concept showed less smiling behavior. This finding is consistent with the implicit association of the "friends" concept with showing emotions and the "strangers" concept with hiding emotions that Küster and Kappas (2006) demonstrated. Surely, more research is needed on such automatic processes in the regulation of expressive behavior.

 ## A SIDE NOTE ON THE METHODOLOGY IN STUDIES ON EMOTION REGULATION

The complexity of disentangling emotion and emotion regulation makes empirical study in this context particularly difficult. A typical paradigm is to instruct/force participants to use a particular regulation strategy (e.g., reappraisal, facial manipulations) during the presentation of an emotion-eliciting stimulus, such as a film. While this seems, on the first view, a viable paradigm to dissect the individual contributions of different regulation strategies, there are different ways to interpret what this experimental situation actually reflects. Foremost, while this could be seen as adding a specific strategy compared to spontaneous viewing of the same material, it can also be reframed as denying the participant other means of regulating her emotional state.

For example, in my own research on emotion regulation (e.g., Kappas, 1989), I noticed that several participants, who were not aware of the presence of a concealed camera and thought that they were being unobserved, used their hands to shield their eyes when confronted with stressful film clips depicting certain medical procedures or burn victims (see Figure 1.1). It is quite interesting that such techniques—usually associated with the behavioral repertoire of children—were shown by college students. Such coping techniques are typically not available to the participant in the well controlled laboratory condition when a specific regulation technique is tested—and also if participants feel observed, or are explicitly instructed not to try to regulate their emotions. Thus, a suppression condition could also be interpreted by (some) participants as a *do not look away and do not try to distract yourself and do not try to think of the contents of the stimulus in other terms* condition. Since the Milgram studies on obedience, it is well known that the experimental situation in a social psychological study is a rather complex affair and the instructions of the experimenters carry a certain

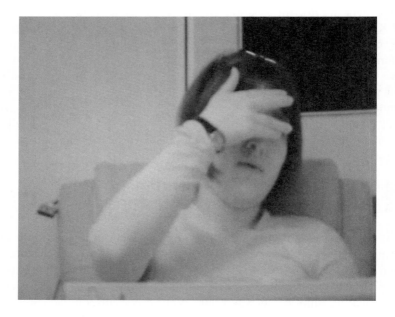

Figure 1.1 A participant might spontaneously use a variety of coping strategies to regulate their emotions. The social situation within the experiment plays an important role in this context. If participants do not feel observed they might use behavioral strategies that they would not use otherwise.

weight due to his/her implied authority (see Spears & Smith, 2001; also Krauss & Fussell, 1996). These aspects could contribute in some cases to create additional stress in participants. In general, such aspects in studies on emotion regulation challenge to some degree the ecological validity of these paradigms and possibly need to be further investigated. Harris (2001) used a complex social condition in which participants had to sing the American national anthem in front of a camera and the experimenter and then watch the recording together with confederates. This study was designed to elicit embarrassment. In one of the two experiments reported, the participants were instructed not to show any expression that could betray their emotions. While this study, in general, is a successful example of using social situations to elicit emotional states in a controlled laboratory context, the suppression instruction was as restrictive as in those mentioned above.

What are the alternatives? This is not easy because while it is possible to provide general instructions to try to inhibit or increase emotions without specifying how to, it is not clear to what degree participants can report after the fact what they exactly did. The same applies of course also to spontaneous control if no instruction is provided at all regarding emotion regulation. If specific techniques were enumerated in a postexperimental questionnaire, this might bias self-report, and if free responses are given, participants might not have the vocabulary to clearly state what they did or remember spontaneously the sequence of events during the experiment. Furthermore, as typically within-subject comparisons are desired, there is the possibility that an enumeration of techniques primes usage in subsequent trials. It is also likely, that if no specific instructions are given participants use multiple strategies (what Gross, 2007, refers to as the "throwing everything you've got at it" strategy, p. 17) in parallel, or sequentially. And yet, is this not what people are likely to do in a real world situation when they try to change ongoing emotional states, be it at a funeral, at the dentist, or in the office when the boss makes a particular remark?

FACIAL FEEDBACK AS ONE ELEMENT IN A RECURSIVE MULTIPLE-LEVEL FEEDBACK SYSTEM FOR THE REGULATION OF INTRA- AND INTERPERSONAL EMOTIONS

Despite the controversial evidence concerning the physiological side-effects of facial control, there is convincing evidence that subjective experience is affected by it. Based on the assumption that facial regulation can have the consequence of up- and down-regulating feelings, Kappas and Descôteaux (2003) suggested that facial feedback may be one factor contributing to intra- and interpersonal emotion. While the effect size of facial modulation may be small (see also Matsumoto, 1987) this does not preclude an important role of such strategies in nested feedback systems. Specifically, there might be significant moments in interaction where facial feedback (as an intrapersonal process) and mimicry (as an interpersonal process; see Dimberg, 1982, 1990 for automatic facial mimicry; Neumann & Strack, 2000 for contagion to affective voices) push the dyadic system into one state or another (also Izard, 1990).

This is particularly relevant as concepts such as display rules (Ekman & Friesen, 1969; Ekman, 2003) might not only regulate what can be shown, but in consequence, via a facial feedback route, affect the emotional state in its entirety. However, it is important to clarify that facial control need not be the consequence of social norms. Or, inversely, that social norms and early social interaction (Rochat & Striano, 1999) are the origin of an individual's attempts to regulate emotion via facial or other expressive behavior.

Specifically Izard (e.g., 1990; also Izard, Ackerman, Schoff, & Fine, 2000) elaborated on the idea that self-regulation via facial regulation would be an emergent property of such a nested feedback system (also Kappas & Descôteaux, 2003). Simply by trial and error, the infant will discover that particular states can be affected in the sense of up- or down-regulation within the first year of life. Added on top of that are social cues in early social interaction (Rochat & Striano, 1999). Furthermore, once the cognitive capacity of the child permits, implicit and explicit rules as to how to behave in a certain context are communicated and reinforced. In other words, the origin of facial control is an emergent property of the biological design of the emotion systems. Added to this are cultural influences which are firstly transmitted in action via early interaction between the child and caregivers, and subsequently cultural norms in larger social contexts, which are transmitted via the reactions of others (feedback), observation, and explicit rules provided by others.

The resulting eliciting situations will thus present a multitude of affordances to regulate expressions, most of which will become highly automatized, do not require attention or effort, and will be fully integrated into each emotion episode. It becomes clear that the attempt to isolate the effect of volitional control, as used in many experimental paradigms on emotion/regulation, is bound to fail ultimately as such a surgical manipulation of the emotion system will not represent emotion/regulation embedded in a normal context. This does not mean that previous studies cannot illuminate some mechanisms, but that such approaches need to be augmented by attempts to better capture the complexity of emotion/regulation in their proper ecological context.

It is also important that the categorical distinction between what people do when they are alone and when they are with others cannot be sustained anymore. The research of Fridlund (see 1994; also Hess et al., 1995) on implicit sociality and recent findings from my own laboratory (Kappas & Küster, 2006; Küster & Kappas, 2006) make clear that there are principal associations between cognitive concepts relating to expressive behavior and interpersonal relationships that mean, in everyday terms, that we are constantly, but to different degrees, accompanied by implicit audiences and interactants. This means that learned associations between particular states and expressive behavior are constantly modulating expressive behavior—even if we are physically alone.

If indeed there can be a situation/social context- and emotion-specific decoupling between feeling, physiology, and expression (Kappas, 2004), then the notion as to whether feedback might also be differentially effective could be raised. In a pilot study we tested whether hysterical laughter, as a case of contagion, could be elicited in the laboratory (Hess, Kappas, & Banse, 1993). The idea is that there is a give-and-take between the coupling of emotional components in the presence of friends that causes externally imposed requirements to regulate expression on the one hand and the bias to express, due to strong emotions, on the other hand, could lead to an oscillation in this complex feedback system that could result in uncontrollable laughter. In the pilot-study dyads had to film a commercial for a fictitious insurance company. The text was written by the pair, but they had to include at the end of the presentation the slogan of the insurance company, which was in fact a tongue twister. While one of the two participants was presenting, the other was sitting at the side with the task to regulate the audio channel. Invariably, presenters got stuck when trying to pronounce the tongue twister. Almost all of the participants started to laugh when they were friends and almost none started to laugh when they were strangers. Friends had to perform repeated takes and extended periods of laughter occurred. Here it is relevant that the necessity to regulate was implicit because of the attempt to film the commercial— no rule or instruction as to regulation was communicated explicitly.

This segment has focused on the role of expression as a regulator of intra- and interpersonal emotion. Of course, similar processes develop as regards deployment of attention to regulate emotion (e.g., Rueda, Posner, & Rothbart, 2005), or appraisal processes. In all of these cases there are processes that will likely emerge by trial and error in early childhood (Izard, 1990) and will be augmented by other layers as the individual grows up. The adult then is characterized by a complex network of recursive multiple-level feedback systems for the implicit and explicit regulation of intra- and interpersonal emotions that makes the distinction of emotion and regulation essentially impossible.

CONCLUSION

The present contribution focuses on a critical evaluation of some of the assumptions underlying research on emotion regulation, as well as experimental methods used in this field. Specifically, the possibility to separate the concepts of emotion and emotion regulation is questioned. This is not the first time this argument has been raised (see Gross & Thompson, 2007) and there are arguments, particularly of a practical nature, that speak towards the usefulness of dealing with these concepts separately. However, particularly if one considers that the anticipation of emotions (Baumeister et al., 2007) as well as the consequences of emotion could be conceptualized as implicit regulation of emotion, as outlined above, then it appears very difficult to insist on separating emotion and regulation. As the science of emotion moves towards social neuroscience (cf. Kappas, 2002), traditional views on the interplay of emotion and regulation are put into question (Barrett, Ochsner, & Gross, 2007). Mutually influencing feedback systems challenge clear notions of cause and effect. Emergent properties of dynamic systems provide an explanation for complex behavioral patterns, without the necessity to invoke (metaphors of) complex rule-books or highly complex executive processes.

However, this chapter is not intended as an exercise in deconstruction. In fact, there are ways forward. Theories are needed that include not only the elicitation but also the regulation of emotion. Such theories need to address the fact that emotions are inherently intra- and interpersonal processes embedded and interacting with a complex net of social structures and culture. Popular theories, such as Ekman's neuro-cultural theory (e.g., Ekman & Friesen, 1969; Ekman, 2003) and recent appraisal theories allude to interpersonal regulation in the guise of display rules, but they do not embed regulation within. They do not allow making clear predictions as to *who will show what to whom in which context* (Kappas, 1996; 1999).

Following the tenets of social neuroscience such an understanding can only emerge from a multilevel analysis of emotion that fully bridges micro-level and macro processes (cf. von Scheve & von Luede, 2005). Of course, this chapter cannot serve this purpose. Instead, it is modestly intended as a reminder of old issues and a—at times perhaps highly—speculative contribution as regards new issues. However, the present volume in its entirety is certainly a step towards a multi-disciplinary and multilevel understanding of emotion/regulation. Developing a truly multilevel theory of emotion/regulation is a daunting task, but in light of the rapidly growing science of emotion (cf. Kappas, 2002) this appears to be a desirable and necessary goal despite all practical concerns.

NOTES

1 While Gross and his colleagues (e.g., Gross & Thompson, 2007) do not include the implicit regulation of emotions in their concept of self-regulation, it would be false to assume that they are only referring to volitional efforts regarding the regulation of emotions. Instead they acknowledge that the processes they refer to can be volitional or automatic, conscious or outside of awareness.

2 A very detailed description of such a hot plate scenario and the reflexes involved in the initial response can be found in Damasio (2000, pp. 71–74).

3 I am using Panksepp's theory here as a short hand to an explicit description of a cascade of responses as it appears plausible today, but see Barrett and Wager (2006) for a critical evaluation of the notion of specialized circuits as proposed by Panksepp.

4 It should be noted here that the cascade of emotional reactions is characterized by different latencies in onset as well as in offset. While some authors (e.g., Scherer, 2001; see also Levenson, 1999) argue that emotions have a synchronizing function, this might be true only from the distance—at a micro level the onset of different components of the emotional cascade is characterized by vastly different onset times ranging from milliseconds in the case of changes in the central nervous system, seconds in the case of peripheral changes mediated by the autonomic nervous system, to changes in the immune system hours or even days later. Similarly, the offsets of these changes in activation are desynchronized. Consider also the discussion of Mauro (1992) on affective dynamics and Mauss, Levenson, McCarter, Wilhelm, and Gross (2005) on the synchronization of physiological responses.

5 A nonhierarchical structure where mutual influences do not assume, as Berridge (2004) puts it, that one structure *bosses* the other.

REFERENCES

Arnold, M. B. (1960). *Emotion and personality. Volume I: Psychological aspects.* New York: Columbia University Press.

Averill, J. R. (1982). *Anger and aggression: An essay on emotion.* New York: Springer.

Averill, J. R. (1992). The structural bases of emotional behavior: A metatheoretical analysis. In M. S. Clark (Ed.), *Emotion. Review of Personality and Social Psychology, 13* (pp. 1–24). Newbury Park, CA: Sage.

Averill, J. R. (1994). Emotions unbecoming and becoming. In P. Ekman & R. J. Davidson (Eds.), *The nature of emotion: Fundamental questions* (pp. 265–269). New York: Oxford University Press.

Averill, J. R. (2006). Good deeds of passion, and bad. *Emotion Researcher, 21,* 3–4.

Bargh, J. A., & Williams, E. L. (2006). The automaticity of social life. *Current Directions in Psychological Science, 15,* 1–4.

Barrett, L. F., Ochsner, K. N., & Gross, J. J. (2007). On the automaticity of emotion. In J. A. Bargh (Ed.), *Social psychology and the unconscious: The automaticity of higher mental processes* (pp. 173–217). New York: Psychology Press.

Barrett L. F., & Wager, T. R. (2006). The structure of emotion: Evidence from neuroimaging studies. *Current Directions in Psychological Science*, *15*, 79–83.

Baumeister, R. F., Vohs, K. D., DeWall, C. N., & Zhang, L. (2007). How emotion shapes behavior: Feedback, anticipation, and reflection, rather than direct causation. *Personality and Social Psychology Review*, *11*, 167–203.

Berridge, K. C. (2004). Motivation concepts in behavioral neuroscience. *Physiology & Behavior*, *81*, 179–209.

Boiten, F. (1996). Autonomic response patterns during voluntary facial action. *Psychophysiology*, *33*, 123–131.

Buck, R. W. (1988). *Human motivation and emotion* (2nd ed.). New York: Wiley.

Buck, R. W. (2000). The epistemology of reason and affect. In J. C. Borod (Ed.), *The neuropsychology of emotion* (pp. 31–55). Oxford: Oxford University Press.

Butler, E. A., Egloff, B., Wilhelm, F. H., Smith, N. C., Erickson, E. A., & Gross, J. J. (2003). The social consequences of expressive suppression. *Emotion*, *3*, 48–67.

Capella, J. N. (1993). The facial feedback hypothesis in human interaction. *Journal of Language and Social Psychology*, *12*, 13–29.

Cornelius, R. R. (1996). *The science of emotion: Research and tradition in the psychology of emotion*. Upper Saddle River, NJ: Prentice Hall.

Cosmides, L., & Tooby, J. (2000). Evolutionary psychology and the emotions. In M. L. Lewis & J. Haviland-Jones (Eds.), *Handbook of Emotions* (2nd ed., pp. 91–115). New York: Guilford.

Damasio, A. R. (2000). *The feeling of what happens: Body and emotion in the making of consciousness*. London: Vintage.

Darwin, C. (1872). *The expression of the emotions in man and animals*. London: Murray.

Dennett, D. C. (1991). *Consciousness explained*. Boston, MA: Little, Brown.

Dethier, V. (1967). The hungry fly. *Psychology Today*, *1*, 64–72.

Dimberg, U. (1982). Facial reactions to facial expressions. *Psychophysiology*, *19*, 643–647.

Dimberg, U. (1990). Facial electromyography and emotional reactions. *Psychophysiology*, *27*, 481–494.

Ekman, P. (2003). *Emotions revealed: Understanding faces and feelings*. London: Weidenfeld & Nicolson.

Ekman, P., Davidson, R. J., Ricard, M., & Wallace, B. A. (2005). Buddhist and psychological perspectives on emotions and well-being. *Current Directions in Psychological Science*, *14*, 59–63.

Ekman, P., & Friesen, W. V. (1969). The repertoire of nonverbal behavior: Categories, origins, usage, and coding. *Semiotica*, *1*, 49–98.

Ekman, P., Levenson, R. W., & Friesen, W. V. (1983). Autonomic nervous system activity distinguishes among emotions. *Science*, *221*, 1208–1210.

Fenske, M. J., & Raymond, J. E. (2006). Affective influences of selective attention. *Current Directions in Psychological Science*, *15*, 312–316.

Ferguson, M. J., & Bargh, J. A. (2004). Liking is for doing: The effects of goal pursuit on automatic evaluation. *Journal of Personality and Social Psychology*, *87*, 557–572.

Forrester, J. W. (1971). Counterintuitive behavior of social systems. *Technology Review*, 73, 52–68.

Forterre, Y., Skotheim, J. M., Dumais, J., & Mahadevan, L. (2005). How the Venus flytrap snaps. *Nature*, *433*, 421–425.

Fridlund, A. J. (1994). *Human facial expression: An evolutionary view.* San Diego, CA: Academic Press.

Frijda, N. H. (1986). *The emotions.* Cambridge: Cambridge University Press.

Goleman, D. P. (1995). *Emotional intelligence: Why it can matter more than IQ for character, health and lifelong achievement.* New York: Bantam Books.

Gross, J. J. (1998a). The emerging field of emotion regulation: An integrative review. *Review of General Psychology*, *2*, 271–299.

Gross, J. J. (1998b). Antecedent- and response-focused emotion regulation: Divergent consequences for experience, expression, and physiology. *Journal of Personality and Social Psychology*, *74*, 224–237.

Gross, J. J., & Levenson, R. W. (1993). Emotional suppression: Physiology, self-report, and expressive behavior. *Journal of Personality and Social Psychology*, *64*, 970–986.

Gross, J. J., & Levenson, R. W. (1997). Hiding feelings: The acute effects of inhibiting positive and negative emotions. *Journal of Abnormal Psychology*, *106*, 95–103.

Gross, J. J., & Thompson, R. A. (2007). Emotion regulation: Conceptual foundations. In J. J. Gross (Ed.), *Handbook of emotion regulation* (pp. 3–24). New York: Guilford.

Harris, C. R. (2001). Cardiovascular responses of embarrassment and effects of emotional suppression in a social setting. *Journal of Personality and Social Psychology*, *81*, 886–897.

Hess, U., Banse, R., & Kappas, A. (1995). The intensity of facial expression is determined by underlying affective state and social situation. *Journal of Personality and Social Psychology*, *69*, 280–288.

Hess, U., Kappas, A., & Banse, R. (1993, May). *Hysterical laughter in the laboratory: Two studies on emotional contagion in an interactive setting.* Paper presented at the 54th Annual Convention of the Canadian Psychological Association, Montreal, Quebec, Canada.

Hess, U., Kappas, A., McHugo, G. J., Lanzetta, J. T., & Kleck, R. E. (1992). The facilitative effect of facial expression on the self-generation of emotion. *International Journal of Psychophysiology*, *12*, 251–265.

Izard, C. E. (1990). Facial expressions and the regulation of emotions. *Journal of Personality and Social Psychology*, *58*, 487–498.

Izard, C. E., Ackerman, B. P., Schoff, K. M., & Fine, S. E. (2000). Self organization of discrete emotions, emotion patterns, and emotion-cognition relations. In M. D. Lewis & I. Granic (Eds.), *Emotion, development, and self-organization: Dynamic systems approaches to emotional development* (pp. 15–36). New York: Cambridge University Press.

Kappas, A. (1989). *Control of emotion.* Unpublished Ph.D. thesis, Dartmouth College, USA.

Kappas, A. (1996). The sociality of appraisals: Impact of social situations on the evaluations of emotion antecedent events and physiological and expressive reactions. In N. H. Frijda (Ed.), *Proceedings of the IXth conference of the International Society for Research on Emotions* (pp. 116–120). Toronto, Ontario, Canada: ISRE Publications.

Kappas, A. (1999, September). *Reconceptualizing the influence of social context on facial displays: Towards a new view of display rules.* Paper presented at the 8th European Conference on Facial Expression - Measurement and Meaning, Saarbrücken, Germany.

Kappas, A. (2001). A metaphor is a metaphor is a metaphor: Exorcising the homunculus from appraisal theory. In K. R. Scherer, A. Schorr, & T. Johnstone (Eds.), *Appraisal processes in emotion: theory, methods, research* (pp. 157–172). New York: Oxford University Press.

Kappas, A. (2002). The science of emotion as a multidisciplinary research paradigm. *Behavioural Processes, 60,* 85–98.

Kappas, A. (2003). What facial activity can and cannot tell us about emotions. In M. Katsikitis (Ed.), *The human face: Measurement and meaning* (pp. 215–234). Dordrecht: Kluwer.

Kappas, A. (2004, October). *Intra- and interpersonal determinants and consequences of facial activation.* Paper presented at the 44th Annual Meeting of the Society for Psychophysiological Research, Santa Fe, NM.

Kappas, A., & Descôteaux, J. (2003). Of butterflies and roaring thunder: Nonverbal communication in interaction and regulation of emotion. In P. Philippot, R. S. Feldman, & E. J. Coats (Eds.), *Nonverbal behavior in clinical settings* (pp. 45–74). New York: Oxford University Press.

Kappas, A., & Küster, D. (2006, October). *Priming "we" or "they" affects level of orbicularis oculi activity in response to funny films: An investigation on the relationship between emotions and facial activity.* Paper presented at the 46th Annual Meeting of the Society for Psychophysiological Research, Vancouver, BC, Canada.

Kappas, A., McHugo, G. J., & Lanzetta, J. T. (1989). Componential control and the modulation of emotional experience. *Psychophysiology, 26,* 37.

Krauss, R. M., & Fussell, S. R. (1996). Social psychological models of interpersonal communication. In E. T. Higgins & A. Kruglanski (Eds.), *Social Psychology: A Handbook of Basic Principles* (pp. 655–701). New York: Guilford.

Kudielka, B. M., & Kirschbaum, C. (2005). Sex differences in HPA axis responses to stress: A review. *Biological Psychology, 69,* 113–132.

Küster, D., & Kappas, A. (2006, May). *Implicit associations between the concepts of friends/strangers with showing/hiding emotions: An indirect investigation on the relationship between emotions and expressions.* Paper presented at the 2nd Meeting of the Consortium of European Research on Emotion (CERE), Louvain-La-Neuve, Belgium.

Lanzetta, J. T., Cartwright-Smith, J., & Kleck, R. E. (1976). Effects of nonverbal dissimulation on emotional experience and autonomic arousal. *Journal of Personality and Social Psychology, 33,* 354–370.

Larsen, J. T., Kasimatis, M., & Frey, K. (1992). Facilitating the furrowed brow: An unobtrusive test of the facial feedback hypotheses applied to unpleasant affect. *Cognition and Emotion, 6,* 321–338.

Lazarus, R. S., & Lazarus, B. N. (1994). *Passion and reason: Making sense of our emotions.* Oxford: Oxford University Press.

Levenson, R. W. (1999). The intrapersonal functions of emotion. *Cognition and Emotion, 13,* 481–504.

Levenson, R. W., & Ekman, P. (2002). Difficulty does not account for emotion-specific heart rate changes in the directed facial action task. *Psychophysiology, 39,* 397–405.

Levenson, R. W., Ekman, P., & Friesen, W. V. (1990). Voluntary facial action generates emotion-specific autonomic nervous system activity. *Psychophysiology, 27,* 363–384.

Lozano, D. I., Crites, S. L., & Aikman, S. N. (1999). Changes in food attitudes as a function of hunger. *Appetite, 32,* 207–218.

Matsumoto, D. (1987). The role of facial response in the experience of emotion: More methodological problems and a meta-analysis. *Journal of Personality and Social Psychology, 52,* 769–774.

Mauro, R. (1992). Affective dynamics: Opponent processes and excitation transfer. In M. S. Clark (Ed.), *Emotion. Review of Personality and Social Psychology, 13* (pp. 150–174). Newbury Park, CA: Sage.

Mauss, I. B., Levenson, R. W., McCarter, L., Wilhelm, F. H., & Gross, J. J. (2005). The tie that binds? Coherence among emotion experience, behavior, and physiology. *Emotion, 5,* 175–190.

McIntosh, D. N. (1996). Facial feedback hypotheses: Evidence, implications, and directions. *Motivation and Emotion, 20,* 121–147.

Mischel, W., Shoda, Y., & Peake, P. K. (1988). The nature of adolescent competencies predicted by preschool delay of gratification. *Journal of Personality and Social Psychology, 54,* 687–696.

Morris, J. S., & Dolan, R. J. (2001). Involvement of human amygdala and orbitofrontal cortex in hunger-enhanced memory for food stimuli. *Journal of Neuroscience, 21,* 5304–5310.

Neumann, R., & Strack, F. (2000). "Mood contagion": The automatic transfer of mood between persons. *Journal of Personality and Social Psychology, 79,* 211–223.

Panksepp, J. (1998). *Affective neuroscience: The foundations of human and animal emotions.* New York: Oxford University Press.

Parkinson, B. (2005). Do facial movements express emotions or communicative motives? *Personality and Social Psychology Review, 9,* 278–311.

Peretz, B., Jacklet, J. W., & Lukowi, K. (1976). Habituation of reflexes in *Aplysia*: Contribution of the peripheral and central nervous systems. *Science, 191,* 396–399.

Philippot, P., Baeyens, C., Douilliez, C., & Francart, B. (2004). Cognitive regulation of emotion: Application to clinical disorders. In P. Philippot & R. S. Feldman (Eds.), *The regulation of emotion* (pp. 71–97). Mahwah, NJ: Erlbaum.

Richards, J. M. (2004). The cognitive consequences of concealing feelings. *Current Directions in Psychological Science, 13,* 131–134.

Richards, J. M., & Gross, J. J. (1999). Composure at any cost? The cognitive consequences of emotion suppression. *Personality and Social Psychology Bulletin, 25,* 1033–1044.

Richards, J. M., & Gross, J. J. (2000). Emotion regulation and memory: The cognitive costs of keeping one's cool. *Journal of Personality and Social Psychology, 79*, 410–424.

Riskind, J. H., & Gotay, C. C. (1982). Physical posture: Could it have regulatory or feedback effects on motivation and emotion? *Motivation and Emotion, 6*, 273–298.

Rochat, P., & Striano, T. (1999). Social-cognitive development in the first year. In P. Rochat (Ed.), *Early social cognition: Understanding others in the first months of life* (pp. 3–34). Mahwah, NJ: Erlbaum.

Rueda, M. R., Posner, M. I., & Rothbart, M. K. (2005). The development of executive attention: Contributions to the emergence of self-regulation. *Developmental Neuropsychology, 28*, 573–594.

Scherer, K. R. (1984). On the nature and function of emotion: A component process approach. In K. R. Scherer & P. Ekman (Eds.), *Approaches to emotion* (pp. 293–317). Hillsdale, NJ: Erlbaum.

Scherer, K. R. (1994). Emotion serves to decouple stimulus and response. In P. Ekman & R. J. Davidson (Eds.), *The nature of emotion: Fundamental questions* (pp. 127–130). New York: Oxford University Press.

Scherer, K. R. (2001). Appraisal considered as a process of multi-level sequential checking. In K. R. Scherer, A. Schorr, & T. Johnstone (Eds.). *Appraisal processes in emotion: Theory, Methods, Research* (pp. 92–120). New York and Oxford: Oxford University Press.

Slovic, P., & Peters, E. (2006). Risk perception and affect. *Current Directions in Psychological Science, 15*, 322–325.

Solomon, R. C. (2000). The philosophy of emotions. In M. Lewis & J. M. Haviland-Jones (Eds.), *Handbook of emotions* (2nd ed., pp. 3–15). New York: Guilford.

Solomon, R. C. (2006). Are we responsible for our emotions? *Emotion Researcher, 21*, 8–9.

Soussignan, R. (2002). Duchenne smile, emotional experience, and autonomic reactivity: A test of the facial feedback hypothesis. *Emotion, 2*, 52–74.

Spears, R., & Smith, H. J. (2001). Experiments as politics. *Political Psychology, 22*, 309–330.

Stemmler, G., (2004). Physiological processes during emotion. In P. Philippot & R. S. Feldman (Eds.), *The regulation of emotion* (pp. 33–70). Mahwah, NJ: Erlbaum.

Stepper, S., & Strack, F. (1993). Proprioceptive determinants of emotional and nonemotional feelings. *Journal of Personality and Social Psychology, 64*, 211–220.

Strack, F., Martin, L. L., & Stepper, S. (1988). Inhibiting and facilitating conditions of the human smile. *Journal of Personality and Social Psychology, 54*, 768–777.

von Scheve, C., & von Luede, R. (2005). Emotion and social structures: Towards an interdisciplinary approach. *Journal for the Theory of Social Behaviour, 35*, 303–328.

Wilson, V. E., & Peper, E. (2004). The effects of upright and slumped postures on the recall of positive and negative thoughts. *Applied Psychophysiology and Biofeedback, 29*, 189–195.

Winkielman, P., & Berridge, K. C. (2004). Unconscious emotion. *Current Directions in Psychological Science, 13*, 120–123.

2 Culture and Automatic Emotion Regulation

Iris B. Mauss, Silvia A. Bunge, and James J. Gross

The authors would like to thank Cendri Hutcherson, Rebecca Ray, Catherine Reed, Sarah Watamura, and Laura Wilhoit for their help with this chapter.

Margot was driving to pick up her nephew from preschool when another driver cut her off and then suddenly slowed down, forcing her to slam on her brakes. You might expect Margot to have become enraged. But she remained quite calm. How could this be? One explanation that leaps to mind is that Margot told herself to calm down, determinedly gripping the steering wheel and clenching her teeth. This explanation comes naturally to the Western mind because it fits well with the venerable Platonian metaphor of passion (e.g., an angry impulse) being reined in by reason (e.g., reminding oneself to be reasonable).

Yet, becoming angry never even crossed Margot's mind. In her native Hawaii, people just don't display anger with other drivers. It is important to note that these rules *didn't enter Margot's mind*—she decreased her anger without making a conscious effort. Interestingly, after spending some time in Southern California, the *same Margot* reports responding with intense rage at similar incursions. This example illustrates how people can regulate their emotions without conscious effort but automatically and according to their socio-cultural context. The aim of the present chapter is to further our understanding of such automatic processes in emotion regulation (AER) by examining what socio-cultural contexts engender AER, and what consequences two types of AER (response-focused versus antecedent-focused) have for individuals' emotional experiences, behaviors, and physiological responses.

EMOTIONS AND EMOTION REGULATION

Before we can talk about emotion *regulation*, we need to define what we mean by *emotion*. We define emotions as multifaceted, whole-organism phenomena that involve changes in the domains of *subjective experience*, *behavior*, and *physiology*. Emotions arise when an individual attends to a situation and evaluates it as directly relevant to his or her goals (Frijda, 1988; Gross & Thompson, 2007). As the row labeled "Emotional Process" in Figure 2.1 (p. 45) illustrates, this definition implies a *chronological sequence* of events, involving, first, a real or imaginary situation; second, attention to and evaluation of the situation (appraisal) by the individual; and, third, an emotional response, usually involving experience, behavior, and physiology.

With an understanding of individuals as agentic beings rather than passive emitters of emotions, researchers have become interested in the ways in which individuals attempt to regulate their emotional responses. We and others define emotion regulation as deliberate or automatic changes in any aspect of the emotional response, including the eliciting situation, attention, appraisals, subjective experience, behavior, or physiology (e.g., Bargh & Williams, 2007; Gross & Thompson, 2007). In order to further categorize types of emotion regulation, an important distinction has been made based on the sequence of events outlined above. Namely, researchers distinguish *response-focused* from *antecedent-focused* emotion regulation strategies (see Figure 2.1; Gross, 1998; Gross & Thompson, 2007). This distinction has important implications, and we therefore describe it next in greater detail.

Response-focused versus antecedent-focused emotion regulation

Response-focused emotion regulatory strategies are mainly directed at emotional responses *after* emotions have been generated. An example of such a process is the act of denying an emotional experience. For example, a person might feel angry (say, for losing a soccer tournament) but not wish to admit these feelings to himself, because they do not adhere to his ideal self (e.g., being a good loser). To do so, he might deny feelings of anger. Similarly, individuals might suppress or mask emotional behaviors after an emotion has been generated. Keeping one's face still when one is sad is an example of such behavioral regulation. Take again our soccer player, who might keep a stony face even when feeling a great deal of sadness and disappointment over losing a critical world cup game. Cognitive engagement or disengagement (e.g., denial) as well as behavioral regulation (e.g., suppression) take place after the emotional tendency itself has been triggered, and thus occur in response to emotional cues (i.e., I realize I am angry and now need to do something about that).

Antecedent-focused emotion regulatory strategies, on the other hand, are mainly directed at aspects that occur *early* in the emotional process. As Figure 2.1 illustrates, they can involve situation selection or modification (e.g., leaving an emotional situation), deployment of attention (e.g., not paying attention to an emotional situation), or cognitive change (e.g., altering of the meaning of an emotional situation; engaging in particular beliefs about the situation). For example, before entering a situation that an individual expects to make her feel angry (e.g., dinner with a not-so-nice relative) she might resolve to pay little attention to provocative remarks or to try to take the perspective of the other person so as to feel less anger (e.g., he talks only about himself because he doesn't have many friends). These regulatory strategies take place in response to situational cues.

Crucially, response-focused versus antecedent-focused emotion regulation strategies are thought to have pervasive and divergent effects on individuals' well-being, social and cognitive functioning, and health. Specifically, altering some components of the emotional response *after* it has come under way (response-focused regulation) might have adverse effects because other components of the emotional response continue to be active and require continued effort to be kept "under control." In contrast, antecedent-focused regulation strategies alter the complete emotional response by intervening *early in the emotional process*. Such strategies seem to have beneficial effects without much cost, because they proactively alter all downstream components of the emotional response (e.g., Côté, 2005; Gross, 1998). Indeed, research on response-focused emotion regulation suggests that it is generally associated with maladaptive effects on individuals' well-being, social and cognitive functioning, or physical health (e.g., Butler et al., 2003; Davidson, MacGregor, Stuhr, Dixon, & MacLean, 2000; Gross & Levenson, 1997; Mauss & Gross, 2004; Muraven, Tice, & Baumeister, 1998). Conversely, antecedent-focused emotion regulation is generally accompanied by a relatively adaptive profile of responding (e.g., Gross & John, 2003; Mauss, Cook, Cheng, & Gross, in press; Ochsner et al., 2004).

Deliberate versus automatic emotion regulation

This research suggests that emotion regulation affects a range of important domains in individuals' lives, and that different types of emotion regulation have quite different patterns of consequences. However, research to date has for the most part focused on *deliberate* types of response-focused versus antecedent-focused emotion regulation (cf. Bargh & Williams, 2007; Davidson et al., 2000; Parkinson & Totterdell, 1999). This is unfortunate, because response-focused versus antecedent-focused *automatic* emotion regulation (AER) might have just as pervasive effects as deliberate emotion regulation. Before we explore this hypothesis, we need to define AER, and explain why we think it may be important.

Most contemporary dual-process models contrast automatic (also called nonconscious, implicit, or impulsive) processes with deliberate (also called controlled, conscious, explicit, or reflective) processes (e.g., Chaiken & Trope, 1999; Sloman, 1996). Deliberate processing requires attentional resources, is volitional, and largely goal-driven. In contrast, automatic processing is initiated by the simple registration of sensory inputs, which in turn activates knowledge structures (schemas, scripts, or concepts) that then shape other psychological functions. Recently, Bargh and colleagues argued that four features characterize automatic processing: absence of subjective awareness, absence of intention, high efficiency, and absence of control (Bargh & Gollwitzer, 1994). A prototypically automatic process is characterized by all four features.

For many functions such as walking or riding a bike, we do not hesitate to agree that they can be performed automatically after they have been thoroughly learned. However, we hesitate to do so for so-called higher-level functions such as self-regulation. After all, until recently self-regulation was thought to be squarely located in the realm of the willful, conscious, and deliberate (cf. Bargh & Gollwitzer, 1994; Wegner, 2002). Thus, at first glance the concept of automatic emotion regulation seems oxymoronic.

However, research by Bargh and others (e.g., Aarts & Dijksterhuis, 2000; Bargh & Gollwitzer, 1994; Glaser & Kihlstrom, 2005) on automatic goal pursuit has challenged the notion that "higher-level" processes can only take place in a deliberate fashion. They propose that the full sequence of goal pursuit—from goal setting to the completion of the goal—can proceed outside of conscious awareness. In a series of studies, Bargh and colleagues show that goals such as the goal to perform well on a cognitive task can indeed be activated and executed without the intervention of conscious awareness (Bargh, Gollwitzer, Lee-Chai, Barndollar, & Trötschel, 2001). Bargh and colleagues explain these findings by postulating that goals (including self-regulation goals) are mentally represented in the same way as are other cognitive constructs. That is, goals correspond to knowledge structures containing information such as conditional information, possible means for attaining the goal, and behavioral procedures to enact those means. Thus, the literature on automatic goal pursuit provides theoretical and empirical precedents for AER.

How could such a process work in the context of emotion regulation? In our opening example, we described an instance in which a driver was able to respond with little anger to a situation that might have provoked a great deal of anger in other persons, *apparently without exerting deliberate effort to make herself less angry*. How are individuals able to regulate their emotions without knowing they are doing so? Following the above considerations, for emotion regulation to take place in an automatic fashion, (a) a percept must be registered, which (b) activates a schema, a concept, a goal, or a script ("don't show this feeling" or "don't pay attention to this situation"), which (c) alters aspects of the emotional response. The initial percept can be the emotion itself (e.g., someone who habitually responds to feelings of anger by suppressing hostile behaviors) or a situational cue (e.g., someone who has learned to decrease anger in the presence of a specific situation). As we describe below, we expect individuals' learning history and socio-cultural context to play an important role in shaping these associative networks. Just like skills, cognitive processing within these networks can become automatized with repeated practice.

Consistent with these considerations, we define AER as changes (either increases or decreases) to any aspect of one's emotion without making a conscious decision to do so, without paying attention to the process of regulating one's emotions, and without engaging in deliberate control. Note that in the present chapter, we are not concerned with the automatic *elicitation* of emotions or the deliberate control of automatic emotional processes. AER can take place after (in response to an emotional cue; response-focused) or before the emotion has been fully triggered (in response to a situational cue; antecedent-focused). Because this last distinction has important functional implications, we will in the following sections separately consider response-focused versus antecedent-focused AER. First, however, we want to explain why we think that socio-cultural contexts matter so much in AER.

Socio-cultural contexts and automatic emotion regulation

As the section above illustrates, which emotion regulatory strategies individuals engage in is a function of their knowledge structures. Knowledge structures, in turn, are profoundly shaped by individuals' socio-cultural context (e.g., Hochschild, 1983; Kitayama, Karasawa, & Mesquita, 2004;

Kitayama & Masuda, 1995; Markus & Kitayama, 1991). Gender, ethnic background, religion, and socioeconomic status are examples of socio-cultural factors that systematically affect—from infancy onward—how in-dividuals think about the world and themselves, including emotions and emotional events (cf. Bruner, 1986; Eisenberg, Smith, Sadovsky, & Spinrad, 2004; Markus & Kitayama, 1991; Mesquita & Albert, 2007; Shweder, 1999; Trommsdorff & Rothbaum, this volume).

Crucially, *automatic* processes might be particularly important for understanding how socio-cultural contexts affect emotion regulation. Be-cause cultural norms and practices are learned early in life, become ha-bitual, and surround us to the point that they appear completely natural and become invisible (Adams & Markus, 2004; Kitayama & Duffy, 2004; Knowles, Morris, Chiu, & Hong, 2001) they have a powerful automatic component. Implicit norms (i.e., notions of what "the right or normal way to be" is) and practices are transmitted to individuals automatically through reinforcement contingencies, by social models, and by individuals' engagement with cultural practices, institutions, and artifacts (cf. Adams & Markus, 2004; D'Andrade, 1984; Gordon, 1989; Mesquita & Albert, 2007; Rudman, 2004).

For example, individuals socialized to decrease emotional responses from early childhood on (e.g., "Anger is an unseemly emotion for a woman," or "Boys don't cry!") would be likely to automatically decrease their emo-tions, without this norm even entering their awareness; on the other hand, individuals to whom emotion regulation is a new, unfamiliar, or more con-flicted concept might engage in it more deliberately (Mesquita & Albert, 2007). Along these lines, Adams and Markus (2004) conclude in their review of cultural psychology that "the more typical case of cultural shap-ing may be as an indirect byproduct of engagement with 'implicit' cultural patterns" (p. 353). Together, these considerations suggest that socio-cultural contexts powerfully shape emotion regulation, and that many of these processes are automatic. In other words, wherever there is a socio-cultural context, there is AER. Against this backdrop, we now turn to the empirical evidence on response-focused and antecedent-focused AER.

RESPONSE-FOCUSED AUTOMATIC EMOTION REGULATION

A first group of emotion regulatory strategies is mainly directed at res-ponses once emotions have been generated (response-focused AER). As is summarized in the right side of the row labeled "Regulatory Mecha-nisms" in Figure 2.1, response-focused AER can involve cognitively en-

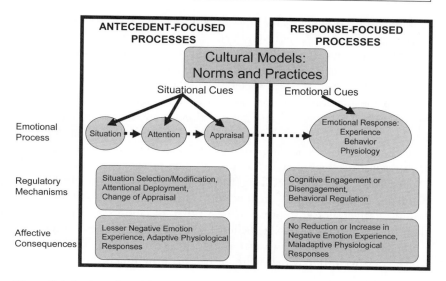

Figure 2.1 Socio-cultural factors, regulatory mechanisms, and affective consequences of two broad types of automatic emotion regulation (AER).

gaging with or disengaging from (e.g., denying) an emotional experience or regulating emotional behaviors after an emotion has been generated (in response to emotional cues). We make the assumption that these processes involve emotion *regulation* rather than simply emotion *reactivity*. We argue that this assumption is a useful one, and provide some empirical evidence for it. However, ultimately more empirical research is needed to fully understand the distinction between emotion reactivity and emotion regulation. With this caveat in mind, we next review, first, the cultural contexts that engender response-focused AER, and, second, laboratory studies that examine its affective consequences.

Socio-cultural considerations

What is the evidence for the conjecture that different cultural contexts engender response-focused AER? It has long been argued that socio-cultural contexts entail *display rules*, or norms about how to display emotions behaviorally (Ekman & Friesen, 1969). As Figure 2.1 illustrates, socio-cultural contexts provide norms about appropriate responses, which are activated in response to emotional cues. An exhaustive description of all socio-cultural contexts with implications for response-focused AER is beyond the scope of this chapter. However, as the following examples will illustrate, contexts such as those delineated by broad societal factors, region, gender, or profession systematically affect response-focused AER.

Much of the research investigating the impact of broader societal factors on emotion regulation has compared "Western" to "Eastern" contexts. For example, many Western societies stress positive aspects of emotions (because they demonstrate one's authentic and unique individuality), and, by extension, generally encourage emotional experience and expression (cf. Markus & Kitayama, 1991; Tsai & Levenson, 1997). In contrast, many East Asian societies more strongly value emotion decrease, especially with respect to "high-activity" emotions such as excitement (e.g., Eid & Diener, 2001; Gudykunst & Ting-Toomey, 1988; Matsumoto, 1990; Tsai, Knutson, & Fung, 2006). In line with this norm, several studies have found relatively lesser expression of a range of emotions in East Asian than in Western contexts (see Scherer, 1997). Notably, these differences were not accompanied by self-reported effortful control of emotions. Thus, societies differ widely with respect to how much they encourage the increase versus decrease of emotions.

Variation across emotions in general, however, is only part of the story. Different cultural contexts also differentially value *specific* emotions for *specific* social relationships (e.g., Matsumoto, Takeuchi, Andayani, Kouznetsova, & Krupp, 1998; Tsai et al., 2006). The regulation of anger, for instance, varies widely in different socio-cultural groups (cf. Briggs, 1970; Stearns & Stearns, 1986; Stratton, 1923). For example, regional differences associated with variations in understandings of honor relate to regulation specifically of anger. As Nisbett and Cohen (1996) detail, in so-called "cultures of honor" such as the American South or some Mediterranean regions, violence and openly expressed hostility are important aspects of defending honor against real or perceived threats (see also Rodriguez Mosquera, Manstead, & Fischer, 2000). Thus, in these contexts relative to others, aggression is encouraged or at least accepted as an aspect of anger.

Positive emotions as well show systematic socio-cultural variation in response-focused regulatory norms. For example, North American cultural contexts place relatively strong value on happiness and its expression (Matsumoto et al., 1998; Sommers, 1984). Happiness is seen as a sign of a "good self" and of psychological well-being (cf. Markus & Kitayama, 1991). In contrast, in other contexts happiness and its behavioral expressions are much less valued. For example, for the Ifaluk (a people living on a Micronesian atoll) happiness is seen as an expression of frivolousness and neglect of duties (Lutz, 1987). Or, in Confucian contexts, harmony among members of a group is strongly valued. Intense personal happiness might counteract that goal, as it may elevate the individual above the group (e.g.,

Heine, Lehman, Peng, & Greenholtz, 2002). Thus, these socio-cultural contexts relatively encourage the *decrease* of happiness while North American contexts relatively encourage the *increase* of happiness.

Individuals' socio-cultural context as delineated by their profession also affects response-focused AER. One early systematic investigation of related processes was conducted in sociological studies of *emotional labor* (that is, emotion regulation at the workplace; Hochschild, 1983). Researchers in this field observed that different professions require *surface acting*, or displays of emotions, to different extents. In particular, service jobs such as airline stewards or waiters, place great value on emotional displays such as "always smile at the customer," especially in contentious situations (e.g., Côté, 2005; Hartel, Ashkanasy, & Zerbe, 2005). Because these contexts are engaged with day-in and day-out, these rules become automatic over time (Hochschild, 1983). Thus, different professions create response-focused AER to different extents.

Together, these considerations suggest that socio-cultural contexts shape individuals' response-focused AER by providing norms about how to handle emotions once they have been triggered. Because humans are in constant engagement with their socio-cultural context, socio-cultural influences—and the automatic regulatory processes they engender—are expected to be quite pervasive. The pervasiveness of these processes makes it important to understand how they work and what affective consequences they have. While no studies have directly assessed socio-cultural differences in AER, the laboratory studies we describe in the following section have examined processes which might help us understand how response-focused AER operates.

Affective consequences of response-focused automatic emotion regulation

How does response-focused AER work, and what might be its affective consequences? The concept of defense in psychodynamic theory (e.g., Freud, 1936; Vaillant, 1977) represents what is probably the first theory of response-focused AER. As formulated by Freud, defensive inhibition of negative emotional experiences is a form of AER that is motivated by the individual's need to keep from awareness emotions that are intolerably painful or incompatible with the ideal self (Freud, 1930/1961). Freud took a negative view of this type of emotion regulation, postulating that this defensive "work" would come at the cost of expenditure of "psychic energy." A type of defensiveness more specific to negative emotions has also been labeled repression, or repressive coping (e.g., Weinberger, 1995).

Several studies support the concept of defenses that are triggered by emotional cues and operate outside of awareness. For example, Shedler and colleagues (Shedler, Mayman, & Manis, 1993) identified participants who reported minimal distress on questionnaires but whose early memories were rated clinically as showing signs of psychological disturbance. The investigators categorized these participants as high in defensiveness. While undergoing a mildly stressful task (e.g., reading aloud), defensive participants showed more indirect signs of anxiety (e.g., stammering or avoiding the content of the stimulus) than other participants, while simultaneously declaring themselves to be the *least* anxious. Importantly, they exhibited greater cardiac reactivity than other participants, indicating that despite their apparent lack of awareness of their anxiety, at some level they nonetheless exhibited greater reactivity.

The correlates of *repression* have been examined with similar paradigms and also point to a relatively maladaptive response profile (e.g., Byrne, Golightly, & Sheffield, 1965; Erdelyi, 2001; Paulhus, Fridhandler, & Hayes, 1997; Weinberger, 1995). Studies indicate that participants high in repression tend to have difficulty recognizing negative emotions (Lane, Sechrest, Riedel, Shapiro, & Kaszniak, 2000). Also, when tested in laboratory inductions of negative emotions such as frustration, participants high in repression tend to report experiencing less negative emotion, but exhibit impaired cognitive and social skills, as well as greater physiological reactivity (e.g., Asendorpf & Scherer, 1983; Brosschot & Janssen, 1998; Schwartz, 1995; Weinberger, 1995).

In a similar vein, Shaver and colleagues (Shaver & Mikulincer, 2007; Shaver, Mikulincer, & Chun, this volume) describe how individuals with avoidant attachment styles (individuals who habitually avoid close emotional relationships) learn as children that the expression of negative emotion does not affect their attachment figures (Cassidy, 1994). Consequently, such individuals learn to inhibit negative emotional cues (cf. Mikulincer & Shaver, 2003), a process that becomes automatized over time. In support of this hypothesis, avoidant individuals show relatively blunted emotional responding on automatic tasks such as lexical decision tasks (Mikulincer, Birnbaum, Woddis, & Nachmias, 2000). Crucially, this process might not entirely resolve their negative emotional reactions. Dozier & Kobak (1992) monitored electrodermal responses while participants recalled memories involving separation or rejection. They found that avoidant individuals had more difficulty generating negative memories. At the same time, avoidant individuals showed increased physiological reactivity during the task, suggesting that there might be an affective cost for cognitive disengagement from the emotion.

In addition to these negative effects of cognitive disengagement, there is evidence that automatic *behavioral* regulation might also have relatively maladaptive consequences for individuals. For example, Egloff and colleagues (Egloff, Schmukle, Burns, & Schwerdtfeger, 2006) examined the correlates of spontaneous (uninstructed and thus relatively automatic) behavioral suppression in a laboratory emotion induction, and found that it did not reduce experience of negative emotions but was associated with greater physiological responding. Field and correlational studies of *surface acting* (changing emotional behaviors without changing the underlying feeling when a situation consistently requires it) suggest a similar conclusion. In general, surface acting is associated with greater negative affect, lesser feelings of authenticity, and greater job strain and rates of burnout (e.g., Brotheridge & Lee, 2003; Côté, 2005; Hochschild, 1983; Montgomery, Panagopolou, de Wildt, & Meenks, 2006).

Together, the studies outlined in this section suggest two conclusions. First, they suggest that socio-cultural factors profoundly shape response-focused AER in a number of ways. Second, the studies on defenses, repression, spontaneous suppression, and surface acting suggest that response-focused AER plays an important role in individuals' affective responding and that it is relatively maladaptive (if not in the short term at least in the long term).

The conclusion that response-focused AER seems to have relatively maladaptive consequences suggests a difficult dilemma: either individuals fully express negative emotions (which might be socially unacceptable or impossible) or they suffer the negative consequences of response-focused AER. Such a simple dichotomy—healthy emotion expression versus unhealthy emotion regulation—is rendered implausible by the existence of at least some individuals who manage to lead quite composed lives without the numerous negative side effects of AER indicated above. How is this possible? The distinction between response-focused and antecedent-focused emotion regulation suggests a solution to this apparent dilemma. Recall that antecedent-focused deliberate emotion regulation seems to have generally more adaptive consequences than response-focused deliberate emotion regulation. Because antecedent-focused emotion regulation resolves emotions *before they are fully triggered*, it does not entail conflict about their expression. Perhaps then, antecedent-focused AER might also be relatively adaptive. Next, we will review empirical studies that provide evidence on this possibility.

ANTECEDENT-FOCUSED AUTOMATIC EMOTION REGULATION

The second main group of automatic regulatory mechanisms (antecedent-focused AER; summarized in the left side of Figure 2.1) have their primary impact on the emotion before the emotional response has been fully generated (Gross, 1998). Antecedent-focused AER is activated according to norms and practices that are provided given a particular situation (in response to situational cues). As is summarized in the row labeled "Regulatory Mechanisms" in Figure 2.1, antecedent-focused AER can involve automatic situation selection or modification (e.g., leaving an emotional situation), attention deployment (e.g., not paying attention to an emotional situation), or appraisal (e.g., altering of the meaning of an emotional situation; engaging in particular beliefs about the situation). In the following sections, we review, first, the socio-cultural contexts that engender antecedent-focused AER, and, second, laboratory evidence that provides insight into its affective consequences.

Socio-cultural considerations

Socio-cultural contexts can affect emotions by way of antecedent-focused AER, including automatic situation selection and modification, attentional deployment, or appraisal. For example, automatic situation selection and modification are thought to vary as a function of cultural contexts. In support of this notion, Kitayama and colleagues (Kitayama, Markus, Matsumoto, & Norasakkunkit, 1997) found that when asked to produce success and failure situations, "Japanese" situations (situations selected by Japanese participants) were rated by independent judges as less self-enhancing, while "American" situations (those selected by American participants) were rated as more self-enhancing. Similarly, Heine et al. (2001) found that Japanese students are more likely to keep engaging in situations that are likely to enhance self-critical views (i.e., those in which failure had been experienced) while American students are more likely to keep engaging in situations that are likely to enhance positive feelings about the self (i.e., those in which success had been experienced). Studies such as these suggest that individuals—depending on their socio-cultural context—might automatically select and modify emotional situations.

Attentional processes as well have been shown to be affected by cultural factors. For example, participants from East Asian contexts tend to direct attention in a number of subtle paradigms automatically at the context, while participants from Western contexts tend to direct their attention to focal objects (Masuda & Nisbett, 2006; Miyamoto, Nisbett,

& Masuda, 2006). In a study directly relevant to emotional situations, Cole and Tamang (1998) examined how mothers report mitigating their 4–5-year-old children's anger. They report that the majority of Tamang (a Nepali culture) mothers would attempt to distract their children from the situation (for example, by giving them food), thus teaching them not to pay attention to anger. These studies make it plausible that cultural contexts guide attention quite automatically in emotional situations.

Socio-cultural norms might also affect automatic appraisal of emotional situations. For example, individuals in cultural contexts that devalue strong emotions (e.g., Rothbaum, Pott, Azuma, Miyake, & Weisz, 2000) might learn over time (by incorporating norms or through observational learning) to appraise various situations as being relatively unimportant to the self and consequently experience relatively weaker emotions. Or, in cultures that value personal control, emotional situations that enhance personal control (e.g., anger-related ones) are likely to be appraised as important and relevant, which might lead to increased anger. In contrast, emotional situations that diminish personal control (e.g., contentment-related ones) are likely to be appraised as less important and relevant, which in turn might lead to decreased contentment (cf. Mesquita & Albert, 2007; Mesquita & Ellsworth, 2001). Along similar lines, Mesquita and Albert (2007) argue that cultural contexts that do not strongly value personal control would lead to less anger, because situations that go against the individual's plans are appraised as less antagonistic to the individual—it is to be expected, after all, that things don't always go the way the individual has planned.

Processes of antecedent-focused AER can of course be combined. For instance, cultures influenced by Buddhist religions, which construct anger as a "destructive" emotion and discourage its experience, provide norms (the self is not important) and habits (meditation on connection with others) that enable individuals to direct attention away from anger-provoking situations as well as provide appraisals that decrease anger (e.g., Nhat Hanh, 2001; Thurman 2006).

Together, these considerations suggest that socio-cultural factors powerfully shape antecedent-focused AER. This raises the question of whether the consequences of this type of AER are indeed more adaptive than those of response-focused AER.

Affective consequences of antecedent-focused automatic emotion regulation

Might antecedent-focused AER be more adaptive than response-focused AER? Four recent lines of investigation suggest that the answer to this question may be "yes." First, in explaining the positivity effect, which refers to the fact that as individuals enter older age, they are better able to regulate their emotions, Carstensen and colleagues (e.g., Carstensen & Mikels, 2005) invoke automatic regulatory processes. They argue that since *deliberate* processing deteriorates in older age, it is likely that more *automatic* emotion regulatory processing is responsible for the positivity effect. Thus, older individuals might make use of AER to their advantage.

Another recent study that conceptualized AER as adaptive was conducted by Jackson and colleagues (Jackson et al., 2003). In this study, participants' resting prefrontal cortex (PFC) EEG activity was measured, which was hypothesized to be a marker of individual differences in AER. As predicted, PFC EEG was associated with smaller emotion-modulated startle in response to negative emotional pictures, indicative of successful AER. Third, Bonanno (2005) has provided data suggesting that emotional avoidance after bereavement can promote *resilience* rather than negative long-term outcomes. Lastly, field studies on emotional labor suggest that *deep acting*, or, changing the way one feels given a particular situation might be associated with positive consequences such as lower levels of burnout and greater levels of job satisfaction (Côté, 2005; Diefendorff & Richard, 2003).

These areas of research are intriguing in that they suggest that AER might be quite adaptive. However, they are limited in some ways. First, in some of these studies, AER was inferred rather than directly measured. Second, these studies do not tell us why these types of AER are more adaptive than other types of AER. These concerns raise the question of whether there might be a more direct way of assessing AER, and whether the distinction between response- and antecedent-focused AER might explain the different patterns of outcomes.

In a study aimed to provide a more direct measure of individual differences in AER, we reasoned that the automatic goal of regulating emotion might be represented as an implicit positive evaluation of emotion regulation. Such individual differences would be likely activated by emotional situations, and would thus likely produce antecedent types of AER. Thus, we developed a variant of the Implicit Association Test (cf. Greenwald, McGhee, & Schwartz, 1998) to assess individual differences in implicit evaluation of emotion regulation (emotion regulation IAT; ER-IAT).

In the ER-IAT, participants are presented with words from the categories *emotion control* (e.g., controlled), *emotion expression* (e.g., expressive), *positive* (e.g., gold), and *negative* (e.g., gloom). Participants have to judge as quickly as possible in which of the four different categories words belong. For example, they have to press the 'a' key whenever they see a word that refers to either emotion control or something positive and press the 'k' key when they see a word that refers to either emotion expression or something negative. Importantly, there are two different blocks of trials: those in which emotion control and positive words share a response key, and those in which emotion control and negative words share a response key. Faster reaction times when categorizing emotion control and positive items together suggest a stronger implicit association between emotion control and positive. Conversely, faster reaction times when categorizing emotion control and negative items together suggest a stronger implicit association between emotion control and negative. A relatively stronger association between emotion control and positive items thus implies implicit positive evaluation of emotion control. By extension, we expected that it would lead to greater likelihood of *engaging in* AER.

Our goal was to put this assertion to the test by assessing whether positive implicit evaluation of emotion control (greater ER-IAT scores) would be associated with experiential, behavioral, and cardiovascular responses to an anger provocation (Mauss, Evers, Wilhelm, & Gross, 2006, study 2). As part of this anger provocation, participants were instructed by an "unfriendly" and "arrogant" experimenter to repeatedly perform a boring yet cognitively straining task. In order to control for the involvement of effortful emotion control, participants were asked after the task to what extent they had tried to control their emotions.

Predictably, most participants became angry during the task. However, those who had greater ER-IAT scores reported relatively less anger experience during this task. In addition, they exhibited a relatively adaptive challenge (as opposed to a threat) cardiovascular activation pattern, characterized by greater sympathetic activation, greater cardiac output, and lower total peripheral resistance (cf. Tomaka, Blascovich, Kelsey, & Leitten, 1993). Apparently, this relative reduction of anger experience happened without conscious effort, because ER-IAT scores were not correlated with self-reported effortful emotion control. These findings indicate that greater positive implicit evaluation of emotion control is associated with affective responses that are consistent with automatic, successful, and physiologically adaptive emotion regulation.

This correlational study of course begs the question of cause and effect, which led us to ask two questions. First, can AER be experimentally manipulated? Second, what would be the affective consequences of experimentally induced AER? To address these questions, we (Mauss, Cook, & Gross, in press) manipulated AER in two studies by priming emotion control versus emotion expression with an adaptation of the Sentence Unscrambling Task (cf. Srull & Wyer, 1979). This task unobtrusively exposed participants to words relating to emotion control or expression, thereby *implicitly* activating (priming) related concepts and goals. Importantly, we first primed emotion regulation, and then provided an emotional context via an anger provocation, maximizing chances that antecedent-focused AER would be engaged. Three domains of affective responding were measured: anger experience, negative emotion experience, and cardiovascular responses.

Results from these studies revealed that indeed priming affected subsequent emotional responding, such that participants primed with emotion control reported less anger than did participants primed with emotion expression. Importantly, participants primed with emotion control reported experiencing slightly lesser global negative emotion experience than those primed with emotion expression and did not exhibit more maladaptive cardiovascular responding. These results imply that, like the individual-difference process associated with ER-IAT scores, situationally induced AER does not invoke a cost.

Together, results from these studies raise the intriguing possibility that people are capable—without conscious effort—of remaining calm, cool, and collected in powerfully negative situations. The relative adaptiveness of this type of AER is in contrast to the maladaptiveness of response-focused AER. How can these two results be reconciled? From the existing studies, we cannot conclusively determine what about these processes makes them maladaptive or adaptive. However, the pattern of responses suggests that individuals using response-focused AER might exhibit an emotional response at some point, which is then decreased. Even though the regulatory processes are automatic, they might thus involve some conflict about the emotion, and some aspects of the emotional response might continue to be active. On the other hand, implicit positive evaluation of emotion regulation and situationally primed values might be activated *early* in the emotional response; they might thus operate in a more antecedent-focused manner, without ever evoking a conflict about the emotion and effectively decreasing all aspects of the emotional response.

Together, the studies reviewed in this section suggest two conclusions. First, they suggest that socio-cultural contexts shape antecedent-focused AER in a number of powerful ways. Second, laboratory studies on implicit evaluation of emotion regulation and automatic goal pursuit suggest that these processes are relatively adaptive.

■ SUMMARY AND CONCLUDING COMMENT

The present chapter is aimed at furthering our understanding of AER. We suggest that AER is shaped by cultural contexts, which provide the individual with implicit norms and automatized practices that can be situation-cued (which situation calls for which emotion regulatory response?) or emotion-cued (which emotion calls for which emotion regulatory response?). Correspondingly, cultural contexts engender antecedent-focused (those mostly taking place before the emotion is fully initiated) or response-focused (those mostly taking place after an emotion is initiated) AER. Importantly, antecedent-focused AER seems to be relatively adaptive while response-focused AER seems to be relatively maladaptive. The notion of an adaptive type of AER is in line with socio-cultural considerations, which suggest that cultural contexts that foster emotion decrease certainly do not lead to generally decreased well-being or psychological functioning. The existence of adaptive AER suggests a possible mechanism for adaptive, socio-culturally mediated emotion regulation. We hope that by providing a conceptual framework for AER, the present overview can help us better understand AER, which will be an important step towards a better understanding of the complex mechanisms by which socio-cultural factors affect emotional responding.

REFERENCES

Aarts, H., & Dijksterhuis, A. (2000). Habits as knowledge structures: Automaticity in goal-directed behavior. *Journal of Personality and Social Psychology*, 78, 53–63.

Adams, G., & Markus, H. R. (2004). Toward a conception of culture suitable for a social psychology of culture. In M. Schaller & C. S. Crandall (Eds.), *The psychological foundations of culture* (pp. 335–360). Mahwah, NJ: Erlbaum.

Asendorpf, J. B., & Scherer, K. R. (1983). The discrepant repressor: Differentiation between low anxiety, high anxiety, and repression of anxiety by autonomic-facial-verbal patterns of behavior. *Journal of Personality and Social Psychology*, 45, 1334–1346.

Bargh, J. A., & Gollwitzer, P. M. (1994). Environmental control of goal-directed action: automatic and strategic contingencies between situations and behavior. *Nebraska Symposium of Motivation*, 41, 71–124.

Bargh, J. A., Gollwitzer, P. M., Lee-Chai, A., Barndollar, K., & Trötschel, R. (2001). The automated will: Nonconscious activation and pursuit of behavioral goals. *Journal of Personality and Social Psychology*, 81, 1014–1027.

Bargh, J. A., & Williams, L. E. (2007). The case for nonconscious emotion regulation. In J. J. Gross (Ed.), *Handbook of emotion regulation* (pp. 429–445). New York: Guilford.

Bonanno, G. A. (2005). Resilience in the face of potential trauma. *Current Directions in Psychological Science*, 14, 135–138.

Briggs, J. L. (1970). *Never in anger: Portrait of an Eskimo family*. Cambridge, MA: Harvard University Press.

Brosschot, J. F., & Janssen, E. (1998). Continuous monitoring of affective-autonomic response dissociation in repressors during negative emotional stimulation. *Personality and Individual Differences*, 25, 69–84.

Brotheridge, C. M., & Lee, R. T. (2003). Development and validation of the Emotional Labour Scale. *Journal of Occupational and Organizational Psychology*, 76, 365–379.

Bruner, J. (1986). *Actual minds, possible worlds*. Cambridge, MA: Harvard University Press.

Butler, E. A., Egloff, B., Wilhelm, F. H., Smith, N. C., Erickson, E. A., & Gross, J. J. (2003). The social consequences of expressive suppression. *Emotion*, 3, 48–67.

Byrne, D., Golightly, C., & Sheffield, J. (1965). The repression-sensitization scale as a measure of adjustment: Relationship with the CPI. *Journal of Consulting Psychology*, 29, 586–589.

Carstensen, L. L., & Mikels, J. A. (2005). At the intersection of emotion and cognition: Aging and the positivity effect. *Current Directions in Psychological Science*, 14, 117–121.

Cassidy, J. (1994). Emotion regulation: Influences of attachment relationships. *Monographs of the Society for Research in Child Development*, 59, 228–283.

Chaiken, S., & Trope, Y. (1999). *Dual-process theories in social psychology*. New York: Guilford.

Cole, P. M., & Tamang, B. L. (1998). Nepali children's ideas about emotional displays in hypothetical challenges. *Developmental Psychology*, 34, 640–646.

Côté, S. (2005). A social interaction model of the effects of emotion regulation on work strain. *Academy of Management Review*, 30, 509–530.

D'Andrade, R. (1984). Cultural meaning systems. In R. A. Shweder & R. A. LeVine (Eds.), *Culture theory. Essays on mind, self, and emotion* (pp. 88–119). New York: Cambridge University Press.

Davidson, K., MacGregor, M. W., Stuhr, J., Dixon, K., & MacLean, D. (2000). Constructive anger verbal behavior predicts blood pressure in a population-based sample. *Health Psychology*, 19, 55–64.

Diefendorff, J. M., & Richard, E. M. (2003). Antecedents and consequences of emotional display rule perceptions. *Journal of Applied Psychology*, 88, 284–294.

Dozier, M., & Kobak, R. R. (1992). Psychophysiology in attachment interviews: converging evidence for deactivating strategies. *Child Development*, 63, 1473–1480.

Egloff, B., Schmukle, S. C., Burns, L. R., & Schwerdtfeger, A. (2006). Spontaneous emotion regulation during evaluated speech tasks: Associations with negative affect, anxiety expression, memory, and physiological responding. *Emotion*, 6, 356–366.

Eid, M., & Diener, E. (2001). Norms for experiencing emotions in different cultures: Inter- and intranational differences. *Journal of Personality and Social Psychology*, 81, 869–885.

Eisenberg, N., Smith, C. L., Sadovsky, A., & Spinrad, T. L. (2004). Effortful control: Relations with emotion regulation, adjustment, and socialization in childhood. In R. F. Baumeister & K. D. Vohs (Eds.), *Handbook of self-regulation: Research, theory, and applications* (pp. 259–282). New York: Guilford.

Ekman, P., & Friesen, W. V. (1969). Nonverbal leakage and clues to deception. *Psychiatry: Journal for the Study of Interpersonal Processes*, 32, 88–106.

Erdelyi, M. H. (2001). Defense processes can be conscious or unconscious. *American Psychologist, 56*, 761–762.

Freud, A. (1936). *The ego and the mechanisms of defense.* New York: International Universities Press.

Freud, S. (1930/1961). Civilization and its discontents. In J. Strachey (Ed. and Trans.), *The standard edition of the complete psychological works of Sigmund Freud* (Vol. 31). New York: Norton.

Frijda, N. H. (1988). The laws of emotion. *American Psychologist, 43*, 349–358.

Glaser, J., & Kihlstrom, J. F. (2005). Compensatory automaticity: Unconscious volition is not an oxymoron. In R. Hassin, J. S. Uleman, & J. A. Bargh (Eds.), *The new unconscious* (pp. 171–195). New York: Oxford University Press.

Gordon, S. L. (1989). The socialization of children's emotions: Emotional culture, competence, and exposure. In C. Saarni & P. L. Harris (Eds.), *Children's understanding of emotion* (pp. 319–349). New York: Cambridge University Press.

Greenwald, A. G., McGhee, D. E., & Schwartz, J. L. K. (1998). Measuring individual differences in implicit cognition: The implicit association test. *Journal of Personality and Social Psychology, 74*, 1464–1480.

Gross, J. J. (1998). Antecedent- and response-focused emotion regulation: Divergent consequences for experience, expression, and physiology. *Journal of Personality and Social Psychology, 74*, 224–237.

Gross, J. J., & John, O. (2003). Individual differences in two emotion regulation processes: Implications for affect, relationships, and well-being. *Journal of Personality and Social Psychology, 85*, 348–362.

Gross, J. J., & Levenson, R. W. (1997). Hiding feelings: The acute effects of inhibiting negative and positive emotion. *Journal of Abnormal Psychology, 106*, 95–103.

Gross, J. J., & Thompson, R. (2007). Emotion regulation: Conceptual foundations. In J. J. Gross (Ed.), *Handbook of emotion regulation* (pp. 3–24). New York: Guilford.

Gudykunst, W. B., & Ting-Toomey, S. (1988). Culture and affective communication. *American Behavioral Scientist, 31*, 384–400.

Hartel, C. E. J., Ashkanasy, N. M., & Zerbe, W. J. (2005). What an emotions perspective of organizational behavior offers. In C. E. Hartel, W. J. Zerbe, & N. M. Ashkanasy (Eds.), *Emotions in organizational behavior* (pp. 359–367). Mahwah, NJ: Erlbaum.

Heine, S. J., Kitayama, S., Lehman, D. R., Takata, T., Ide, E., Leung, C., et al. (2001). Divergent consequences of success and failure in Japan and North America: An investigation of self-improving motivations and malleable selves. *Journal of Personality and Social Psychology, 81*, 599–615.

Heine, S. J., Lehman, D. R., Peng, K., & Greenholtz, J. (2002). What's wrong with cross-cultural comparisons of subjective Likert scales?: The reference-group effect. *Journal of Personality and Social Psychology, 82*, 903–918.

Hochschild, A. (1983). *The managed heart.* Berkeley, CA: University of California Press.

Jackson, D. C., Mueller, C. J., Dolski, I., Dalton, K. M., Nitschke, J. B., Urry, H. L., et al. (2003). Now you feel it, now you don't: Frontal brain electrical asymmetry and individual differences in emotion regulation. *Psychological Science, 14,* 612–617.

Kitayama, S., & Duffy, S. (2004). Cultural competence—tacit, yet fundamental: Self, social relations, and cognition in the United States and Japan. In R. J. Sternberg & E. L. Grigorenko (Eds.), *Culture and competence* (pp. 55–87). Washington, DC: American Psychological Association.

Kitayama, S., Karasawa, M., & Mesquita, B. (2004). Collective and personal processes in regulating emotions: Emotion and self in Japan and the United States. In P. Philippot & R. S. Feldman (Eds.), *The regulation of emotion* (pp. 251–273). Mahwah, NJ: Erlbaum.

Kitayama, S., Markus, H. R., Matsumoto, H., & Norasakkunkit, V. (1997). Individual and collective processes in the construction of the self: Self-enhancement in the United States and self-criticism in Japan. *Journal of Personality and Social Psychology, 72,* 1245–1267.

Kitayama, S., & Masuda, T. (1995). Reappraising cognitive appraisal from a cultural perspective. *Psychological Inquiry, 6,* 217–223.

Knowles, E. D., Morris, M. W., Chiu, C.-Y., & Hong, Y.-Y. (2001). Culture and the process of person perception: Evidence for automaticity among East Asians in correcting for situational influences on behavior. *Personality and Social Psychology Bulletin, 27,* 1344–1356.

Lane, R. D., Sechrest, L., Riedel, R., Shapiro, D. E., & Kaszniak, A. W. (2000). Pervasive emotion recognition deficit common to alexithymia and the repressive coping style. *Psychosomatic Medicine, 62,* 492–501.

Lutz, C. A. (1987). Engendered emotion: Gender, power, and the rhetoric of emotional control in American discourse. In C. A. Lutz & L. Abu-Lughod (Eds.), *Language and the politics of emotion* (pp. 69–91). Cambridge: Cambridge University Press.

Markus, H. R., & Kitayama, S. (1991). Culture and the self: Implications for cognition, emotion, and motivation. *Psychological Review, 98,* 224–253.

Masuda, T., & Nisbett, R. E. (2006). Culture and change blindness. *Cognitive Science, 30,* 381–399.

Matsumoto, D. (1990). Cultural similarities and differences in display rules. *Motivation and Emotion, 14,* 195–214.

Matsumoto, D., Takeuchi, S., Andayani, S., Kouznetsova, N., & Krupp, D. (1998). The contribution of individualism vs. collectivism to cross-national differences in display rules. *Asian Journal of Social Psychology, 1,* 147–165.

Mauss, I. B., Cook, C. L., Cheng, J. Y. J., & Gross, J. J. (in press). Individual differences in cognitive reappraisal: Experiential and physiological responses to an anger provocation. *International Journal of Psychophysiology.*

Mauss, I. B., Cook, C. L., & Gross, J. J. (in press). Automatic emotion regulation during anger provocation. *Journal of Experimental Social Psychology.*

Mauss, I. B., Evers, C., Wilhelm, F. H., & Gross, J. J. (2006). How to bite your tongue without blowing your top: Implicit evaluation of emotion regulation predicts affective responding to anger provocation. *Personality and Social Psychology Bulletin, 32,* 589–602.

Mauss, I. B., & Gross, J. J. (2004). Emotion suppression and cardiovascular disease: Is hiding feelings bad for your heart? In L. R. Temoshok, I. Nyklicek, & A. Vingerhoets (Eds.), *Emotional expression and health* (pp. 62–81). New York: Brunner-Routledge.

Mesquita, B., & Albert, D. (2007). The cultural regulation of emotions. In J. J. Gross (Ed.), *Handbook of emotion regulation* (pp. 486–503). New York: Guilford.

Mesquita, B., & Ellsworth, P. C. (2001). The role of culture in appraisal. In K. R. Scherer, A. Schorr, & T. Johnstone (Eds.), *Appraisal processes in emotion* (pp. 233–248). New York: Oxford University Press.

Mikulincer, M., Birnbaum, G., Woddis, D., & Nachmias, O. (2000). Stress and accessibility of proximity-related thoughts: Exploring the normative and intra-individual components of attachment theory. *Journal of Personality and Social Psychology, 78,* 509–523.

Mikulincer, M., & Shaver, P. R. (2003). The attachment behavioral system in adulthood: Activation, psychodynamics, and interpersonal processes. In M. P. Zanna (Ed.), *Advances in experimental social psychology* (Vol. 35, pp. 53–152). San Diego, CA: Academic Press.

Miyamoto, Y., Nisbett, R. E., & Masuda, T. (2006). Culture and the physical environment: Holistic versus analytic perceptual affordances. *Psychological Science, 17,* 113–119.

Montgomery, A. J., Panagopolou, E., de Wildt, M., & Meenks, E. (2006). Work–family interference, emotional labor and burnout. *Journal of Managerial Psychology, 21,* 36–51.

Muraven, M., Tice, D. M., & Baumeister, R. F. (1998). Self-control as limited resource: Regulatory depletion patterns. *Journal of Personality and Social Psychology, 74,* 774–789.

Nhat Hanh, T. (2001). *Anger: Wisdom for cooling the flames.* New York: Riverhead Books.

Nisbett, R. E., & Cohen, D. (1996). *Culture of honor: The psychology of violence in the south.* Boulder, CO: Westview Press.

Ochsner, K. N., Knierim, K., Ludlow, D. H., Hanelin, J., Ramachandran, T., Glover, G., et al. (2004). Reflecting upon feelings: An fMRI study of neural systems supporting the attribution of emotion to self and other. *Journal of Cognitive Neuroscience, 16,* 1746–1772.

Parkinson, B., & Totterdell, P. (1999). Classifying affect-regulation strategies. *Cognition and Emotion, 13,* 277–303.

Paulhus, D. L., Fridhandler, B., & Hayes, S. (1997). Psychological defense: Contemporary theory and research. In R. Hogan, J. A. Johnson, & S. R. Briggs (Eds.), *Handbook of Personality Psychology* (pp. 543–579). San Diego, CA: Academic Press.

Rodriguez Mosquera, P. M., Manstead, A. S. R., & Fischer, A. H. (2000). The role of honor-related values in the elicitation, experience, and communication of pride, shame, and anger: Spain and the Netherlands compared. *Personality and Social Psychology Bulletin, 26,* 833–844.

Rothbaum, F., Pott, M., Azuma, H., Miyake, K., & Weisz, J. (2000). The development of close relationships in Japan and the United States: Paths of symbiotic harmony and generative tension. *Child Development, 71*, 1121–1142.

Rudman, L. A. (2004). Sources of implicit attitudes. *Current Directions in Psychological Science, 13*, 79–82.

Scherer, K. R. (1997). The role of culture in emotion-antecedent appraisal. *Journal of Personality and Social Psychology, 73*, 902–922.

Schwartz, G. E. (1995). Psychobiology of repression and health: A systems approach. In J. L. Singer (Ed.), *Repression and dissociation: Implications for personality theory, psychopathology, and health* (pp. 405–434). Chicago: University of Chicago Press.

Shaver, P. R., & Mikulincer, M. (2007). Adult attachment strategies and the regulation of emotion. In J. J. Gross (Ed.), *Handbook of emotion regulation* (pp. 446–465). New York: Guilford.

Shedler, J., Mayman, M., & Manis, M. (1993). The illusion of mental health. *American Psychology, 48*, 1117–1131.

Shweder, R. A. (1999). Why cultural psychology? *Ethos, 27*, 62–73.

Sloman, S. A. (1996). The empirical case for two systems of reasoning. *Psychological Bulletin, 119*, 3–22.

Sommers, S. (1984). Reported emotions and conventions of emotionality among college students. *Journal of Personality and Social Psychology, 46*, 207–215.

Srull, T. K., & Wyer, R. S. (1979). The role of category accessibility in the interpretation of information about persons: Some determinants and implications. *Journal of Personality and Social Psychology, 37*, 1660–1672.

Stearns, C. Z., & Stearns, P. N. (1986). *Anger: The struggle for emotional control in America's history*. Chicago: University of Chicago Press.

Stratton, G. M. (1923). *Anger: Its religious and moral significance*. New York: Macmillan.

Thurman, R. (2006). *Anger: The seven deadly sins*. New York: Oxford University Press.

Tomaka, J., Blascovich, J., Kelsey, R. M., & Leitten, C. L. (1993). Subjective, physiological, and behavioral effects of threat and challenge appraisal. *Journal of Personality and Social Psychology, 65*, 248–260.

Tsai, J. L., Knutson, B., & Fung, H. H. (2006). Cultural variation in affect valuation. *Journal of Personality and Social Psychology, 90*, 288–307.

Tsai, J. L., & Levenson, R. W. (1997). Cultural influences of emotional responding: Chinese American and European American dating couples during interpersonal conflict. *Journal of Cross-Cultural Psychology, 28*, 600–625.

Vaillant, G. (1977). *Adaptation to life*. Boston, MA: Little, Brown.

Wegner, D. M. (2002). *The illusion of conscious will*. Cambridge, MA: MIT Press.

Weinberger, D. A. (1995). The construct validity of the repressive coping style. In J. L. Singer (Ed.), *Repression and dissociation: Implications for personality theory, psychopathology, and health* (pp. 337–386). Chicago: University of Chicago Press.

3 Emotion-Related Regulation: Biological and Cultural Bases

Claire Hofer and Nancy Eisenberg

This research was supported by a grant from the National Institutes of Mental Health (2 R01 MH60838) to Nancy Eisenberg.

Emotion regulation is of obvious importance in most, if not all, cultures. Individuals who are able to regulate their emotion, and thus their behavior, in a manner that achieves goals and/or conforms with cultural expectations should have an evolutionary and social advantage. Thus, emotion regulation would be expected to have a biological basis. In addition, because social expectations and demands vary across groups and cultures, it is important to examine if individual differences in regulation are associated with positive outcomes in a variety of cultures. In this chapter, we review research relevant to the biological bases of emotion-related regulation, family correlations of emotion regulation, and the relations of emotion-related regulation to socialization and developmental outcomes in several cultures. Due to space limitations, our review is selective and is focused to a considerable degree on our own work. In addition, we focused primarily, albeit not solely, on individual differences in measures of dispositional emotion-related self-regulation. We start with some conceptual and measurement considerations, prior to reviewing relevant empirical literature.

THE CONSTRUCT OF EMOTION-RELATED REGULATION

People define emotion regulation in a variety of ways. According to Gross (1998), "Emotion regulation refers to the process by which individuals influence which emotions they have, when they have them, and how they experience and express these emotions" (p. 275). Definitions of emotion regulation differ in regard to whether they include regulation by extrinsic factors (e.g., parental behavior) or only processes within the individual. Gross and Thompson (2007) suggested that these two aspects of emotion regulation should be differentiated by the use of the terms "extrinsic" and "intrinsic." They also proposed that the construct of emotion regulation includes a variety of processes, especially situation selection, situation modification, attentional deployment, cognitive change, and response modulation.

Our definition of emotion-related regulation is similar to Gross and Thompson's (2007) definition of intrinsic emotion regulation. Emotion-related self-regulation (henceforth called emotion-related regulation or emotion regulation for brevity) refers to processes used to manage and change if, when, and how (e.g., how intensely) one experiences emotions and emotion-related motivational and physiological states, as well as how emotions are expressed behaviorally (i.e., response modulation; Eisenberg, Hofer, & Vaughan, 2007). We frequently have used the term *emotion-related* regulation because, unlike some investigators, we include in our definition the regulation of behavior associated with emotion, as well as the regulation of emotion reactivity. We also selected this designation because many of the processes frequently involved in emotion-related regulation are also used for the regulation of other aspects of functioning (see below).

In our view, emotion-related self-regulation should be confined to processes that can be willfully controlled. However, we also believe that aspects of self-regulation may, over time, become automatic and executed without much conscious awareness in many contexts, even though the individual should be able to shift into an aware mode when needed (Eisenberg, Hofer, et al., 2007; also see Gross & Thompson, 2007). Like some others (e.g., Gross & Thompson, 2007), we believe that emotion-related regulation is used in the service of biological and social adaptation and to achieve individual goals, although it may not always be adaptive.

In many studies of children's regulation, investigators have used behavioral measures of persistence (e.g., Eisenberg, Fabes, Guthrie, & Reiser, 2000), executive functioning (e.g., assessing the ability to deploy and switch attention; e.g., Blair, 2003), the abilities to inhibit or activate behavior, or delay of gratification skills (e.g., Kochanska, Murray, & Harlan, 2000). Other researchers have used a variety of questionnaires, including self- and other-reports of individual differences in the abilities to focus attention and inhibit or activate behavior. We, like some others (e.g., Kochanska et al., 2000), believe that the abilities to willfully manage attention and behavior partly reflect a dispositional, temperamentally based capacity called *effortful control*. Rothbart defines effortful control as "the efficiency of executive attention—including the ability to inhibit a dominant response and/or to activate a subdominant response, to plan, and to detect errors" (Rothbart & Bates, 2006, p. 129). Thus, effortful control involves the ability to willfully deploy attention (i.e., willful attention focusing and shifting) and to inhibit or activate behavior (labeled inhibitory and activational control, respectively), especially when a person prefers not to do so but needs to do so to adapt to the context or to achieve a goal. By definition, some executive functioning skills such as effortful deployment of attention, integrating of information attended to, inhibitory control, and planning are involved in effortful control. Although effortful control can be used for self-regulation of behavior or cognitive processes that are not very emotional, it is intimately involved in emotion regulation (Rothbart & Bates, 2006). Effortful control contributes to the individual's dispositional capacity for self-regulation; however, this capacity may or may not be reflected in specific behavior in a given context.

THE BIOLOGICAL BASES OF EFFORTFUL CONTROL AND SELF-REGULATION

As already noted, effortful control is viewed as one of the major components of temperament, defined as "constitutionally based individual differences in reactivity and self-regulation, in the domains of affect, activity, and attention" (Rothbart & Bates, 2006, p. 100). Rothbart and Bates (2006) use the term *constitutional* to "refer to the biological bases of temperament, influenced over time by heredity, maturation, and experience" (p. 100). Thus, temperament, including effortful control, generally is viewed as having both biological and environmental bases.

The genetic basis of temperament, including effortful control, has been supported in a number of studies. For example, in twin studies, Goldsmith and colleagues (Goldsmith, Buss, & Lemery, 1997) have found evidence for genetic as well as unshared and shared environmental influences on effortful control. In a study of young adult twins in Japan, Yamagata et al. (2005) found support for the genetic bases of attentional, activational, and inhibitory effortful control (heritability estimates ranged from .31 for inhibitory control to .44 for attentional control), as well as for unshared (but not shared) environmental effects. In another body of work, investigators are finding that the executive attention network, the basis of effortful control, has a strong genetic component (e.g., Fan, Wu, Fossella, & Posner, 2001).

Posner and Rothbart (2007) have argued that areas of the anterior cingulate gyrus and lateral ventral and prefrontal areas (as well as basal ganglia) underlie the general executive attentional network and effortful control. The midline frontal areas (especially the anterior cingulate gyrus) are also believed to regulate brain areas like the amygdala that are more clearly implicated in the reactive aspects of negative affect. There is now mounting evidence in studies of brain activity that the cingulate gyrus is activated when people engage in tasks tapping executive control of attention (e.g., Fan, McCandliss, Sommer, Raz, & Posner, 2002) or are experiencing emotion (Ochsner, Bunge, Gross, & Gabrieli, 2002).

With the new knowledge provided by research on the human genome, investigators are now starting to identify genes that are linked to executive attention and related processes. The anterior cingulate is only a synapse away from the ventral tegmental area, a major source of dopamine (a neurotransmitter), and there are numerous dopamine receptors in the brain (Rothbart & Bates, 2006). Thus, a number of candidate genes believed to affect dopamine, serotonin, and related neurotransmitters have been studied in relation to attention, including t-HTTLPR, DRD4, DAT1, COMT, and MAOA.

The first gene is called SERT (which is a promoter of the serotonin transporter). Parts of this gene (e.g., 5-HTTLPR) affect the availability of the neurotransmitter serotonin in the spaces between nerve cells (neurons). Levels of serotonin are thought to interact with other factors to influence mood and behavior (e.g., shyness), and the well-known drug Prozac affects serotonin levels. Human cells with the long 5-HTTLPR allele produce higher concentrations of serotonin transporter than cells with any short alleles. People with 1 or 2 short alleles exhibit greater amygdala neuronal activity in response to fearful stimuli (Hariri et al., 2002) and/or simply respond less to neutral stimuli (which often are compared to negative stimuli; Canli et al., 2005). They also tend to have reduced gray matter volume in limbic regions critical for processing of negative emotion, particularly in the perigenual cingulate and amygdala (Pezawas et al., 2005). Recently the short allele was also associated with decreased volume and gray matter density in the anterior cingulate and frontal cortical areas (Canli et al., 2005), suggesting a role in executive control/effortful control.

Dopamine is a neurotransmitter that appears to be especially central in modulating executive attention (Posner & Rothbart, 2007). DRD4 affects dopamine receptors and is associated with attention (Goldberg & Weinberger, 2004). The DRD4 gene is expressed predominantly in the prefrontal cortex and preferentially influences prefrontal gray matter volume (Durston et al., 2005). Among normal adults, the 4-repeat allele has a relation with executive attention (conflict networks), with the 4,7 allele combination being associated with the greatest difficulty (2,2 was best; Fossella, Posner, Fan, Swanson, & Pfaff, 2002). Auerbach et al. (1999) found that infants with long DRD4 alleles had lower scores on negative emotionality and distress to limitations than those with short alleles, although there is also some evidence of a link between the 7-repeat allele and attention deficit hyperactivity disorder (ADHD) (Faraone, Doyle, Mick, & Biederman, 2001). Thus, findings for DRD4 are mixed, but DRD4 likely is relevant for executive attention (Goldberg & Weinberger, 2004).

DAT1 (Dopamine transporter 1) affects the availability of the neurotransmitter dopamine in the synapses between neurons). Variations in this gene are thought to influence attentional capacity and behavior. Rueda, Rothbart, McCandliss, Saccomanno, and Posner (2005) found that the DAT1 10-repeat allele was associated with better executive attention in children, although the sample size was very small. The combination of long with short alleles appears to be particularly problematic and might be responsible for inconsistent prior findings (e.g., in Fan et al., 2002; Posner, personal communication, May 2, 2006).

COMT (catechol-O-methyl-transferase), involved in dopamine degradation, influences levels of dopamine in the brain, especially in the prefrontal cortex (PFC). Metabolizing dopamine via COMT may be particularly important for low activation of dopamine in the PFC, judging from the relation of COMT to reduced dopamine synthesis in the brain (Meyer-Lindenberg et al., 2005). The COMT gene has a common functional bi-allelic polymorphism that is associated with poor PFC (executive) function (Akil et al., 2003). In some research, adults with two Methionine (Met) alleles (vs. Valine alleles), which presumably allows more dopamine to become available at the synapse, performed best on executive functioning tasks. Individuals with one Met and one Val allele were intermediate, and those with two Val alleles performed most poorly (Egan et al., 2001; Goldberg et al., 2003), especially when the demand for attentional control was high (Blasi et al., 2005). The Met/Met genotype also has been associated with some measures of children's prefrontal cognitive functioning (Diamond, Briand, Fossella, & Gehlbach, 2004; but cf. Fossella, Sommer, et al., 2002). However, people with more Met alleles also show increased limbic and prefrontal activation to unpleasant stimuli (Smolka et al., 2005).

The MAOA (monoamine oxidase A) gene encodes an enzyme that metabolizes neurotransmitters such as dopamine, serotonin, and norepinephrine and, thus, affects the amount of these transmitters that are active in the brain. There is evidence that the shorter 3-repeat allele and/or the variants associated with lower enzyme expression (2, 3, or 5 repeats vs. 3.5

or 4 repeats; Meyer-Lindenberg et al., 2006) are linked with less efficient executive attention (Fan, Fossella, Sommer, Wu, & Posner, 2003), especially for men (Fossella, Sommer, et al., 2002), as well as impaired cingulate activation during cognitive inhibition and a hyper-responsive amygdala during emotional arousal (Meyer-Lindenberg et al., 2006).

In summary, although research findings are complex and changing as the field has emerged, there is initial reason to believe that the executive attention skills involved in effortful control and emotion-related regulation have a genetic basis. This is to be expected given the obvious adaptive advantage of these skills for human beings. In the next few years it is likely that we will know much more about the role of specific genes in executive attention and, thus, in individual differences in the regulation of emotion.

 ENVIRONMENTAL INFLUENCES ON EMOTION-RELATED REGULATION

As already discussed, the behavioral genetics findings suggest that environmental factors have an influence on capacities related to emotion-related regulation, especially effortful attentional and behavioral control. It is likely that numerous levels of environmental factors influence the development of emotion regulation; indeed, effortful control has been related to factors such as family stress and risk (Evans & English, 2002), culture (Trommsdorff & Rothbaum, this volume), and parenting. In this section of the chapter, we provide some examples of findings regarding parenting found in research in North America, followed by findings in other countries and cultures.

Illustrative findings regarding the socialization correlates of emotion regulation in North America

In general, supportive parenting has been positively related to children's emotion regulation, as assessed with discrete behaviors or dispositional measures of effortful control. Early in life, mothers who have more negative caregiving styles tend to have children who use less adaptive strategies for coping with emotion—when frustrated, for example, they are more likely to orient to and manipulate an object that they are not allowed to have and less likely to direct their attention away from the denied object (i.e., to distract themselves; Calkins, Smith, Gill, & Johnson, 1998). In contrast, when mothers tend to use positive guiding behaviors, their infants are more likely to use strategies such as distraction (Calkins & Johnson, 1998). Gilliom, Shaw, Beck, Schonberg, and Lukon (2002) found that warm, supportive parenting (versus more hostile or punitive parenting) when children were 1.5 years of age predicted children's ability to shift their attention from a frustrating situation at 3.5 years of age. Kochanska and colleagues (Kochanska et al., 2000; Kochanska & Knaack, 2003) have obtained similar results in a series of studies with young children; responsive parenting has been positively related to children's effortful control whereas mothers' power assertion has been negatively related to young children's effortful control. Consistent with the notion that sensitive parenting is related to the emergence of emotion regulation, children with a secure attachment exhibit better emotion regulation (Gilliom et al., 2002; see Calkins, 2004).

Similar findings have been obtained in studies of school-age children. Affective quality of parenting (e.g., positive affect, warmth) generally has been related to school-age children's level of effortful control, sometimes even when controlling for prior levels of EC when predicting across time (e.g., Brody & Ge, 2001). For example, Eisenberg et al. (2005) found that parental warmth and the expression of positive affect when interacting with their children predicted their teacher- and parent-reported effortful control two years later (also see Valiente et al., 2006), whereas parental reported negative expressivity has been negatively related to children's effortful control (e.g., Eisenberg, Gershoff, et al., 2001). Parental warmth has been linked to young school children's appropriate expression of affect (Isley, O'Neil, Clatfelter, & Parke, 1999) and to their regulation of positive affect (Davidov & Grusec, 2006). In addition, parental acceptance of children's negative emotionality has been positively related to their emotion regulation (Ramsden & Hubbard, 2002), whereas parental punitive responses have been related to suboptimal coping (Eisenberg, Fabes, & Murphy, 1996).

Numerous factors may account for the relations between the affective quality of parenting and children's regulatory capacities. Hoffman (2000) argued that parents' hostile or punitive negative expressivity is likely to elicit affective overarousal in their children, which undercuts regulation and learning in the specific context. Children who are overaroused are likely to have difficulties focusing and/or shifting their attention as needed, and their developing attentional and behavioral self-regulation skills may be compromised. Negatively aroused children are also less likely to take advantage of parental attempts to scaffold their emerging attentional and behavioral regulatory skills (e.g., through joint attention in the early years; Raver & Leadbeater, 1995). In contrast, when parents are warm and supportive, children are unlikely to be overaroused and are better able to respond to parental efforts to focus their attention and guide their behavior. In addition, as suggested by a number of researchers (e.g., Dix, 1991; Hoffman, 2000), children are more disposed to process their parents' messages, internalize parents' expectations for desirable behavior (e.g., inhibiting undesirable behavior and paying attention), and control their emotions and behaviors when their parents are positive and supportive rather than negative. The argument is that they may be more *motivated*, as well as better able, to attend to and learn from interactions with, and scaffolding provided by, warm parents.

Parental warmth and positive expressivity have also been associated with children's having a secure attachment (Contreras, Kerns, Weimer, Gentzler, & Tomich, 2000), and security of attachment is believed to foster regulated behavior, in part because the child has greater psychological resources for dealing with negative emotions and events. Children with more secure attachments are likely to be better at understanding others' emotions (see Thompson, 2006), which can contribute to the development and maintenance of emotion-related self-regulation. In fact, warm parents are relatively likely to allow their children to express their feelings and to participate in emotion-coaching and parental acceptance of emotion and discussions of emotion have been related to children's emotion regulation (e.g., Gottman, Katz, & Hooven, 1997).

Warm, positive parents are likely to evoke positive emotion in their children, and positive mood promotes creativity, attention, and flexibility in thinking and problem solving (Fredrickson, 2003). Consequently, when parenting maintains children's positive affectivity, it is likely to foster effortful control and active attempts to regulate. In addition, parents who express relatively high levels of positive emotion and are supportive are likely to model constructive ways to manage stress and relationships, including the regulation of emotional responses to stress (Power, 2004) and inappropriate behavior (Halberstadt, Crisp, & Eaton, 1999). Moreover, they may further foster children's regulation by promoting the predictability of the environment (Brody & Ge, 2001) and by protecting children from exposure to potentially stressful events (Power, 2004).

Parents' attempts to regulate young children's emotions also have been associated with higher levels of emotion regulation in young children. For example, in a study of 30-month-olds, Putnam, Spritz, and Stifter (2002) found that mothers of those children who refrained from touching a forbidden toy tended to use distraction as a technique during that period, whereas mothers of children who transgressed used more nondistracting strategies. Moreover, Spinrad, Stifter, Donelan-McCall, and Turner (2004) found that mothers' attempts to regulate their children's affect at 30 months were positively related to children's appropriate emotional displays in response to disappointment (e.g., hiding negative affect and expressing positive affect) at age 5 (an analogous relation was not found at 18 months). Mothers' soothing at 18 months was particularly related to children's use of distraction at 5 years of age (interestingly, mothers' use of distraction was negatively related), whereas mothers' specific strategies (rather than general use of strategies) were unrelated to children's self-regulation at age 5. Parenting practices that scaffold or supplement children's regulation may not only reduce children's arousal, but also help them to develop appropriate means of doing so themselves.

In summary, there is mounting evidence in Western societies that parents' socialization styles and behaviors are associated with individual differences in children's abilities to regulate their emotions and behaviors. An important issue is whether similar relations have been found in other countries.

 EMOTION REGULATION, CORRELATES, AND CULTURE

Culture (values, norms, and beliefs that are shared and transmitted socially, see Bugental & Grusec, 2006) can be conceptualized on different dimensions. A common classification of culture uses the individualist–collectivist or independent–interdependent dichotomy (Markus & Kitayama, 1991; see also Bugental & Grusec, 2006). Independent cultures value separation of the self and autonomy whereas interdependent cultures focus on the group rather than the self and value interrelatedness and connection. Recently, Kagitcibasi (2005) debated the independent–interdependent dichotomy and suggested that autonomy and relatedness are not incompatible (see also Oyserman, Coon, & Kemmelmeier, 2002). She introduced a third class of cultures, which can be called autonomous–related. Autonomous–related cultures value interpersonal relatedness but also value autonomous functioning. Based on a cross-cultural study of German, Euro-American, Greek, Cameroonian Nso, Gujarati farmers, urban Indian, urban Chinese, urban Mexican, and urban Costa Rican women, Keller et al. (2006) provided additional support for Kagitcibasi's model as applied to cultural models of parenting. Although Kagitcibasi's three dimensions of cultures can be useful, it has not yet been widely used and therefore, most studies described here classified countries on one of the common two dimensions.

It has been argued that self-regulation may be less important or valued in cultures that value interdependence (see Trommsdorff & Rothbaum, this volume). However, interdependence often requires subjugating one's own desires for the benefit of the group. Cultures may differ in the degree to which they are concerned about self-regulation in young children or in the degree to which other people are typically used as sources of soothing or modulation of emotion (see Trommsdorff & Rothbaum, this volume). However, given the emphasis on others' needs and the group in societies that are relatively interdependent or collectivist in their orientation, we would argue that self-regulation may be more valued and required for compliance with normative expectations than is true in cultures that value autonomy and the independent self.

Eisenberg, Zhou, Liew, Champion, and Pidada (2006) proposed a conceptual model of culture, emotion regulation, and children's functioning in the peer context (which can be adjusted to social functioning in general). In this model and based on previous studies, we suggested that, among other things, culture influences attitudes and beliefs about emotion and its regulation, which influences the socialization of emotion. Emotion-related regulation is thought to be affected by both socialization of emotion and cultural attitudes/beliefs. Emotion-related regulation in turn affects children's social functioning (see Eisenberg, Zhou, et al., 2006, for a complete version of the model). Although the distinction between interdependent–independent cultures might be useful in hypothesizing differences in emotion-related regulation and its correlates, based on our conceptual model, we would argue that there are many differences in attitudes and beliefs about emotions and emotion regulation even within independent and interdependent cultures. We believe that it also is useful to investigate the specific cultural attitudes, beliefs, and emotion-related behaviors (e.g., discussion of emotion) to understand if and how emotion regulation, including its socialization influences and prediction of social outcomes, differs based on the cultural context.

Socialization practices and emotion regulation across cultures

Cultural models are thought to shape socialization goals and parenting practices (see Bugental & Grusec, 2006; Kagitcibasi, 2005; Keller et al., 2006). And although not equally documented across cultures, it is somewhat well established that parents' socialization styles and behaviors vary from culture to culture (see Cole, Dennis, Martin, & Hall, this volume; see Trommsdorff & Rothbaum, this volume). For example, Wu et al. (2002) reported that Chinese parents are more authoritarian than European American parents. In multiple studies, Bornstein and colleagues reported differences in parenting practices across Europe, Asia, the Middle East, South America, and North America (e.g., Bornstein et al., 1998). However, an important issue is whether those differences in parenting attitudes and practices lead to differences in emotion-related regulation.

Although it is not as widely documented how such differences in socialization relate to individual differences in emotion-related regulation, some studies demonstrate that socialization does relate to emotion regulation across cultures and, in many cases, in a manner that is similar to that found in North America. However, there might be differences in the mean levels and the meaning of emotion regulation across cultures.

Differences in socialization can be observed at multiple levels. First, culture likely affects the expectations that parents might have about when children should develop specific emotion-related skills, which might affect their parenting practices and the age at which children develop skills to regulate their emotions. In fact, Joshi and MacLean (1997) found that maternal expectations in regard to child development differed across countries. Among other differences, they found that Indian mothers reported that they expected their child to be proficient at controlling their emotions and at being compliant at an older age than did Japanese and English mothers. This might impact their parenting practices and therefore the development of children's emotion regulation. These findings support our belief that the interdependent–independent classification of culture might not be a sufficient framework when addressing the research question of emotion regulation across cultures. Although India and Japan can be both classified as interdependent cultures (Marshall, 1997; Hofstede, 1991), Japanese mothers' expectations were closer to those of English mothers than those of Indian mothers.

Even though differences might be observed across cultures in the mean level of emotion regulation and in the contexts in which emotion regulation might be expected, the adaptive value of emotion-related regulation and some of the relations of parenting practices to regulation might be somewhat universal (Eisenberg, Zhou, et al., 2006). Keller, Lohaus, et al. (2004) compared early parenting practices in West Africa, India, Costa Rica, Greece, and Germany. They coded for the amount of body contact, body stimulation, object stimulation and face-to-face contact that mothers displayed during a free-play situation with their 3-month-old babies. They identified two styles of parenting: a proximal parenting style (characterized by more body contact and body stimulation) that was associated with the interdependent countries and a distal parenting style (characterized by more face to face and object stimulation) that was associated with the independent countries. Using these styles of parenting as predictors for children's self-regulation (compliance to requests and compliance to prohibition) at 18 to 20 months, Keller, Yovsi, et al. (2004) reported that in general, children who experienced a more proximal parenting style displayed higher self-regulation. Furthermore, they noted that the culture-specific socialization practices influenced children's development of self-regulation: 18- to 20-month-old toddlers were more self-regulated in Nso Cameroon (where proximal parenting style was displayed) than in Costa Rica (where proximal and distal parenting styles were displayed) and, in turn, Costa Rican children were more self-regulated than Greek children (where a distal parenting style was displayed).

Although Keller, Lohaus, et al. (2004) reported differences in the mean levels of emotion regulation as a function of socialization practices, the relations between types of parenting and children's regulation appear somewhat universal. In a study of 7–10-year-old Chinese children, relations between parenting styles and children's effortful control were investigated (Zhou, Eisenberg, Wang, & Reiser, 2004). The authors assessed parents' reported authoritative and authoritarian parenting styles. In general, they found that parents who were more authoritarian tended to have children lower on effortful control and higher on negative emotionality (as measured by children's proneness to anger and frustration) and that authoritative parenting was related to somewhat higher effortful control in children (as reported by parents).

Similarly, in China, Chang, Schwartz, Dodge, and McBride-Chang (2003) found that mothers' and fathers' harsh parenting was related to lower emotion regulation in kindergarteners. In a study of Indonesian children, Eisenberg, Liew, and Pidada (2001) reported that, as in the United States, parental expression of negative emotion related negatively to third grade children's emotion regulation as assessed by attentional control and inhibitory control. In addition, in a study comparing American and Japanese families, although Kobayashi-Winata & Power (1989) reported differences in parenting techniques between the two cultures, they also found that for both cultures, compliance was associated negatively with punishment and physical intervention as parenting practices. Overall, these findings suggest similarities with the US on the influences of socialization onto emotion-related regulation.

However, contrary to findings reported in the US (Eisenberg, Gershoff, et al., 2001), Eisenberg, Liew, et al. (2001) found no relation between parental positive expressiveness and children's emotion regulation in their study of Indonesian third graders. They suggested that because control of emotion is strongly valued on the island of Java, Indonesia (Mulder, 1989), the expression of intense positive emotion is not valued. Thus, this finding highlights the importance of understanding the cultural values and attitudes of a culture toward emotions before investigating relations among socialization and emotion regulation.

Investigators examining the relations of socialization to children's regulation in countries typically referred to as independent provide further support for the universality of the processes relating socialization to emotion regulation. For example, a study with 16-year-old German adolescents (Zimmermann, 1999) found that secure attachment representation, as measured by the adult attachment interview, was related to more adaptive emotion regulation. Emotion regulation was measured using a task on which adolescents answered questions tapping adaptive emotion regulation after hearing stories about social rejection or social failure.

In a study of French high school students, Champion (2003) reported that adolescents' family environment predicted their effortful control, such that adolescents in a supportive family environment (i.e., high connection between parents and adolescents, parents monitoring adolescents, and positive expressiveness in the family) tended to be more regulated whereas adolescents in an unsupportive family environment (parents using psychological control towards their children, and negative expressiveness in the family) tended to be less regulated. These findings also support some similarity in the relation between socialization and children's emotion regulation in France and the United States despite differences in parenting practices (such as the belief of French mothers that their parenting practices have very little influence on their children's development; Bornstein et al., 1998). French families also tend to be less nuclear than in North America and have strong intergenerational bonds (Claes, Lacourse, Bouchard, & Luckow, 2001). Therefore, it is also possible that differences in the socialization processes and the way children learn about emotions, display rules, and emotion regulation strategies can be observed and that French children learn from many people in different complementary ways.

Emotion regulation and social functioning across cultures

Numerous studies in Western cultures have shown that well-regulated children are more socially adjusted (e.g., Eisenberg, Cumberland, et al., 2001; Eisenberg et al., 2005; Valiente et al., 2006; see also Rothbart & Bates, 2006, for a review). To the extent that culture likely affects emotion-related regulation, it is of interest to examine if the positive relations between regulation and adjustment are observed across the globe. Based on knowledge from the cultural influences of socialization and its relations to emotion regulation, one would expect that although what is considered adjustment and the importance of emotion regulation might differ across culture, the mechanism by which adaptive emotion regulation and adjustment are positively associated would be observed somewhat universally.

In fact, similar to findings in the United States, in China, Zhou et al. (2004) and Eisenberg, Ma, Chang, Zhou, West, and Aiken (2007) found that high effortful control predicted higher social functioning (i.e., lower externalizing and internalizing problem behaviors and higher social competence) in 7–10-year-old children. Furthermore, effortful control appeared to mediate the relation between authoritarian parenting and children's social functioning in China (Zhou et al., 2004). Similarly, Chang et al. (2003) found support for low emotion regulation as a mediator of the relation between harsh parenting and children's aggression with a sample of Chinese kindergarteners. In Indonesia, Eisenberg, Liew, et al. (2001) and Eisenberg, Pidada, and Liew (2001) found that, similar to findings in North America, emotion-related regulation predicted higher social adjustment in third graders. Regulation also appeared to mediate the relation between parenting and children's social functioning such that parents who expressed more negative emotions had children who were less regulated, which in turn predicted lower popularity and higher externalizing problems (Eisenberg, Liew, et al., 2001). Furthermore, boys' regulation when they were in third grade still predicted their social adjustment three years later (Eisenberg, Liew, & Pidada, 2004). Finally, in a study of South African 6-year-old children, Barbarin, Richter, and DeWet (2001) found that children's resilience (which is linked to effortful control; see Eisenberg, Spinrad, et al., 2004) was important in their social functioning. Specifically, children's resilience (measured by a scale assessing children's adaptability and tolerance to frustration—both of which can be considered aspects of regulation) served as a buffer against the effects of violence on children's internalizing and externalizing problems, and academic motivation.

In other Western cultures, similar findings have also been reported. In France, effortful control in high school students tended to relate to higher popularity and lower externalizing and internalizing behavior problems (Champion, 2003). In another Western country (New Zealand), Caspi, Henry, McGee, Moffit, and Silva (1995) reported that behavior problems such as externalizing and, to a lesser extent, internalizing in adolescents were predicted by poor emotion regulation (i.e., lack of control: poor attention span, emotional lability, negativism, and restlessness) measured in early childhood (at 3 and 5 years of age). In Australia, adjustment at 12 years of age was predicted by self-regulation capacities from 1 to 10 years of age (Prior, Smart, Sanson, & Oberklaid, 2001). Similarly, in Iceland, Hart, Hofmann, Edelstein, and Keller (1997) found that resilient children at 7 years of age display less externalizing or internalizing problem behaviors and did better academically in adolescence than their peers who were overcontrolled or undercontrolled at 7. Thus, there appears to be cross-cultural support for the importance of emotion regulation skills in social adjustment.

Immigration and emotion-related regulation

The potential influences of culture on the relations between socialization, emotion regulation, and adjustment do not stop with the geographical limits of a country. Within the United States, for example, there are many subcultures (see Parke & Buriel, 2006). Some differences in socialization and social adjustment of some subcultures have been documented (see Parke & Buriel, 2006). However, in many US studies, subcultures are often grouped together and labeled "minorities" and few investigators have looked at differences in emotion regulation and its correlates within those subcultures.

Furthermore, when people migrate to a new country, they are faced with the challenge of adjusting to a new culture. Emotion-related regulation skills have been shown to be crucial in the prediction of intercultural adjustment. For example, Yoo, Matsumoto, and LeRoux (2006) found that the emotion regulation of international college students from a wide variety of countries from Europe, Asia, and South and Central America (as measured by a questionnaire) positively predicted their adjustment concurrently (i.e., less anxiety, culture shock, depression, and hopelessness, and more contentment and satisfaction with life), 2 months later (as rated by others as more friendly and lower anxiety), and 9 months later (i.e., indicated by less anxiety, culture shock, depression, homesickness, and hopelessness, more contentment and satisfaction with life, higher self-ratings of adjustment).

SUMMARY

This chapter highlights the biological bases of emotion-related regulation and environmental and cultural influences on emotion-related regulation. Studies in the United States have used a multitude of measures to assess emotion-related regulation in infants, children, adolescents, and adults. However, researchers need to create purer measures of emotion regulation (see Eisenberg, Champion, & Ma, 2004) that are not confounded with other constructs (e.g., adjustment, reactive control). Recently, some studies have focused on the biological bases of emotion-related regulation. Areas of the brain and specific genes have been identified as playing a role in emotion regulation skills. As research and knowledge of biological bases of emotion regulation increases, researchers will need to further address interactions between genes and the environment in the development of emotion regulation. Furthermore, because it is difficult to identify genetic influences that are independent of the environment (Moore, 2002), it would be interesting to see if identical genes can be linked to emotion regulation skills (such as executive attention) in a variety of countries.

In the US, relations between parenting and children's regulation skills have been widely reported across multiple age groups. It appears that, although there are differences among socialization beliefs and practices across cultures, there is also some degree of universality in the processes involved in the influence of socialization on emotion-related regulation. Furthermore, emotion-related regulation does appear to be adaptive across cultures, as positive relations between regulation and adjustment have been reported in many studies with different age groups worldwide. It is likely that the magnitude of some of those relations and mean levels varies across cultures (e.g., see Eisenberg, Zhou, et al., 2006); however, the pattern of relations appears somewhat universal.

Studies differ widely in the measures of socialization, emotion regulation, and adjustment used. As a result, the cross-cultural comparisons are limited. There is a pressing need for more systematic cultural research that statistically assess the viability of using North American-based measures in other countries and their equivalence. And researchers need to further address the meaning of emotion regulation itself in different cultures. Finally, although studies have investigated a variety of cultures, many cultures and subcultures are still not represented. The findings highlighted here suggest that emotion-related regulation is central to individuals' social functioning and needs in most (if not all) cultures and should be further investigated in non-Western countries.

REFERENCES

Akil, M., Kolachana, B. S., Rothmond, D. A., Hyde, T. M., Weinberger, D. R., & Kleinman, J. E. (2003). Catechol-O-Methyltransferase genotype and dopamine regulation in the human brain. *Journal of Neuroscience, 23*, 2008–2013.

Auerbach, J., Geller, V., Lezer, S., Shinwell, E., Belmaker, R. H., Levine, J., et al. (1999). Dopamine D4 receptor (D4DR) and serotonin transporter promoter (5-HTTLPR) polymorphisms in the determination of temperament in 2-month-old infants. *Molecular Psychiatry, 4*, 369–373.

Barbarin, O. A., Richter, L., DeWet, T. (2001). Exposure to violence, coping resources, and psychological adjustment of South African children. *American Journal of Orthopsychiatry, 71*, 16–25.

Blair, C. (2003). Behavioral inhibition and behavioral activation in young children: Relations with self-regulation and adaptation to preschool in children attending Head Start. *Developmental Psychobiology, 42*, 301–311.

Blasi, G., Mattay, V. S., Bertolino, A., Elevag, B., Callicott, J. H., Das, S., et al. (2005). Effect of catechol-O-methyltransferase val158-met genotype on attentional control. *Journal of Neuroscience, 25*, 5038–5045.

Bornstein, M., Haynes, M., Azuma, H., Galperin, C., Maital, S., Ogino, M., et al. (1998). A cross-national study of self-evaluations and attributions in parenting: Argentina, Belgium, France, Israel, Italy, Japan, and the United States. *Developmental Psychology, 34*, 662–676.

Brody, G. H., & Ge, X. (2001). Linking parenting processes and self-regulation to psychological functioning and alcohol use during early adolescence. *Journal of Family Psychology, 15*, 82–93.

Bugental, D. B., & Grusec, J. E. (2006). Socialization processes. In N. Eisenberg (Ed.), *Handbook of child psychology. Vol. 3. Social, emotional, and personality development* (6th ed., pp. 366–428). New York: Wiley.

Calkins, S. D. (2004). Early attachment processes and the development of emotional self-regulation. In R. F. Baumeister & K. D. Vohs (Eds.), *Handbook of self-regulation: Research, theory, and applications* (pp. 324–339). New York: Guilford.

Calkins, S. D., & Johnson, M. J. (1998). Toddler regulation of distress to frustrating events: Temperamental and maternal correlates. *Infant Behavior and Development, 21*, 379–395.

Calkins, S. D., Smith, C. L., Gill, K. L., & Johnson, M. C. (1998). Maternal interactive style across contexts: Relations to emotional, behavioral, and physiological regulation during toddlerhood. *Social Development, 7*, 350–369.

Canli, T., Omura, K., Haas, B. W., Fallgatter, A., Constable, R. T., & Lesch, K. P. (2005). Beyond affect: A role for genetic variation of the serotonin transporter in neural activation during a cognitive attention task. *Proceedings of the National Academy of Sciences, 102*, 12224–12229.

Caspi, A., Henry, B., McGee, R. O., Moffitt, T. E., & Silva, P. A. (1995). Temperamental origins of child and adolescent behavior problems: From age three to age fifteen. *Child Development, 66*, 55–68.

Champion, C. (2003). *The role of socialization, control, and resiliency in French adolescents' social functioning.* Master's thesis, Arizona State University.

Chang, L., Schwartz, D., Dodge, K. A., & McBride-Chang, C. (2003). Harsh parenting in relation to child emotion regulation and aggression. *Journal of Family Psychology, 17*, 598–606.

Claes, M., Lacourse, E., Bouchard, C., & Luckow, D. (2001). Adolescents' relationships with members of the extended family and non-related adults in four countries: Canada, France, Belgium and Italy. *International Journal of Adolescence and Youth, 9*, 207–225.

Contreras, J., Kerns, K. A., Weimer, B. L., Gentzler, A. L., & Tomich, P. L. (2000). Emotion regulation as a mediator of associations between mother-child attachment and peer relationships in middle childhood. *Journal of Family Psychology, 14*, 111–124.

Davidov, M., & Grusec, J. E. (2006). Untangling the links of parental responsive-
ness to distress and warmth to child outcomes. *Child Development, 77*, 44–58.
Diamond, A., Briand, L., Fossella, J., & Gehlbach, L. (2004). Genetic and neuro-
chemical modulation of prefrontal cognitive functions in children. *American
Journal of Psychiatry, 161*, 125–132.
Dix, T. (1991). The affective organization of parenting: Adaptive and maladap-
tive processes. *Psychological Bulletin, 110*, 3–25.
Durston, S., Fossella, J. A., Casey, B. J., Hulshoff Pol, H. E., Galvan, A., Schnack,
H. G., et al. (2005). Differential effects of DRD4 and DAT1 genotype on fronto-
striatal gray matter volumes in a sample of subjects with attention deficit hyperactivity disorder, their unaffected siblings, and controls. *Molecular Psychiatry,
10*, 678–685.
Egan, M. F., Goldberg, T. E., Kolachana, B. S., Callicott, J. H., Mazzanti, C. M.,
Straub, R. E., et al. (2001). Effect of COMT Val108/158 Met genotype on frontal lobe function and risk for schizophrenia. *Proceedings of the National Academy of Sciences, 98*, 6917–6922.
Eisenberg, N., Champion, C., & Ma, Y. (2004). Emotion-related regulation: An
emerging construct. *Merrill-Palmer Quarterly, 50*, 236–259.
Eisenberg, N., Cumberland, A., Spinrad, T. L., Fabes, R. A., Shepard, S. A., Reiser,
M., et al. (2001). The relations of regulation and emotionality to children's externalizing and internalizing problem behavior. *Child Development, 72*, 1112–1134.
Eisenberg, N., Fabes, R. A., Guthrie, I. K., & Reiser, M. (2000). Dispositional
emotionality and regulation: Their role in predicting quality of social functioning. *Journal of Personality and Social Psychology, 78*, 136–157.
Eisenberg, N., Fabes, R. A., & Murphy, B. C. (1996). Parents' reactions to children's negative emotions: Relations to children's social competence and comforting behavior. *Child Development, 67*, 2227–2247.
Eisenberg, N., Gershoff, E. T., Fabes, R. A., Shepard, S. A., Cumberland, A. J.,
Losoya, S. H., et al. (2001). Mothers' emotional expressivity and children's behavior problems and social competence: Mediation through children's regulation. *Developmental Psychology, 37*, 475–490.
Eisenberg, N., Hofer, C., & Vaughan, J. (2007). Effortful control and its socio-
emotional consequences. In J. J. Gross (Ed.), *Handbook of emotion regulation*
(pp. 287–306). New York: Guilford.
Eisenberg, N., Liew, J., & Pidada, S. U. (2001). The relations of parental emotional expressivity with quality of Indonesian children's social functioning.
Emotion, 1, 116–136.
Eisenberg, N., Liew, J., & Pidada, S. U. (2004). The longitudinal relations of
regulation and emotionality to quality of Indonesian children's socioemotional
functioning. *Developmental Psychology, 40*, 790–804.
Eisenberg, N., Ma, Y., Chang, L., Zhou, Q., West, S. G., & Aiken, L. (2007).
Relations of effortful control, reactive undercontrol, and anger to Chinese children's adjustment. *Development and Psychopathology, 19*, 385–409.
Eisenberg, N., Pidada, S. U., & Liew, J. (2001). The relations of regulation and
negative emotionality to Indonesian children's social functioning. *Child Development, 72*, 1747–1763.

Eisenberg, N., Spinrad, T. L., Fabes, R. A., Reiser, M., Cumberland, A., Shepard, S. A., et al. (2004). The relations of effortful control and impulsivity to children's resiliency and adjustment. *Child Development, 75*, 25–46.

Eisenberg, N., Zhou, Q., Liew, J., Champion, C., & Pidada, S. U. (2006). Emotion, emotion-related regulation, and social functioning. In X. Chen, D. French, & B. Schneider (Eds.), *Peer relationships in cultural context* (pp. 170–197). New York: Cambridge University Press.

Eisenberg, N., Zhou, Q., Spinrad, T. L., Valiente, C., Fabes, R. A., & Liew, J. (2005). Relations among positive parenting, children's effortful control, and externalizing problems: A three-wave longitudinal study. *Child Development, 76*, 1055–1071.

Evans, G. W., & English, K. (2002). The environment of poverty: Multiple stressor exposure, psychophysiological stress, and socioemotional adjustment. *Child Development, 73*, 1238–1248.

Fan, J., Fossella, J. A., Sommer, T., Wu, Y., & Posner, M. I. (2003). Mapping the genetic variation of executive attention onto brain activity. *Proceedings of the National Academy of Sciences, 100*, 7406–7411.

Fan, J., McCandliss, B. D., Sommer, T., Raz, A., & Posner, M. I. (2002). Testing the efficiency and independence of attentional networks. *Journal of Cognitive Neuroscience, 14*, 340–347.

Fan, J., Wu, Y., Fossella, J., & Posner, M. I. (2001). Assessing the heritability of attentional networks. *BMC Neuroscience, 2*, 14.

Faraone, S. V., Doyle, A. E., Mick, E., & Biederman, J. (2001). Meta-analysis of the association between the 7-repeat allele of the dopamine D4 receptor gene and attention deficit hyperactivity disorder. *American Journal of Psychiatry, 158*, 1052–1057.

Fossella, J., Posner, M. I., Fan, J., Swanson, J. M., & Pfaff, D. W. (2002). Attentional phenotypes for the analysis of higher mental function. *The Scientific World Journal, 2*, 217–223.

Fossella, J., Sommer, T., Fan, J., Wu, Y., Swanson, J. M., Pfaff, D. W., et al. (2002). Assessing the molecular genetics of attention networks. *BMC Neuroscience, 3*, 14.

Fredrickson, B. L. (2003). The value of positive emotions. *American Scientist, 9*, 330–335.

Gilliom, M., Shaw, D. S., Beck, J. E., Schonberg, M. A., & Lukon, J. L. (2002). Anger regulation in disadvantaged preschool boys: Strategies, antecedents, and the development of self-control. *Developmental Psychology, 38*, 222–235.

Goldberg, T. E., Egan, M. F., Gscheidle, T., Coppola, R., Weickert, T., Kolachana, B. S., et al. (2003). Executive subprocesses in working memory. Relationship to catechol-O-methyltransferase Val158Met genotype and schizophrenia. *Archives of General Psychiatry, 60*, 889–896.

Goldberg, T. E., & Weinberger, D. R. (2004). Genes and the parsing of cognitive processes. *Trends in Cognitive Sciences, 8*, 325–335.

Goldsmith, H. H., Buss, K. A., & Lemery, K. S. (1997). Toddler and childhood temperament: Expanded content, stronger genetic evidence, new evidence for the importance of environment. *Developmental Psychology, 33*, 891–905.

Gottman, J. M., Katz, L. F., & Hooven, C. (1997). *Meta-emotion: How families communicate emotionally.* Mahwah, NJ: Erlbaum.

Gross, J. J. (1998). The emerging field of emotion regulation: An integrative review. *Review of General Psychology, 2,* 271–299.

Gross, J. J., & Thompson, R. A. (2007). Emotional regulation: Conceptual foundations. In J. J. Gross (Ed.), *Handbook of emotion regulation* (pp. 3–24). New York: Guilford.

Halberstadt, A. G., Crisp, V. W., & Eaton, K. L. (1999). Family expressiveness: A retrospective and new directions for research. In P. Philippot, R. S. Feldman, & E. Coats (Eds.), *The social context of nonverbal behavior* (pp. 109–155). New York: Cambridge University Press.

Hariri, A. R., Mattay, V. S., Tessitore, A., Kolachana, B., Fera, F., Goldman, D., et al. (2002). Serotonin transporter genetic variation and the response of the human amygdale. *Science, 297,* 400–403.

Hart, D., Hofmann, V., Edelstein, W., & Keller, M. (1997). The relation of childhood personality types to adolescent behavior and development: A longitudinal study of Icelandic children. *Developmental Psychology, 2,* 195–205.

Hoffman, M. L. (2000). *Empathy and moral development: Implications for caring and justice.* New York: Cambridge University Press.

Hofstede, G. (1991). *Cultures and organizations: Software of the mind.* New York: McGraw-Hill.

Isley, S. L., O'Neil, R., Clatfelter, D., & Parke, R. D. (1999). Parent and child expressed affect and children's social competence: Modeling direct and indirect pathways. *Developmental Psychology, 35,* 547–560.

Joshi, M. S., & MacLean, M. (1997). Maternal expectations of child development in India, Japan, and England. *Journal of Cross-Cultural Psychology, 28,* 219–234.

Kagitcibasi, C. (2005). Autonomy and relatedness in cultural context: Implications for self and family. *Journal of Cross-Cultural Psychology, 36,* 403–422.

Keller, H., Lamm, B., Abels, M., Yovsi, R., Borke, J., Jensen, H., et al. (2006). Cultural models, socialization goals, and parenting ethnotheories. A multicultural analysis. *Journal of Cross-Cultural Psychology, 37,* 155–172.

Keller, H., Lohaus, A., Kuensemueller, P., Abels, M., Yovsi, R., Voelker, S., et al. (2004). The bio-culture of parenting: Evidence from five cultural communities. *Parenting: Science and Practice, 4,* 25–50.

Keller, H., Yovsi, R., Borke, J., Kartner, J., Henning, J., & Papaligoura, Z. (2004). Developmental consequences of early parenting experiences: Self-recognition and self-regulation in three cultural communities. *Child Development, 75,* 1745–1760.

Kobayashi-Winata, H., & Power, T. G. (1989). Child rearing and compliance: Japanese and American families in Houston. *Journal of Cross-Cultural Psychology, 20,* 333–356.

Kochanska, G., & Knaack, A. (2003). Effortful control as a personality characteristic of young children: Antecedents, correlates, and consequences. *Journal of Personality, 71,* 1087–1112.

Kochanska, G., Murray, K., & Harlan, E. (2000). Effortful control in early childhood: Continuity and change, antecedents, and implications for social development. *Developmental Psychology, 36,* 220–232.

Markus, H. R., & Kitayama, S. (1991). Culture and the self: Implications for cognition, emotion, and motivation. *Psychological Review, 98,* 224–253.

Marshall, R. (1997). Variances in levels of individualism across two cultures and three social classes. *Journal of Cross-Cultural Psychology, 28,* 490–495.

Meyer-Lindenberg, A., Buckholtz, J. W., Kolachana, B., Hariri, A. R., Pezawas, L., Blasi, G., et al. (2006). Neural mechanisms of genetic risk for impulsivity and violence in humans. *Proceedings of the National Academy of Sciences, 103,* 6269–6274.

Meyer-Lindenberg, A., Kohn, P. D., Kolachana, B., Kippenhan, S., McInerney-Leo, A., Nussbaum, R., et al. (2005). Midbrain dopamine and prefrontal function in humans: Interaction and modulation by *COMT* genotype. *Nature Neuroscience, 8,* 594–596.

Moore, D. S. (2002). *The dependent gene: The fallacy of "nature vs. nurture."* New York: Holt.

Mulder, N. (1989). *Individual and society in Java: A cultural analysis.* Yogyakarta: Gadjah Mada University Press.

Ochsner, K. N., Bunge, S. A., Gross, J. J., & Gabrieli, J. D. E. (2002). Rethinking feelings: An fMRI study of the cognitive regulation of emotion. *Journal of Cognitive Neuroscience, 14,* 1215–1229.

Oyserman, D., Coon, H. M., & Kemmelmeier, M. (2002). Rethinking individualism and collectivism: Evaluation of theoretical assumptions and meta-analyses. *Psychological Bulletin, 128,* 3–72.

Parke, R. D., & Buriel, R. (2006). Socialization in the family: Ethnic and ecological perspectives. In N. Eisenberg (Ed.), *Handbook of child psychology. Vol. 3. Social, emotional, and personality development* (6th ed., pp. 429–504). New York: Wiley.

Pezawas, L., Meyer-Lindenberg, A., Drabant, E. M., Verchinski, B. A., Munoz, K. E., Kolachana, B. S., et al. (2005). 5-HTTLPR polymorphism impacts human cingulated-amygdala interactions: A genetic susceptibility mechanism for depression. *Nature Neuroscience, 8,* 828–834.

Posner, M. I., & Rothbart, M. K. (2007). Research on attention networks as a model for the integration of psychological science. *Annual Review of Psychology, 58,* 1–23.

Power, T. G. (2004). Stress and coping in childhood: The parents' role. *Parenting, 4,* 271–317.

Prior, M., Smart, D., Sanson, A., & Oberklaid, F. (2001). Longitudinal predictors of behavioural adjustment in pre-adolescent children. *Australian and New Zealand Journal of Psychiatry, 35,* 297–307.

Putnam, S. P., Spritz, B. L., & Stifter, C. A. (2002). Mother-child coregulation during delay of gratification at 30 months. *Infancy, 3,* 209–225.

Ramsden, S. R., & Hubbard, J. A. (2002). Family expressiveness and parental emotion coaching: Their role in children's emotion regulation and aggression. *Journal of Abnormal Child Psychology, 30,* 657–667.

Raver, C. C., & Leadbeater, B. J. (1995). Factors influencing joint attention between socio-economically disadvantaged adolescent mothers and their infants. In C. Moore & P. Dunham (Eds.), *Joint attention: Its origins and role in development* (pp. 251–271). Hillsdale, NJ: Erlbaum.

Rothbart, M. K., & Bates, J. E. (2006). Temperament. In N. Eisenberg (Ed.), *Handbook of child psychology. Vol. 3. Social, emotional, and personality development* (6th ed., pp. 99–166). New York: Wiley.

Rueda, M. R., Rothbart, M. K., McCandliss, B. D., Saccomanno, L., & Posner, M. I. (2005). Training, maturation, and genetic influences on the development of executive attention. *Proceedings of the National Academy of Sciences, 102,* 14931–14936.

Smolka, M. N., Schumann, G., Wrase, J., Grusser, S. M., Flor, H., Mann, K., et al. (2005). Catechol-O-Methyltransferase val158-met genotype affects processing of emotional stimuli in the amygdale and prefrontal cortex. *Journal of Neuroscience, 25,* 836–842.

Spinrad, T. L., Stifter, C. A., Donelan-McCall, N., & Turner, L. (2004). Mothers' regulation strategies in response to toddlers' affect: Links to later emotion self-regulation. *Social Development, 13,* 40–55.

Thompson, R. A. (2006). The development of the person: Social understanding, relationships, conscience, self. In N. Eisenberg (Ed.), *Handbook of child psychology. Vol. 3. Social, emotional, and personality development* (6th ed., pp. 24–98). New York: Wiley.

Valiente, C., Eisenberg, N., Spinrad, T. L., Reiser, M., Cumberland, A., Losoya, S. H., et al. (2006). Relations among mothers' expressivity, children's effortful control, and their problem behaviors: A four-year longitudinal study. *Emotion, 6,* 459–472.

Wu, P., Robinson, C. C., Yang, C., Hart, C. H., Olsen, S. F., Porter, C. L., et al. (2002). Similarities and differences in mothers' parenting of preschoolers in China and the United States. *International Journal of Behavioral Development, 26,* 481–491.

Yamagata, S., Takahashi, Y., Kijima, N., Maekawa, H., Ono, Y., & Ando, J. (2005). Genetic and environmental etiology of effortful control. *Twin Research and Human Genetics, 8,* 300–306.

Yoo, S. H., Matsumoto, D., & LeRoux, J. A. (2006). The influence of emotion recognition and emotion regulation on intercultural adjustment. *International Journal of Intercultural Relations, 30,* 345–363.

Zhou, Q., Eisenberg, N., Wang, Y., & Reiser, M. (2004). Chinese children's effortful control and dispositional anger/frustration: Relations to parenting styles and children's social functioning. *Developmental Psychology, 40,* 352–366.

Zimmerman, P. (1999). Structure and functions of internal working models of attachment and their role for emotion regulation. *Attachment & Human Development, 1,* 291–306.

PART II

Culture and Social Interaction: Markers in the Development of Emotion Regulation

4 Development of Emotion Regulation in Cultural Context

Gisela Trommsdorff and Fred Rothbaum

This study was supported by a grant to the first author by the Deutsche Forschungsgemeinschaft (TR 169/14–2). We thank Michael Boiger for his careful copy-editing of the manuscript.

Emotions have usually been studied with regard to three components: cognitive-experiential ("feelings"), behavioral-expressive (e.g., facial expression), and physiological-biochemical (physical states). The concept of emotion regulation refers to the process of altering stimuli and modulating responses that have their basis in these components (Eisenberg, 2004; Thompson, 1994). "Emotion regulation refers to the process by which individuals influence which emotions they have, when they have them, and how they experience and express these emotions" (Gross, 1998b, p. 275). This view is in line with Campos's (Campos, Campos, & Barrett, 1989) notion that an understanding of emotions necessarily entails an understanding of emotion regulation. Emotion regulation is an aspect of self-regulation, which includes efforts to manage behavioral as well as emotional responses.

To date, most studies on the development of emotion regulation have been conducted in the United States and other Western countries. Therefore, it is unclear whether the findings obtained can be generalized to other cultures (see critical comments by Cole, 1996; Eisenberg, Liew, & Pidada, 2004; Rubin, 1998).

We assume that emotion regulation is related to a person's self-construal and to his/her goals. Research has pointed to culture-specific construals of the self—with an independent self more emphasized and valued in the West and an interdependent self more emphasized and valued in much of the rest of the world (Markus & Kitayama, 1991, 1994). Therefore, in this chapter we explore the implications of cultural differences in self-construal for the study of emotion regulation and its development.

We also assume that regulatory behavior (like any other behavior) strives to achieve certain goals. This idea is basic to general motivation theories (e.g., McClelland, 1961), to the goal-oriented approach on self-regulation by Carver and Scheier (1998), and the goal-oriented approach of regulatory fit by Higgins and Spiegel (2004). In case of cultural differences in goal orientation, differences in emotion regulation are expected.

Our focus is on cultural differences in emotion regulation, which we presume pertain to differences in the sense of self and the goals sought. We are particularly interested in independent vs. interdependent conceptions of self and the pursuit of promotion vs. prevention goals. The independent self highly values promotion goals involving individual autonomy, self-enhancement, and overt expression of emotions. The interdependent self highly values prevention goals including accommodation to familiar other persons and norms, fulfillment of obligations, self-effacement, and public suppression of emotions. The processes and outcomes of emotion regulation should depend upon these different conceptions of self and goals.

We assume that persons growing up in a cultural context where the independent self is more valued than the interdependent self will develop regulatory abilities serving the goal of enhancing the independent self—to perceive and experience the self as positive and having efficacy. In contrast, where the interdependent self is more valued, persons will develop regulatory abilities serving the goal of preventing hurt to others' interests or threatening the group—to perceive and experience relational harmony, based on shared efficacy. This view challenges a widely held assumption in most Western research on emotion and self-regulation that the major goal of regulatory processes is to achieve positive emotions and a positive view on the self (Baumeister & Heatherton, 1996; Fredrickson & Losada, 2005; King, Hicks, Krull, & Gaiso, 2006). Our primary objective is to review evidence of cultural differences in child-rearing conditions and to highlight links between them and cultural differences in the development of self, goals, and most importantly, emotion regulation.

This chapter is structured into two main sections, on emotion regulation in cultural context and culture-specific socialization conditions for emotion regulation. First though we briefly review assumptions and findings from Western research on emotion regulation that are often treated as universal but which cultural evidence indicates are not. In a final section, we summarize our evidence and suggest consequences for a culture-informed theory on emotion regulation.

ASSUMPTIONS UNDERLYING RESEARCH ON EMOTION REGULATION IN THE WEST

Theory and research on emotion regulation and its development has dramatically increased during the past two decades (historical overview by Eisenberg, 2004). Most definitions of emotion regulation highlight its adaptive nature and its relation to emotion generation (Campos et al., 1989; Mauss, Bunge, & Gross, this volume) and emotional competence (Cole, Martin, & Dennis, 2004; Cole, Dennis, Martin, & Hall, this volume; Eisenberg & Spinrad, 2004; Gross, 2002; Gross & John, 2003; Saarni, 1999, 2001).

Western theories and research on emotion regulation focus on the maintenance of positive emotions (especially pride/esteem), and avoidance of negative emotions (especially those associated with ego threat, anxiety, and depression). Later in this chapter, we will suggest that there are different assumptions about emotion regulation in non-Western cultures. What is experienced as desirable and as undesirable is closely related to the cultural model of the self. The desire to prolong, intensify, or terminate emotions depends upon one's self-construal, situational demands, and cultural factors.

The factors that are typically most important in successful emotion regulation in the West are self-esteem, optimism, and self-efficacy. We will attempt to show that these factors are much less emphasized in non-Western cultures.

The intentional execution of emotion regulation results from attentional focus and effortful control (Kochanska, 1998), the activation of the "cool" system—the "know" system as opposed to the "hot" or "go" system (Metcalfe & Mischel, 1999; Mischel & Ayduk, 2004), various coping strategies (reappraisal, cognitive restructuring) and the modification of emotional expression. Thinking about an event in a way that cools its emotional quality induces less physiological activation than does suppression of one's emotion (Gross, 1998a; Mauss et al., this volume). These studies suggest that suppression of negative emotions has relatively negative effects, a conclusion that we reexamine in light of cultural evidence.

Since children's emotionality and their capacity for emotion regulation are associated with their social adjustment and competence in childhood and later development (Caspi, Roberts, & Shiner, 2005; Rothbart & Bates, 1998), there has been much attention to links between emotion regulation (which is one type of self-regulation) and behavioral regulation (other types of self-regulation). Both imply efforts to alter ongoing activity. Some research has dealt with the question whether there is a mutually supportive relationship between emotional and behavioral regulation, i.e., with respect to the activation of the "cool" system in delay (Mischel & Ayduk, 2004). The major link between emotional and behavioral self-regulation as studied in previous research is the motive to maintain one's positive self-esteem.

However, the evidence mentioned above and elaborated below challenges the universal validity of this assumption. The above dynamics may be quite different in East Asia where there is much less emphasis on a positive self-concept (e.g., Heine, Lehman, Markus, & Kitayama, 1999).

▣ EMOTION REGULATION IN CULTURAL CONTEXT

Cultural differences in emotion regulation are assumed to be influenced by the respective distinct scripts of emotion and self (Cole & Tamang, 1998; Cole, Tamang, & Shrestha, 2006). The experience, the expression, and the regulation of emotions may vary according to cultural scripts or cultural models of self (Markus, Mullally, & Kitayama, 1997), of agency (Markus & Kitayama, 2002), and of emotions (Mesquita & Markus, 2004; Kitayama & Markus, 1994, 1995, 2000). Accordingly, the developmental conditions for achieving the culturally adaptive forms of "optimal" emotion regulation can differ.

Focus on an independent versus interdependent model of self

The Western world favors an independent model of self which is autonomous, unique, distinctive, characterized by stable and internal attributes, and which values individual self-enhancement. In contrast, in many non-Western cultures, there is an emphasis on an interdependent model of self which is more relational, contextual, and socially situated (DeVos, 1973; Lewis, 1995).

To the extent that the self is defined in terms of the relationship of which the self is a part, the person gives priority to adjusting self to the relationship, to fitting in, to controlling or holding back internal wishes and emotions in order to insure interpersonal harmony. To the extent that the self is a separate and distinct person, priority is given to authentic expression of one's emotions and inner feelings even when this may adversely affect social harmony or give rise to interpersonal conflict. Accordingly, in the case of the interdependent self, positive emotions are experienced when the self is in harmony and in accord with other persons. In the case of the independent self, positive emotions are experienced when individuals assert their preferences and negotiate to defend their rights even though conflict is likely.

Focus on positive versus negative outcomes

Most research on emotion regulation is based on the assumption that the overarching goal of emotion regulation is to protect and enhance one's self-esteem, personal efficacy, and individuality; this is related to the goal of increasing positive emotions and avoiding negative emotions in order to improve one's well-being. These assumptions are in line with evidence that promotion goals are more prevalent in cultures favoring independence as compared to interdependence (Elliot, Chirkov, Kim, & Sheldon, 2001) and with influential Western theories of motivation (Bandura, 1997; Carver & Scheier, 1990, 1998; Ryan & Deci, 2000).

Research on cultural differences in self-esteem (e.g., Heine et al., 2001; Kitayama, Markus, Matsumoto, & Norasakkunkit, 1997) shows less positive effects of enhanced views of the self for Asian people than for people from Western societies, and less negative effects of failure on self-esteem (overview by Lehmann, Chiu, & Schaller, 2004). Asian as compared to US persons rather engage in more self-effacement and self-criticism, and in less individual (but more group-oriented) self-enhancement (Lehman et al., 2004). This implies cultural differences in emotion and emotion regulation after failure and success.

Focus on promotion versus prevention goals

Recent findings indicate that cultural differences in emotion regulation are due to differences in "regulatory fit" (Higgins, 1998, 2000). Persons "experience a *regulatory* fit when they pursue goals in ways that fit their regulatory orientation, and this regulatory fit increases the value of what they are doing" (Higgins, 2000, p. 1219). Regulatory fit has accordingly been conceptualized as "the increased motivational intensity that results when there is a match between the manner in which a person pursues a goal and his or her goal orientation" (Aaker & Lee, 2006, p. 15).

Lee, Aaker, and Gardner (2000) explore links between cultural differences in promotion goals (i.e., pursuit of gains) and prevention goals (i.e., avoidance of losses and fulfillment of obligations) on the one hand and independent and interdependent construals of self on the other. Westerners' emphasis on an independent self, positive distinctiveness, autonomy, self-enhancement, and a positive bias in information more generally, is

more consistent with a focus on promotion goals. In contrast, an emphasis on an interdependent self, harmony, and a negativity bias (Heine &
Lehman, 1997) may be more consistent with a focus on prevention goals.
Persons with these goals focus on negative aspects of the self in order to
avoid hurting group harmony or social relatedness. There is evidence that
interdependent self-construals are positively related and independent self-
construals are negatively related to the pursuit of avoidance goals (Elliot
et al., 2001).

The tendency of Japanese, as compared to Americans, to believe that
failure has more impact on self-esteem (Kitayama et al., 1997) may help
explain their prevention focus and their strategies for self-regulation (Lee
et al., 2000). The focus on failure and on prevention goals no doubt relates to their greater concern with ought–self comparisons—i.e., a focus
on differences between others' social norms or "oughts," and the actual
self. These tendencies relate to their interdependent self-construal. Duty
and obligation, and a focus on reducing the discrepancy between one's
current behavior and what one "ought" to do, are key features of prevention goals. Lee et al. (2000) demonstrate that, when an interdependent self is experimentally activated, more prevention-focused emotional
responses occur, particularly along the anxiety dimension. Thus, self-
construal, as well as culture and situation (e.g., failure, social obligations)
can be seen as important moderators of regulatory focus. We assume that
the prevention as compared to the promotion focus encourages inhibition of expression of emotions, and a preference for socially engaged
emotions, such as shame in contrast to pride.

Promotion and prevention focused goals can influence a variety of behaviors. Quite a different situation requiring emotion regulation is helping
(or avoiding to help) when experiencing another person in need (Trommsdorff, Friedlmeier, & Mayer, 2007). Promotion-focused concerns (helping) are more pronounced in cultures where the model of independence
prevails, in contrast to prevention-focused goals (refraining from helping in order to avoid hurting the victim inadvertently, e.g., by causing the
victim to lose face) in contexts where interdependence prevails.

Focus on developmental and performance goals

According to Dweck's (1999; Grant & Dweck, 2001, 2003) goal theory
of personality, the kind of goal one pursues influences attribution and
emotion regulation processes after failure. Dweck differentiates between
developmental/learning goals which are based in incremental views of
self and which she shows are highly adaptive, and performance/judgment

goals which are based in entity views of self and which are frequently maladaptive.

Grant and Dweck (2001) as well as other investigators find that East Asians are more likely to hold incremental views of self and manifest greater effort, but at the same time they emphasize performance and judgment goals—a pattern that has not emerged in Western samples. Given the repeated finding in the West of associations between incremental views of self, learning goals, and effective regulation of negative emotion (Grant & Dweck, 2001, 2003), these cultural differences in the relationship between views of self and goal pursuit have important implications for research on emotion regulation.

Focus on disengaging versus engaging emotions

Kitayama, Markus, and Kurokawa (2000) have demonstrated that cultural differences in positive emotion (feeling good) are based on qualitatively different experiences. In Japan, "interpersonally engaged" behavior and related emotions (e.g., empathy and shame) are experienced as relatively more positive; in the US "interpersonally disengaged" behavior and emotions (e.g., pride and anger) are experienced as authentic and relatively more positive. Socially engaged emotions result from empathizing with, and fulfilling the expectations of, others, e.g., by perfecting one's roles and duties and by acting as a responsible member of the social group. Kwan, Bond, and Singelis (1997) have shown that for people from Hong Kong as compared to the United States, a person's engagement in harmonious relationships contributes more to subjective well-being and good feelings. In closely knit communities where members value the regulation of negative emotions so as not to disturb others, empathy allows for an understanding of the other person's emotions even when these are not openly expressed. Empathy and expectations of empathy are critical in such contexts.

In the case of an interdependent self, shame can partly compensate for failing to fulfill others' (e.g., parents') expectations and for causing harm to the collective "face" (e.g., family). Shame allows the group to excuse the failure (Mesquita & Karasawa, 2004). Shame pertains to self–ought comparisons (self's fulfillment of standards and norms one ought to meet) whereas pride is more concerned with self-chosen standards and self-ideal comparisons (self's fulfillment of self-selected ideals) (Creighton, 1990; Wang, 2005). Not surprisingly, shame is more emphasized and is more accepted by Asians than by Westerners (Creighton, 1990).

In contrast to empathy and shame, socially disengaging emotions such

as pride and anger reflect and reinforce the individual's sense of autonomy and desire for self-assertion which is consistent with the Western
focus on the need to protect self's freedom, individual rights, and opportunities. These emotions relate to self-reports of general well-being
by persons from the US (Elliot et al., 2001; Kitayama & Markus, 2000;
Kitayama et al., 2000). West versus non-West differences in the emphasis on rights versus duties have been documented by Chiu, Dweck, Tong,
and Fu (1997).

Focus on deactivating versus activating emotion

According to Bowlby (1973) interactions with significant others are the
basis for the development of different attachment-related strategies of
affect regulation. Mikulincer, Shaver, and Pereg (2003) suggest that hyperactivating strategies involving overdependence on the relationship with
the caretaker and a low trust in one's own competence to regulate distress
are characteristic of persons high in anxious ambivalence (cf. also Shaver,
Mikulincer, & Chun, this volume). Deactivating strategies involving the
denial of attachment needs to prevent further distress are characteristic of
persons high in anxious avoidance.

Cross-cultural studies on attachment have shown cultural differences in
attachment insecurity, with greater incidence of avoidant-dismissive attachment types in the West and greater incidence of ambivalent-preoccupied
types in several other cultures (van IJzendoorn & Sagi, 1999). This suggests
that deactivating strategies for emotion regulation may be more common
in the West and that hyperactivating strategies may be more common in
other cultures. This assumption is consistent with the findings of more emphasis on self-reliance in the West and on heightened dependency in other
cultures. The latter dynamics may explain the reports of greater expression of distress (as contrasted to physiological measures) in non-Western
as compared to Western children (Norasakkunkit, 2003; Trommsdorff &
Friedlmeier, 2006; Trommsdorff et al., 2006).

Focus on expressing versus suppressing emotions

In Western cultures it is often assumed that open expression of emotions
(e.g., early family emotional discourse) fosters children's emotional
competence. However, Asians are more likely to inhibit expression of
emotion, at least in public, formal contexts, so as not to disturb others.
They are also less likely to seek social support in part because of concern

about upsetting others and disrupting harmony (Taylor et al., 2004). The question arising here is how findings of Asians' "hyperactivation" and "dependency" on caregivers fit with their lower levels of emotional expression and support seeking.

Empirical results show that Chinese do not differ from American adults in their physiological reactions but usually show a lower frequency, intensity, and duration of emotional expression (Chen et al., 1998). Our own studies show that Japanese children express their distress and anxiety more with intimate others (mothers) and more nonverbally in contrast to Westerners who express their distress more publicly and more verbally (Trommsdorff & Friedlmeier, 1993, 1999). Also, German preschool children express their frustration openly while Indian children are less overt in their displays (Trommsdorff, 2006b; Trommsdorff, Mishra, von Suchodoletz, Heikamp, & Merkel, 2006).

In the United States, suppression of emotion is typically seen as a maladaptive form of regulation (Gross, 1999, 2002; Gross & John, 2003; John & Gross, 2004). By contrast, in societies where the interdependent self is more emphasized and valued, "suppression" may be more accepted and considered a key strategy for achieving social harmony and appropriately accommodating oneself to external circumstances. Inhibition has been seen as a valid indicator of culturally adaptive behavior for Chinese children (Chen et al., 1998), or as maturity (see Mulder, 1992, for Javanese people; Lebra, 1994; Azuma, 1986, for Japan).

Focus on autonomy and intrapersonal regulation versus harmony and interpersonal regulation

Most Western research on the development of emotion regulation assumes that the underlying process is the development of autonomy and personal well-being. In contrast the developmental goal for regulation in many non-Western countries is rather centered around harmony and the group's well-being.

Self-determination theory (SDT), as well as most other Western theories of development, assume that universally people strive for autonomy, which is a cornerstone of optimal internalization (Deci & Ryan, 2000; Ryan & Deci, 2000). SDT assumes that regulation that is autonomous is internalized and experienced as authentic. This view is in line with the widely accepted Western assumption that regulation follows a developmental course from interpersonal (between caregiver and infant) to intrapersonal regulation (independent from others) (Thompson, 1999). The desired developmental outcome in the West is to achieve independence in

one's regulatory abilities (Holodynski & Friedlmeier, 2006) and to succeed in the "passage from coregulation to self-regulation" (Mikulincer
et al., 2003, p. 93). In non-Western cultures, by contrast, the desirable
developmental outcome entails interpersonal, socially engaged, and em-
pathy- and contextually-based regulation. Such interpersonal regulation
will be internalized as the culturally appropriate mode of regulation.
Non-Western perspectives focus on the development of accommoda-
tive and interpersonal regulatory processes and/or processes that focus
on self–environment relations, as opposed to the development of intrapersonal regulation. We review evidence of these differences in the next
section.

 ## SOCIALIZATION AND THE DEVELOPMENT OF EMOTION REGULATION

Fostering self-esteem and striving for positive emotions in the West

A recurring theme in the Western socialization literature is the need to
foster positive emotions and positive beliefs about self and the world, including but not limited to happiness, personal mastery and a positive sense
of self (e.g., confidence, worth, esteem, and efficacy). Accordingly, there is
considerable emphasis in the West on providing positive as opposed to negative feedback, including praise and verbal expressions of love (Henderlong & Lepper, 2002; Rothbaum & Trommsdorff, 2007; Wang, 2005,
p. 60; Wang, Wiley, & Chiu, 2007).

Western socialization investigators depict self-esteem as a hub of child
development—many roads lead to it and from it. Children's self-esteem is
supported by a range of positive parenting practices and it supports children's sense of autonomy, uniqueness, and other aspects of the independent self (Chao, 1994; Wang et al., 2007). Whereas European-American
mothers view self-esteem as crucial to children's healthy development,
Taiwanese mothers view it as unimportant or as leading to vulnerabilities such as frustration, stubbornness, and unwillingness to be corrected
(Miller, Wang, Sandel, & Cho, 2002).

Throughout the Western literature on praise, the focus is on the development of personal autonomy and self-esteem—on intrinsic and internal
motivation. The possibility that praise may motivate children to sustain
social approval is seen negatively because such motivation is regarded as
extrinsic and transient (Wang, 2005; Wang et al., 2007).

In giving feedback, Western caregivers seek to maximize positive, internal, stable, and generalized attributions for successful behavior ("you are good at this"), and to minimize negative, internal, and stable attributions for failure ("you are not good at this"). Positive and internal attributions support a positive evaluation of self. Stable and generalized attributions support the Western sense of self as consistent across time and place/context—as a fixed entity entailing enduring dispositions and traits, as opposed to continuously changing depending on the situation or person at hand (Ji, Nisbett, & Su, 2001).

Fostering face and accepting negative emotions in non-Western cultures

Asian parents, compared to Western parents, are less likely to provide positive stable, internal, and generalized attributions for children's behavior (Trommsdorff & Kornadt, 2003). They are relatively more likely to emphasize self-critical attributions and self-improvement (Miller et al., 2002). More generally, they place less value on enhancing self-esteem and more value on preserving self-face (Fung, 1999). Whereas self-esteem depends upon one's own views of one's ability, traits, and other stable characteristics, self-face depends upon others' views of one's efforts for self-improvement and strategies to accommodate to specific persons and situations. Asian parents are less likely to encourage children's positive self-evaluations; indeed, face tends to be more positive when the individual engages in self-effacement (Kitayama et al., 1997). That is, others view self more positively when self downplays self's positive qualities.

The goal in non-Western communities is to instill a sense of the child as malleable and as needing to exert effort to improve self and fulfill external standards rather than a sense of the child as a distinct and capable entity that pursues self-determined standards. The failure to live up to external standards leads to shame which is a major motivator ensuring renewed efforts to adhere to external standards. Accordingly shame is seen more positively by Asian than Western socialization agents (Fung, 1999).

There is reason to suspect that Western parents' and teachers' efforts to foster self-esteem and other markers of positive self-evaluation are reinforced by the wider society, as are non-Western socialization agents' efforts to foster self-criticism. When viewing and coding tapes of parent–child dinnertime interaction, Chinese-American coders as compared to European-American coders were more likely to regard parents' criticism of their children and their social comparison feedback as appropriate means to improve children's interpersonal relationships and to help them avoid mistakes; the European-American coders were more likely to view critical parent behaviors as intrusive and damaging children's self-esteem and individuality (Wang et al., 2007).

Pride versus shame, self-chosen versus assigned behavior, and promotion versus prevention goals

Praise is valued in the West because it fosters self-esteem which, in turn, fosters an independent self. The goal of Western parents is to foster the child's unique, distinctive qualities which are manifested in the child's spontaneous, self-determined choices and behaviors. Not surprisingly, then, Western children prefer and persist more on tasks that they have freely chosen and on which they have previously succeeded (promotion goals) as opposed to those assigned to them that they are obligated to perform and on which they have previously failed (prevention goals). Just the opposite pattern exists for Asian children (Iyengar & Lepper, 1999). This relates to findings that there is greater preference and persistence (a) at freely chosen tasks among Westerners, who value promotion goals and (b) at assigned tasks among East Asians, who value prevention goals (Iyengar & Lepper 1999; Lee et al., 2000).

Several developmental-cultural theorists have highlighted Western parents' tendency to emphasize promotion goals—ways in which their children can increase their gains. This is seen in Western parents' focus on ways of enhancing their children's sense of self and their children's "self maximization" (Harwood, Miller, & Irizarry, 1995). Self-maximization refers to the realization of the greatest possible fulfillment of the child's potential—a potential which arises from self's positive dispositions and traits. Each child is assumed to know best how to maximize his/her potential; while parents play an important facilitating role, ultimately children must rely on their own preferences and beliefs to chart their own course and realize their greatest gains. Research by Wang et al. (in press) indicates that a clear majority of US parents but only a minority of Chinese parents use praise to foster children's self-initiated behavior. That is, US parents' praise reinforces behavior that is determined by the child as opposed to by the parent or by social norms.

Pride is so valued in the West because it motivates and reflects the pursuit of self-selected promotion goals such as self-enhancement and self-maximization. As a positive but disengaging emotion, pride creates distance between self and others, and does so in the interests of identifying and charting self-determined goals that maximize self-interests. Pride is only encouraged in non-Western cultures when the person's achievements are attributed to the joint efforts of the group (social honor) (Markus &

Kitayama, 2002). Otherwise, pride is avoided in these communities because it indicates social distance between the person and others.

Western parents avoid shame because it undermines children's positive self-evaluations and self-determination and because it reinforces dependence on norms and others' evaluations. Indeed shame is treated as a destructive socialization practice in the West because it undermines self-selected goals (reviewed in Barber, 2002), just as praise is considered destructive by Asian parents when it undermines self-improvement or when it prioritizes self- over other-selected goals. Praise that is clearly intended to reinforce children's adherence to social expectations is actually preferred and used more often by Asian-American than by Euro-American parents (Wang et al., 2007). Interestingly, the expressions used by Chinese parents to praise their children refer to obeying, listening, understanding, and following norms. Shame is seen positively in Asia because of the value placed on socially engaging emotions.

One of the reasons that shame has a less negative, and more positive, meaning to Asian parents and children than to their US counterparts is that Asians have a more malleable view of self (Heine et al., 2001). Shame motivates behavioral change in Asians because the presumption is that the person is able to bring their behavior in line with others' standards and social norms. Shame that occurs in the context of a more fixed and entity-based view of self, which is more prevalent in the West, has a more deleterious effect on the child.

Another socially engaging emotion that may be especially valued by parents in non-Western cultures is empathy. In some communities, adults' empathy and their expectation that children will reciprocate empathy are cornerstones of their socialization practices (Clancy, 1986). When caregivers explicitly request that their children reciprocate empathy, children from non-Western communities are more likely than Western children to respond positively and to indulge the request. For example, when mothers say "If you cared about me, you would not do things to cause me to worry" African-American and Hispanic children feel more loved than controlled whereas European-American children feel manipulated and controlled (Mason, Walker-Barnes, Tu, Simons, & Martinez-Arrue, 2004; Wang et al., 2007).

The role of autonomy and control in socialization

Several Western investigators consider the socialization of autonomy as critical in fostering adaptation and self-regulation; restrictions on the child's autonomy are seen as undermining development (e.g., Ryan &

Deci, 2000; Dweck, 1999). However, different cultural models of self lead to different assumptions about the importance of autonomy in the development of emotion regulation.

In her description of the internalization process in Japan, Lewis (1989) highlights both the indulgence that young children experience, especially from parents, and the social control that is enforced, especially by peers. In Japan, teachers exercise authority indirectly, by setting up the environment, engaging children as monitors and models, and using psychological control more so than direct behavioral intervention. All of these practices are designed to foster children's harmony with, as opposed to autonomy from, others and one's context.

Indirect control methods by parents, as seen in asking questions rather than issuing commands, and in exercising authority through intermediaries (e.g., siblings and peers), combined with indulgence by highly empathic caregivers, helps explain how non-Western socialization agents exert their influence. They also rely upon psychological control (Rothbaum, Pott, Azuma, Miyake, & Weisz, 2000). Such control is considered a serious infringement of the child's autonomy in the West because it violates the psychological boundary between caregiver and child (Barber, 2002). Coercion is also seen as a serious violation of the child's autonomy because it does not respect the child's personal rights (e.g., for self-expression; to receive an explanation and to understand the adult's decision) (Baumrind, 1971, 1989). The key factor distinguishing acceptable from unacceptable control in the West is whether or not the control respects the parent–child boundary and children's autonomy.

Not surprisingly, the form of control that is most accepted in the West is "firmness"—i.e., control that is clear and consistent—in large part because it respects the parent–child boundary and the child's autonomy (Baumrind, 1971, 1989). This type of respect is of much less concern to caregivers in other cultures. They are more likely to use positive (empathy) and negative forms of psychological control, and they show little regard for firmness—as seen in inconsistent and even contradictory behavior (Choi & Nisbett, 2000; Wang et al., 2007). These practices reflect their relatively greater concern with children's adapting to social and situational constraints and their lesser concern with supporting children's autonomy.

For their part, children in other cultures are more willing to accept their parents' control. They are less invested in preserving emotional autonomy. Their sense of well-being is more dependent on the ability to be responsive to social standards and expectations, which is fostered by parental control, and less dependent on self-esteem, which is fostered by support for self-determination and for autonomy (Kwan et al., 1997).

The above differences help explain profound cultural differences in the meaning, experience, and expression of warmth. Warmth in the West is associated with autonomy support—inverse relationships between warmth and control have consistently been found, both in parents' and children's perceptions and in observed behavior. A parent who is warm would not undermine the child's autonomy and too much control in itself nullifies warmth. By contrast, warmth in most other cultures is directly related to control. Warmth is expressed in large part as exercise of control (Trommsdorff, 1995; Rothbaum & Trommsdorff, 2007).

Fostering learning versus performance goals

According to Dweck (1999), praise only contributes to improved regulation when the feedback leads to learning goals. This theory has important cultural implications, because there are cultural differences in learning goals. Parenting goals in East Asia center on self-improvement, education, filial piety, obedience, and discipline. These goals are closely tied to the Chinese concept of "*guan*" which means "to train." *Guan* has considerable influence on children's self-concept and their development of self-regulation (see Chao, 1994, 2000; Chen, 2001; Cheah & Rubin, 2003; Li, 2002). It is closely tied to judgments of whether one is conforming to social roles and related standards of social, in contrast to individual, performance. Guan is associated with adherence to social expectations (prevention goals) rather than with self-selected standards of achievement (promotion goals).

Dweck's (1999) goal-based model has proven highly generative in the West, but it may require modification when applied to other communities, particularly Asian communities. All development (learning) goals have in common an emphasis on effort, incremental change, and a de-emphasis on entity views. Yet the socialization practices giving rise to these goals may vary across cultures. Learning as opposed to performance goals are more likely to occur when caregivers praise the child's effort rather than ability, thus fostering the child's investment in self-improvement. Asian parents are more likely to praise effort than are Western parents whose praise focuses on children's initiative. Asian parents believe that the child is malleable and must accommodate to others' expectations and external reality. Therefore, they continuously convey to their child the need to improve the self so as to align with social expectations (Chao, 1994; Rothbaum, Pott, et al., 2000). This belief system is the foundation for learning goals in Asian societies.

Different dynamics operate in the West. Several studies indicate that the Western child's orientation to pleasing others and living up to their standards undermines learning goals (Dweck, 1999). Depending on others' approval or evaluation is more consistent with performance goals. The tendency of Western caregivers to view the child as a stable, dispositional entity, consisting of enduring traits, and their use of feedback reflecting this belief may also explain why Western adults' approval motivates children's efforts to *prove* the self (performance goals). Asian children are repeatedly encouraged to change themselves so as to accommodate to external standards and changing situations, and they are more likely to respond to adults' feedback by seeking to *improve* the self (learning goals).

In short, the antecedents and consequences of learning and performance goals must be considered as part of a pattern of socialization beliefs and practices in a given cultural context. Because learning as opposed to performance goals have been shown to lead to greater ability to regulate negative affect (Dweck, 1999), it is essential that we understand the relationship between caregiving practices and learning goals in different communities.

Attachment and emotion regulation

A substantial body of research in the US and Western Europe indicates a relationship between: (a) sensitive parenting and caregivers' emotional availability, (b) children's secure attachment, and (c) the development of emotion competence including the ability to effectively regulate negative emotions, particularly anxiety (Thompson, 1999). Securely attached children are more emotionally open to negative feelings, are not overexpressive, and show a greater ability to tolerate distress aroused by separation stimuli (Shouldice & Stevenson-Hinde, 1992).

The characteristics of caretaking that foster security and adaptive regulatory skills include sensitivity, support, warmth, responsiveness, non-intrusiveness, and positive emotion (Morelli & Rothbaum, 2007). Sensitive responding by caretakers is seen as essential in helping the child manage distress (Ainsworth, Blehar, Waters, & Wall, 1978). The sensitive caregiver helps the child to develop secure as contrasted with insecure patterns of attachment. The latter include an avoidant pattern, involving exploration in the absence of a secure base and deactivation of negative emotions, as well as an ambivalent pattern, involving exploration and hyperactivation of negative emotions (Emde & Easterbrooks, 1985; Laible & Thompson, 2000; Mikulincer et al., 2003; Thompson, 1999).

There are cultural differences in the incidence of avoidant-dismissive (more common in the West) and ambivalent-preoccupied (more common in non-Western cultures, including Japan and Israel) attachment patterns (van IJzendoorn & Sagi, 1999). Even though secure attachment is prevalent, and described as preferable by mothers in most if not all communities, the function of attachment security may vary across culture. Attachment theorists presume a close link between the attachment and exploration systems, and between security and autonomy more generally (van IJzendoorn & Sagi, 1999); this association is less clear in Asian, Hispanic, and African communities (Rothbaum & Morelli, 2005). In some non-Western cultures, attachment security may be less related to exploration and more related to dependence (or interdependence) and belonging (see review by Morelli & Rothbaum, 2007).

For persons with an independent self, attachment security is closely linked with exploration in infancy, and with autonomy later in development (Rothbaum, Weisz, Pott, Miyake, & Morelli, 2000). A defining feature of Western security is trust in new relationships (Rothbaum & Trommsdorff, 2007). The valuing of exploration and autonomy is consistent with the Western emphasis on intrapersonal emotion regulation, independent from the mother. In contrast, for the interdependent self, security in social relations is not primarily based on trust but rather on the belief in the continuity and the satisfying quality of existing relationships, which are long-term, stable, and guaranteed/assured (Kitayama, 2001; Kitayama & Markus, 1994, 1995, 2000; Rothbaum & Kakinuma, 2004; Rothbaum & Trommsdorff, 2007).

While support of the independent self (e.g., autonomy fostering) seems to be the optimal caretaking strategy for fostering secure attachment in Western cultures, support of the interdependent self may be optimal for fostering secure attachment in non-Western cultures. In the latter cultures, sensitive parenting focuses on establishing and maintaining the bond between the caretaker and the child. Here, control and extreme closeness (symbiotic quality), rather than autonomy fostering and non-intrusiveness, are key (Rothbaum & Trommsdorff, 2007).

In the next two sections we provide evidence that sensitive caregiving in non-Western communities may differ from sensitive caregiving in the West, and we suggest ways in which those differences may relate to cultural differences in attachment and the regulation of negative emotions such as anxiety, frustration, and distress.

Culture-specific forms of sensitive caretaking: physical closeness

An often reported characteristic of caretaking in many non-Western countries is the close body contact between mothers and their infant children (Rogoff, 2003; Roopnarine & Carter, 1992). This includes prolonged physical contact such as occurs in many African societies where children are often carried to save them from the dangerous environment (LeVine, 1988). Another indicator of physical closeness is the several year period of children sleeping together with their mothers (Morelli, Rogoff, Oppenheim, & Goldsmith, 1992).

Observational studies in non-Western communities indicate the importance of close body contact between mother and child for "successful" regulatory development (Keller et al., 2004) while Western investigators consistently suggest that prolonged body contact leads to overdependence of the child on the caregiver. According to Western socialization beliefs, parents must facilitate the progression from dependence to autonomy, self-efficacy, and self-determination, and too much dependence or too much delay in shifting to independence undermine regulation (Shweder et al., 1998).

Yet there is evidence that physical closeness in early childhood may induce effective emotion regulation. Closeness ensures that the child's expression and regulation of emotion is under constant surveillance of the caretaker who provides near constant proximity and near complete satisfaction of basic needs (Mulder, 1992). In non-Western communities, interpersonal regulation may be valued even into adulthood, and there is correspondingly less emphasis on the shift to intrapersonal regulation. In contrast, in Western countries, children are encouraged to soothe themselves (e.g., by suckling on objects) beginning in infancy.

In their famous cross-cultural study on early child development, Whiting and Whiting (1975) distinguished "back and hip cultures," where there are very high levels of physical closeness, from "crib or cradle cultures" where the infant spends most of the time in a crib or is heavily swaddled and thus separate from the caregiver. More than 80% of the cultures of tropical South America, sub-Saharan Africa, tropical Asia, and Pacific islands have been characterized by close body contact between mother and infant and frequent holding. In contrast, 80% of the societies from the temperate and frigid zones use cradles and heavy swaddling (Whiting, 1981). Close body contact between the mother and the child provides a symbiotic relationship which diminishes infants' stress responses.

Even in close-contact cultures, stressful experiences occur. In these cultures, 2-year-old children are often weaned from the back and lap of the mother. The caregiver helps to regulate the ensuing distress by engaging the child in social responsibilities, interdependent action, and socially engaged emotions. For example, Kikuyu children in Kenya are encouraged to practice nurturant behavior to other family members (Whiting, 1990). Physical contact is one of several practices fostering closeness and connectedness.

Extremely close and symbiotic emotional connections are manifested in

Japan as "amae" (Doi, 1973; Rothbaum & Kakinuma, 2004; Yamaguchi, 2004). Yamaguchi (2004) defines amae as the "presumed acceptance of one's inappropriate behavior on request" (p. 29). Indulgence of inappropriate behavior is a manifestation of the closeness of the relationship. The above authors cite evidence that desirable amae is associated with secure attachment. Yet there are also differences—amae is more associated with voluntary compliance, cooperation, and receptivity whereas secure attachment is more associated with autonomy, self-esteem, and self-assertion (Rothbaum & Kakinuma, 2004).

Amae and empathy can be seen as preconditions for successful socially engaged coregulation of emotions. Amae facilitates indirect control by the mother since the child does not perceive the mother as forcing the child to comply. High responsiveness and empathy of mothers motivate the child to willingly comply and facilitate the child's emotion regulation. The latter takes the form of mother–child coregulation (Fogel, 1993) in cultures preferring interdependent relationships.

Qualities similar to amae (dependence and enmeshment) are reported in Korea (Choi, 1992) and other East Asian cultures. Emotional closeness provides security and serves as the basis for later social and emotional regulation (Rothbaum & Kakinuma, 2004). In these communities, there appears to be a positive relationship between physical closeness and emotion regulation, *at least as long as the caretaker is present*. The question then arises whether high levels of physical closeness may thwart "independent" emotion regulation—i.e., regulation in situations where the caregiver is absent.

Studies show that Japanese and German toddlers need their mother's intervention to regulate their emotions. However, the German preschoolers can regulate distress independently from their mothers better than can their Japanese age-mates (Trommsdorff & Friedlmeier, 1999), and they are better able to regulate distress when their mother is absent (Japanese children are better able to regulate when their mother is present) (see also Trommsdorff, 1995; Trommsdorff & Friedlmeier, 2006). Successful emotion regulation can either be based on intra- or on interpersonal regulation strategies depending on the prevailing cultural model of independence or interdependence.

Proactive/anticipatory versus reactive/responsive sensitivity

The association between mothers' sensitivity and children's ability to regulate distress depends upon the cultural context (Friedlmeier & Trommsdorff, 1999; Trommsdorff & Friedlmeier, 1993, 2006). Japanese mothers show more "proactive sensitivity"; they pay extensive attention to the child, they anticipate the emotional reactions of the child, and they start to soothe the infant before he or she signals negative emotions. German mothers are more likely to respond after their child expresses his/her distress. As noted by LeVine and Miller (1990), crib and cradle children learn to express their need before their caretaker intervenes. By contrast, the constant contact between back and hip children and their mothers enables mothers to discern very subtle cues and to provide proactive care. Trommsdorff and Friedlmeier (2006) found that German mothers' reactive sensitivity (responsiveness) was less successful than Japanese mothers' proactive sensitivity in inducing their children's regulation of distress. German mothers reacted to the child's distress and disappointment by focusing on these emotions, thus increasing the child's awareness of her own emotions and heightening distress. In contrast, Japanese mothers reacted before their child expressed distress and distracted him or her before the child appraised the situation as frustrating. This kind of proactive sensitivity proved quite successful in helping Japanese children regulate their negative emotions at a very early stage. By contrast, German children became fully engaged in their negative emotions because they needed to wait for their mothers' reactions to engage in reappraisal and because of their mothers' focus on their negative emotions. This is in line with research by Gross (1999, 2002) showing that reappraisal of emotions is most effective before the emotion is fully developed.

Similar findings have been reported by Rothbaum, Nagaoka, and Ponte (2006). Japanese teachers were more likely than US teachers to emphasize the importance of anticipating children's needs; US teachers emphasized the importance of responsiveness—i.e., waiting until children expressed their needs. Wang et al. (in press) provide evidence that Chinese-American mothers commonly give praise in anticipation of the child's "correct" behavior; this kind of praise is virtually non-existent among European Americans. Such anticipatory proactive sensitivity may foster interdependence, by increasing children's empathy and their readiness to fulfill social expectations. Furthermore, Japanese mothers' proactive sensitivity can be seen as part of their general preference for prevention goals.

Fostering the expression versus suppression of negative emotion

In communities favoring interdependence as compared to independence an important goal for children's socialization is fostering empathy. Several authors underline this developmental goal (e.g., Mulder, 1992, for Javanese people; Azuma, 1986, for Japanese). Fogel, Stevenson, and Messinger (1992, p. 46) found that Japanese, as compared to American, mothers were more likely to promote their children's empathic understanding of a social situation by appealing to the child's feelings and pointing out consequences of the child's action for others. This is in line with studies comparing German and Japanese mother–child interactions (Trommsdorff & Kornadt, 2003). Rothbaum et al. (2000) refer to evidence that Japanese parents value "reading others' minds." This is a good example of socializing empathy. These findings help explain why US mothers expected earlier verbal assertiveness and social skills in their children, and why Japanese mothers expected earlier emotional maturity as evidenced by the modulation of expressivity of their children (Hess, Kashiwagi, Azuma, Price, & Dickson, 1980; Rothbaum & Trommsdorff, 2007).

These differences in emotion regulation are consistent with findings involving Japanese and German mothers' responses to conflict arising from the child's disappointment or frustration (Trommsdorff & Kornadt, 2003). Japanese as compared to German mothers are less likely to attribute bad intentions to their child; they attribute their child's undesirable behavior to immaturity and lack of understanding. In the context of interdependence, the child tends to feel what the mother expects. The Japanese child observes that the mother does not react to conflict (disobedience) with anger, but instead gives in to the child so as to maintain a sense of unity. The behavior modeled by the mother, the mother's empathic interpretation of the child's behavior, and the child's investment in repairing the bond facilitate the child's regulation of negative affect (e.g., anger or disappointment about not "winning" a conflict). German mothers, by contrast, believe that their child wants to impose her/his own will and to demonstrate independence. This belief in the child's obstinacy and willfulness, as well as mothers' greater modeling of anger, contribute to the escalation of conflicts in mother–child interactions, thus inducing less regulation of negative emotions.

The Japanese mother coaches her child to view conflict as a disruption in the bond and to seek to restore harmony, whereas the Western mother coaches her child to view conflict as a matter of contested wills and to seek negotiation while maintaining autonomy (cf. Kuczynski, 2003). Japanese or Balinese as compared to German adolescents report less conflicts with parents (Trommsdorff, 1992, 1995). Regulation in Japan is undermined by negative feedback from others—negative face—because it is associated with failure in relational harmony; by contrast, regulation in the West is undermined by negative self-esteem because it is associated with diminished autonomy.

Expressiveness, and in particular direct verbal communication, is more common in US than in Chinese and Japanese homes and classrooms (Kim & Markus, 2002; Rothbaum, Pott, et al., 2000; Tobin, Wu, & Davidson, 1989). Chinese and Japanese children engage in fewer overt emotional interchanges (Gudykunst, Ting-Toomey, & Chua, 1988; Lin & Fu, 1990) and are trained to manage their own emotions and restrict their emotional expressions (Chen et al., 1998). In several cultures favoring interdependence, very expressive individuals are seen as socially immature and poorly regulated (e.g., Ho, 1986, for Chinese; Mulder, 1992, for Javanese), suggesting that children's expressivity is not encouraged. Unlike their Western counterparts, Chinese parents and children tend not to view emotional expressiveness as an important attribute of "happy" families (Chen et al., 1998; Shek, 2001).

Interestingly, the above cultural differences are magnified under conditions of positive caregiving. Maternal warmth fosters the development of inhibition of emotions in Chinese children and it fosters the development of open expression in Canadian children. In both cases, warmth ultimately leads to positive outcomes: inhibition in Chinese children is associated with high peer acceptance and high ratings of psycho-social adjustment, while inhibition does not lead to these positive outcomes for Canadian children (Chen et al., 1998). Sensitive caretaking and maternal warmth encourage the development of regulatory functions that are valued in the respective cultural context, e.g., inhibition in the traditional Chinese family, and self-assertion/expression in the Canadian family.

In recent years, dramatic socio-economic and cultural changes have led to a decreased valuing of inhibition in China as well as to weaker and at times negative associations between shyness/inhibition and social adjustment (Chen, Cen, Li, & He, 2005). These findings serve to underscore the complex ways in which values, local circumstances (including economic conditions and social change), and caregiving practices influence the adaptiveness of different forms of emotion regulation.

Fostering interpersonal versus intrapersonal regulation of emotion

The above findings indicate that Japanese mothers' indirect teaching, empathy, acceptance, close body contact, and prolonged proximity constitute the basis for a sense of oneness and merger between mother and child (e.g., "amae"). The extremely close bond allows the child to develop socially engaged emotions and to regulate emotions successfully, especially in the mother's presence (interdependent regulation). In contrast, for the Western child, awareness and expression of one's own will and the belief that mother and child are independent agents in the negotiation of conflict, foster the development of disengaged emotions. To regulate emotions the child must openly express them when the mother is present and the child must deal with them "on one's own" when she is not (intrapersonal regulation). This lesser reliance on the caretaker and greater self-reliance are closely associated with socialization practices fostering self-esteem and self-confidence. Cultural differences in fostering children's esteem and confidence may explain Miller, Wiley, Fung, and Liang's (1997) findings that Taiwanese mothers frequently reported children's transgressions while US mothers generated positive portraits of their children. Similarly, Weisz, Chaiyasit, Weiss, Eastman, and Jackson (1995) found that Thai parents and teachers report as much problem behavior as their US counterparts even though independent observers report much greater incidence of such behavior in the US.

Another socialization technique to foster intra- in contrast to interpersonal regulation is focusing on internal mental processes as opposed to interpersonal behavior. Wang and Fivush (2005) demonstrate that, when providing feedback about emotionally salient events, Chinese parents, as compared to their Euro-American counterparts, focus more on the social interaction and acceptance of social norms, thus underscoring the importance of maintaining interpersonal relationships. Euro-American mothers are more likely to adopt a "cognitive approach" to emotion regulation, emphasizing the cause of children's feeling states (i.e., intrapersonal processes); Chinese mothers are more likely to adopt a "behavioral approach" to emotion regulation, emphasizing discipline and proper conduct as well as the need to maintain the relationship (i.e., interpersonal processes).

Wang and Fivush (2005) also found that Chinese mothers value harmonious and balanced social interactions as a goal for emotion development and regulation more than did US mothers. Mother–child conversations about past experiences of negative emotions reveal that US mothers prefer their children to develop an autonomous sense of self and regulate negative emotions through emotional understanding. In contrast, conversations of Chinese dyads indicate that emotion regulation is based on relatedness and acceptance of social norms.

These results are similar to findings from an observational study comparing German and Indian mothers' reactions to their children's disappointment (Trommsdorff, Mishra, et al., 2006; Trommsdorff, 2006a). German mothers who imitated their children's negative emotions usually increased the disappointment of their child. In contrast, Indian mothers who adopted a behavioral approach succeeded in reducing the child's negative emotions; they focused their child's attention on joint rule-oriented activity as well as on their relationship with the child.

These findings highlight the interaction of cultural values and caregiving practices in determining the effective regulation of children's negative emotions. Mothers living in cultures which foster independent self-construals focus their child's attention more often on his/her own emotion, or foster an emotionally distancing form of reappraisal of (e.g., joking about) the situation thereby reversing the emotional reaction. This is a strategy that they can practice and ultimately employ on their own (intrapersonal regulation). The strategy switches the quality of the expression of emotion from disappointment to joy, thus making use of the situation to boost the child's self-confidence and self-assurance. Mothers from cultures with interdependent self-construals focus their child's attention away from his/her own emotion often through distraction and focus instead on a joint activity or on the relationship per se (interpersonal regulation). These mothers make use of the situation by pointing out to the child the value of fulfilling one's obligations and showing proper behavior. Thus, stressful situations and negative emotions experienced by the child are used by parents to simultaneously promote socialization goals and positive emotions.

These studies present evidence for cultural differences in the development of emotion regulation. Not all cultures follow the pathway of increasing intrapersonal regulation often assumed by Western investigators. The pathway of interpersonal regulation seems more appropriate in cultural contexts favoring interdependence. Questions about the effectiveness of different forms of sensitivity in fostering emotion regulation should be considered in the context of prevailing cultural values. When caregivers' behavior is sensitively aligned with these values, their children develop culturally appropriate emotion regulation.

▤ SUMMARY AND CONCLUSIONS

In a cultural context where the model of interdependence prevails, emotion regulation centers on socially engaging emotions, on the well-being of other persons, and on maintaining harmony in the group. Attempts to maintain security are largely dependent on acceptance by the group. In contrast, in a cultural context where the model of independence prevails, emotion regulation centers on socially disengaging emotions, on self-esteem, and on individuals' well-being. The development of emotion regulation in non-Western cultures is related to empathy, interpersonal accommodation, and norm orientation. The development of emotion regulation in Western cultures is related to autonomy and self-expression (see Table 4.1).

Table 4.1 Cultural differences in emotion regulation and socialization

	Western Countries	Non-Western Countries
Culture and emotion regulation		
Goal of emotion regulation: positive vs. negative (self and emotion)	Self-enhancement; self-serving bias; self-esteem Increase positive emotion Reappraise negative emotion as positive	Self-criticism; self-effacement; face Modulate positive emotion Acknowledge (accept and transcend) negative emotions
Goal of emotion regulation: promotion vs. prevention	Promotion focus; Self-maximizing; Personal ideals	Prevention focus; Group maximizing; Social oughts
Valued emotions	Socially disengaging (pride, anger)	Socially engaging (empathy, shame)
Attachment and negative emotion	Deactivate negative (prove self-reliance) Self-regulation/self-comforting	Hyperactive negative (gain support from others) Coregulation/seek indulgence
Valued expression	Open; Be authentic	Suppressed; Don't disrupt harmony
Regulatory process	Intrapersonal; Autonomous and entity-based	Interpersonal; Accommodative and context-based
Culture and socialization		
Goal of emotion regulation: positive vs. negative (self and emotion)	Fostering self-esteem, striving for positive emotions	Fostering face, accepting negative emotions
Goal of emotion regulation: promotion vs. prevention	Pride, self-chosen behavior and promotions goals Autonomy-fostering caregiving	Shame, behaving in accord with others' expectations, prevention goals Controlling caregiving
Attachment and negative emotion	Distal contact Reactive/responsive sensitivity	Physical closeness Proactive/anticipatory
Valued expression	Expression of negative emotions	Suppression of negative emotions
Regulatory process	Interpersonal vs. intrapersonal regulation Accomodative, context-based	Interpersonal/coregulation

The socialization and development of emotion regulation differs in these cultural contexts. In Western cultures, the most important goal for the development of emotion regulation usually is to promote one's autonomy and affirm positive views of the self. The most important goal for emotion regulation in many non-Western cultures is to adapt to social expectations and obligations by accommodating the individual self and protecting the collective self (see Table 4.1). Feeling with the other, understanding the emotions of the other, and taking into account social rules, social roles, and duties is the primary pathway to the development of emotion regulation in cultures favoring the model of interdependence.

Throughout this chapter we have emphasized ways in which members of Western or non-Western communities regulate emotion. In so doing, we have glossed over important differences between Western communities and between non-Western communities. Equally or more important, we have neglected differences *within* cultures.

Cultures are not homogenous systems (see critical review by Oyserman, Coon, & Kemmelmeier, 2002), and descriptions of values on the cultural level should be differentiated from belief systems on the subgroup and individual level (e.g., cohort effects and differences related to socio-economic status have to be taken into account; Trommsdorff, Mayer, & Albert, 2004). Therefore, it makes sense to assess emotion regulation of individuals within as well as between cultures. An interesting study would be to test whether different ways of regulating emotion occur during goal-oriented behavior, depending on the respective goal preference. Cultural differences in the priority given to beliefs in independence and interdependence can be seen as a cultural frame which influences social customs and formal institutions and thereby permeates socialization and the development of emotions (see Table 4.1 for a summary of the cultural differences).

We end this chapter by considering two findings that have interesting implications for one another. First, suppression/lack of expression of negative emotion is more common and more valued in non-Western cultures. Second, emotional distress is more common in those non-Western cultures (see Trommsdorff et al., 2007, for children). If, as we claim, people in non-Western cultures are more effective at suppressing negative emotions, why do they experience more distress? There is evidence that this distress is situation-specific. It is most likely to occur in unfamiliar situations (i.e., in novel circumstances in which people cannot rely on previous experience and social norms), and in situations where people are likely to "let their guard down" (i.e., in informal situations and/or in the presence of intimate others). Even though non-Westerners are more effective at suppressing (or not expressing) emotions, they apparently pay a price for exercising this strategy. Yet, the price paid is limited to particular situations, suggesting that the adverse effects of suppression may be less robust among non-Western individuals.

There is reason to believe that the price paid for suppression is suppression rebound—the tendency of suppressed thoughts and feelings to reassert themselves, due to effortless monitoring processes. While the function of monitoring is to enable suppression (maintaining vigilance for the to-be-avoided thoughts) the inadvertent effect is to increase awareness of the very thoughts one wishes to ignore. Wenzlaff and Wegner's (2000) work on suppression provides ample evidence of this rebound dynamic, at least in Western communities. The findings reviewed above suggest that these dynamics may be universal, or at least that they also occur in several non-Western communities. The finding that, in non-Western communities, these dynamics are manifest only in particular situations points to the likely interplay of universal dynamics (suppression rebound) and culturally influenced processes (the limited situations in which rebound manifests itself and, thus, the decreased likelihood of its occurrence). Our focus throughout this chapter has been the prevalence of that interplay.

REFERENCES

Aaker, J. L., & Lee, A. Y. (2006). Understanding regulatory fit. *Journal of Marketing Research, 43*, 15–19.

Ainsworth, M. D. S., Blehar, M. C., Waters, E., & Wall, S. (1978). *Patterns of attachment: A psychological study of the strange situation.* Hillsdale, NJ: Erlbaum.

Azuma, H. (1986). Why study child development in Japan? In H. W. Stevenson, H. Azuma, & K. Hakuta (Eds.), *Child development and education in Japan* (pp. 3–12). New York: Freeman.

Bandura, A. (1997). *Self-efficacy: The exercise of control.* New York: Freeman.

Barber, B. K. (Ed.) (2002). *Intrusive parenting: How psychological control affects children and adolescents.* Washington, DC: American Psychological Association.

Baumeister, R. F., & Heatherton, T. F. (1996). Self-regulation failure: An overview. *Psychological Inquiry, 7*, 1–15.

Baumrind, D. (1971). Current patterns of parental authority. *Developmental Psychology, 4*, 1–103.

Baumrind, D. (1989). Rearing competent children. In W. Damon (Ed.), *Child development today and tomorrow* (pp. 349–378). San Francisco, CA: Jossey-Bass.

Bowlby, J. (1973). *Attachment and loss. Vol. 2. Separation: Anxiety and anger.* New York: Hogarth Press.

Campos, J. J., Campos, R. G., & Barrett, K. C. (1989). Emergent themes in the study of emotional development and emotion regulation. *Developmental Psychology, 25*, 394–402.

Carver, C. S., & Scheier, M. F. (1990). Principles of self-regulation: Action and emotion. In E. T. Higgins & R. M. Sorrentino (Eds.), *Handbook of motivation and cognition: Foundations of social behavior* (Vol. 2, pp. 3–52). New York: Guilford.

Carver, C. S., & Scheier, M. F. (1998). *On the self-regulation of behavior.* New York: Cambridge University Press.

Caspi, A., Roberts, B. W., & Shiner, R. L. (2005). Personality development: Stability and change. *Annual Review of Psychology, 56,* 453–484.

Chao, R. K. (1994). Beyond parental control and authoritarian parenting style: Understanding Chinese parenting through the cultural notion of training. *Child Development, 65,* 1111–1119.

Chao, R. K. (2000). Cultural explanations for the role of parenting in the school success of Asian-American children. In R. Taylor & M. Wang (Eds.), *Resilience across contexts: Family, work, culture, and community* (pp. 333–363). Mahwah, NJ: Erlbaum.

Cheah, C. S. L., & Rubin, K. H. (2003). European American and mainland Chinese mothers' socialization beliefs regarding preschoolers' social skills. *Parenting: Science & Practice, 3,* 1–21.

Chen, H. (2001). Parents' attitudes and expectations regarding science education: Comparisons among American, Chinese-American, and Chinese families. *Adolescence, 36,* 305–313.

Chen, X., Cen, G., Li, D., & He, Y. (2005). Social functioning and adjustment in Chinese children: The imprint of historical time. *Child Development, 76,* 182–195.

Chen, X., Hastings, P. D., Rubin, K. H., Chen, H., Cen, G., & Stewart, S. L. (1998). Child-rearing attitudes and behavioral inhibition in Chinese and Canadian toddlers: A cross-cultural study. *Developmental Psychology, 34,* 677–686.

Chiu, C., Dweck, C. S., Tong, J. Y., & Fu, J. H. (1997). Implicit theories and conceptions of morality. *Journal of Personality & Social Psychology, 73,* 923–940.

Choi, I., & Nisbett, R. E. (2000). Cultural psychology of surprise: Holistic theories and recognition of contradiction. *Journal of Personality and Social Psychology, 79,* 890–905.

Choi, S. H. (1992). Communicative socialization processes: Korea and Canada. In S. Iwawaki, Y. Kashima, & K. Leung (Eds.), *Innovations in cross-cultural psychology* (pp. 103–121). Lisse: Swets & Zeitlinger.

Clancy, P. M. (1986). The acquisition of communicative style in Japanese. In B. B. Schieffelin & E. Ochs (Eds.), *Language socialization across cultures* (pp. 213–250). New York: Cambridge University Press.

Cole, M. (1996). *Culture in mind.* Cambridge, MA: Harvard University Press.

Cole, P. M., Martin, S. E., & Dennis, T. A. (2004). Emotion regulation as a scientific construct: Methodological challenges and directions for child development research. *Child Development, 75,* 317–333.

Cole, P. M., & Tamang, B. L. (1998). Nepali children's ideas about emotional displays in hypothetical challenges. *Developmental Psychology, 34,* 640–646.

Cole, P. M., Tamang, B. L., & Shrestha, S. (2006). Cultural variations in the socialization of young children's anger and shame. *Child Development, 77,* 1237–1251.

Creighton, M. R. (1990). Revisiting shame and guilt cultures: A forty-year pilgrimage. *Ethos, 18,* 279–307.

Deci, E. L., & Ryan, R. M. (2000). The "what" and "why" of goal pursuits: Human needs and the self-determination of behavior. *Psychological Inquiry, 11,* 227–268.

DeVos, G. A. (1973). *Socialisation for achievement: Essays on the cultural psychology of the Japanese.* Berkeley, CA: University of California Press.

Doi, T. (1973). *The anatomy of dependence.* Tokyo: Kodansha.

Dweck, C. S. (1999). *Self-theories: Their role in motivation, personality, and development.* Philadelphia, PA: Psychology Press.

Eisenberg, N. (2004). Emotion-related regulation: An emerging construct. *Merrill-Palmer Quarterly, 50,* 236–259.

Eisenberg, N., Liew, J., & Pidada, S. U. (2004). The longitudinal relations of regulation and emotionality to quality of Indonesian children's socioemotional functioning. *Developmental Psychology, 40,* 790–804.

Eisenberg, N., & Spinrad, T. L. (2004). Emotion-related regulation: Sharpening the definition. *Child Development, 75,* 334–339.

Elliot, A. J., Chirkov, V. I., Kim, Y., & Sheldon, K. M. (2001). A cross-cultural analysis of avoidance (relative to approach) personal goals. *Psychological Science, 12,* 505–645.

Emde, R. N., & Easterbrooks, M. A. (1985). Assessing emotional availability in early development. In W. K. Frankenburg, R. N. Emde, & J. W. Sullivan (Eds.), *Early identification of children at risk: An international perspective* (pp. 79–101). New York: Plenum.

Fogel, A. (1993). *Development through relationships: Origins of communication, self, and culture.* Chicago: University of Chicago Press.

Fogel, A., Stevenson, M. B., & Messinger, D. (1992). A comparison of the parent–child relationship in Japan and the United States. In J. L. Roopnarine & D. Bruce (Eds.), *Annual advances in applied developmental psychology: Vol. 5. Parent–child socialization in diverse cultures* (pp. 25–51). Norwood, NJ: Ablex.

Fredrickson, B. L., & Losada, M. F. (2005). Positive affect and the complex dynamics of human flourishing. *American Psychologist, 60,* 678–686.

Friedlmeier, W., & Trommsdorff, G. (1999). Emotion regulation in early childhood: A cross-cultural comparison between German and Japanese toddlers. *Journal of Cross-Cultural Psychology, 30,* 684–711.

Fung, H. (1999). Becoming a moral child: The socialization of shame among young Chinese children. *Ethos, 27,* 180–209.

Grant, H., & Dweck, C. S. (2001). Cross-cultural response to failure: Considering outcome attributions with different goals. In F. Salili, C. Chiu, & Y.-Y. Hong (Eds.), *Student motivation: The culture and context of learning* (pp. 203–219). New York: Kluwer.

Grant, H., & Dweck, C. S. (2003). Clarifying achievement goals and their impact. *Journal of Personality and Social Psychology, 85,* 541–553.

Gross, J. J. (1998a). Antecedent- and response-focused emotion regulation: Divergent consequences for experience, expression, and physiology. *Journal of Personality and Social Psychology, 74,* 224–237.

Gross, J. J. (1998b). The emerging field of emotion regulation: An integrative review. *Review of General Psychology, 2,* 271–299.

Gross, J. J. (1999). Emotion regulation: Past, present, future. *Cognition & Emotion*, *13*, 551–573.

Gross, J. J. (2002). Emotion regulation: Affective, cognitive, and social consequences. *Psychophysiology*, *39*, 281–291.

Gross, J. J., & John, O. P. (2003). Individual differences in two emotion regulation processes: Implications for affect, relationships, and well-being. *Journal of Personality and Social Psychology*, *85*, 348–362.

Gudykunst, W. B., Ting-Toomey, S., & Chua, E. (1988). *Culture and interpersonal communication*. Thousand Oaks, CA: Sage.

Harwood, R. L., Miller, J. G., & Irizarry, N. L. (1995). *Culture and attachment: Perceptions of the child in context*. New York: Guilford.

Heine, S. J., Kitayama, S., Lehman, D. R., Takata, T., Ide, E., Leung, C., et al. (2001). Divergent consequences of success and failure in Japan and North America: An investigation of self-improving motivations and malleable selves. *Journal of Personality and Social Psychology*, *81*, 599–615.

Heine, S. J., & Lehman, D. R. (1997). Culture, dissonance, and self-affirmation. *Personality & Social Psychology Bulletin*, *23*, 389–400.

Heine, S. J., Lehman, D. R., Markus, H. R., & Kitayama, S. (1999). Is there a universal need for positive self-regard? *Psychological Review*, *106*, 766–794.

Henderlong, J., & Lepper, M. R. (2002). The effects of praise on children's intrinsic motivation: A review and synthesis. *Psychological Bulletin*, *128*, 774–795.

Hess, R. D., Kashiwagi, K., Azuma, H., Price, G. G., & Dickson, W. P. (1980). Maternal expectations for mastery of developmental tasks in Japan and the United States. *International Journal of Psychology*, *15*, 259–271.

Higgins, E. T. (1998). Promotion and prevention: Regulatory focus as a motivational principle. In M. P. Zanna (Ed.), *Advances in experimental social psychology* (Vol. 30, pp. 1–46). San Diego, CA: Academic Press.

Higgins, E. T. (2000). Making a good decision: Value from fit. *American Psychologist*, *55*, 1217–1230.

Higgins, E. T., & Spiegel, S. (2004). Promotion and prevention strategies for self-regulation: A motivated cognition perspective. In R. F. Baumeister & K. D. Vohs (Eds.), *Handbook of self-regulation: Research, theory, and applications* (pp. 171–187). New York: Guilford.

Ho, D. Y. F. (1986). Chinese patterns of socialization: A critical review. In M. H. Bond (Ed.), *The psychology of the Chinese people* (pp. 1–37). Oxford: Oxford University Press.

Holodynski, M., & Friedlmeier, W. (2006). *Development of emotions and emotion regulation*. New York: Springer.

Iyengar, S. S., & Lepper, M. R. (1999). Rethinking the value of choice: A cultural perspective on intrinsic motivation. *Journal of Personality and Social Psychology*, *76*, 349–366.

Ji, L.-J., Nisbett, R. E., & Su, Y. (2001). Culture, change, and prediction. *Psychological Science*, *12*, 450–456.

John, O. P., & Gross, J. J. (2004). Healthy and unhealthy emotion regulation: Personality processes, individual differences, and life span development. *Journal of Personality*, *72*, 1301–1333.

Keller, H., Lohaus, A., Kuensemueller, P., Abels, M., Yovsi, R. D., Voelker, S., et al. (2004). The bio-culture of parenting: Evidence from five cultural communities. *Parenting: Science and Practice, 4*, 25–50.

Kim, H. S., & Markus, H. R. (2002). Freedom of speech and freedom of silence: An analysis of talking as a cultural practice. In R. A. Shweder, M. Minow, & H. R. Markus (Eds.), *Engaging cultural differences: The multicultural challenge in liberal democracies* (pp. 432–452). New York: Russell Sage Foundation.

King, L. A., Hicks, J. A., Krull, J. L., & Gaiso, A. K. (2006). Positive affect and the experience of meaning in life. *Journal of Personality and Social Psychology, 90*, 179–196.

Kitayama, S. (2001). Culture and emotion. In N. J. Smelser & P. B. Baltes (Eds.), *International encyclopedia of the social and behavioral sciences* (pp. 3134–3139). Oxford: Elsevier.

Kitayama, S., & Markus, H. R. (Eds.) (1994). *Emotion and culture: Empirical studies of mutual influence.* Washington, DC: American Psychological Association.

Kitayama, S., & Markus, H. R. (1995). Culture and self: Implications for internationalizing psychology. In N. R. Goldberger & J. B. Veroff (Eds.), *The culture and psychology reader* (pp. 366–383). New York: New York University Press.

Kitayama, S., & Markus, H. R. (2000). The pursuit of happiness and the realization of sympathy: Cultural patterns of self, social relations, and well-being. In E. Diener & E. M. Suh (Eds.), *Culture and subjective well being* (pp. 113–161). Cambridge, MA: MIT Press.

Kitayama, S., Markus, H. R., & Kurokawa, M. (2000). Culture, emotion, and well-being: Good feelings in Japan and the United States. *Cognition & Emotion, 14*, 93–124.

Kitayama, S., Markus, H. R., Matsumoto, H., & Norasakkunkit, V. (1997). Individual and collective processes in the construction of the self: Self-enhancement in the United States and self-criticism in Japan. *Journal of Personality and Social Psychology, 72*, 1245–1267.

Kochanska, G. (1998). Mother–child relationship, child fearfulness, and emerging attachment: A short-term longitudinal study. *Developmental Psychology, 34*, 480–490.

Kuczynski, L. (Ed.). (2003). *Handbook of dynamics in parent–child relations.* Thousand Oaks, CA: Sage.

Kwan, V. S. Y., Bond, M. H., & Singelis, T. M. (1997). Pancultural explanations for life satisfaction: Adding relationship harmony to self-esteem. *Journal of Personality and Social Psychology, 73*, 1038–1051.

Laible, D. J., & Thompson, R. A. (2000). Attachment and self-organization. In M. D. Lewis & I. Granic (Eds.), *Emotion, development, and self-organization: Dynamic systems approaches to emotional development* (pp. 298–323). New York: Cambridge University Press.

Lebra, T. S. (1994). Mother and child in Japanese socialization: A Japan–U. S. comparison. In P. M. Greenfield & R. R. Cocking (Eds.), *Cross-cultural roots of minority child development* (pp. 259–274). Hillsdale, NJ: Erlbaum.

Lee, A. Y., Aaker, J. L., & Gardner, W. L. (2000). The pleasures and pains of distinct self-construals: The role of interdependence in regulatory focus. *Journal of Personality and Social Psychology, 78*, 1122–1134.

Lehman, D. R., Chiu, C., & Schaller, M. (2004). Psychology and culture. *Annual Review of Psychology, 55*, 689–714.

LeVine, R. A. (1988). Human parental care: Universal goals, cultural strategies, individual behavior. In R. A. LeVine & P. M. Miller (Eds.), *New directions for child development: Vol. 40. Parental behavior in diverse societies* (pp. 3–12). San Francisco, CA: Jossey-Bass.

LeVine, R. A., & Miller, P. M. (1990). Commentary. *Human Development, 33*, 73–80.

Lewis, C. C. (1989). From indulgence to internalization: Social control in the early school years. *Journal of Japanese Studies, 15*, 139–157.

Lewis, M. D. (1995). Cognition-emotion feedback and the self-organization of developmental paths. *Human Development, 38*, 71–102.

Li, J. (2002). A cultural model of learning: Chinese "heart and mind for wanting to learn." *Journal of Cross-Cultural Psychology, 33*, 248–269.

Lin, C. C., & Fu, V. R. (1990). A comparison of child-rearing practices among Chinese, immigrant Chinese, and Caucasian-American parents. *Child Development, 61*, 429–433.

Markus, H. R., & Kitayama, S. (1991). Culture and the self: Implications for cognition, emotion, and motivation. *Psychological Review, 98*, 224–253.

Markus, H. R., & Kitayama, S. (1994). The cultural construction of self and emotion: Implications for social behavior. In S. Kitayama & H. R. Markus (Eds.), *Emotion and culture: Empirical studies of mutual influence* (pp. 89–130). Washington, DC: American Psychological Association.

Markus, H. R., & Kitayama, S. (2002). Models of agency: Sociocultural diversity in the construction of action. In V. Murphy-Berman & J. Berman Lincoln (Eds.), *The 49th Annual Nebraska Symposium on Motivation: Cross-cultural differences in perspectives on self* (pp. 1–57). Lincoln, NE: University of Nebraska Press.

Markus, H. R., Mullally, P. R., & Kitayama, S. (1997). Selfways: Diversity in modes of cultural participation. In U. Neisser & D. A. Jopling (Eds.), *The conceptual self in context: Culture, experience, self-understanding* (pp. 13–61). New York: Cambridge University Press.

Mason, C. A., Walker-Barnes, C. J., Tu, S., Simons, J., & Martinez-Arrue, R. (2004). Ethnic differences in the affective meaning of parental control behaviors. *Journal of Primary Prevention, 25*, 59–79.

McClelland, D. C. (1961). *The achieving society*. Princeton, NJ: Van Nostrand.

Mesquita, B., & Karasawa, M. (2004). Self-conscious emotions as dynamic cultural processes. *Psychological Inquiry, 15*, 161–166.

Mesquita, B., & Markus, H. R. (2004). Culture and emotion: Models of agency as sources of cultural variation in emotion. In A. S. R. Manstead, N. Frijda, & A. Fischer (Eds.), *Feelings and emotions: The Amsterdam Symposium* (pp. 341–358). New York: Cambridge University Press.

Metcalfe, J., & Mischel, W. (1999). A hot/cool-system analysis of delay of gratification: Dynamics of willpower. *Psychological Review, 106*, 3–19.

Mikulincer, M., Shaver, P. R., & Pereg, D. (2003). Attachment theory and affect regulation: The dynamics, development, and cognitive consequences of attachment-related strategies. *Motivation & Emotion, 27,* 77–102.

Miller, P. J., Wang, S., Sandel, T., & Cho, G. E. (2002). Self-esteem as folk theory: A comparison of European American and Taiwanese mothers' beliefs. *Parenting: Science and Practice, 2,* 209–239.

Miller, P. J., Wiley, A. R., Fung, H., & Liang, C.-H. (1997). Personal storytelling as a medium of socialization in Chinese and American families. *Child Development, 68,* 557–568.

Mischel, W., & Ayduk, O. (2004). Willpower in a cognitive-affective processing system: The dynamics of delay of gratification. In R. F. Baumeister & K. D. Vohs (Eds.), *Handbook of self-regulation: Research, theory, and applications* (pp. 99–129). New York: Guilford.

Morelli, G. A., Rogoff, B., Oppenheim, D., & Goldsmith, D. (1992). Cultural variation in infants' sleeping arrangements: Questions of independence. *Developmental Psychology, 28,* 604–613.

Morelli, G. A., & Rothbaum, F. (2007). Situating the person in relationships: Attachment relationships and self-regulation in young children. In S. Kitayama & D. Cohen (Eds.), *Handbook of cultural psychology* (pp. 500–527). New York: Guilford.

Mulder, N. (1992). *Individual and society in Java: A cultural analysis.* Yogyakarta: Gadjah Mada University Press.

Norasakkunkit, V. (2003). *Self-construal priming and emotional distress: Testing for cultural biases in the concept of distress.* Unpublished doctoral dissertation, University of Massachusetts, Boston.

Oyserman, D., Coon, H. M., & Kemmelmeier, M. (2002). Rethinking individualism and collectivism: Evaluation of theoretical assumptions and meta-analyses. *Psychological Bulletin, 128,* 3–72.

Rogoff, B. (2003). *The cultural nature of human development.* New York: Oxford University Press.

Roopnarine, J. L., & Carter, D. B. (Eds.) (1992). *Parent–child socialization in diverse cultures.* Norwood, NJ: Ablex.

Rothbart, M. K., & Bates, J. (1998). Temperament. In N. Eisenberg (Ed.), *Handbook of child psychology: Vol. 3. Social, emotional, and personality development* (5th ed., pp. 105–176). New York: Wiley.

Rothbaum, F., & Kakinuma, M. (2004). Amae and attachment: Security in cultural context. *Human Development, 47,* 34–39.

Rothbaum, F., & Morelli, G. (2005). Attachment and culture: Bridging relativism and universalism. In W. Friedlmeier, P. Chakkarath, & B. Schwarz (Eds.), *Culture and human development: The importance of cross-cultural research for the social sciences* (pp. 99–123). Hove, UK: Psychology Press.

Rothbaum, F., Nagaoka, R., & Ponte, I. C. (2006). Caregiver sensitivity in cultural context: Japanese and U. S. teachers' beliefs about anticipating and responding to children's needs. *Journal of Research in Childhood Education, 21,* 23–39.

Rothbaum, F., Pott, M., Azuma, H., Miyake, K., & Weisz, J. R. (2000). The development of close relationships in Japan and the United States: Paths of symbiotic harmony and generative tension. *Child Development, 71*, 1121–1142.

Rothbaum, F., & Trommsdorff, G. (2007). Do roots and wings complement or oppose one another? The socialization of relatedness and autonomy in cultural context. In J. E. Grusec & P. Hastings (Eds.), *The handbook of socialization* (pp. 461–489). New York: Guilford.

Rothbaum, F., Weisz, J. R., Pott, M., Miyake, K., & Morelli, G. (2000). Attachment and culture: Security in the United States and Japan. *American Psychologist, 55*, 1093–1104.

Rubin, K. H. (1998). Social and emotional development from a cultural perspective. *Developmental Psychology, 34*, 611–615.

Ryan, R. M., & Deci, E. L. (2000). Self-determination theory and the facilitation of intrinsic motivation, social development, and well-being. *American Psychologist, 55*, 68–78.

Saarni, C. (1999). *The development of emotional competence.* New York: Guilford.

Saarni, C. (2001). Epilogue: Emotion communication and relationship context. *International Journal of Behavioral Development, 25*, 354–356.

Shek, D. T. L. (2001). Chinese adolescents and their parents' views on a happy family: Implications for family therapy. *Family Therapy, 28*, 73–104.

Shouldice, A. E., & Stevenson-Hinde, J. (1992). Coping with security distress: The Separation Anxiety Test and attachment classification at 4.5 years. *Journal of Child Psychology and Psychiatry, 33*, 331–348.

Shweder, R. A., Goodnow, J., Hatano, G., LeVine, R. A., Markus, H. R., & Miller, P. (1998). The cultural psychology of development: One mind, many mentalities. In R. M. Lerner (Ed.), *Handbook of child psychology: Vol. 1. Theoretical models of human development* (5th ed., pp. 865–937). Hoboken, NJ: Wiley.

Taylor, S. E., Sherman, D. K., Kim, H. S., Jarcho, J., Takagi, K., & Dunagan, M. S. (2004). Culture and social support: Who seeks it and why? *Journal of Personality and Social Psychology, 87*, 354–362.

Thompson, R. A. (1994). Emotion regulation: A theme in search of definition. In N. A. Fox (Ed.), *The development of emotion regulation: Biological and behavioural considerations* (pp. 25–52). Chicago: University of Chicago Press.

Thompson, R. A. (1999). Early attachment and later development. In J. Cassidy & P. R. Shaver (Eds.), *Handbook of attachment: Theory, research, and clinical applications* (pp. 265–286). New York: Guilford.

Tobin, J. J., Wu, D. Y. H., & Davidson, D. H. (1989). *Preschool in three cultures: Japan, China, and the United States.* New Haven, CT: Yale University Press.

Trommsdorff, G. (1992). Values and social orientations of Japanese youth in intercultural comparison. In S. Formanek & S. Linhart (Eds.), *Japanese biographies: Life histories, life cycles, life stages* (pp. 57–81). Vienna: Verlag der Österreichischen Akademie der Wissenschaften.

Trommsdorff, G. (1995). Person-context relations as developmental conditions for empathy and prosocial action: A cross-cultural analysis. In T. A. Kindermann & J. Valsiner (Eds.), *Development of person-context relations* (pp. 113–146). Hillsdale, NJ: Erlbaum.

Trommsdorff, G. (2006a). Parent–child relations over the life-span. A cross-cultural perspective. In K. H. Rubin & O. B. Chung (Eds.), *Parenting beliefs, behaviors, and parent–child relations: A cross-cultural perspective* (pp. 143–183). New York: Psychology Press.

Trommsdorff, G. (2006b). Development of emotions as organized by culture. *ISSBD Newsletter, 49*, 1–4.

Trommsdorff, G., & Friedlmeier, W. (1993). Control and responsiveness in Japanese and German mother–child interactions. *Early Development and Parenting, 2*, 65–78.

Trommsdorff, G., & Friedlmeier, W. (1999). Emotionale Entwicklung im Kulturvergleich [The cultural comparison of emotional development]. In W. Friedlmeier & M. Holodynski (Eds.), *Emotionale Entwicklung: Funktion, Regulation und soziokultureller Kontext von Emotionen* (pp. 275–293). Heidelberg: Spektrum.

Trommsdorff, G., & Friedlmeier, W. (2006). *Cultural differences in emotion regulation and maternal sensitivity.* Manuscript under review.

Trommsdorff, G., Friedlmeier, W., & Mayer, B. (2007). Sympathy, distress, and prosocial behavior of preschool children in four cultures. *International Journal of Behavioural Development, 31*, 284–293.

Trommsdorff, G., & Kornadt, H.-J. (2003). Parent–child relations in cross-cultural perspective. In L. Kuczynski (Ed.), *Handbook of dynamics in parent–child relations* (pp. 271–306). Thousand Oaks, CA: Sage.

Trommsdorff, G., Mayer, B., & Albert, I. (2004). Dimensions of culture in intra-cultural comparisons: Individualism/collectivism and family-related values in three generations. In H. Vinken, J. Soeters, & P. Ester (Eds.), *Comparing cultures: Dimensions of culture in a comparative perspective* (pp. 157–184). Leiden: Brill.

Trommsdorff, G., Mishra, R. C., von Suchodoletz, A., Heikamp, T., & Merkel F. (2006). Emotion regulation of Indian and German preschool children. Unpublished raw data.

van IJzendoorn, M. H., & Sagi, A. (1999). Cross-cultural patterns of attachment: Universal and contextual dimensions. In J. Cassidy & P. R. Shaver (Eds.), *Handbook of attachment: Theory, research, and clinical applications* (pp. 713–734). New York: Guilford.

Wang, Q., & Fivush, R. (2005). Mother–child conversations of emotionally salient events: Exploring the functions of emotional reminiscing in European-American and Chinese families. *Social Development, 14*, 473–495.

Wang, Y. (2005). *Comparing parent–child dinnertime interactions in two cultures.* Unpublished doctoral dissertation, University of Illinois at Urbana-Champaign.

Wang, Y., Wiley, A. R., & Chiu, C. (in press). Independence-supportive praise versus interdependence promoting praise. *International Journal of Behavioral Development.*

Weisz, J. R., Chaiyasit, W., Weiss, B., Eastman, K., & Jackson, E. (1995). A multimethod study of problem behaviour among Thai and American children in school: Teacher reports versus direct observation. *Child Development, 66*, 402–415.

Wenzlaff, R. M., & Wegner, D. M. (2000). Thought suppression. *Annual Review of Psychology, 51*, 59–91.

Whiting, B. B., & Whiting, J. W. M. (1975). *Children of six cultures: A psycho-cultural analysis*. Cambridge, MA: Harvard University Press.

Whiting, J. W. M. (1981). Environmental constraints on infant care practices. In R. J. Munroe, R. L. Munroe, & B. B. Whiting (Eds.), *Handbook of cross-cultural human development* (pp. 155–180). New York: Garland.

Whiting, J. W. M. (1990). Adolescent rituals and identity conflicts. In J. W. Stigler, R. A. Shweder, & G. Herdt (Eds.), *Cultural psychology: Essays on comparative human development* (pp. 357–365). New York: Cambridge University Press.

Yamaguchi, S. (2004). Further clarifications of the concept of amae in relation to dependence and attachment. *Human Development, 47*, 28–33.

5

Adult Attachment Theory, Emotion Regulation, and Prosocial Behavior

Phillip R. Shaver, Mario Mikulincer, and David S. Chun

Attachment theory (Ainsworth & Bowlby, 1991; Bowlby, 1982) is a theory of the developmental origins of individual differences in emotion regulation within the context of close relationships. Early studies based on the theory (e.g., Ainsworth, Blehar, Waters, & Wall, 1978) were concerned with human infants' "attachment to" or "emotional bonding with" their mothers, because individual differences in relational orientations and affect-regulation strategies were thought to begin in infancy. In recent years, however, much of the emphasis has shifted to emotional attachments in adolescents and adults, including attachment to romantic or marital partners, and to individual differences in emotion regulation associated with different patterns of attachment or "attachment styles" (Mikulincer & Shaver, 2007, in press). In the present chapter, we outline attachment theory, review psychological and neuropsychological research on attachment-related individual differences in emotion regulation, and show how security-related regulation processes foster mental health and prosocial mental states and behaviors.

Various typologies and dimensional conceptions of individual differences in "attachment style" have been proposed. One of the conceptual schemes used most often by researchers in personality and social psychology is a model proposed originally by Bartholomew (1990) and developed further by Fraley and Shaver (2000) and Mikulincer and Shaver (2003). According to this model, attachment styles can be viewed as regions in a two-dimensional space defined by anxious attachment and avoidant attachment, with low scores on these dimensions representing a dispositional sense of attachment security or a secure attachment style. In recent years, experimental research—both behavioral and brain-oriented (e.g., using functional magnetic resonance imaging, or fMRI)—has revealed some of the dynamics of emotion regulation related to these dimensions of attachment style. Along with insights and findings about emotion regulation generally, research on adult attachment indicates that attachment security and associated emotion-regulation processes foster effective coping with stress, development of prosocial values, and socially desirable interpersonal and group behavior.

 ATTACHMENT THEORY AND THE CONSTRUCT OF ATTACHMENT STYLE

According to Bowlby (1973, 1980, 1982), human beings and many nonhuman primates are born with an innate psychobiological system (the *attachment behavioral system*) that motivates them to seek proximity to significant others (*attachment figures*) in times of need as a way of protecting themselves from threats and alleviating distress. Bowlby (1973) also described important individual differences in attachment-system functioning that result from social experiences with attachment figures beginning in childhood. Interactions with attachment figures who are available and responsive in times of need promote a sense of attachment security—"felt security" (Sroufe & Waters, 1977)—based on expectations that attachment figures will be available and helpful when needed. These expectations are organized into relatively stable *working models*: mental representations of self and others in the context of close relationships.

When attachment figures are not reliably available and supportive, however, a sense of security is not attained, negative working models of self and/ or others are formed, and strategies of affect regulation other than normal proximity seeking are engaged. These *secondary attachment strategies* can be conceptualized in terms of two roughly orthogonal dimensions, avoidance and anxiety. A person's position on the first dimension, *avoidance*, reflects the extent to which he or she distrusts relationship partners' goodwill and strives to maintain behavioral independence and emotional distance from partners. The second dimension, attachment-related *anxiety*, reflects the degree to which a person worries that a partner will not be available in times of need. People who score low on these two dimensions are said to be secure or securely attached.

Attachment styles begin to be formed in interactions with primary caregivers during early childhood, as a large body of research has shown (Cassidy & Shaver, 1999), but Bowlby (1988) claimed that memorable interactions with other people throughout life can alter a person's working models and move him or her from one region of the two-dimensional space to another. Moreover, although attachment style is often conceptualized as a single global orientation toward close relationships, and can definitely be measured as such (e.g., Brennan, Clark, & Shaver, 1998), a person's attachment orientation is rooted in a complex cognitive and affective network that includes many different episodic, context-related, and relationship-specific, as well as fairly general attachment representations (Mikulincer & Shaver, 2003). In fact, research shows that attachment style can change, subtly or dramatically, depending on natural or experimentally induced contexts and recent experiences (e.g., Baldwin, Keelan, Fehr, Enns, & Koh Rangarajoo, 1996; Mikulincer & Shaver, 2001).

ATTACHMENT-SYSTEM FUNCTIONING AND EMOTION REGULATION IN ADOLESCENCE AND ADULTHOOD

When an adolescent or adult finds him- or herself in a threatening or stressful situation, perceiving that attachment figures are unavailable or unresponsive compounds the distress (as also occurs in infancy; Bowlby, 1982). This state of insecurity forces a decision about the viability of further (more active, more intense) proximity seeking as a protective strategy. The appraisal of proximity as feasible or essential—because of attachment history, temperamental factors, or contextual cues—results in energetic, insistent attempts to attain proximity, support, and love. These attempts are called *hyperactivating strategies* (Cassidy & Kobak, 1988) because they involve up-regulation of the attachment system, including constant vigilance and intense concern until an attachment figure is perceived to be adequately available and supportive.

Hyperactivating strategies include strident attempts to elicit a partner's involvement, care, and support through crying, begging, clinging, and controlling behaviors (Davis, Shaver, & Vernon, 2003) and overdependence on relationship partners as a source of protection (Shaver & Hazan, 1993). Hyperactivating strategies cause a person to remain perpetually vigilant about threat-related cues and cues of attachment figures' unavailability, the two kinds of cues that activate the attachment system (Bowlby, 1973). Hence, once they become the focus of a person's attention, they more or less guarantee that the attachment system will remain continuously active. These aspects of attachment-system hyperactivation account for many of the empirically documented correlates of attachment anxiety (Mikulincer & Shaver, 2003, in press).

Hyperactivation also intensifies negative emotional responses to threats.

Anxiously attached individuals often perceive negative emotions as congruent with their attachment goals and therefore sustain or exaggerate them. Such people are guided by an unfulfilled wish to get attachment figures to pay attention and provide more reliable protection, which causes them to intensify their bids for love and care. As a result, hyperactivating strategies can intensify emotions associated with crying out for attention and care, such as jealousy and anger, or implicitly emphasize a person's vulnerability, helplessness, and neediness, such as sadness, anxiety, fear, and shame. This kind of emotional expression runs counter to typical conceptualization of emotion regulation in terms of *down*-regulation of distress. In the case of anxiously attached persons, however, "regulation" can also include distress intensification.

How is anxious hyperactivation sustained? One way is to exaggerate appraisals, perceptually heightening the threatening aspects of even fairly minor threats, hold onto pessimistic beliefs about one's inability to manage distress, and attribute threat-related events to uncontrollable causes and global personal inadequacies. Another regulatory technique is to shift attention to internal indicators of distress (engaging in what Lazarus and Folkman, 1984, called "emotion-focused coping"). This involves hypervigilant attention to the physiological changes associated with emotion, heightened recall of threat-related feelings, and rumination on actual and potential threats. Another strategy is to intensify negative emotions by making self-defeating decisions and taking ineffective courses of actions that are likely to end in failure. All of these strategies create a self-amplifying cycle of distress, which is maintained by ruminative thoughts even after a threat subsides. As a result, anxious individuals have ready access to undesirable emotions, their cognitive system is often burdened by distress, and their stream of consciousness is clogged with threat-related ideation.

Appraising proximity seeking as unlikely to alleviate distress results in deliberate deactivation of the attachment system, inhibition of the quest for support, and commitment to handling distress alone, especially distress arising from the failure of attachment figures to be available and responsive. These strategies of affect regulation are called *deactivating* (Cassidy & Kobak, 1988) because their goal is to keep the attachment system down-regulated, to avoid the frustration and pain of attachment-figure unavailability. Deactivating strategies include avoidance of intimacy and dependence in close relationships and maximization of emotional distance from others, and suppression of attachment-related thoughts, feelings, concerns, and wishes. These strategies account for the empirically documented correlates of attachment avoidance (Mikulincer & Shaver, 2003, 2007).

Avoidant defenses include inhibition of emotional states that are incongruent with the goal of keeping one's attachment system deactivated. These inhibitory efforts are directed mainly at fear, anxiety, anger, sadness, shame, guilt, and distress, because such emotions are triggered by threats and can cause unwanted activation of the attachment system. In addition, anger implies emotional involvement in a relationship, and such involvement may be incongruent with an avoidant person's commitment to self-reliance (Cassidy, 1994). Moreover, fear, anxiety, sadness, shame, and guilt can be interpreted as signs of weakness or vulnerability, which contradict an avoidant person's sense of strength and independence. Avoidant individuals may even feel uncomfortable with joy and happiness, because they encourage interpersonal closeness and may be interpreted by a relationship partner as indications of investment in the relationship (Cassidy, 1994). Like secure people, avoidant ones attempt to down-regulate threat-related emotions. But whereas secure people's regulatory attempts usually promote accurate perception, effective communication, and relationship maintenance, avoidant people's efforts are aimed at minimizing perceived threats, closeness, and interdependence, regardless of the deleterious effects on a relationship.

Inability or unwillingness to deal openly with the causes of painful emotional states confines avoidant people to a single regulatory path: suppressing emotion or dissociating oneself from its manifestations in experience and behavior (by using what Lazarus & Folkman, 1984, called "distancing coping" and Gross, 1999, called "response-focused emotion regulation"). These regulatory efforts consist of denial or suppression of emotion-related thoughts and memories, diversion of attention from emotion-related material, suppression of emotion-related action tendencies, and inhibition or masking of verbal and nonverbal expressions of emotion. By preventing the conscious experience and expression of emotions, avoidant individuals make it less likely that emotional experiences will be integrated into their memory structures or that they will use the experiences effectively in information processing and behavior.

EMPIRICAL EVIDENCE FOR ATTACHMENT-RELATED EMOTION REGULATION STRATEGIES

There is extensive empirical evidence for the theoretical ideas outlined in the previous section. Here, we will review several examples that link the theoretical analysis with the diverse kinds of emotion regulation that have been studied to date.

Experiencing and managing death anxiety

Adult attachment researchers have examined how attachment styles are related to the experience and management of specific emotional states. For example, a number of studies conducted in Mikulincer's laboratory have examined attachment-style differences in the strength of death anxiety, measured in terms of overt statements on questionnaires (Florian & Mikulincer, 1998; Mikulincer, Florian, & Tolmacz, 1990), less conscious, indirect indicators of death anxiety (e.g., responses to projective Thematic Apperception Test (TAT) cards; Mikulincer et al., 1990), and the accessibility or inaccessibility of death-related thoughts in the context of laboratory experiments (e.g., the number of death-related words a person produces in a word completion task; Mikulincer & Florian, 2000; Mikulincer, Florian, Birnbaum, & Malishkowitz, 2002).

Attachment-anxious individuals (identified with self-report measures, such as those created by Brennan et al., 1998) intensify death concerns and keep death-related thoughts active in working memory. That is, attachment anxiety is associated with heightened fear of death at both conscious and unconscious levels, as well as heightened accessibility of death-related thoughts even when no death reminder is present. Avoidant individuals suppress death concerns and show signs of dissociation between their conscious claims and unconscious dynamics. For example, attachment-related avoidance (again, assessed with self-report measures) is related to both low levels of self-reported fear of death and heightened death-related anxiety assessed with a projective TAT measure.

Attachment-style differences have also been noted in the meanings people assign to death or the process of dying (Florian & Mikulincer, 1998; Mikulincer et al., 1990). Anxiously attached people tend to attribute their fear to a dreaded loss of social identity after death (e.g., "People will forget me"), whereas avoidant people tend to attribute their anxiety to the unknown nature of death, dying, and any experiences that may occur after death (e.g., "Uncertainty about what to expect"). These findings are compatible with the two kinds of secondary attachment strategies discussed earlier. Anxious people hyperactivate worries about rejection and abandonment, viewing death as yet another relational setting in which they may be abandoned or forgotten. Avoidant people try to remain self-reliant and in control, which leads to fear of the uncertain and unknown aspects of death, which threaten loss of control.

A related line of research has linked attachment theory with "terror management theory" (Greenberg, Pyszczynski, & Solomon, 1997), or TMT for short. According to TMT, human beings' knowledge that they are destined to die, coexisting with strong wishes to perceive themselves as special, important, and immortal, makes it necessary for them to engage in self-promotion, defend their cultural worldview, and deny their mortality, physicality, and animality. Much creative research has shown that experimentally induced death reminders lead to more negative reactions to moral transgressors and more hostile and derogatory responses to members of out-groups (see Greenberg et al., 1997, for a review). However, Mikulincer and colleagues have shown that this reaction is more characteristic of attachment-insecure than of secure individuals. For example, experimentally induced death reminders produced more severe judgments and punishments of moral transgressors and greater willingness to die for a cause only among insecurely attached people, either anxious or avoidant (Caspi-Berkowitz, 2003; Mikulincer & Florian, 2000). Securely attached people were not affected by death reminders, did not recommend harsher punishments for transgressors following a mortality salience induction, and were generally averse to endangering people's lives to protect cultural values.

Some of the studies reveal special ways in which securely attached adults react to death reminders. Mikulincer and Florian (2000) found that secure people reacted to mortality salience with an increased sense of symbolic immortality—a transformational, constructive strategy that, while not solving the unsolvable problem of death, leads a person to invest in his or her children's care and to engage in creative, growth-oriented activities whose products will live on after one's death. Secure people also react to mortality salience with heightened attachment needs—a more intense desire for intimacy in close relationships (Mikulincer & Florian, 2000) and greater willingness to engage in social interactions (Taubman Ben-Ari, Findler, & Mikulincer, 2002).

Experiencing and managing anger

Adult attachment researchers have also studied connections between attachment style and the experience and management of anger. In Bowlby's (1973) analysis of emotional reactions to separation, he viewed anger as a functional response to separation from an attachment figure, insofar as it succeeded in gaining the attention of an unreliable figure or caused the figure to become more available. Anger is functional to the degree that it is not intended to hurt or destroy the attachment figure but only to discourage his or her frustrating or frightening behavior and to reestablish a warm and satisfying relationship. However, Bowlby (1973, 1988) also noted that anger sometimes becomes so intense that it alienates the partner or becomes vengeful rather than corrective. In particular, Bowlby

(1988) discussed how some cases of family violence can be understood as exaggerated forms of otherwise functional behavior. For example, he characterized certain coercive behaviors within close relationships (including battering) as strategies for controlling the other and precluding separation. In Bowlby's (1988) view, although violent and uncontrollable outbursts of anger may have functional roots (being evolutionarily "designed" to discourage a partner's negative behavior), it is dysfunctional when it becomes so extreme that it destroys a relationship one is attempting to maintain.

Bowlby's analysis of the complex, multifaceted nature of anger is consistent with other theoretical perspectives on anger which view it as motivated by either constructive or destructive goals, expressible in functional or dysfunctional ways, resulting in positive or negative relational behaviors, eliciting positive or negative responses from a relationship partner, and having positive or negative effects on a relationship (e.g., Averill, 1982; Tangney et al., 1996). Functional forms of anger are motivated by constructive goals (e.g., maintaining a relationship, bringing about a beneficial change in a partner's behavior), are typically expressed in the form of focused complaints and problem-solving discussions, and do not entail animosity, hostility, or hatred. In contrast, dysfunctional forms of anger include resentment toward one's partner, deliberately injuring the partner emotionally or physically, and seeking revenge, which can easily weaken emotional bonds (Tangney et al., 1996).

Functional expressions of anger seem to be typical of securely attached people. They attempt to deal with negative emotions in a constructive, transformational manner while maintaining stable and satisfying relationships; they have positive working models of others and believe that others' negative behavior can be corrected through discussion. Indeed, Mikulincer (1998) found that, when confronted with anger-provoking events, secure people held optimistic expectations about their partner's subsequent behavior (e.g., "He/she will accept me") and made well-differentiated, reality-attuned appraisals of their partner's intentions. Only when there were clear contextual cues, provided by the experimenter, indicating that a partner actually had acted with hostile intent did secure people attribute hostility to the partner and react with anger. Moreover, secure people's accounts of anger-eliciting events were characterized by the constructive goal of repairing a relationship, engaging in adaptive problem solving, and experiencing positive affect following the temporary period of discord.

The constructive nature of secure people's anger has also been demonstrated in a recent study by Zimmermann, Maier, Winter, and Grossmann (2001). In this study, adolescents performed a frustrating, difficult cognitive task with the help of a friend, and the researchers assessed reports of disappointment and anger during the task as well as disruptive behavior toward the friend (e.g., rejection of the friend's suggestions without discussion). The results indicated that disappointment and anger were associated with more frequent disruptive behavior only among insecurely attached adolescents (identified with the Adult Attachment Interview, a narrative measure of attachment style; Hesse, 1999). Among securely attached adolescents, these emotions were associated with less rather than more disruptive behavior. Therefore, secure people's anger seemed to be well regulated and channeled in useful directions.

Theoretically, avoidant individuals' attempts to sidestep negative emotions include suppressing anger, which might indicate vulnerability or over-involvement in a relationship. This anger suppression might result in anger being expressed in unconscious or unattended ways, which might include showing "unexplained" hostility toward a partner (what Mikulincer, 1998, labeled *"dissociated anger"*). In support of this view, he found that although individuals scoring high on avoidant attachment did not report overly intense specific anger in reaction to another person's negative behavior, they scored higher on a more general hostility measure and exhibited intense physiological arousal during stressful interactions. They also reported using distancing strategies to cope with potentially anger-provoking events and attributed hostility to a partner even when there were clear contextual cues (provided by the experimenter) concerning the partner's nonhostile intent.

Anxiously attached individuals' intensification of negative emotions and tendency to ruminate about threats can fuel intense and prolonged bouts of anger. However, their fear of separation and desperate desire for others' love may hold their resentment and anger in check and redirect it toward the self. As a result, anxious people's anger can include a complex mixture of resentment, hostility, self-criticism, fear, sadness, and depression. Mikulincer (1998) provided evidence for this characterization of anxiously attached people's anger experiences: Their recollections of anger-provoking life experiences included an uncontrollable flood of angry feelings, persistent rumination on these feelings, and sadness and despair following conflicts. Mikulincer (1998) also found that anxious people held more negative expectations about others' responses during anger episodes and tended to make more undifferentiated, negatively biased appraisals of a relationship partner's intentions. They attributed hostility to their partner and reacted in kind, even when there were ambiguous cues (in the experiment) concerning hostile intent. There is also evidence in other studies that attachment anxiety is associated with anger, aggression, and hostility (e.g., Buunk, 1997; Calamari & Pini, 2003; Zimmerman, 2004).

The dysfunctional nature of anxious people's anger has also been observed in studies of dyadic interactions. Simpson, Rholes, and Phillips (1996) found that attachment anxiety was associated with displaying and reporting more anger and hostility while discussing an unresolved problem with a dating partner. And in a study of support seeking, Rholes, Simpson, and Orina (1999) found no association between attachment anxiety and anger toward a dating partner while waiting for an anxiety-provoking activity, but after the participant was told that she would not really have to undergo the expected stress, attachment anxiety was associated with anger toward the partner. Interestingly, this was particularly true if participants had been more upset during the "waiting" period and had sought more support from their partner. It therefore seems that anxious participants' strong need for reassurance counteracted, or led to suppression of, angry feelings and expressions during support seeking, but after support was no longer necessary the angry feelings surfaced, reflecting hyperactivating strategies that perpetuate distress.

Anxious people's problems in anger management have also been documented using physiological measures. Diamond and Hicks (2005) exposed young men to two anger-provoking experimental inductions (performance of serial subtraction accompanied by discouraging feedback from the experimenter; recollection of a recent anger-eliciting event) and measured reports of anxiety and anger during and after the inductions. They also recorded participants' vagal tone (indexed by resting levels of respiration-related variability in heart rate), a common indicator of parasympathetic down-regulation of negative emotion. Diamond and Hicks found that attachment anxiety was associated with lower vagal tone—a sign that the parasympathetic nervous system responded less quickly and flexibly to the stressful tasks and that attachment-anxious participants recovered poorly from frustration and anger. In addition, attachment anxiety was associated with self-reports of distress and anger during and after the anger-induction tasks, and vagal tone mediated the association between attachment anxiety and reports of anger.

Romantic jealousy

Adult attachment studies have also explored associations between attachment strategies and romantic jealousy. In general, secure people tend to report less jealousy (e.g., Buunk, 1997; Collins & Read, 1990; Hazan & Shaver, 1987; Radecki-Bush, Farrel, & Bush, 1993; Sharpsteen & Kirkpatrick, 1997), milder emotional reactions to jealousy-provoking events (e.g., Guerrero, 1998; Radecki-Bush et al., 1993; Sharpsteen & Kirkpatrick, 1997), fewer interfering thoughts and worries in response to these events (Guerrero, 1998), and greater use of constructive coping strategies, such as openly discussing matters with one's partner and attempting to put the relationship back on a better course (Guerrero, 1998).

Attachment anxious people tend to experience jealousy in intense and dysfunctional ways, allowing it to ignite other negative emotions, overwhelm thought processes, and erode relationship quality. They score high on measures of jealousy (e.g., Buunk, 1997; Collins & Read, 1990; Hazan & Shaver, 1987; Radecki-Bush et al., 1993; Sharpsteen & Kirkpatrick, 1997); experience fear, guilt, shame, sadness, and anger along with jealousy (Guerrero, 1998; Radecki-Bush et al., 1993; Sharpsteen & Kirkpatrick, 1997); report higher levels of suspicion and worry in jealousy-eliciting situations (Guerrero, 1998); and cope by expressing hostility toward one's partner and engaging in more surveillance (mate-guarding) behavior (Guerrero, 1998).

Avoidant individuals, like their secure counterparts, report low levels of jealousy and do not react to jealousy-eliciting events with strong negative emotions or disrupted thinking. But they are the least likely to engage in coping efforts aimed at restoring relationship quality (Guerrero, 1998). Instead, they prefer to avoid discussing the problem and seem, at the moment, to overlook the problem (Guerrero, 1998). This is another example of deactivating strategies and is likely to contribute to relationship cooling and dissolution.

Neuroscience studies of attachment and emotion regulation

Attachment-related patterns of emotion regulation have been examined in a variety of studies, using different measures of attachment style, different experimental interventions, and different kinds of outcome measures. Because the availability of fMRI as an assessment technique now makes it possible to investigate some of the brain processes underlying attachment effects, relevant studies are beginning to appear in the literature.

In one recent study, Gillath, Bunge, Shaver, Wendelken, and Mikulincer (2005) built upon prior behavioral studies of attachment style and thought suppression (e.g., Fraley & Shaver, 1997) and examined neural processes underlying the ability to suppress negative thoughts and associated emotions. Participants were asked, while lying in an MRI scanner, to think and then to suppress thoughts about both neutral and emotion-provoking experiences with a relationship partner, including previous and imagined losses (e.g., a breakup, the death of one's partner). In general, all participants showed activation in the anterior cingulate cortex (ACC) and medial prefrontal cortex (MPFC) when asked to suppress either a neutral or an emotional experience, as had been found in earlier studies (e.g., Phan et al., 2005; Wyland, Kelley, Macrae, Gordon, & Heatherton, 2003).

Of greater interest here, participants who scored low on avoidant attachment deactivated other brain regions (e.g., lateral prefrontal cortex, or LPFC, and subcollosal cingulate cortex, or SCC) while activating the ACC and MPFC, but avoidant individuals did not. This lack of deactivations had been noted in previous studies (e.g., Binder et al., 1999; Hester et al., 2004; Mazoyer et al., 2001; Shulman et al., 1997) and associated with poor performance on certain cognitive tasks, and on particular trials within these tasks. This may help to explain results obtained by Mikulincer, Dolev, and Shaver (2004) in a study of avoidant suppression of loss-related thoughts. Avoidant people seemed to be good at suppressing such thoughts until an additional cognitive task, or "load," was added. Under a high cognitive load, they tended to lose control of both loss-related thoughts and negative self-relevant traits.

In the Gillath, Bunge, et al. (2005) study, anxious individuals showed greater activation in emotion-related brain areas such as the anterior temporal pole (ATP) and lower activation in control-related frontal regions such as the orbitofrontal cortex (OFC) when thinking about relationship losses, suggesting that one reason for their intense negative emotions in everyday life is high activation of emotion circuitry combined with undercontrol or insufficient emotion regulation. The reciprocal relation between activation in emotion-related and control regions of the brain has been documented in several studies (Beer, Shimamura, & Knight, 2004; Lévesque et al., 2003; Ochsner, Bunge, Gross, & Gabrieli, 2002; Ochsner & Gross, 2005), but without much focus on individual differences. Gillath, Bunge, et al. (2005) found that the correlations between anxious attachment, high ATP activation while thinking about losses, and low OFC activation were so high that the inverse correlation between activation in the ATP and OFC, which is expected based on anatomical connections, dropped to insignificance when attachment anxiety scores were statistically controlled.

These results suggest that clinical interventions that lowered emotionality and/or increased self-regulatory skill would be especially helpful for attachment-anxious individuals. The results also suggest that fMRI could be used to monitor the success or failure of such clinical interventions.

Another recent study, although not specifically focused on attachment theory, investigated the neural correlates of handholding and threat regulation. Coan, Schaefer, and Davidson (2006), found that when married women whose brains were being monitored in an MRI scanner were threatened with periodic electric shocks, several stress- and emotion-related brain regions showed increased activation. These levels of activation, however, were decreased when the women held their spouse's hand. (For example, activation in the ventral ACC, posterior cingulate, and left caudate decreased significantly.) Moreover, the wife's level of marital satisfaction (but not the husband's) moderated some of the brain activation effects, indicating that the wife's sense of security in the marriage determined how comforting it was to hold her partner's hand while under threat. Informal discussions with one of the authors of this study (Coan) revealed that attachment style measures were also included in the study and yielded interesting and theory-consistent effects that will be reported in a subsequent paper. Thus, there would seem to be a bright future for social neuroscience studies of hypotheses derived from attachment theory and previous behavioral studies of attachment and emotion-regulation.

 ## THE ATTACHMENT SYSTEM IN RELATION TO THE CAREGIVING SYSTEM

Besides providing a detailed analysis of the hypothesized "attachment behavioral system," Bowlby (1982) proposed additional behavioral systems as a way of accounting for motivated behavior that previous psychodynamic theories had attributed to drives or instincts. Among these other behavioral systems were an exploration system, to account for infants' and children's tendency to explore their environments and learn new skills when provided by a good attachment figure with a sense of security (Ainsworth et al., 1978), and a caregiving system, to account for attachment figures' seemingly innate responsiveness to infants and other people in need. Bowlby also discussed an affiliation system (related to play and leisure interactions at later ages) and a sexual system, to account for sexual attraction and sexual relationships. Here, because we are interested in connections between attachment security or insecurity, on one hand, and prosocial feelings, values, and behavior, on the other, we give special attention to the caregiving system.

Defining the caregiving behavioral system

Among attachment researchers, caregiving is viewed not only as the primary ingredient in parental behavior, but also as a major contributor to romantic and marital relationships, and as a key constituent of all forms of prosocial behavior. For young children, parents are usually the primary providers of protection, support, and security, and differences in the way they fulfill or abdicate this role have dramatic effects on their children's socio-emotional development in general, and on their attainment of felt security in particular. Similarly, romantic partners are frequently called upon to provide comfort, assistance, and security to one another in times of need, and the quality of the support they are willing and able to provide is one of the major determinants of relationship quality and stability (Collins & Feeney, 2000; Collins, Guichard, Ford, & Feeney, 2006).

According to attachment theory, the aim of the caregiving behavioral system is to reduce others' suffering, protect them from harm, and foster their growth and development (e.g., Collins et al., 2006; George & Solomon, 1999; Gillath, Shaver, & Mikulincer, 2005; Kunce & Shaver, 1994). In other words, the caregiving system is designed to accomplish the two major functions of a security-providing attachment figure: to meet another person's needs for protection and support in times of danger or distress (which Bowlby, 1982, called providing a "safe haven") and to support that person's exploration, autonomy, and growth when exploration is safe and viewed by the explorer as desirable. (Bowlby called this function "provision of a secure base for exploration").

Although we assume that everyone is born with the potential to become an effective caregiver, the smooth and effective operation of the caregiving system depends on several intra- and interpersonal factors. For example, caregiving can be impaired by emotional states, beliefs, and concerns in the mind of a potential caregiver that inhibit sensitivity and responsiveness to another person's needs. It can also be impaired by a careseeker's failure to express needs appropriately, by his or her rebuff of a caregiver's helping attempts, or by external obstacles to support provision. As Collins et al. (2006) noted, "It is clear that effective caregiving is a difficult process that is likely to be easier for some people than for others, and in some relationships compared to others" (p. 160).

Attachment style, emotion regulation, and caregiving

Bowlby (1982) noticed that different behavioral systems can interfere with each other. Because of the urgency and priority of threats to oneself (especially during early childhood), for example, activation of the attachment system is likely to disrupt smooth operation of the exploration system. A threatened or frightened child usually terminates exploration and quickly devotes all of his or her energy to attaining protection from an attachment figure. This kind of disruption or interference can also occur in caregiving situations (Kunce & Shaver, 1994), because a potential caregiver may feel so threatened that obtaining care for him- or herself seems more urgent than providing it to others. At such times even adults are likely to be so focused on their own vulnerability that they lack the mental resources necessary to attend compassionately to others' needs for help and care. Only when some degree of safety is attained and a sense of attachment security is restored can most people perceive others not only as sources of security and support, but also as human beings who need and deserve comfort and support.

Securely attached individuals' positive working models and sense of felt security also sustain effective care provision in nonfamily situations. Their comfort with closeness and interdependence allows them to approach others in need, which is important because it is usually necessary to accept others' need for sympathy, support, and sometimes physical assistance in order to help them through a crisis (Lehman, Ellard, & Wortman, 1986). Secure people's effective emotion-regulation skills help them maintain their own emotional stability while addressing another person's needs, a task that can otherwise generate great personal distress (Batson, 1991). Positive models of self also sustain a sense of control and confidence in one's ability to cope with a partner's distress and reduce one's own distress.

Attachment theorists have also suggested that insecure people's deficits in emotion regulation can lead to difficulties in providing effective care (Collins et al., 2006; George & Solomon, 1999; Mikulincer & Shaver, 2005; Shaver & Hazan, 1988). Although anxiously attached people may have some of the skills and qualities necessary for effective caregiving (e.g., comfort with intimacy and closeness), their deficits in emotion regulation may result in personal distress that interferes with sensitive and responsive care. Their tendency to intensify distressing emotions can trigger disruptive memories when they encounter other people's pain and suffering, which draws attention inward rather than outward toward what might be done for someone else. If this state is prolonged during a crisis, it can lead to emotional overload, "burnout," and exhaustion. Anxiously attached people easily become sidetracked by self-focused worries and concerns and hence may fail to maintain the good judgment and psychological boundaries necessary to help in sensitively appropriate ways. Moreover, their excessive need for closeness may cause them to become overly involved and intrusive, and their lack of self-confidence can make it difficult for them to adopt the role of care provider (Collins et al., 2006).

Avoidant individuals, who often try to distance themselves from interaction partners, especially ones who signal neediness and dependency, are likely to react coolly or unresponsively to needy others and avoid being "sucked in" by empathy and compassion. They do not approve expressions of need and vulnerability, in themselves or their relationship partners, and have little desire to get entangled with someone who seems needy. For them, besides being a "hassle" and a drain on personal resources, a distressed person threatens to become a mirror of the self's own weaknesses and suppressed weaknesses and vulnerabilities. When obliged by social norms or interpersonal commitments to help others, avoidant people are likely to grumble about the burden, express disapproval, lack sympathy and compassion, and behave insensitively. Moreover, their reactions to another person's suffering are likely to take the form of pity rather than compassion, which means viewing the sufferer as inferior to oneself and excusing oneself from suffering while perhaps showing disgust or disdain (Ben-Ze'ev, 1999).

In short, although hyperactivating and deactivating strategies lead to opposite patterns of emotion regulation (intensification versus suppression), both result in dysfunctional emotion regulation and caregiving. Security-based regulation of one's emotions, in contrast, allows caregivers to deal effectively with the tension and discomfort associated with another person's pain and distress, thereby promoting effective care provision. Deficient emotion regulation can overwhelm care providers with intense personal distress, causing them to slip over into the role of the needy person rather than the care provider, or to physically, emotionally, or cognitively distance themselves from a needy other to reduce their own distress, even if this means abdicating the caregiving role. The following section reviews some of the evidence supporting this theoretical analysis.

 ## ATTACHMENT, COMPASSION, AND PROSOCIAL BEHAVIOR

Studies of preschoolers show that attachment insecurities measurable during infancy predict less empathic concern for an adult stranger's or other children's distress later on, as indicated by teachers' ratings and researchers' observations of children's behavior (e.g., Kestenbaum, Farber, & Sroufe, 1989; van der Mark, van IJzendoorn, & Bakermans-Kranenburg, 2002). Moreover, secure attachment to parents during adolescence had been found to contribute positively to compassionate, empathic responses to needy people (e.g., Laible, Carlo, & Raffaelli, 2000; Markiewicz, Doyle, & Brendgen, 2001). These findings led researchers to explore the possibility that emotion regulation strategies associated with attachment style would influence prosocial values, intergroup tolerance, and altruistic behavior in adults.

Self-transcendent values

In three experiments, Mikulincer, Gillath, et al. (2003) found theoretically predictable attachment-related differences in value orientations.
Avoidant attachment (measured with a self-report questionnaire) was
inversely associated with endorsing two self-transcendent values, ben-
evolence (concern for close others) and universalism (concern for all
humanity), supporting the expectation that avoidance fosters lack of
concern for others' needs. In addition, experimentally priming mental
representations of attachment-figure availability, as compared with posi-
tive-affect or neutral primes, strengthened endorsement of these two
prosocial values.

Altruistic helping

In a recent series of studies, Mikulincer, Shaver, Gillath, and Nitzberg
(2005) examined the decision to help or not to help a person in distress.
In the first two experiments, participants watched a confederate while she
performed a series of increasingly aversive tasks. As the study progressed,
the confederate became very distressed by the aversive tasks, and the
actual participant was given an opportunity to take the distressed person's
place, in effect sacrificing self for the welfare of another. Shortly before
the scenario just described, participants were primed with either representations of attachment-figure availability (the name of a participant's
security provider) or attachment-unrelated representations (the name of
a close person who does not function as an attachment figure, the name
of a mere acquaintance). This priming procedure was conducted at either
a subliminal level (rapid presentation of the name of a specific targeted
person) or supraliminal level (asking people to recall an interaction with
the targeted person). At the point of making a decision about replacing
the distressed person, participants completed brief measures of compassion and personal distress.

   In both studies, avoidant attachment was related to lower compassion
and lower willingness to help the distressed person. Attachment anxiety
was related to heightened personal distress, but not to either compassion
or willingness to help. In addition, subliminal or supraliminal priming of
representations of a security-provider figure decreased personal distress
and increased participants' compassion and willingness to take the place
of a distressed other.

Intergroup hostility

Mikulincer and Shaver (2001) examined the effects of manipulated felt security on the regulation of intergroup hostility. Children as young as 3 years of age have shown that a secure attachment style with their primary caregiver was associated with increased exploration, curiosity, empathy, and reduced fear of strangers. Perhaps, having this sense of security may allow adults to be open to unfamiliar others without fear and, as a result, exhibit caregiving behaviors. In a series of five experiments conducted in Israel, Mikulincer, and Shaver (2001) primed participants, supraliminally or subliminally, with thoughts and feelings related to attachment security by having them imagine being cared for by a loved one or quickly presenting them with words such as *love*, *hug*, and *secure*. Participants' feelings were then assessed toward a variety of out-groups (as viewed by the secular, Jewish university students who participated in the studies): Israeli Arabs, Ultra-Orthodox Jews, Russian immigrants, and homosexuals. Attachment style was measured beforehand and relevant control conditions such as positive mood were included.

As expected, security enhancement, whether induced supraliminally or subliminally, eliminated the difference between attitudes toward in-group and out-group members. Similar effects did not occur for neutral primes or positive primes that were unrelated to love and affection. In addition, the results were not attributable to changes in positive mood. Anxious attachment was consistently related to perceiving out-group members as threatening. Finally, the interaction between security priming and dispositional attachment style was not significant, suggesting that security enhancement increases out-group tolerance in all people.

In summary, across a wide variety of correlational and experimental studies, attachment security has been associated with greater compassion, greater openness to others, and greater willingness to help someone in need. Avoidant attachment has been consistently associated with lower levels of compassion and altruistic helping. Anxious attachment has been associated with heightened personal distress that did not translate into greater willingness to help. All of these results support the hypothesis that altruistic motivations for caregiving and the ability to provide sensitive, responsive care are conditional upon a certain degree of attachment security and the associated ability to regulate emotions.

The neuroscience of attachment, compassion, and altruism

There is as yet no neuroscience research on the links we have discussed in previous sections between attachment style, compassion or empathy, and prosocial behavior. But there is a very interesting emerging literature on the neuroscience of empathy which could fruitfully be extended into the domain of attachment research. As explained by Decety and Jackson (2006) in a recent overview:

> A handful of fMRI studies have indicated that the observation of pain in others is mediated by several brain areas that are implicated in processing the affective and motivational aspects of one's own pain. In one study, participants received painful stimuli and observed signals indicating that their partner, who was present in the same room, had received the same stimuli (Singer et al., 2004). The [anterior] ACC, the insula, and the cerebellum were active during both conditions. In another study, participants were shown photographs depicting body parts in painful or neutral everyday-life situations, and were asked to imagine the level of pain that these situations would produce (Jackson, Meltzoff, & Decety, 2005). In comparison to neutral situations, painful conditions elicited significant activation in regions involved in the affective aspects of pain processing, notably the ACC and the anterior insula. (p. 55)

Other studies have identified some of the brain regions involved in adopting another person's perspective. Ruby and Decety (2004) asked study participants to imagine how they would feel if they were in certain situations and how their mothers would feel in the same situations. When participants adopted their mother's perspective, there was notable activation in the frontopolar cortex, the ventromedial PFC, the medial PFC, and the right inferior parietal lobule—areas that have been associated in previous studies with taking another person's perspective. Regions involved in emotional processing, including the amygdala and the temporal poles, were activated in conditions that would provoke emotions in oneself or one's mother.

Decety and Jackson (2006) also mention, however, that other brain regions activate differently in the self and mother cases, indicating that empathy and personal distress, or emotional contagion, are not necessarily the same, as found in some of the studies we reviewed, which showed that anxious attachment is associated with personal distress in reaction to another's pain, whereas secure attachment is not. Moreover, there are hints in recent research concerning how avoidant individuals might avoid becoming empathic with another person's pain or suffering. Recent fMRI studies (e.g., Kalisch et al., 2005) have revealed regions in the antero-lateral and medial PFC that are associated with reappraising situations so as to deny their self-relevance. Thus, there are numerous methodological models available for studying the brain correlates, or underpinnings, of attachment-style differences in compassion and empathy.

▮ CONCLUDING COMMENTS

We have reviewed extensive evidence suggesting a link between attachment-related differences in emotion regulation and prosocial behavior. Attachment security and the ability to regulate emotions is associated with a variety of prosocial feelings and caregiving behaviors, including self-transcendent values, compassion and altruism toward people who are suffering, and increased tolerance for out-group members. A stable prosocial stance seems to be based on a foundation of attachment security, and it can be enhanced by contextual manipulations of security. Security makes it easier to focus on other people's needs, perceive those needs and the options for meeting them accurately, and act effectively. In contrast, attachment insecurity is associated with self-concerns that interfere with accurate and empathic perception of others' needs, which makes effective altruism less likely.

We have shown how the attachment-related influences on emotion regulation can be studied using social-cognition research paradigms and emerging neuroscience methods. Much still needs to be learned about how security can be enhanced on a longer-term basis, as we know often happens with effective education, coaching, and psychotherapy (Mikulincer & Shaver, in press).

REFERENCES

Ainsworth, M. D. S., Blehar, M. C., Waters, E., & Wall, S. (1978). *Patterns of attachment: Assessed in the strange situation and at home.* Hillsdale, NJ: Erlbaum.
Ainsworth, M. D. S., & Bowlby, J. (1991). An ethological approach to personality development. *American Psychologist, 46,* 333–341.
Averill, J. R. (1982). *Anger and Agression.* New York: Springer.
Baldwin, M. W., Keelan, J. P. R., Fehr, B., Enns, V., & Koh Rangarajoo, E. (1996). Social-cognitive conceptualization of attachment working models: Availability and accessibility effects. *Journal of Personality and Social Psychology, 71,* 94–109.
Bartholomew, K. (1990). Avoidance of intimacy: An attachment perspective. *Journal of Social and Personal Relationships, 7,* 147–178.
Batson, C. D. (1991). *The altruism question: Toward a social-psychological answer.* Hillsdale, NJ: Erlbaum.

Beer, J. S., Shimamura, A. P., & Knight, R. T. (2004). Frontal lobe contribution to executive control of cognitive and social behavior. In M. S. Gazzaniga (Ed.), *Cognitive neuroscience* (Vol. 3, 3rd ed., pp. 1091–1104). Cambridge, MA: MIT Press.

Ben-Ze'ev, A. (1999). Mercy, pity, and compassion. In A. Brien (Ed.), *The quality of mercy* (pp. 132–145). Amsterdam: Rodopi.

Binder, J. R., Frost, J. A., Hammeke, T. A., Bellgowan, P. S. F., Rao, S. M., & Cox, R. W. (1999). Conceptual processing during the conscious resting state: A functional MRI study. *Journal of Cognitive Neuroscience, 11*, 80–93.

Bowlby, J. (1973). *Attachment and loss: Vol. 2. Separation: Anxiety and anger*. New York: Basic Books.

Bowlby, J. (1980). *Attachment and loss: Vol. 3. Sadness and depression*. New York: Basic Books.

Bowlby, J. (1982). *Attachment and loss: Vol. 1. Attachment* (2nd ed.). New York: Basic Books. (Original ed. 1969.)

Bowlby, J. (1988). *A secure base: Clinical applications of attachment theory*. London: Routledge.

Brennan, K. A., Clark, C. L., & Shaver, P. R. (1998). Self-report measurement of adult attachment: An integrative overview. In J. A. Simpson & W. S. Rholes (Eds.), *Attachment theory and close relationships* (pp. 46–76). New York: Guilford.

Buunk, B. P. (1997). Personality, birth order, and attachment styles as related to various types of jealousy. *Personality and Individual Differences, 23*, 997–1006.

Calamari, E., & Pini, M. (2003). Dissociative experiences and anger proneness in late adolescent females with different attachment styles. *Adolescence, 38*, 287–303.

Caspi-Berkowitz, N. (2003). *Mortality salience effects on the willingness to sacrifice one's life: The moderating role of attachment orientations*. Unpublished doctoral dissertation, Bar-Ilan University, Ramat Gan, Israel.

Cassidy, J. (1994). Emotion regulation: Influences of attachment relationships. *Monographs of the Society for Research in Child Development, 59*, 228–283.

Cassidy, J., & Kobak, R. R. (1988). Avoidance and its relationship with other defensive processes. In J. Belsky & T. Nezworski (Eds.), *Clinical implications of attachment* (pp. 300–323). Hillsdale, NJ: Erlbaum.

Cassidy, J., & Shaver, P. R. (Eds.) (1999). *Handbook of attachment: Theory, research, and clinical applications*. New York: Guilford.

Coan, J. A., Schaefer, H. S., & Davidson, R. J. (2006). Lending a hand: Social regulation of the neural response to threat. *Psychological Science, 17*, 1032–1039.

Collins, N. L., & Feeney, B. C. (2000). A safe haven: An attachment theory perspective on support seeking and caregiving in intimate relationships. *Journal of Personality and Social Psychology, 78*, 1053–1073.

Collins, N. L., Guichard, A. C., Ford, M. B., & Feeney, B. C. (2006). Responding to need in intimate relationships: Normative processes and individual differences. In M. Mikulincer & G. S. Goodman (Eds.), *Dynamics of romantic love: Attachment, caregiving, and sex* (pp. 149–189). New York: Guilford.

Collins, N. L., & Read, S. J. (1990). Adult attachment, working models, and relationship quality in dating couples. *Journal of Personality and Social Psychology, 58*, 644–663.

Davis, D., Shaver, P. R., & Vernon, M. L. (2003). Physical, emotional, and behavioral reactions to breaking up: The roles of gender, age, emotional involvement, and attachment style. *Personality and Social Psychology Bulletin, 29*, 871–884.

Decety, J., & Jackson, P. L. (2006). A social neuroscience perspective on empathy. *Current Directions in Psychological Science, 15*, 54–58.

Diamond, L. M., & Hicks, A. M. (2005). Attachment style, current relationship security, and negative emotions: The mediating role of physiological regulation. *Journal of Social and Personal Relationships, 22*, 499–518.

Florian, V., & Mikulincer, M. (1998). Symbolic immortality and the management of the terror of death: The moderating role of attachment style. *Journal of Personality and Social Psychology, 74*, 725–734.

Fraley, R. C., & Shaver, P. R. (1997). Adult attachment and the suppression of unwanted thoughts. *Journal of Personality and Social Psychology, 73*, 1080–1091.

Fraley, R. C., & Shaver, P. R. (2000). Adult romantic attachment: Theoretical developments, emerging controversies, and unanswered questions. *Review of General Psychology, 4*, 132–154.

George, C., & Solomon, J. (1999). Attachment and caregiving: The caregiving behavioral system. In J. Cassidy & P. R. Shaver (Eds.), *Handbook of attachment: Theory, research, and clinical applications* (pp. 649–670). New York: Guilford.

Gillath, O., Bunge, S. A., Shaver, P. R., Wendelken, C., & Mikulincer, M. (2005). Attachment-style differences in the ability to suppress negative thoughts: Exploring the neural correlates. *Neuroimage, 28*, 835–847.

Gillath, O., Shaver, P. R., & Mikulincer, M. (2005). An attachment-theoretical approach to compassion and altruism. In P. Gilbert (Ed.), *Compassion: Conceptualizations, research, and use in psychotherapy* (pp. 121–147). London: Brunner-Routledge.

Greenberg, J., Pyszczynski, T., & Solomon, S. (1997). Terror management theory of self-esteem and cultural worldviews: Empirical assessments and conceptual refinements. In M. P. Zanna (Ed.), *Advances in experimental social psychology* (Vol. 29, pp. 61–141). San Diego, CA: Academic Press.

Gross, J. J. (1999) Emotion and emotion regulation. In O. P. John & L. A. Pervin (Eds.), *Handbook of personality: Theory and research* (2nd ed., pp. 525–552). New York: Guilford.

Guerrero, L. K. (1998). Attachment-style differences in the experience and expression of romantic jealousy. *Personal Relationships, 5*, 273–291.

Hazan, C., & Shaver, P. R. (1987). Romantic love conceptualized as an attachment process. *Journal of Personality and Social Psychology, 52*, 511–524.

Hesse, E. (1999). The Adult Attachment Interview: Historical and current perspectives. In J. Cassidy & P. R. Shaver (Eds.), *Handbook of attachment: Theory, research, and clinical applications* (pp. 395–433). New York: Guilford.

Hester, R. L., Murphy, K., Foxe, J. J., Foxe, D. M., Javitt, D. C., & Garavan, H. (2004). Predicting success: patterns of cortical activation and deactivation prior to response inhibition. *Journal of Cognitive Neuroscience, 16*, 776–785.

Jackson, P. L., Meltzoff, A. N., & Decety, J. (2005). How do we perceive the pain of others: A window into the neural processes involved in empathy. *Neuroimage, 24,* 771–779.

Kalisch, R., Wiech, K., Critchley, H. D., Seymour, B., O'Doherty, J. P., Oakley, D. A., et al. (2005). Anxiety reduction through detachment: Subjective, physiological, and neural effects. *Journal of Cognitive Neuroscience, 17,* 874–883.

Kestenbaum, R., Farber, E. A., & Sroufe, L. A. (1989). Individual differences in empathy among preschoolers: Relation to attachment history. In N. Eisenberg (Ed.), *Empathy and related emotional competence. New directions for child development,* No. 44 (pp. 51–64). San Francisco, CA: Jossey-Bass.

Kunce, L. J., & Shaver, P. R. (1994). An attachment-theoretical approach to caregiving in romantic relationships. In K. Bartholomew & D. Perlman (Eds.), *Advances in personal relationships: Attachment processes in adulthood* (Vol. 5, pp. 205–237). London: Jessica Kingsley.

Laible, D. J., Carlo, G., & Raffaelli, M. (2000). The differential relations of parent and peer attachment to adolescent adjustment. *Journal of Youth and Adolescence, 29,* 45–59.

Lazarus, R. S., & Folkman, S. (1984). *Stress, appraisal, and coping.* New York: Springer.

Lehman, D. R., Ellard, J. H., & Wortman, C. B. (1986). Social support for the bereaved: Recipients' and providers' perspectives of what is helpful. *Journal of Consulting and Clinical Psychology, 54,* 438–446.

Lévesque, J., Eugène, F., Joanette, Y., Paquette, V., Mensour, B., Beaudoin, G., et al. (2003). Neural circuitry underlying voluntary suppression of sadness. *Biological Psychiatry, 53,* 502–510.

Markiewicz, D., Doyle, A. B., & Brendgen, M. (2001). The quality of adolescents' friendships: Associations with mothers' interpersonal relationships, attachments to parents and friends, and prosocial behaviors. *Journal of Adolescence, 24,* 429–445.

Mazoyer, B., Zago, L., Mellet, E., Bricogne, S., Etard, O., Houde, O., et al. (2001). Cortical networks for working memory and executive functions sustain the conscious resting state in man. *Brain Research Bulletin, 54,* 287–298.

Mikulincer, M. (1998). Adult attachment style and individual differences in functional versus dysfunctional experiences of anger. *Journal of Personality and Social Psychology, 74,* 513–524.

Mikulincer, M., Dolev, T., & Shaver, P. R. (2004). Attachment-related strategies during thought suppression: Ironic rebounds and vulnerable self-representations. *Journal of Personality and Social Psychology, 87,* 940–956.

Mikulincer, M., & Florian, V. (2000). Exploring individual differences in reactions to mortality salience: Does attachment style regulate terror management mechanisms? *Journal of Personality and Social Psychology, 79,* 260–273.

Mikulincer, M., Florian, V., Birnbaum, G., & Malishkevich, S. (2002). The death-anxiety buffering function of close relationships: Exploring the effects of separation reminders on death-thought accessibility. *Personality and Social Psychology Bulletin, 28,* 287–299.

Mikulincer, M., Florian, V., & Tolmacz, R. (1990). Attachment styles and fear of personal death: A case study of affect regulation. *Journal of Personality and Social Psychology, 58*, 273–280.

Mikulincer, M., Gillath, O., Sapir-Lavid, Y., Yaakobi, E., Arias, K., Tal-Aloni, L., et al. (2003). Attachment theory and concern for others' welfare: Evidence that activation of the sense of secure base promotes endorsement of self-transcendence values. *Basic and Applied Social Psychology, 25*, 299–312.

Mikulincer, M., & Shaver, P. R. (2001). Attachment theory and intergroup bias: Evidence that priming the secure base schema attenuates negative reactions to out-groups. *Journal of Personality and Social Psychology, 81*, 97–115.

Mikulincer, M., & Shaver, P. R. (2003). The attachment behavioral system in adulthood: Activation, psychodynamics, and interpersonal processes. In M. P. Zanna (Ed.), *Advances in experimental social psychology* (Vol. 35, pp. 53–152). New York: Academic Press.

Mikulincer, M., & Shaver, P. R. (2005). Mental representations of attachment security: Theoretical foundation for a positive social psychology. In M. W. Baldwin (Ed.), *Interpersonal cognition* (pp. 233–266). New York: Guilford.

Mikulincer, M., & Shaver, P. R. (2007). *Attachment patterns in adulthood: Structure, dynamics, and change.* New York: Guilford.

Mikulincer, M., Shaver, P. R., Gillath, O., & Nitzberg, R. A. (2005). Attachment, caregiving, and altruism: Boosting attachment security increases compassion and helping. *Journal of Personality and Social Psychology, 89*, 817–839.

Ochsner, K. N., Bunge, S. A., Gross, J. J., & Gabrieli, J. D. E. (2002). Rethinking feelings: An fMRI study of the cognitive regulation of emotion. *Journal of Cognitive Neuroscience, 14*, 1215–1229.

Ochsner, K. N., & Gross, J. J. (2005). The cognitive control of emotion. *Trends in Cognitive Sciences, 9*, 242–249.

Phan, K. L., Fitzgerald, D. A., Nathan, P. J., Moore, G. J., Uhde, T. W., & Tancer, M. E. (2005). Neural substrates for voluntary suppression of negative affect: A functional magnetic resonance imaging study. *Biological Psychiatry, 57*, 210–219.

Radecki-Bush, C., Farrell, A. D., & Bush, J. P. (1993). Predicting jealous responses: The influence of adult attachment and depression on threat appraisal. *Journal of Social and Personal Relationships, 10*, 569–588.

Rholes, W. S., Simpson, J. A., & Orina, M. (1999). Attachment and anger in an anxiety-provoking situation. *Journal of Personality and Social Psychology, 76*, 940–957.

Ruby, P., & Decety, J. (2004). How would you feel versus how do you think she would feel? A neuroimaging study of perspective taking with social emotions. *Journal of Cognitive Neuroscience, 16*, 988–999.

Sharpsteen, D. J., & Kirkpatrick, L. A. (1997). Romantic jealousy and adult romantic attachment. *Journal of Personality and Social Psychology, 72*, 627–640.

Shaver, P. R., & Hazan, C. (1988). A biased overview of the study of love. *Journal of Social and Personal Relationships, 5*, 473–501.

Shaver, P. R., & Hazan, C. (1993). Adult romantic attachment: Theory and evidence. In D. Perlman & W. Jones (Eds.), *Advances in personal relationships* (Vol. 4, pp. 29–70). London: Jessica Kingsley.

Shulman, G. L., Fiez, J. A., Corbetta, M., Buckner, R. L., Meizin, F. M., Raichle, M. E., et al. (1997). Common blood flow changes across visual tasks: II. Decreases in cerebral cortex. *Journal of Cognitive Neuroscience, 9,* 648–663.

Simpson, J. A., Rholes, W. S., & Phillips, D. (1996). Conflict in close relationships: An attachment perspective. *Journal of Personality and Social Psychology, 71,* 899–914.

Singer, T., Seymour, B., O'Doherty, J., Kaube, H., Dolan, R. J., & Frith, C. D. (2004). Empathy for pain involves the affective but not sensory components of pain. *Science, 303,* 1157–1162.

Sroufe, L. A., & Waters, E. (1977). Attachment as an organizational construct. *Child Development, 48,* 1184–1199.

Tangney, J. P., Hill-Barlow, D., Wagner, P. E., Marschall, D. E., Borenstein, J. K., Sanftner, J., et al. (1996). Assessing individual differences in constructive versus destructive responses to anger across the lifespan. *Journal of Personality and Social Psychology, 70,* 780–796.

Taubman Ben-Ari, O., Findler, L., & Mikulincer, M. (2002). The effects of mortality salience on relationship strivings and beliefs: The moderating role of attachment style. *British Journal of Social Psychology, 41,* 419–441.

van der Mark, I. L., van IJzendoorn, M. H., & Bakermans-Kranenburg, M. J. (2002). Development of empathy in girls during the second year of life: Associations with parenting, attachment, and temperament. *Social Development, 11,* 451–468.

Wyland, C. L., Kelley, W. M., Macrae, C. N., Gordon, H. L., & Heatherton, T. F. (2003). Neural correlates of thought suppression. *Neuropsychologia, 41,* 1863–1867.

Zimmermann, P. (2004). Attachment representations and characteristics of friendship relations during adolescence. *Journal of Experimental Child Psychology, 88,* 83–101.

Zimmermann, P., Maier, M. A., Winter, M., & Grossmann, K. E. (2001). Attachment and adolescents' emotion regulation during a joint problem-solving task with a friend. *International Journal of Behavioral Development, 25,* 331–343.

6

Themes in the Development of Emotion Regulation in Childhood and Adolescence and a Transactional Model

Maria von Salisch

How emotion regulation develops over the course of childhood and adolescence, may be told as a short story and as a long story. Think about a baby crying hard. When you do this, you will remember how irritable infants tend to be and your memory may bring up the sound of the baby's distraught voice. At age 5, the same child may still show an explosive temper from time to time, but in general his or her emotional expressions have become much more restrained. And ten years later as an adolescent, the same youngster may have become quite successful in *not* letting you know which emotion he or she is feeling at the moment. The short story thus captures the general age-trend of an increasing minimization of the expression of most emotions in most situations (Holodynski, 2004; Saarni, 1984; Underwood, Hurley, Johanson, & Mosley, 1999).

How do youngsters manage to control their emotional expressions? Which strategies help them to do so? And which strategies do they use to regulate their emotions when they arise? That is the long story. It tells about developmental influences on the regulation of emotion, about the socialization of emotion regulation, and about the development of interindividual differences. In order to keep definitions straight, I would like first to present a process model about how emotions are generated, followed by a definition of emotion regulation and a discussion of some of the difficulties involved in studying developmental changes in emotion regulation. Then I will present four themes in the development of emotion regulation and will illustrate them with relevant studies. This will culminate in a transactional model of emotional development that puts the four themes presented before under one overarching perspective.

◼ HOW ARE EMOTIONS GENERATED?

James Gross's (1999) process model on how emotions are typically generated has the advantage of integrating research results from the functionalist and the structuralist traditions of research on emotions. While most
research in the functionalist tradition focused on the appraisal of antecedent conditions (e.g., Lazarus, 1991; Scherer, 1984), research in the
structuralist tradition tended to concentrate on the "output" side, that
is, on the modulation of behavioral signs of emotions, such as facial expressions (e.g., Ekman's 1972 research on display rules). As described by
Gross (1999) and Mauss, Bunge, and Gross (this volume), today most
psychologists would agree that emotions contain different components
that are activated at different times: Antecedent conditions in the form
of internal signals from the body or psychological systems, or cues from
an external situation are first perceived by the person and then filtered by
appraisal processes. Depending on how the antecedent cue is appraised,
different emotion prototypes are generated. Because individuals tend
to appraise antecedent events in different ways, the "same" antecedent
event may result in different emotion prototoypes.

Emotion prototypes are part of the latent reaction tendencies within
the person that cannot be observed. In the simplified process model they
influence three types of reaction tendencies, that is, the subjective experiences of emotion, the expression program in face and behavior, and the
physiological reactions (Stemmler, 2004). Latent reactions are in turn
modulated when turned into manifest reactions that can be observed or
otherwise collected. The "output" of these modulations are self-reports
of emotions, expressive behavior (facial expressions, gestures, but also
body movements, possibly touch and locomotion), as well as physiological reactions in the central and in the autonomic nervous systems. Some
emotion researchers—like Frijda (1986)—add action readiness as a motivational component that steers the resulting behavior into one or the
other direction.

As stated before, this model is rather elegant because it integrates ideas
about the modulation of expressive behavior with ideas on appraisal
processes, emotion prototypes, etc. that have been proposed by emotion
researchers standing in the functionalist tradition. Especially appealing
seems to be the time line implied in this model, that is, the idea that appraisal processes typically occur before modulation processes. In Gross's
(1999) process model, emotions thus tend to proceed in a linear fashion.
This may be an oversimplification on two accounts:

(1) When emotions are intense, people tend to reappraise their emotions, often and over again. With strong emotions, therefore, more than

one iteration through the emotion cycle of perception → appraisal → generation of an emotion prototype → latent reaction tendencies → manifest reaction tendencies is to be expected (Lewis, 1995). In other words, in the light of new perceptions or ideas, individuals slowly change their appraisals of these very important emotions. For example, the painful emotions generated in the final break-up of a marriage may thus change with successive reappraisals of the conditions that led up to them.

(2) Reciprocal processes between the components were not included in the model (i.e., not only feedforward loops, but also feedback loops that change settings in "earlier" steps in the generation of an emotion). Thus, phenomena such as facial feedback (Soussignan, 2002) are not covered in this model. Additional processes are discussed in this volume by Kappas; Greenberg and Vandekerckhove; and Philippot, Neumann, and Vrielynck.

James Gross's (1999) process model focuses on the generation of emotions in adult individuals. How emotions are embedded in the interactions with (significant) other persons is not part of this model. A first step in this direction has been taken by Butler and Gross (2004) when they summarized the distancing effects the (voluntary) suppression of emotional expressions of adults have on their adult interaction partners (Gross & John, 2003). This is akin to the disturbing effects of an adult's still face on her baby's well-being (Weinberg, Tronick, Cohn, & Olson, 1999). However, the influence long-time relationship partners exert on children's emotional development over time has not been modeled yet. That is unfortunate because the way parents and peers socialize children's appraisals and shape their behaviors are key questions in emotional development. The transactional model presented at the end of this chapter attempts to answer some of these questions by outlining some aspects of children's emotional development while interacting with a stable social partner.

EMOTION REGULATION AND ITS MEASUREMENT

For children, emotion regulation often means self-soothing or dampening emotional arousal. This way of influencing which emotions are experienced and expressed is likely to take place at least at three points in time in Gross's (1999) process model (cf. also Eisenberg, Spinrad, & Smith, 2004):

(1) By attending or not attending to antecedent conditions (of an internal or an external kind). Thus, children do or do not pay attention to their father's play face, to their feelings of anger when observing an injus-

tice, or to their accelerated heart beat when walking alone in the woods at night. In addition, adults are in a better condition than children when it comes to influencing the probability of encountering external antecedent conditions—they can cope proactively. Individuals who know that they become very afraid in horror movies are likely to avoid watching them.

(2) By choosing one way of appraising antecedent conditions over another one. Individuals vary in how they evaluate situations: children who suffer from a hostile attribution bias typically assume that another child who spilled some water over their watercolor picture has done this in order to ruin their picture, while other children consider this to be an accident or even understand that the spilling occurred out of prosocial motives, such as when the other child tried to help with the picture (Crick & Dodge, 1994). Depending on how the antecedent events are appraised, different intensities of one emotion—in this case anger (von Salisch, 2000)—will result. In some antecedent conditions different emotion prototypes are generated in the same situation. A recent study, for example, showed that blocking a nonsocial or a social goal in infants generated mostly anger expressions, but a few expressions of sadness resulted that were correlated with an increase in cortisol levels (Lewis & Ramsay, 2005).

(3) By modulating their latent reaction tendencies people may tailor their public expression of their subjective experience of an emotion according to their standards of social desirability or other aspects of their self-concept (Harter, 1999). In addition, children and adults alike tend to change their expressive behavior according to display rules (e.g., Cole, 1986; Cole, Dennis, Martin, & Hall, this volume; Saarni, 1984; Shaver, Mikulincer, & Chun, this volume). Emotion-related physiological reactions can also be modulated by means of physical exercise, psychotropic drugs, or other body-oriented techniques, such as yoga or meditation (Cahn & Polich, 2006).

Since emotions can be regulated at different points in time, it may be difficult to differentiate between emotion and emotion regulation. Methodological problems arise because currently measurement can take place only at the output end of the emotion process. Therefore, appraisals can only be generated in retrospect which, of course, limits their reliability. In addition, these retrospective accounts are self-reports which make them subject to further distortions (Averill, 1982). In the process model, reciprocal relationships between components are difficult to disentangle, especially when moving "backward" in the model. Finally, cumulative effects are possible in the sense that appraisals, subjective experiences, expressions, and physiological reactions involved in emotions may change with increasing numbers of iterations through the emotion process. Cumulative effects of this sort may be observed in toddlers' temper tantrums: many frustrated attempts to reach a goal lead to high irritability and outbursts of anger. Or take the example of adults who "work themselves up" to a specific emotion in order to fulfill feeling rules required in their workplace (Poder, this volume), such as being a charming flight attendant (Hochschild, 1983).

This and other evidence raises the principal question of whether all emotions are regulated—at least in adults. Even though researchers have not yet charted the "natural history of the emotion process" (preferably at different points in the life span), there is a debate within developmental psychology on whether it is possible for people to experience "pure" (i.e., unregulated) emotions (Campos, Frankel, & Camras, 2004). Because evidence for emotion regulation is hard to come by, after a review of the research literature Cole, Martin, and Dennis (2004) and Cole et al. (this volume) recommended (1) measuring emotions and supposed regulation strategies in an independent manner; (2) analyzing the temporal sequence (i.e., the increase, maintenance or decrease of an emotional expression after using different regulation strategies); (3) comparing emotional displays under different (experimental) conditions; and (4) using multiple and convergent measures of emotions (i.e., measuring more than one component of the emotion at the same time).

In addition, the motivation and the ability to regulate an emotion need to be differentiated because individuals may be able to regulate an emotion but may not be motivated to do so (e.g., Davis, 1995).

In the following, I will outline four important themes in the developmental literature on emotion regulation that may serve as a framework guiding further research. Further details and an expansion into life-span development can be found in von Salisch and Kunzmann (2005). In presenting the empirical examples that are designed to illustrate these themes I have tried to select studies that adhere to the methodological standards proposed by Cole et al. (2004), but given the state of affairs, this has not always been possible.

 ## THEME 1: FUNDAMENTAL CHANGES IN EMOTIONAL DEVELOPMENT IN CHILDHOOD AND ADOLESCENCE

In the course of development the repertoire of strategies for emotion regulation increases. This expansion can be observed especially in childhood and adolescence, because the developing neuropsychological functions, the acquisition of language and a theory of mind, as well as the growing capacities for moral reasoning and metacognition each open up new possibilities of experiencing, expressing, and regulating emotions.

This first theme is concerned with general emotional development in childhood and adolescence. It is grounded on the assumption that youngsters are active in producing their development because they process emotionally-relevant situations differently, depending on their level of physiological, cognitive, and emotional development (Lerner, 2002). Children's reactions to the regulatory attempts of their parents and caretakers thus depend on their level of general development. These general developmental changes go hand in hand with young people's abilities to experience, express, and regulate their emotions. One of the consequences of passing the milestones of general development is a growing repertoire of regulatory strategies. In the following I will illustrate this point with three examples.

Rapid expansion of the regulatory repertoire in infancy

One of the first abilities to regulate emotions in ontogenetic development centers around the voluntary deployment of attention (Rothbart & Bates, 1998). When babies are overstimulated they tend to turn their head away from the source of their discomfort because starting at about 3 months of age, infants are able to control the movements of their head. Thus the first emotion regulation strategy to appear in ontogenesis is oriented toward "controlling" the antecedent conditions, i.e., the emotion-generating input. In the second half of infants' first years of life their repertoire of emotion regulation strategies rapidly expands. This is demonstrated in the results of a study by Buss and Goldsmith (1998) who examined 148 infants of 6, 12, and 18 months of age—unfortunately only in cross-sectional analyses.

In their laboratory study Buss and Goldsmith (1998) brought their infants into standardized situations that had previously been established to generate moderate levels of fear and anger. In one of the two anger-eliciting laboratory paradigms, the child's arm is restrained by an adult and in the other an attractive toy is taken out of the child's reach and placed behind a barrier. To induce fear, during one situation a remote-controlled spider crawls toward the child, and a mechanical dog behaves in an unpredictable way in the second situation. In order to keep the children involved in the laboratory procedure, situations eliciting joy and other positive emotions were interspersed between the anger- and the fear-stimulating situations.

Buss and Goldsmith (1998) were among the first to analyze the temporal sequence of the unfolding emotion episode. Their research strategy centered on the question of which regulation strategies reduced the intensity of children's vocal and facial expressions of fear or anger. Buss and Goldsmith (1998) focused on strategies that were successful in bringing down infants' and toddlers' negative emotions more than predicted by chance. In doing so, they made a point of measuring children's emotional expressions largely independently from their emotions. At 6 months of age, expressions of fear were only reduced when children actively withdrew from a frightening stimulus. Expressions of anger did not increase any further when they distracted themselves by looking at some other toy. These two strategies are geared toward regulating the perception of antecedent conditions. Thus, regulating the intensity of an emotion-inducing "input"—either by creating physical distance or by shifting one's attention—seems to be the first effective strategy in the regulation of negative emotions to appear in ontogenetic development.

When children were tested at 12 and 18 months of age, quite a different pattern emerged. After their first birthday a variety of strategies proved to be effective in reducing the children's anger over time. The toddlers' anger was not only reduced when they distanced themselves, but also when they used problem-solving, in the sense that they now reached for the inaccessible toy or touched the barrier that was part of the experimental setup. A soothing effect also resulted when the toddlers engaged the adults by means of social referencing, i.e., by looking at their mother or at the experimenter for help or guidance with this frustrating situation (Sorce, Emde, Campos, & Klinnert, 1985). All these strategies could be observed when the infants were 12 months old. No further increase in the repertoire was noted between 12 and 18 months of age. With respect to fear, a similar expansion of the repertoire was observed, although the pattern was less clear.

To sum up Buss and Goldsmith's (1998) findings: due to the shifts in neuropsychological functioning as well as in cognitive and emotional development, the repertoire of emotion regulation strategies of these very young children greatly increased in the second half of their first year of life. Whether the complexity of these strategies and the flexibility of their use also increased in this time remains to be shown in future research.

Emotion talk and emotion regulation in the preschool years

Further changes in emotional experience and emotion regulation are introduced when children become capable of forming words to verbally express their emotional states. This happens in the course of children's second year of life. As demonstrated by a series of home observations by Dunn and colleagues, children are increasingly able to refer to inner states which include feelings, but also other states, such as sensations and volitions (Dunn, Bretherton, & Munn, 1987). While toddlers at 18 months of age made an average of 0.8 utterances about their inner states, by 24 months they mentioned 4.7 words that related to their feelings and other inner states. Thus, within six months, children made almost six times more remarks about their feelings, sensations, and volitions (Dunn et al., 1987).

At the same time, talking with the mother and an older sibling about the causes and consequences of the child's feelings also increased from an average of 0.9 utterances (at 18 months) to 2.3 utterances (at 24 months). These increases are considerable. They are also steeper than the "normal" increase in verbal utterances to be observed at this age (Dunn et al., 1987). In other words, in the months leading up to their second birthday, toddlers increasingly talk about what is important to them, first of all about emotions and other inner states of themselves, and about other family members.

Being able to verbalize subjective feelings may not only change children's reports of their emotions but may also impinge on their experience of these inner states. Applying verbal labels to emotional experiences may oversimplify the preverbal experiences of these emotions (Stern, 2002), especially early on, when children's vocabulary is quite limited. Words may nevertheless help children (and adults, for that matter) in pulling together their often diffuse emotional experiences. Moreover, verbal expressions may make fleeting experiences more accessible to reflection and memory. When children become able to express their inner feelings in words, they become capable of transcending the momentary nature of their emotional experience. This advantage, however, may be offset by the fact that the verbal labels applied have been constructed together with their caretakers (who are members of a certain culture that posits certain definitions and constellations of emotions). When parents mislabel one (or all) of their children's emotions on a regular basis, children may later have a hard time in understanding their own emotional experiences and in sharing them with social partners who, of course, will tend to use different words (Crittenden, 1993).

When children are able to express their needs and desires with words, they should be better able to regulate negative emotions, because misunderstandings with others—which often generate negative emotions—can be avoided. With words it also becomes possible to communicate with others about one's own emotions and about those of the other person. In these meta-emotion discussions, past and future emotional experiences can be included in the discourse and children can be coached on the expression and regulation of their emotions (Gottman, Katz, & Hooven, 1997). One of the long-standing hypotheses in the field of developmental emotion regulation has therefore been that with the acquisition of language children should be better able to regulate their (negative) emotions (Kopp, 1989). Evidence for this is circumstantial, as a reduction in expressions of anger and distress within the family was not observed in the child's second year of life, but only later, when the child was 3 and 4 years and older (Dunn, Creps, & Brown, 1996).

Although with increasing age all children tend to talk more about their feelings, there are large differences between families in how often they talk about children's emotions. In 75 minutes of observation time, Dunn and colleagues noted between none and 27 utterances about internal states when the (younger) child was 33 months of age (Dunn, Brown, Slomkowski, Tesla, & Youngblade, 1991). The more often children at this age talked about their feelings (and the causes of these feelings) with their mother and their older sibling, the better developed was their ability to engage in affective perspective taking 7 months later. Thus, children who more often talked about feelings in their families were later better able to label the emotions of a puppet protagonist—even when the emotions the puppet showed did not coincide with their own emotions in the same situation. Emotion talk remained important in predicting advanced capabilities in affective perspective taking over time, even when other indicators such as the family's social class or the mean length of verbal utterances between mother and child, were included in the analyses. The central role of emotion-related discussions for the development of children's understanding of emotions was recently confirmed by De Rosnay, Pons, Harris, and Morell (2004).

Why are family discussions about feelings helpful in advancing children's affective perspective taking? By talking about emotions and other inner states, parents give their children the message that their feelings are worthy of their attention. In addition, they can help their children to adopt appraisals of antecedent conditions that tend to decrease the intensity of their emotions. When talking about feelings parents also tend to give their children direct advice on how they can manage to reduce their negative emotions (such as "when you are angry, count to ten") (Gottman et al., 1997). Long-term consequences of advanced affective perspective taking at age 3 include longer times in cooperative play with a friend at age 4 (Slomkowski & Dunn, 1996), and a more advanced understanding of emotions (Brown & Dunn, 1996) and moral issues (Dunn, Brown, & Maguire, 1995) in school-age children.

In sum, finding words for emotional experiences should change the subjective experience of these feelings. Talking about them makes children more susceptible to adult influences in regard to the appraisal of (inner and outer) antecedent conditions that influence which emotion prototype is generated. In addition, family talk about emotions tends to revolve around which emotion words are appropriate to express in which situation. Thus having the capacity to verbalize emotions and to communicate about them with close others enlarges children's repertoire of regulatory strategies significantly. Further research is needed that looks not only at the quantity of emotion talk in families, but also at its quality. Especially pressing seem to be studies that examine what consequences ensue when children's emotions are consistently mislabeled by their caretakers.

Reappraisal increases in middle childhood

Another set of antecedent-oriented regulation strategies in Gross's (1999) process model focuses on children's appraisal and reappraisal of emotion-inducing events. Although rudimentary appraisals may be already apparent in infancy (Lewis & Ramsay, 2005), very little work has looked into the developmental changes in children's appraisals. Even less research has been conducted on the development of reappraisals. Therefore evidence from related studies needs to be extrapolated.

A number of studies using systematic variations in hypothetical situations suggest that in middle childhood children's appraisals of anger-generating conditions tend to grow in complexity. While 5-year-olds are generally able to understand that anger may have been aroused by incorrect assumptions about a person (theory of mind) (Harris, 1989), school-age children are capable of taking into account the intentions of a person who has frustrated them. This enables them to distinguish between provocations that are motivated by hostility and others that have come about by misunderstanding or by negligence (Stadler, Janke, & Schmidt-Atzert, 1997). Reappraising an anger-provoking event to be the result of negligence on the part of the perpetrator should reduce the intensity of children's anger. Starting in second grade, children also are able to evaluate the controllability of a situation (Graham, Doubleday, & Guarino, 1984).

Now, when they realize that an anger-provoking situation was not controllable, they can excuse the anger-instigating event, as when a friend did not keep his promise to come by the child's house because he had to go shopping with his mother. Reappraisals in the form of excuses should also serve to lower the intensity of their anger. In the course of their later primary-school years, children learn to take into account the motives

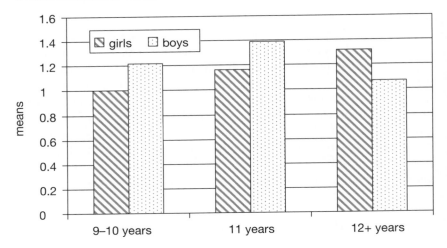

Figure 6.1 Use of reappraisal strategies when angry at a friend by age and gender.

behind other persons' anger-arousing behavior. Children now realize that anger-generating events (such as pushing them) may be motivated by prosocial motives of the instigator (such as saving them from the approaching school bus they had not noticed). These types of attributions open up another category of reappraisals that should reduce the intensity of their anger because the action is legitimized by the perpetrator's benevolent motives (Olthof, Ferguson, & Luiten, 1989). Over the course of about five years, children are thus theoretically able to take an ever wider array of reappraisals into account when evaluating the anger-generating behavior of a friend. These reappraisals should generally help them to downregulate their anger (von Salisch, 2000).

My own research (von Salisch, 2000, 2001; von Salisch & Vogelgesang, 2005, 2006) focuses on how children regulate their anger at a friend of their own gender. For this research we developed a questionnaire on Children's Strategies of Anger Regulation toward a friend (SAR-C) that included nine strategies of anger regulation, among them reappraisal of the anger-provoking event. In a cross-sectional study, we asked N = 124 children between 9 and 12 years of age to fill in the SAR-C (Study 3).

As shown in Figure 6.1, reappraisal increased for all children up to 11 years of age and then increased again only for girls. Even though the univariate ANOVA was neither significant for age (F(1, 127) = 1.0) nor for gender (F(1, 128) < 1.0), the interaction between age and gender proved to be significant (F (1, 128) = 3.12, p = .048, eta = .05). This interaction effect was replicated with a more heterogeneous sample from middle- and lower-class neighborhoods of former East and West Berlin (KUHL). In this longitudinal study spanning grades 3, 4, and 6, the repeated measures MANOVA was again not significant for age (Pillais-Trace $F(2, 109)$ < 1). However, gender effects were pronounced (Pillais-Trace $F(1, 110)$ = 12.98, p < .000, eta = .11) and the interaction between age and gender was significant as a trend (Pillais-Trace $F(2, 109)$ = 2.23, p < .10, eta = .04).

Taken together, these two studies suggest that virtually all children, and then girls alone, tend to use reappraisal strategies when they are angry at a friend of their own gender more often over time. Children are thus increasingly capable of using reappraisals to downregulate their anger at their friend. That reappraisals are more often used by the 12-year-old girls than by the boys may have to do with the fact that some reappraisals are akin to unfounded self-blame, such as blaming oneself because "one could have known that the friend always behaved in this impossible manner." Thoughts of this kind are symptomatic of depression which is more prevalent in girls than in boys at this age (Steinberg, 2002). Preliminary evidence suggests that these reappraisals are not conducive to mental health (von Salisch & Vogelgesang, 2006). Thus, it is no surprise that the preference for reappraisal strategies decreases in adolescence (von Salisch & Vogelgesang, 2005). Further research is needed to chart the various reappraisals, to examine how often they are used by boys and by girls, and which developmental sequelae result from their habitual use.

On the preceding pages, I have outlined only some of the more obvious changes in the experience, the expression and the regulation of emotions that take place over the course of childhood. In adolescence, the repertoire further increases, when considering that taking alcohol and other drugs offers new opportunities to regulate—or perhaps rather numb—strong emotions.

 ## THEME 2: THE DEVELOPMENT OF EMOTION REGULATION PROCEEDS IN A MULTIDIMENSIONAL WAY

Over the course of childhood the ways in which emotions are typically regulated change. While behavioral strategies for the control of expressive behaviors are learned in early childhood, cognitive strategies gain in importance in the preschool years and thereafter. Because behavioral strategies are implicit in nature, regulation strategies of this type seem to develop earlier than the explicit knowledge about them.

Behavioral strategies employed in emotion regulation involve modeling or contingency learning of the expressive behavior of the parent. For example, high correlations between the child's and the mother's lip biting behavior that increased up to the child's second birthday have been reported (Malatesta, Culver, Tesman, & Shepard, 1989). In addition, children learn by reinforcement (Saarni & von Salisch, 1993). Parents tend to evaluate the appropriateness of their children's emotional expressions (von Salisch, 2001), but children also seem to be able to mask their expressive behavior at quite a young age for their own instrumental reasons. One study showed that by age 3, most children were capable of masking the fact that they have looked at an attractive toy when they were not supposed to (Lewis, Stanger, & Sullivan, 1989). Emotion-related physiological reactions may also be influenced by the behavioral strategies caretakers usually employ to soothe their charges' ruffled feelings, but this needs to be corroborated by further research. All behavioral strategies tend to apply to the "expressive end" of the emotion process and they are hard to verbalize. Cognitive strategies, in contrast, are generally easier to access verbally. In Gross's (1999) model they should be most effective in changing the appraisals of antecedent conditions or in redefining subjective experiences of an emotion. In the following, I would like to illustrate the point that some behavioral strategies develop years before their cognitive representation.

Masking disappointment and talking about it

Behavioral strategies to mask disappointment tend to develop quite early in ontogenetic development. The second study of Cole's (1986) experiment managed to generate disappointment in 20 girls who were between 3 and 4 years of age. To that end, the children were first asked to rank order ten possible rewards for their work. After the children had done some of this task the experimenter told them that they were very helpful and gave them their favorite reward. After doing some more work, disappointment was instilled in the children because they now received the prize they had earlier rated as the least attractive one. In the social condition the experimenter stayed in the room but did not start an interaction with the child. In the nonsocial condition, the experimenter left the room right after giving the inappropriate gift to the child so that she was alone in the room while her reactions were videotaped. Systematic coding of these tapes indicated that the girls displayed more positive than negative emotions in the social condition. When they were alone, however, they displayed fewer emotions and among them more negative than positive emotions. In masking their disappointment with a smile (and perhaps a nice "thank you") these 3–4-year-old girls demonstrated a behavioral strategy for regulating their disappointment.

In the next part of the experiment, the children were interviewed on their knowledge of facial expressions and the use of display rules in other situations in which children's expectations were violated (i.e., when there was a discrepancy between the subjective experience and the expression of emotion in the protagonist). This interview probed the semantic representation of the behavioral strategies designed to hide disappointment. Results indicate that 94% of the children were capable of labeling the protagonists' ill feelings in hypothetical stories, 65% were able to voice the child protagonist's disappointment or negative emotion about the unattractive gift and 50% were of the impression that the experimenter "must know" about the children's disappointment—even though the children had not said a word about it. Only one out of the 20 children in this study was aware that the experimenter knew how the children in the stories felt because of their (facial) expressions.

Thus, although 3- and 4-year-olds attempt to hide their disappointment in their faces, they are typically unable to verbalize the consequences of this benevolent deception. This is generally achieved only two to three years later (Josephs, 1993). All in all, children first learn behavioral strategies designed to control their expressive displays before they become aware of it and are able to verbalize it. When they become aware that their own emotional expressions can be purposefully misleading, many doors to influencing other peoples' emotions open up; emotion regulation thus also increases in complexity. Future research should focus on the conditions that are conducive to this aspect of understanding emotions.

THEME 3: EMOTION REGULATION SHIFTS FROM INTERPERSONAL TO INTRAPERSONAL REGULATION

While the influence of parents and caretakers on the regulation of emotions is rather substantial at the beginning of life, over the course of development more and more situations and emotions are mastered by the children themselves. Interpersonal regulation shifts from parents to agemates, such as peers and friends, and in adolescence further to romantic partners.

Since there are many studies that demonstrate children's growing powers of self-regulation as well as parents' socialization of children's emotion regulation (e.g., Denham, 1999; Eisenberg et al., 2004), it is important to discuss the shift in interpersonal regulation away from caretakers to peers occurring around the time children enter primary school. In these years of middle childhood peers become increasingly important people in children's lives (Youniss, 1980). Evidence for a shift in the interpersonal regulation from parents and adult caretakers to peers is more indirect as no studies have been published that have measured children's emotions and their emotion regulation separately. This is indeed a difficult undertaking because the emotional expressions of school-age children tend to be more muted than in earlier years—especially in a laboratory where children tend to feel "watched" by video cameras. Because school-age children are well on their way to becoming experts in the modulation of their expressive displays (Holodynski, 2004; Underwood et al., 1999), it is no longer possible to examine the temporal sequence of their emotions and purported emotion regulation strategies. At this age, however, it is possible to profit from their growing insights into their emotion processes. School-age children thus tend to produce much more reliable answers when asked about their emotion-related cognitions and regulation strategies than preschoolers.

Example: School-age children's expectations when they show anger, sadness, or pain to others

A vignette study by Zeman and Garber (1996) explored the expectations that first- to fifth-graders harbored when showing anger, sadness, or pain on their faces in the presence of different categories of onlookers. Each of the 192 children in this experiment listened to three stories in which a child protagonist experienced anger, sadness, and pain. Between the children it varied whether the mother, the father, a peer (not the best friend), or nobody watched while the child in the story expressed the relevant feeling on his or her face, so that children in each experimental condition were exposed. Each group of children was exposed to only one story for each emotion. After listening to every story the children were asked how intensely they would show this emotion in the presence of the different audiences when they were in the protagonist's situation. Although there were some differences between the emotions, participants agreed across all three negative emotions that they would express these emotions in lower intensity in front of their peers than with their parents or when alone. Further studies corroborate that children expected the least understanding from their peers when showing feelings of vulnerability (but this also depended on gender and emotion type) (von Salisch, 2001). When children have learned that expressions of vulnerability (and also anger) are not suited for the eyes and ears of their peers, their motivation to control their facial expressions of emotions should increase, but this requires further exploration.

This example demonstrates the influence of peers on children's expression of emotions, but whether these peer influences work through the same "mechanisms" as parents' influences on children's emotional development is largely unknown. More specifically, research on emotion modeling and instrumental learning in the peer context, as well as emotion talk in peer groups, is sorely needed.

THEME 4: EMOTION REGULATION DEVELOPS DIFFERENTIALLY

So far, most of the evidence on emotion regulation is based on cross-sectional studies. Therefore we cannot estimate how large the effects of interindividual differences (e.g., temperament or quality of attachment) on intraindividual changes in emotion regulation will be. To answer these questions we will need longitudinal studies with precise measurements of the different emotion components.

Up to now we have considered developmental processes that can be observed in all youngsters, but interindividual differences are likely to change the trajectory of this "normal" emotional development. They can be expected at various points in Gross's (1999) process model. For example, from the first days of life human beings tend to vary in their thresholds of perception, in their physiological reactivity to emotion-arousing stimuli, and possibly also in their emotional expressivity (i.e., temperament) (Eisenberg & Fabes, 1992; Rothbart & Bates, 1998). Beginning in the preschool years, individual differences in appraisals become apparent. Some preschoolers, for example, are more likely than others to suspect hostile intentions in other people's harmful behavior which makes them prone to experience feelings of anger (and to show aggressive behavior) more often than children who tend to attribute more benevolent motivations (Crick & Dodge, 1994). Finally, children differ in their ability to put their subjective emotional experiences into words. Some children are simply more verbal than others. What is needed is a longitudinal study that examines the influence of these and other interindividual differences on the development of the different emotion components and the relationships between these components over time. Such a systematic consideration of interindividual differences could shed light on further developmental mechanisms.

THE TRANSACTIONAL MODEL OF EMOTIONAL DEVELOPMENT

When talking about the development of emotions and emotion regulation, interpersonal influences have to be taken into account because emotion communication lies at the heart of many of the changes observed. No

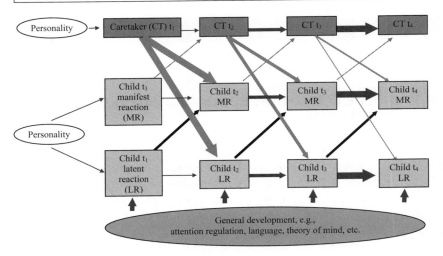

Figure 6.2 A transactional model of emotional development.

model of emotional development is complete without considering development at the level of the interaction episodes in which adult caretakers (and later on peers) react to children's emotional expressions (and vice versa). The transactional model of emotional development presented in Figure 6.2 borrows children's latent and manifest emotional reactions from Gross's (1999) model and puts them in a framework of socialization by adding an adult caretaker as a second person who influences the child's emotional appraisals, reactions, and regulatory strategies and is influenced by them.

Let us review this transactional model that allows us to take a conclusive, though innovative look at the four themes advanced earlier in this chapter. The general development of emotions, that was the first topic of discussion, can be found at the bottom of the diagram. We can see the child's latent and manifest emotional reactions as they proceed over time (t1 → t2 . . .). The arrows between the time points that grow thicker over time are meant to indicate that through thousand-fold repetitions children become more entrenched in their own way of reacting emotionally, both at the latent and at the manifest level. The arrows that start from "general development," which is captured in the oval at the bottom, suggest that children's emotional development is influenced by other accomplishments that typically occur in the course of child and adolescent development. Developmental changes in neuropsychological functions, cognitions, and language, are thus expected to influence children's emotional development.

The second theme that outlined the shift from behavioral to cognitive strategies of emotion regulation with age is also illustrated. While children's manifest reactions (such as their expressive behavior) are targeted by caretakers early in life with the aim of modulating the child's outward reactions in accordance with the prescriptions of their own family, culture, and society, latent reactions are influenced at a later point in life, i.e. starting not until t2. When verbal exchanges with the child become possible, emotion talk that is geared toward guiding the child in her appraisals and reappraisals takes on center stage.

The shift from interpersonal to intrapersonal emotion regulation that was the third theme is echoed by drawing the lines that mark the socializing influence of the caretaker thinner at successive points in time. This is meant to indicate a decreasing influence of parents and caretakers on children's emotional development over a longer period of time. The fact that parents and other adult caretakers as the principal "agents of socialization" are supplemented by peers, friends, and later romantic partners, could not be included in the transactional model without vastly increasing its complexity. Children's increasing powers of self-regulation are symbolized by the growing thickness of the arrows connecting the children's latent reactions and manifest reactions at successive time points. Thicker arrows suggest the increasing tendency of behavior to perpetuate or its increasing resistance to change. Additionally, the topmost lines going upward illustrate that children's manifest emotional reactions tend to influence their caretakers in return.

Theme 4, which addressed differential development, is captured by including the child's personality on the left side of the model. Differences in children's biological dispositions that can be found as early as the neonatal period are expected to influence their perception of emotional events, their threshold of reactivity, and the intensity of their (physiological) emotional reactions. Differential influences of caretakers on children's emotional development are the main theme of attachment theory (cf. Shaver et al., this volume). They are part of this transactional model insofar as caretakers' own experiences of more or less sensitive parenting and their state of mind regarding attachment can be subsumed under their personality.

This transactional model of emotional development is a framework that organizes different lines of research in a cohesive and comprehensive way. General development, the development of interindividual differences, and the influence of caretakers and "significant others" on children's and adolescents' emotional development are conceptualized in this transactional model. Most empirical work can address only a portion of the associations outlined in the model. Gathering the empirical evidence necessary to answer the many research questions implied in this conceptualization of emotional development, will be a task for the future. Given the complexity of the model, it will often be quite a challenge.

REFERENCES

Averill, J. (1982). *Anger and aggression.* New York: Springer.

Brown, J. R., & Dunn, J. (1996). Continuities in emotion understanding from three to six years. *Child Development, 67,* 789–802.

Buss, K. A., & Goldsmith, H. (1998). Fear and anger regulation in infancy: Effects on the temporal dynamics of affective expression. *Child Development, 69,* 359–374.

Butler, E., & Gross, J. J. (2004). Hiding feelings in social contexts: Out of sight is not out of mind. In P. Philippot & R. S. Feldman (Eds.), *The regulation of emotion* (pp. 101–126). Mahwah, NJ: Erlbaum.

Cahn, B. R., & Polich, J. (2006). Meditation states and traits: EEG, ERP, and neuroimaging studies. *Psychological Bulletin, 132,* 180–211.

Campos, J., Frankel, C., & Camras, L. (2004). On the nature of emotion regulation. *Child Development, 75,* 377–394.

Cole, P. M. (1986). Children's spontaneous control of facial expression. *Child Development, 57,* 1309–1321.

Cole, P. M., Martin, S. A., & Dennis, T. A. (2004). Emotion regulation as a scientific construct: Methodological challenges and directions for child development research. *Child Development, 75,* 317–333.

Crick, N., & Dodge, K. A. (1994). A review and reformulation of social information-processing mechanisms in children's social adjustment. *Psychological Bulletin, 115,* 74–101.

Crittenden, P. (1993). Peering into the black box: An exploratory treatise on the development of self in young children. In D. Cicchetti & S. L. Toth (Eds.), *Rochester Symposium on Development and Psychopathology. Vol. 5. The self and its disorders* (pp. 51–75). Rochester, NY: University of Rochester Press.

Davis, T. (1995). Gender differences in masking negative emotions: Ability or motivation? *Developmental Psychology, 31,* 660–667.

De Rosnay, M., Pons, F., Harris, P., & Morrell, J. (2004). A lag between understanding false belief and emotion attribution in young children: Relationships with linguistic ability and mothers' mental state language. *British Journal of Developmental Psychology, 22,* 197–218.

Denham, S. A. (1999). *Emotional development in young children.* New York: Guilford.

Dunn, J., Bretherton, I., & Munn, P. (1987). Conversations about feeling states between mothers and their young children. *Developmental Psychology, 23,* 132–139.

Dunn, J., Brown, J., & Maguire, M. (1995). The development of children's moral sensibility: Individual differences and emotional understanding. *Developmental Psychology, 31,* 649–659.

Dunn, J., Brown, J., Slomkowski, C., Tesla, C., & Youngblade, L. (1991). Young children's understanding of other people's feelings and beliefs: Individual differences and their antecedents. *Child Development, 62,* 1352–1366.

Dunn, J., Creps, C., & Brown, J. (1996). Children's family relationships between two and five: Developmental changes and individual differences. *Social Development, 5,* 230–250.

Eisenberg, N., & Fabes, R. (1992). Emotion, self-regulation, and the development of social competence. In M. Clark (Ed.), *Review of personality and social psychology. Vol. 14* (pp. 119–150). Newbury Park, CA: Sage.

Eisenberg, N., Spinrad, T., & Smith, C. L. (2004). Emotion-related regulation: Its conceptualization, relations to social functioning, and socialization. In P. Philippot & R. S. Feldman (Eds.), *The regulation of emotion* (pp. 277–306). Mahwah, NJ: Erlbaum.

Ekman, P. (1972). Universals and cultural differences in facial expressions of emotion. In J. Cole (Ed.), *Nebraska Symposium on Motivation* (pp. 115–161). Lincoln, NE: University of Nebraska Press.

Frijda, N. H. (1986). *The emotions.* Cambridge: Cambridge University Press.

Gottman, J. M., Katz, L. F., & Hooven, C. (1997). *Meta-emotion: How families communicate emotionally.* Hillsdale, NJ: Erlbaum.

Graham, S., Doubleday, C., & Guarino, P. (1984). The development of relations between perceived controllability and the emotions of pity, anger and guilt. *Child Development, 55,* 561–565.

Gross, J. J. (1999). Emotion regulation: Past, present, and future. *Cognition & Emotion, 13,* 551–573.

Gross, J. J., & John, O. P. (2003). Individual differences in two emotion regulation processes: Implications for affect, relationships, and well-being. *Journal of Personality and Social Psychology, 55,* 348–362.

Harris, P. (1989). *Children and emotion: The development of psychological understanding.* Cambridge, MA: Blackwell.

Harter, S. (1999). *The construction of the self: A developmental perspective.* New York: Guilford.

Hochschild, A. R. (1983). *The managed heart.* Berkeley, CA: University of California Press.

Holodynski, M. (2004). The miniaturization of expression in the development of emotional self-regulation. *Developmental Psychology, 40,* 16–28.

Josephs, I. (1993). *The regulation of emotional expression in preschool children.* Münster: Waxmann.

Kopp, C. B. (1989). Regulation of distress and negative emotions: A developmental view. *Developmental Psychology, 25,* 343–354.

Lazarus, R. S. (1991). *Emotion and adaptation.* Oxford: Oxford University Press.

Lerner, R. M. (2002). *Concepts and theories of human development.* Mahwah, NJ: Erlbaum.

Lewis, M., & Ramsay, D. (2005). Infant emotional and cortisol responses to goal blockage. *Child Development, 76,* 518–530.

Lewis, M., Stanger, C., & Sullivan, M. W. (1989). Deception in 3-year-olds. *Developmental Psychology, 25,* 439–443.

Lewis, M. D. (1995). Cognition-emotion feedback and the self-organization of developmental paths. *Human Development, 38,* 71–102.

Malatesta, C. Z., Culver, C., Tesman, J. R., & Shepard, B. (1989). *The development of emotion expression during the first two years of life. Monographs of the Society for Research in Child Development, Vol. 54.* Chicago: University of Chicago Press.

Olthof, T., Ferguson, T., & Luiten, A. (1989). Personal responsibility antecedents of anger and blame reactions in children. *Child Development, 60*, 1328–1336.

Rothbart, M. K., & Bates, J. E. (1998). Temperament. In N. Eisenberg (Ed.), *Handbook of child psychology. Vol. 3. Social, emotional, and personality development* (5th ed., pp. 105–176). New York: Wiley.

Saarni, C. (1984). An observational study of children's attempts to monitor their expressive behavior. *Child Development, 55*, 1504–1513.

Saarni, C., & Salisch, M. von (1993). The socialization of emotional dissemblance. In M. Lewis & C. Saarni (Eds.), *Lying and deception in everyday life* (pp. 106–125). New York: Guilford.

Salisch, M. von (2000). *Wenn Kinder sich ärgern . . . Emotionsregulierung in der Entwicklung.* Göttingen: Hogrefe.

Salisch, M. von (2001). Children's emotional development: Challenges in their relationships to parents, peers, and friends. *International Journal of Behavioral Development, 25*, 310–319.

Salisch, M. von, & Kunzmann, U. (2005). Emotionale Entwicklung über die Lebensspanne. In J. Asendorpf (Ed.), *Soziale, emotionale und Persönlichkeitsentwicklung* (pp. 1–74). Göttingen: Hogrefe.

Salisch, M. von, & Vogelgesang, J. (2005). Anger regulation among friends: Assessment and development from childhood to adolescence. *Journal of Social and Personal Relationships, 37*, 317–330.

Salisch, M. von, & Vogelgesang, J. (2006). *Anger regulation in friendship and self-evaluation of acceptance among friends (and peers): A longitudinal study on the direction of effects.* Manuscript under review.

Scherer, K. R. (1984). Emotion as a multicomponent process. In P. Shaver (Ed.), *Review of personality and social psychology, Vol. 5* (pp. 37–63). Beverly Hills, CA: Sage.

Slomkowski, C. L., & Dunn, J. (1996). Young children's understanding of other people's beliefs and feelings and their connected communication with friends. *Developmental Psychology, 32*, 442–447.

Sorce, J. F., Emde, R. N., Campos, J., & Klinnert, M. D. (1985). Maternal emotional signaling: Its effects on the visual cliff behavior of 1-year-olds. *Developmental Psychology, 21*, 195–200.

Soussignan, R. (2002). Duchenne smile, emotional experience, and autonomic reactivity. A test of the facial feedback hypothesis. *Emotion, 2*, 52–74.

Stadler, C., Janke, W., & Schmidt-Atzert, L. (1997). Der Einfluss der Intentionsattribuierung auf aggressives Verhalten im Vorschulalter. *Zeitschrift für Entwicklungspsychologie und pädagogische Psychologie, 29*, 43–61.

Steinberg, L. (2002). *Adolescence* (6th ed.). New York: Knopf.

Stemmler, G. (2004). Physiological processes during emotion. In P. Philippot & R. S. Feldman (Eds.), *The regulation of emotion* (pp. 33–70). Mahwah, NJ: Erlbaum.

Stern, D. N. (2002). *The first relationship: Infant and mother.* Cambridge, MA: Harvard University Press.

Underwood, M., Hurley, J., Johanson, C., & Mosley, J. (1999). An experimental, observational investigation of children's responses to peer provocation: Developmental and gender differences in middle childhood. *Child Development*, *70*, 1428–1446.

Weinberg, K., Tronick, E. Z., Cohn, J., & Olson, K. (1999). Gender differences in emotional expressivity and self-regulation during infancy. *Developmental Psychology*, *35*, 175–188.

Youniss, J. (1980). *Parents and peers in social development*. Chicago: University of Chicago Press.

Zeman, J., & Garber, J. (1996). Display rules for anger, sadness, and pain: It depends on who is watching. *Child Development*, *67*, 957–973.

PART III

What Is and What Is Expected: Psychopathology and Emotion Regulation

7

Emotion Regulation and the Early Development of Psychopathology

Pamela M. Cole, Tracy A. Dennis, Sarah E. Martin, and

Sarah E. Hall

The concept of emotion regulation has assumed a central place in contemporary Western science, particularly in the field of psychology, including the subdisciplines of clinical and developmental psychology. Although there is no consensus as to its definition, emotion regulation is generally described as the modulation of one or more component processes of emotion (e.g., changes in appraisal, expression, experience, readiness to act; Campos, Mumme, Kermoian, & Campos, 1994; Cole, Martin, & Dennis, 2004; Gross, 1998a; Mauss, Bunge, & Gross, this volume; Thompson, 1994). The concept is especially appealing within the framework of developmental psychopathology. This framework provides an overarching perspective for understanding how normal developmental processes lead to adaptive outcomes, under what conditions those same processes are compromised and lead to maladaptive outcomes, how early risk for problematic outcomes are exacerbated or ameliorated over the course of development, and how typical and atypical developmental trajectories inform each other (Cicchetti & Cohen, 2006).

The concept of emotion regulation has become a prominent focus of research conducted within the developmental psychopathology framework. The reason for this is that the concept of emotion regulation integrates an apparent contradiction. Specifically, it provides a conceptual basis for understanding how emotional functioning plays a primary role in both adaptive outcomes, such as psychological competencies tolerating frustration while maintaining interest and curiosity in a difficult task (Saarni, 1999; Shonkoff & Phillips, 2000) and maladaptive outcomes, such as hostile defiance, persistent irritability, or hopelessness (Cole, Michel, & Teti,

1994; Keenan, 2000). That is, the concept of emotion regulation provides a way to understand how emotions can be central to psychological adaptation and competence and yet deeply implicated in the development of psychopathology. It also provides a central focus to understanding how both individual differences and environmental conditions influence the manner in which emotions organize adaptive or maladaptive behavior.

In this chapter, we briefly discuss the importance of studying emotion regulation in order to understand the development of psychological competence and psychopathology and the need for well-designed behavioral observation research to achieve this aim. We first provide some background on the concept of emotion regulation in regard to both typical and atypical development and then describe the dimensions of emotion regulation that are pertinent to clinical risk. With the aid of a clinical case example, we then offer testable predictions about how children at risk for depression can be distinguished from typically developing children on the basis of behavioral observations.

 ## EMOTIONS AS BOTH ADAPTIVE AND MALADAPTIVE

Contemporary emotion theories emphasize the adaptive function of emotions. Generally speaking, what we observe in ourselves and others as emotion states are the visible phases of an ongoing processing of information, the tip of the iceberg so to speak, of a particular type of processing focused on how one is faring relative to one's goals and circumstances. This information processing is of a particular type that distinguishes it from other forms of information processing (e.g., judging distances). Specifically, emotion processing involves appraising our circumstances in light of our goals for well-being and readying us to act accordingly to regain or maintain our goals (Arnold, 1960; Barrett & Campos, 1987; Frijda, 1986; Lazarus, 1991). Although emotions like anger, sadness, and guilt are often viewed as undesirable, contemporary emotion theories point out that they allow us to enact behavior that preserves or regains our sense of well-being. For example, anger allows an individual to act assertively to correct a problem and even prevent its recurrence. Sadness allows a person to cease futile action and relinquish a goal, typically eliciting comfort and support from others. Guilt allows a person to modify or repair action when self-interested action compromises the well-being of another; it prevents future errors, communicates regret to others, and typically elicits forgiveness and relationship repair.

These same adaptive processes, however, clearly have the capacity to compromise psychological health and development under certain conditions. Individuals who are having significant psychological problems evidence significant emotional difficulties. For example, when emotions rise to the level that others are aware of them, we readily see how those emotions can endanger the individuals' relationships or interfere with their ability to engage in productive activity and prolong ill-feeling toward the self and others, even if the emotions serve some immediate goal to regain a sense of well-being. An adult, for example, may have difficulty recognizing his own anxiety (and, therefore, have difficulty managing an emotion he does not recognize), feel chronically unhappy, become irritable with himself and others, and have a cascade of interpersonal and personal difficulties that he cannot resolve because he is caught in an emotional quicksand. Indeed, most forms of psychopathology in children and adults are characterized by emotional symptoms (Cole et al., 1994; Keenan, 2000).

Within the developmental psychopathology framework, the goal of research on emotion regulation is to understand how individuals typically acquire the ability to manage anxiety and other emotions, such that they serve both their immediate goals and progress toward adaptive long-term developmental outcomes. That is, the goal is to understand how the adaptive qualities of emotional functioning evolve to lead to productive, happy adult lives and, from this normative perspective, to understand how disabling patterns of emotion develop and are corrected. Returning to the case of anxiety, it is a functional emotional response to perceived or anticipated risks and dangers to well-being. In typically developing children, anxiety helps a child hesitate to approach a novel or uncertain situation, to work harder to plan and prepare for activities that others will observe, and to resist acting on impulses and desires because they appropriately fear the consequences of criticism, embarrassment, or retribution. Indeed, a lack of appropriate anxiety is thought to be an underlying problem of some behavioral disorders (Kagan, 1994; Raine, Reynolds, Venables, Mednick, & Farrington, 1998).

Anxiety and other negative emotions, however, can paralyze or disorganize behavior. For example, in children who are referred to clinics, we often see anxiety persisting or amplifying in ways that interfere with children's transition to school or to separate comfortably from their parents, their ability to play easily with friends, the degree to which they can focus on learning materials, and their ability to cease worrying about risks and dangers long enough to fall asleep or enjoy going outside to play. Empirical evidence in studies of highly shy or inhibited children reveals how high levels of anxiety about approaching a novel, uncertain situation (e.g., a small group of unfamiliar children of the same age; Rubin, Cheah, & Fox, 2001) overwhelms their natural desire to play and be accepted by others. There are also children who present with behavior management problems, such as noncompliance and defiance, whose problem behaviors are fueled by anxiety and a need to feel in control of situations. In these cases, anxiety is less paralyzing and more disorganizing of social behavior or the ability to work in a focused way on a task. It is important to state, at this juncture, that children with significant problems do attempt to regulate their emotions. What is most interesting is that their regulatory attempts are often not adequate to the challenge of modulating anxiety. In short, anxiety is useful in many ways for most individuals but, if poorly regulated, can become disabling. The dynamics of such emotional responses—duration, intensity, and recovery time—are characteristic of problems with emotion regulation that appear to mark risk for a range of social-emotional and behavioral problems.

In sum, analysis of the pathways from a basic adaptive emotion to a variety of different adaptive and maladaptive developmental outcomes is an important area of study. The concept of emotion regulation is particularly helpful in understanding these various developmental trajectories. The concept provides a way to conceptualize how emotions can both be fundamentally adaptive, serving our ability to function well in an ever-changing environment and, under certain conditions (genetic predispositions and environmental risks), lead to a range of difficulties; it is the way in which emotions are regulated that is crucial to understand in predicting current and future adjustment and maladjustment.

CHALLENGES IN THE SCIENTIFIC STUDY OF EMOTION REGULATION

The breadth and richness of the concept of emotion regulation has led to an enthusiastic embrace by developmental and clinical scientists but also considerable confusion and debate as to the precise meaning of the term. Too often, empirical studies equate "regulation" with positive or neutral emotional expression and "dysregulation" with relatively higher levels of expression of one or more negative emotions. That is, they equate the valence of emotion with the quality of regulation, rendering negative emotions a problematic status even though theories argue that all emotions serve adaptive functions (e.g., Barrett & Campos, 1987; Lazarus, 1991; Sroufe, 1995).

Most recognize the overly simplistic nature of such an approach, but the complexity of the concept of emotion regulation is daunting when one attempts to study it with observational methods. It is beyond the scope of this chapter to detail those challenges, but several issues have plagued scientific progress, including the inherent regulatory aspects of emotions (e.g., anger organizes particular actions), whether any emotion is ever wholly unregulated, what exactly an emotion is, and how we measure emotion independently of regulatory processes (Cole et al., 2004). Emotion regulation is best understood to be a dynamic phenomenon, unfolding in a nonlinear fashion within and across multiple levels of functioning (affect, cognition, and behavior) (e.g., Campos et al., 1994; Fogel & Thelen, 1987; Saarni, Mumme, & Campos, 1998). Even at the physical level, nonlinear, dynamic qualities are observed in neurological substrates of emotional processing, in which cortical and subcortical brain regions influence each other via feedback loops and the forward and backward flow of information (Lewis, 2005; Tucker et al., 2003) . That is, the process of generating changes in emotional state and the process of regulating emotional state co-occur at a physiological level such that the "emotions" we observe, in others or in ourselves, are already products of both emotion generation and emotion regulation. The precise nature of emotions, the nature of the relation between component processes (appraisal and readiness to act), and the nature of regulatory influences remains to be clarified. Such clarification will require advances in the form of increasingly sophisticated experiments and development of new technologies.

As these thorny issues are worked out scientifically, there is and will continue to be widespread use of behavioral observations to infer emotion regulation in children. Clinical practitioners, child care providers, teachers, and parents rely on their observations of child behavior in real time to gain insight into a child's motivations and needs and to determine how to help them be effective in their self-regulation of emotions. Such behavioral methods are especially critical when studying young children, for whom it is difficult or impossible to employ nonbehavioral methods (e.g., self-report, fMRI). It is also well known that the emotional relationships and experiences of the first five years of life are crucial in the development of emotional health and competence (Denham, 1998; Kopp, 1989; Saarni, 1999; Shonkoff & Phillips, 2000; Sroufe, 1995), making this developmental period especially relevant to the study of emotion regulation and the emergence of psychopathology.

Thus, there will continue to be reliance on behavioral observations to understand young children's emotion regulation both in practice and in science. Yet to effectively and validly infer emotion regulation from the sequential flow of a young child's behavior in real-time, real-world contexts, it is essential to have clearly stated conceptual formulations and operational definitions of emotion regulation that lead to clearly specified predictions tested with methods of behavioral assessment.

The use of behavioral sequences, however, is provocative in that it risks implying a model in which emotion and its regulation are two distinct entities that occur in a linear, temporal progression (first an emotional reaction and then an independent regulator of that emotion). As stated above, it is clear that emotion regulation is a dynamic, nonlinear phenomenon. As such, the clinician or researcher who attempts to infer emotion regulation by observing behavior in time and sequence is faced with two related problems: (1) the observer cannot easily disentangle the ebb and flow of a child's emotional responses from the array of regulatory influences that are occurring, and (2) the observed behavior exists in a stream of person–environment transactions rendering any start point of an observation somewhat arbitrary.

Thus, despite enormous advances in both behavioral techniques and affective neuroscience that will shed light on the nature of emotion and emotion regulation, we recognize a continuing need for more sophisticated ways to infer emotion regulation from a child's behavior. To this end, we conceive of emotion regulation as changes in an emotional reaction in a situational context and advocate studying those changes using converging measures, situation-behavior relations, and temporal relations between the nature of expressive behavior and strategic attempts by the child or another to regulate emotion (for further detail, see Cole et al., 2004). This includes observing changes in the intensity, duration, and valence of emotion based on behavior in situational context, making judgments about the effect of dominant emotions on the organization or disorganization of behavior, and assessing a child's anticipating and avoiding emotional reactions (Cole et al., 1994; Thompson, 1994). It is our goal to use observations of child behavior, in time and sequence, to help us to infer that a dynamic emotion regulation process has unfolded in a particular, predictable way. Finally, we advocate applying such behavioral observation methods to the assessment of both typically developing children and those whose emotional functioning has become impaired, namely children who have or are at risk for having psychopathology. As we discuss shortly, such an approach provides a more complete understanding of both basic emotional development by examining a broader range of individual differences but also permits the examination of atypical emotional development in light of typical development. From these viewpoints, we aim to articulate and empirically test specific predictions about the role of emotion regulation in the development of psychological competence and early psychopathology.

FROM MOMENT-TO-MOMENT EMOTION REGULATION TO STABLE, INDIVIDUALIZED PATTERNS OF ER

The observation of moment-to-moment changes in emotion in context can detail the mechanisms by which stable patterns of emotion regulation evolve. These pathways are yet not well understood and must be further delineated in order to clarify what variations in emotional functioning constitute normal variability and when and how certain variations become stable, organized dysfunctional patterns of emotion regulation. Such individualized patterns of emotion regulation develop over time as moment-to-moment experiences accumulate; even without conscious attention, certain ways of regulating emotion serve immediate needs, and, therefore, the probability that they will recur and become characteristic of the child's functioning is increased. Styles of emotion regulation emerge as individual experiences lead to organized preferences for certain emotions and certain regulatory strategies (e.g., Davidson, 2005; Gross, 1998a, b; Izard, Youngstrom, Fine, Mostow, & Trentacosta, 2006; Malatesta & Wilson, 1988; Sroufe, 1995) such that we come to describe not the behavior of the moment but the person as emotionally well-regulated or prone to emotional dysregulation. Emotion–behavior sequences in which emotions are followed by inappropriate or ineffective behaviors will become characteristic patterns of emotion regulation if they succeed in meeting short-term or secondary goals (e.g., a child throws a temper tantrum when candy is taken away, but receives comfort in its place).

Individuals who suffer from psychopathological functioning appear to develop emotion regulation patterns that involve either overregulating and/or underregulating certain emotional responses. For example, one pathway to serious misconduct is hypothesized to be the development of a pattern of underregulating anger but overregulating emotions that are often experienced as creating vulnerability, such as sadness or anxiety (Cole, Hall, & Radzioch, in press). In an effort to avoid feeling those latter feelings, a tendency to generate anger when actually feeling sad or anxious can develop (see also Cole et al., in press). This response may often be inappropriate to a given situation, for example, showing anger when one suffers a saddening loss. A child who generally becomes angry when it is more appropriate (age typical, expected in the situation, acceptable to adults) to be deeply disappointed may have a greater likelihood of behaving in aggressive or antisocial ways, even though the circumstances that trigger a strong emotional response may initially elicit sadness or anxiety.

The emotion regulation story is also not limited to the reduction of negative emotion (Cole et al., 1994). Some children show a surprising lack of expected positive emotions during enjoyable situations such as play. A child who experiences and expresses little positive emotion when it is socially appropriate to do so may be at specific risk for depression (Shankman et al., 2005). Both types of context-inappropriate emotion— the presence of unexpected emotions or the lack of expected emotions —are thought to reflect clinical risk depending on the specific nature of under- or overregulation (e.g., Buss, Davidson, Kalin, & Goldsmith, 2004; Zahn-Waxler et al., 1994).

LINKS BETWEEN OBSERVED BEHAVIOR, PATTERNS OF EMOTION REGULATION, AND CLINICAL DISORDER

Our developmental psychopathology orientation leads us to predict child outcomes from individualized patterns of emotion regulation. That is, we are keenly interested in how a child's efforts to regulate emotion (i.e., achieve goals for well-being) devolve into chronic psychological distress and functional impairment (Cicchetti, Ganiban, & Barnett, 1991; Maughan & Cicchetti, 2002). Theory suggests (Calkins, 1994; Kopp, 1989) and evidence indicates (e.g., Blair, Denham, Kochanoff, & Whipple, 2004; Cole, 1986; Denham et al., 2003; Fabes & Eisenberg, 1992; Stansbury & Sigman, 2000) that between the ages of 3 and 5 years, children acquire the ability to self-regulate emotions and that individual differences in the quality and style of emotion regulation distinguish the typically developing child from children with emerging behavioral and emotional disorders (Cole, Zahn-Waxler, & Smith, 1996; Gilliom, Shaw, Beck, Schonberg, & Lukon, 2002; Silk, Shaw, Forbes, Lane, & Kovacs, 2006).

These growing capacities are strongly linked to earlier and concurrent efforts by parents to bolster and redirect children's independent attempts at emotional self-regulation (Berlin & Cassidy, 2003; Cole, Teti, & Zahn-Waxler, 2003; Stansbury & Zimmerman, 1999). Children at risk for psychopathology may show a reduced capacity to benefit from caregiver attempts. Indeed, children may show escalation of negative emotions rather than the expected decreases. Yet, there remains insufficient empirical evidence to document the specific nature of emotional dysregulation, what differentiates early emotional dysregulation that represents a transient, developmental phase from that which signals risk, and the precise mechanisms by which emerging patterns of emotion regulation lead to specific clinically significant outcomes.

To illustrate, we present a case of a 4-year-old boy who was referred for services and diagnosed with major depressive disorder. The description has been written to protect the anonymity of the child and his family. The case was selected because it typified a class of early childhood psychopathology that is, unfortunately, common in our practices. In our presentation, we highlight several stylized patterns of emotion regulation that characterize the child's functioning and provide hypotheses for why preschool age children with clinical depression should differ from typically developing children of this age and from children with different clinical presentations (e.g., attention deficit disorder). The description is based on parental observations of the child's behavior at home, teacher observations of the child's behavior at preschool, and the clinic staff's observations of the child's behavior in the clinic. To our way of thinking, the case portrays a pattern of emotional dysregulation that is characteristic of and specific to childhood depression. The child had frequent, prolonged episodes of irritability, dysphoria, and a loss of interest and enjoyment. However, what aspects of this child's functioning point to difficulty with emotion regulation? They are the following:

(a) Context-inappropriate emotion, namely anger and sadness in situations most children enjoy
(b) Emotion-behavior sequences in which emotional responses are followed by inappropriate rather than appropriate, acceptable behavior
(c) Episodes of negative emotions that are longer and more intense in which age-appropriate self-regulatory strategies (e.g., distraction, making bids for help) are not deployed or, when deployed, they fail to reduce or resolve distress
(d) Difficulty recovering from negative emotion even when responsible, sensitive adults use appropriate caregiving strategies, including increases in negative emotions to efforts that should lead to decreases.

A CLINICAL EXAMPLE

Clinical cases provide rich material for forming hypotheses about the development of specific emotion regulation difficulties. In the last section of this chapter, we tie together aspects of emotion regulation that appear to distinguish typical and atypical functioning and the examples provided in the case study. Together they offer testable hypotheses about how depressed preschoolers should differ from typically developing 4-year-olds.

Andrew's mother tearfully called the clinic, expressing helplessness and deep concerns about her 4-year-old son's unmanageable and aggressive behavior. She and her husband felt they could not control their son's behavior. Andrew opposed their attempts to direct, correct, and influence his behavior. When they made an attempt to direct him, he not only failed to comply with their instructions but became intensely angry and hostilely refused to do as they wished. In addition, he had frequent and intense conflicts with his 3-year-old sister such that they feared he might harm her.

There was converging evidence from different observers that Andrew not only had frequent episodes of opposition and conflict but that his behavior appeared to be fueled by persistent irritability and intense emotional reactivity, even in response to what could be regarded as minor frustrations or interpersonal disagreement. Moreover, the descriptions were noteworthy in that it was evident that Andrew's anger did not organize his behavior into effective problem-solving. Rather, once angry, he grew increasingly agitated and became unruly or aggressive. During his most escalated outbursts, he would become reckless and destructive, throwing or breaking household objects within reach, even his own toys and belongings.

As described thus far, Andrew's behavior is consistent with that of children whose behavior meets criteria for oppositional defiant disorder. Additional observations, however, led to considering the likelihood that Andrew was experiencing major depression. Notably, his verbalizations during angry outbursts often included statements that family members hated him and that he himself wished he were dead. Further, when his angry and agitated subsided, the boy became tearful and withdrawn for extended periods, i.e., hours and even days. Efforts to soothe, help, and cheer him were met with renewed anger and agitation. In addition, he no longer appeared to enjoy activities that he once did, and he showed waning interest in any play and family activities.

In the clinic, Andrew was quiet and reserved. He complied with the therapist's requests but never initiated conversation or play. In fact, he showed no interest in the play materials. He made very little eye contact and no attempt, even nonverbally, to engage the therapist. With a skillful clinician, most young children eventually begin to explore play materials and warm up to the clinician who is kind and friendly. Andrew continued to avoid interaction and activity. For example, in a task where he was asked to complete stories, his narratives were brief and unelaborated although it was known from parent and teacher reports that he was skilled verbally. His teacher described Andrew as generally unhappy, difficult to engage in enjoyable activities, and easily upset by events that most children found to be minor irritations. His play at school was typically solitary, lacking much joy or pleasure, and his peer relations were fraught with conflict because he was so easily frustrated by their behavior.

Context-inappropriate emotion

It is generally easy for adults to predict the emotional responses of 4-year-olds to the situations they encounter. Emotional reactions that occur in contexts that do not typically elicit those reactions may be indicative of clinical risk (e.g., Buss et al., 2004; Zahn-Waxler et al., 1994). For example, children typically enjoy game-like laboratory procedures such as story-telling and interacting with puppets, but children who are at clinical risk will often show a lack of enjoyment or even a negative emotion in a situation that typically would not elicit fear or anger. The case illustration suggests that a depressed preschooler is less likely to enjoy activities that are typically fun, inviting, and interesting.

Emotion leads to inappropriate action

Anger in a typically developing 4-year-old child most often leads to instrumental efforts to achieve a desired goal. Those efforts fall along a continuum of social appropriateness from negotiating and arguing to whining, crying, and tantrums (Potegal, Kosorok, & Davidson, 2003). Often, however, 4-year-olds' understanding of rules and their desire to preserve their relationships facilitate their ability to deploy strategies to either inhibit inappropriate behavior or give up their protests (Kopp, 1989). When they are tired or hungry or unwell, they may be less likely to deploy strategies and may become more intensely upset, requiring adult efforts for resolving the distress. Those adult efforts are typically effective, if not immediately. In our lab, we have unpublished data that shows that the typically developing 4-year-old who becomes frustrated trying to overcome an obstacle to a goal tends to express mild frustration (e.g., pressed lips, furrowed brows, vocal expressions of exasperation and sighs) that are immediately followed by persistence or attempts at alternative problem-solving. The case description in contrast reveals a child whose anger reliably has a disorganizing rather than organizing effect on his behavior. Specifically, Andrew's anger and distress repeatedly undermined interactions with his environment, manifesting in conflictual and aggressive encounters and destructive behaviors.

Relative lack of effective self-regulatory strategies

The average 4-year-old can manage ordinary frustrations and disappointments associated with peers and siblings (e.g., Fantuzzo, Sekino, & Cohen,

2004), school work (e.g., Howse, Calkins, Anastopoulos, Keane, & Shelton, 2003), or adult requests and directions (e.g., Feldman & Klein, 2003). These associations between emotion regulation and competent behavior imply that children are using regulatory strategies that are effective in modulating their frustration and disappointment. Indeed, there is a small body of evidence that shows that very young children (ages 2 through 5) have a repertoire of strategies (e.g., engaging in an enjoyable activity, distracting themselves from a desirable object they cannot have) that effectively help them tolerate frustration and even become emotionally positive in the face of a blocked goal (Grolnick, Bridges, & Connell, 1996; Silk et al., 2006). In contrast, Andrew demonstrates an extremely restricted repertoire for coping with negative emotions, relying primarily on defiance and social withdrawal to accomplish his goals and thereby manage his anger, frustration, and anxiety. Such efforts likely serve to reduce his immediate distress, but at a clear cost. More adaptive and competent intra- and interpersonal coping alternatives (e.g., support-seeking, rudimentary problem-solving) are largely absent from his strategy repertoire.

Ineffectiveness of appropriate regulatory efforts by caregivers

There is evidence, from infancy through the preschool age years, that sensitive efforts to redirect and soothe a young child's distress are related to the quality of the child's self-regulation (Berlin & Cassidy, 2003; Calkins, Smith, Gill, & Johnson, 1998; Cole et al., 2003; Diener & Mangelsdorf, 1999; Stansbury & Zimmerman, 1999). That is, typically, when children cannot deploy an effective strategy to modulate their distress, caregivers such as parents, other adult family members, and child care providers attempt to reduce the child's distress by helping the child achieve the goal, teaching the child how to cope with the situation, comforting the child, or instructing the child to stop or do something else. Ordinarily, these parenting strategies are effective in reducing the child's distress and, although the developmental mechanisms are not well known, it is clear that parenting plays a role in promoting healthy emotion regulation in children. It is also clear that children differ in their temperamental predispositions and that this influences what parenting strategies are most effective in helping them deal with their emotions (Dennis, 2006; Kennedy, Rubin, Hastings, & Maisel, 2004). However, in most cases, adults find ways to tailor their efforts to reduce child distress and teach coping strategies that are successful. In the case illustration, we see that one aspect of the parents' desperation is that their attempts to support their child seem to exacerbate rather than decrease the child's negative emotions. Although it is beyond the scope of the chapter to describe the socialization of emotion regulation and the family dynamics of the case, it is often the case that ordinarily effective strategic attempts to reduce a child's distress are more often ineffective with children who are developing early psychopathology.

CONCLUSIONS

Emotion regulation is an appealing construct because it allows us to examine how basic adaptive processes contribute to the development of psychological competence and health but also understand how these processes can play such a poignant role in the development of psychopathology. There are, however, a number of challenges to studying emotion regulation. Because it is a complex phenomenon, it is difficult to generate adequate behavioral methods that test significant individual differences in emotion regulation. As a result, many empirical studies have tended to conflate emotion with emotion regulation (e.g., interpret higher scores on negative emotion as evidence of poor emotion regulation), such that one could only conclude that negative emotions are undesirable when they are adaptive processes that have evolved and endured as a key part of human functioning. Advances in theory and method may resolve some of the thorny definitional and methodological issues that confront emotion regulation researchers, but for many researchers—and practitioners—who work with children, behavioral observations will continue to play an important role in our drawing conclusions about individual patterns of emotion regulation and dysregulation. An important feature of behavioral assessment of emotion regulation is that it (a) lends itself to use in research with children who may not be able to participate in other methods (e.g., fMRI, highly controlled experimental designs) and (b) offers a translational bridge between scientific evidence and practical use by teachers, parents, and clinicians. Ideally, behavioral studies of emotion regulation will not only shed light on the developmental trajectories by which emotion influences both adaptive and maladaptive outcomes but will do so in a way that allows such research to be readily adapted to practical assessment strategies in real-world contexts.

In this chapter, we attempt to portray the real-world difficulties that children can present to illustrate how it is not emotion per se but difficulty regulating emotion that compromises psychological health. Elsewhere we have described the qualities of emotional functioning that are associated with being an emotionally well-regulated person (Cole et al., 1994) and the transactional pathways by which risk and stress influence the nature of individual patterns of emotion regulation (Chaplin & Cole, 2005). In this chapter, we highlight four specific dimensions of emotion regulation that can be inferred from behavioral observations, showing the qualities of regulation that distinguish children at clear clinical risk from children who appear to be developing normally. The contrasts provide a set of concepts and suggest methods of measurement that can be used to test hypotheses about individual differences in emotion regulation, using a case of a young child with a major depressive disorder to illustrate the contrast. This approach is consistent with a developmental psychopathology perspective because it incorporates multiple levels of analysis (affective, cognitive, behavioral, and contextual), conceptualizes how normal developmental processes can lead to both adaptive and maladaptive outcomes, and addresses the interplay of risk and resilience in the development of psychopathology.

In brief, the case study illustrates the general point that children whose developing emotion regulation patterns reflect psychological risk are more likely:

(a) to evidence emotions that are not typical in a given context (e.g., failing to enjoy activities that most children enjoy or getting angry when most children would be sad),

(b) to behave inappropriately, rather than within the bounds of acceptability to parents, teachers, and/or society (e.g., be aggressive rather than assertive when angry, become disruptive and hostile when sad or anxious),

(c) to have fewer effective and appropriate strategies for regulating emotion (e.g., less capacity to shift attention away from a problem that cannot be solved appropriately), and

(d) to have difficulty recovering from negative emotion even when responsible, sensitive adults use appropriate caregiving strategies.

This list of observable emotion regulation risk factors was not intended to be exhaustive; rather, it provides an example of how hypotheses concerning emotion regulation can tap several important factors in the development and maintenance of psychopathology. Our clinical case example focused on stable individual differences in emotion regulation that may reflect risk for major depressive disorder, including the context-inappropriate overregulation of sadness and happiness, and, following angry outbursts, experiences of sadness that were intense, long-lasting, and slow to rebound. In addition, Andrew's regulatory attempts were often ineffective or inappropriate, and he did not seem able to benefit even from his parents' competent attempts to help him manage his distress.

This approach, which characterizes multiple domains of emotion regulation in relation to distinct disorders, has the potential to move the understanding of mental health and illness forward if it is grounded in empirical evidence and if it proceeds in light of clinical practice. For example, future research can develop and refine hypotheses by examining which aspects of emotion regulation are "active ingredients" in creating risk or resilience for a range of disorders; these patterns then can be compared between typically developing children and clinical samples. Such a program of research could readily inform the development of more targeted and effective treatments; treatments that frame psychopathology in terms of normal emotional processes that have become disorganized, and that serve to enhance emotion regulatory strengths and ameliorate emotion regulatory risks.

REFERENCES

Arnold, M. B. (1960). *Emotion and personality. Volume 1: Psychological aspects.* New York: Columbia University Press.

Barrett. K. C., & Campos, J. J. (1987). Perspectives on emotional development II: A functionalist perspective to emotions. In J. Osofsky (Ed.), *Handbook of infant development* (2nd ed., pp. 555–578). New York: Wiley.

Berlin, L. J., & Cassidy, J. (2003). Mothers' self-reported control of their preschool children's emotional expressiveness: A longitudinal study of associations with infant–mother attachment and children's emotion regulation. *Social Development, 12,* 477–495.

Blair, K. A., Denham, S. A., Kochanoff, A., & Whipple, B. (2004). Playing it cool: Temperament, emotion regulation, and social behavior in preschoolers. *Journal of School Psychology, 42,* 419–443.

Buss, K. A., Davidson, R. J., Kalin, N. H., & Goldsmith, H. H. (2004). Context-specific freezing and associated physiological reactivity as a dysregulated fear response. *Developmental Psychology, 40,* 583–594.

Calkins, S. D. (1994). Origins and outcomes of individual differences in emotion regulation. In N. A. Fox (Ed.), *The development of emotion regulation: Biological and behavioral considerations. Monographs of the Society for Research in Child Development, 59* (2–3, Serial No. 240), 53–72.

Calkins, S. D., Smith, C. L., Gill, K. L., & Johnson, M. C. (1998). Maternal interactive style across contexts: Relations to emotional, behavioral, and physiological regulation during toddlerhood. *Social Development, 7,* 350–369.

Campos, J. J., Mumme, D. L., Kermoian, R., & Campos, R. G. (1994). A functionalist perspective on the nature of emotion. In N. A. Fox (Ed.), *The development of emotion regulation: Biological and behavioral considerations. Monographs of the Society for Research in Child Development, 59* (2–3, Serial No. 240), 284–303.

Chaplin, T. M., & Cole, P. M. (2005). The role of emotion regulation in the development of psychopathology. In B. L. Hankin & J. R. Z. Abela (Eds.), *Development of psychopathology: A vulnerability-stress perspective* (pp. 49–74). Thousand Oaks, CA: Sage.

Cicchetti, D., & Cohen, D. J. (2006). *Developmental psychopathology* (2nd ed.). Hoboken, NJ: Wiley.

Cicchetti, D., Ganiban, J., & Barnett, D. (1991). Contributions from the study of high-risk populations to understanding the development of emotion regulation. In J. Garber & K. A. Dodge (Eds.), *The development of emotion regulation and dysregulation* (pp. 15–48). New York: Cambridge University Press.

Cole, P. M. (1986). Children's spontaneous control of facial expression. *Child Development, 57*, 1309–1321.

Cole, P. M., Hall, S. E., & Radzioch, A. M. (in press). Emotional dysregulation and the development of serious misconduct. In S. Olson & A. Sameroff (eds.), *Regulatory processes in the development of behavior problems: Biological, behavioral, and social-ecological interactions.* New York: Cambridge University Press.

Cole, P. M., Martin, S. E., & Dennis, T. A. (2004). Emotion regulation as a scientific construct: Methodological challenges and directions for child development research. *Child Development, 75*, 317–333.

Cole, P. M., Michel, M. K., & Teti, L. O. (1994). The development of emotion regulation and dysregulation: A clinical perspective. In N. Fox (Ed.), *The development of emotion regulation: Biological and behavioral considerations. Monographs of the Society for Research in Child Development, 59* (2–3, Serial No. 240), 73–100.

Cole, P. M., Teti, L. O., & Zahn-Waxler, C. (2003). Mutual emotion regulation and the stability of conduct problems between preschool and early school age. *Development and Psychopathology, 15*, 1–18.

Cole, P. M., Zahn-Waxler, C., & Smith, K. D. (1996). Expressive control during a disappointment: Variations related to preschoolers' behavior problems. *Developmental Psychology, 30*, 835–846.

Davidson, R. J. (2005). Well-being and affective style: Neural substrates and biobehavioural correlates. In F. A. Huppert, N. Baylis, & B. Keverne (Eds.), *The science of well-being* (pp. 107–139). New York: Oxford University Press.

Denham, S. A. (1998). *Emotional development in young children.* New York: Guilford.

Denham, S. A., Blair, K. A., DeMulder, E., Levitas, J., Sawyer, K., Auerbach-Major, S., et al. (2003). Preschool emotional competence: Pathway to social competence? *Child Development, 74*, 238–256.

Dennis, T. (2006). Emotional self-regulation in preschoolers: The interplay of child approach reactivity, parenting, and control capacities. *Developmental Psychology, 42*, 84–97.

Diener, M. L., & Mangelsdorf, S. C. (1999). Behavioral strategies for emotion regulation in toddlers: Associations with maternal involvement and emotional expressions. *Infant Behavior and Development, 22*, 569–583.

Fabes, R. A., & Eisenberg, N. (1992). Young children's coping with interpersonal anger. *Child Development, 63*, 116–128.

Fantuzzo, J., Sekino, Y., & Cohen, H. L. (2004). An examination of the contributions of interactive peer play to salient classroom competencies for urban Head Start children. *Psychology in the Schools, 41*, 323–336.

Feldman, R., & Klein, P. S. (2003). Toddlers' self-regulated compliance to mothers, caregivers, and fathers: Implications for theories of socialization. *Developmental Psychology, 39*, 680–692.

Fogel, A., & Thelen, E. (1987). Development of early expressive and communicative action: Reinterpreting the evidence from a dynamic systems perspective, *Developmental Psychology, 23*, 747–761.

Frijda, N. (1986). *The emotions*. New York: Cambridge University Press.

Gilliom, M., Shaw, D. S., Beck, J. E., Schonberg, M. A., & Lukon, J. L. (2002). Anger regulation in disadvantaged preschool boys: Strategies, antecedents, and the development of self-control. *Developmental Psychology, 38*, 222–235.

Grolnick, W. S., Bridges, L. J., & Connell, J. P. (1996). Emotion regulation in two-year-olds: Strategies and emotional expression in four contexts. *Child Development, 67*, 928–941.

Gross, J. J. (1998a). Sharpening the focus: Emotion regulation, arousal, and social competence. *Psychological Inquiry, 9*, 287–290.

Gross, J. J. (1998b). Antecedent- and response-focused emotion regulation: Divergent consequences for experience, expression, and physiology. *Journal of Personality and Social Psychology, 74*, 224–237.

Howse, R. B., Calkins, S. D., Anastopoulos, A. D., Keane, S. P., & Shelton, T. L. (2003). Regulatory contributors to children's kindergarten achievement. *Early Education and Development, 14*, 101–119.

Izard, C. E., Youngstrom, E. A., Fine, S. E., Mostow, A. J., & Trentacosta, C. J. (2006). Emotions and developmental psychopathology. In D. Cicchetti & D. J. Cohen (Eds.), *Developmental psychopathology. Vol 1. Theory and method* (2nd ed., pp. 244–292). Hoboken, NJ: Wiley.

Kagan, J. (1994). *Galen's prophecy*. New York: Basic Books.

Keenan, K. (2000). Emotion dysregulation as a risk factor for child psychopathology. *Clinical Psychology: Science and Practice, 7*, 418–434.

Kennedy, A. E., Rubin, K. H., Hastings, P. D., & Maisel, B. (2004). Longitudinal relations between child vagal tone and parenting behavior: 2 to 4 years. *Developmental Psychobiology, 45*, 10–21.

Kopp, C. B. (1989). Regulation of distress and negative emotions: A developmental view. *Developmental Psychology, 25*, 343–354.

Lazarus, R. S. (1991). *Emotions and adaptation*. New York: Oxford University Press.

Lewis, M. D. (2005). Bridging emotion theory and neurobiology through dynamic systems modeling. *Behavioral and Brain Sciences, 28*, 169–245.

Malatesta, C. Z., & Wilson, A. (1988). Emotion/cognition interaction in personality development: A discrete emotions, functionalist analysis. *British Journal of Social Psychology, 27*, 91–112.

Maughan, A., & Cicchetti, D. (2002). Impact of child maltreatment and interadult violence on children's emotion regulation abilities and socioemotional adjustment. *Child Development, 73*, 1525–1542.

Potegal, M., Kosorok, M. R., & Davidson, R. J. (2003). Temper tantrums in young children: 2. Tantrum duration and temporal organization. *Journal of Developmental and Behavioral Pediatrics, 24,* 148–154.

Raine, A., Reynolds, C., Venables, P. H., Mednick, S. A., & Farrington, D. P. (1998). Fearlessness, stimulation-seeking, and large body size at age 3 years as early predispositions to childhood aggression at age 11 years. *Archives of General Psychiatry, 55,* 745–751.

Rubin, K. H., Cheah, C. S. L., & Fox, N. A. (2001). Emotion regulation, parenting and display of social reticence in preschoolers. *Early Education and Development, 12,* 97–115.

Saarni, C. (1999). *The development of emotional competence.* New York: Guilford.

Saarni, C., Mumme, D. L., & Campos, J. J. (1998). Emotional development: Action, communication, and understanding. In N. Eisenberg (Ed.), *Handbook of child psychology. Vol. 3. Social, emotional, and personality development* (5th ed., pp. 237–309). Hoboken, NJ: Wiley.

Shankman, S. A., Tenke, C. E., Bruder, G. E., Durbin, E. C., Hayden, E. P., & Klein, D. N. (2005). Low positive emotionality in young children: Association with EEG asymmetry. *Development and Psychopathology, 17,* 85–98.

Shonkoff, J. P., & Phillips, D. A. (2000). *From neurons to neighborhoods: The science of early childhood development.* Washington, DC: National Academy Press.

Silk, J. S., Shaw, D. S., Forbes, E. E., Lane, T. L., & Kovacs, M. (2006). Maternal depression and child internalizing: The moderating role of child emotion regulation. *Journal of Clinical Child and Adolescent Psychology, 35,* 116–126.

Sroufe, A. (1995). *Emotional development: The organization of the early years.* New York: Cambridge University Press.

Stansbury, K., & Sigman, M. (2000). Responses of preschoolers in two frustrating episodes: Emergence of complex strategies for emotion regulation. *Journal of Genetic Psychology, 161,* 182–202.

Stansbury, K., & Zimmerman, L. K. (1999). Relations among child language skills, maternal socializations of emotion regulation, and child behavior problems. *Child Psychiatry & Human Development, 30,* 121–142.

Thompson, R. A. (1994). Emotion regulation: A theme in search of definition. In N. A. Fox (Ed.), *The development of emotion regulation: Biological and behavioral considerations. Monographs of the Society for Research in Child Development, 59* (2–3, Serial No. 240), 25–52.

Tucker, D. M., Luu, P., Desmond, R. E., Jr., Hartry-Speiser, A., Davey, C., & Fleisch, T. (2003). Corticolimbic mechanisms in emotional decisions. *Emotion, 3,* 127–149.

Zahn-Waxler, C., Cole, P. M., Richardson, D. T., Friedman, R. J., Michel, M. K., & Belouad, F. (1994). Social problem solving in disruptive preschool children: Reactions to hypothetical situations of conflict and distress. *Merrill-Palmer Quarterly, 40,* 98–119.

8

Emotion Information Processing and Affect Regulation: Specificity Matters!

Pierre Philippot, Aurore Neumann, and Nathalie Vrielynck

For a long time, psychotherapy models have neglected emotion, considering it as the by-product of unconscious conflicts or of irrational beliefs, or as a too subjective notion to be considered by a truly scientific approach to psychotherapy. Yet, most people seeking psychotherapeutic help suffer from emotion they cannot regulate (Peper & Vauth, this volume). This truism has lately impacted on recent conceptions of psychotherapy, and emotion deregulation is now considered as a key feature in most psychopathological disorders (Greenberg & Vandekerckhove, this volume). For instance, Barlow (Barlow, Allen, & Choate, 2004; Moses & Barlow, 2006) has proposed a new unified treatment for a large scope of psychopathological disorders that is based on emotion science. According to Barlow, the common ground of many psychopathological conditions is that some emotions are perceived as uncontrollable and/or intolerable. People are then attempting to suppress and avoid these emotions. However, as one cannot avoid an internal state such as emotion, suppression and avoidance coping strategies are doomed to failure and result in increased distressing emotion, feeding forward the sense of uncontrollability and intolerability. A vicious circle is thus initiated that precipitates, and ultimately maintains, emotional distress.

In this perspective, a central concern for clinical intervention is the development of the ability to regulate such distressing emotions, rather than attempting to avoid or suppress them. The present chapter is based on the premise that emotion regulation is partly determined by how emotional information is processed. In other words, the way we think and ruminate about our emotions is conceived of as a main determinant of our ability to regulate them. This notion is not entirely new and has already been proposed by scholars who investigated the efficacy factors of intervention based on exposure. For instance, Foa and McNally (1996) have proposed that considering the type of emotional information processing during exposure is central for understanding therapeutic efficacy.

In the present chapter, we will focus on one dimension of emotional information processing that has shown its relevance for emotion regulation in general and psychopathology in particular: the specificity versus generality at which emotional information is processed. Specificity refers to the activation of detailed and precise information about specific and unique emotional experiences that are well circumscribed in time in episodes lasting less (and often much less) than a day. Generality refers to the activation of generic information about emotion. It can refer to features that tend to be repeatedly experienced during a given emotion (i.e., prototypic emotional information, e.g., the type of tense body sensation I feel each time I get angry) or to abstract information about extended periods of time (e.g., how I felt during my honeymoon).

First, we will review research that has shown that several emotional disorders are characterized by an overgenerality bias in emotional information processing. Next, the naïve theories that might sustain this bias will be investigated. The validity of the naïve theories will be questioned on the basis of a cognitive model of emotion regulation based on multi-level theories of emotion. Then, we will review our own research program that examined the regulatory consequences of processing emotional information at a specific or overgeneral level. Finally, the implications for psychopathology and clinical interventions will be discussed.

SPECIFICITY: A RELEVANT DIMENSION IN EMOTIONAL INFORMATION PROCESSING

Two lines of research have investigated overgenerality in processing emotional information, one has focused on depression, the other on anxiety and worry. In the field of depression, Williams (1996) has evidenced that depressed individuals suffer from an overgenerality bias in retrieving personal memories of past emotional experiences (e.g., Williams, 1996; Williams, Stiles, & Shapiro, 1999) as well as in imagining possible future experiences (Williams et al., 1996). For instance, when asked to recall experiences of anger, depressed individuals tend to report overgeneral events (e.g., "when I am with my girlfriend") rather than specific events (e.g., "last Sunday, I had an argument with my neighbor whose dog was endlessly barking"). This overgenerality bias has also been observed in other clinical populations, such as bipolar depression, posttraumatic and acute stress disorders, or schizophrenia (e.g., van Vreeswijk & de Wilde, 2004). Further, several studies have reported that this lack of memory specificity is correlated with impaired social problem solving (e.g., Goddard, Dritschel, & Burton, 1996). Williams (1996) has proposed that, by remaining at a general—and thus more abstract—level of information, individuals attempt to avoid the reactivation of acute and painful emotions felt during specific personal experiences.

In the field of anxiety, Borkovec (Borkovec & Inz, 1990; Stoeber & Borkovec, 2002) has observed that worries are essentially a verbal thought activity that tends to remain at an overgeneral and abstract level. Quite similarly to Williams (1996), he conceptualizes this overgeneral processing as a coping strategy to avoid somatic activation and imagery associated with negative affect. Further, Stoeber and Borkovec (2002) argue that overgeneral processing can lead to maintenance of anxiety because it results in a failure in emotional processing: Too general and abstract emotional information would be impossible to disconfirm and modify. Consequently, these authors consider that processing more specifically and concretely emotional information is useful for improving problem solving and facilitating emotional processing.

In sum, although the notions of generality and specificity of processing have been defined and operationalized differently according to the authors, the literature suggests that overgeneral processing of emotional information is related to the maintenance of emotional disorders. For instance, overgenerality applied to past emotional experiences would be associated with depression vulnerability, while overgenerality in future projections would characterize anxious rumination. This suggests that specific processing might lead to emotional change and better emotional regulation, but that it would bear a cost : the activation of acute emotional feelings.

LAY THEORIES ABOUT THE EMOTIONAL CONSEQUENCES OF SPECIFYING PERSONAL EXPERIENCES

These psychological theories are congruent to laypeople's naïve beliefs. In a series of studies (e.g., Philippot, Baeyens, & Douilliez, 2006), we have documented that people tend to believe that specifying (that is, examining in detail) one's emotional experience increases its intensity, as compared to considering it in a more general way. Specifically, different groups of participants were asked to report how the intensity of their emotion would evolve, minute after minute, if they were thinking about an emotional experience for ten minutes. In some studies, people were requested to imagine that they were thinking about an emotional memory, in other studies that they were thinking about an upcoming experience (e.g., thinking about an upcoming stressful talk they would have to give). Some participants were instructed to imagine that they would be thinking of the emotional experience from a general perspective, without trying to analyze or to detail their emotions; other participants were instructed to imagine that they would be thinking of the emotional experience with the greatest possible details, imagining all the scenarios and different emotions that could arise. In all these studies, people reported the same pattern of results. When imagining thinking in a general way about their emotion, people expect to experience an average intensity of emotion that remains stable in time. However, when imagining thinking about it in a specific way, people expect that their emotional intensity would increase steadily and be significantly greater than in the general condition.

We further investigated whether this naïve theory is also true for people suffering from emotional disorders. Indeed, one could argue that, when thinking about a negative experience, people suffering from an emotional disorder might select its more negative aspects and catastrophize its consequences (Beck, Emery, & Greenberg, 1985). One could thus predict that people suffering from emotional disorders might expect more intense negative emotion when thinking about a negative event. However, it is unclear whether a clinical population would differentiate in the same way the impact of specifying versus remaining general about emotion processing. One could indeed argue that remaining general in emotional processing fosters the generalization of a negative experience to many experiences, and entails these more negative expectations. On the other hand, one could counter-argue that specifying a negative experience should generate acuter distress in clinical populations, and thus more negative expectations (e.g., Williams, 1996). Thus, there are arguments in favor of more negative expectations in clinical populations for either specifying or generalizing. It may also be that these two modes are not distinguished by clinical populations as they are by healthy people.

To investigate this alternative, we compared out-patients suffering from social phobia to a healthy control group in a task in which they imagine that they would be thinking about an important speech they would have to give the next day (Philippot et al., 2006). Like in the other studies, participants had to imagine that they would be thinking either in a general or in a specific way about what could happen during the talk. They had to report how their anxiety would evolve in each condition. The results revealed that, quite expectedly, social phobics forecast overall more anxiety than healthy controls, but also, and more interestingly, that they hold even more contrasted expectations between the specific and general condition than healthy controls. Indeed, while in the general processing condition, social phobics and healthy controls are both similarly expecting a stable level of anxiety, the former expect a steadier and more continuous increase of anxiety than the latter in the specific processing condition.

In sum, healthy individuals as well as people suffering from emotional disorders expect that processing their emotional experiences at a specific level increases the intensity of their affects. The latter are even expecting a more severe increase in emotional intensity than the former. These naïve theories offer a rational accounting for the fact that people are likely to avoid thinking in specific details about painful experiences. They are offering support to the notion that overgenerality in processing personal experiences is an avoidant coping strategy (Borkovec & Hu, 1990; Williams, 1996).

QUESTIONING THE NAÏVE THEORY

However, one could question the validity of the naïve theory claim that specifying one's (negative) experience results in deleterious effects for emotion regulation. As developed in the preceding paragraphs, overgenerality in processing personal experiences characterizes many clinical populations. Further, several authors have demonstrated that overgenerality in retrieving autobiographical memories is associated with poor interpersonal problem solving skills (Goddard et al., 1996). Thus, in the long run, most authors would agree that, as with any avoidant coping strategies, the overgenerality bias has more deleterious effects to one's well being and emotional health than the tendency to process specifically one's personal experiences.

Could the naïve theory also be invalid for short term consequences? There is some empirical evidence suggesting that this might indeed be the case. For instance, Taylor, Pham, Rivkin, and Armot (1998) have demonstrated that imagining in specific details coping with an upcoming exam leads to better problem solving and emotional management than imagining the happiness that would be felt if the exam was a success. Similarly, recent clinical approaches to emotion regulation, such as mindfulness-based approaches, stress the importance of fully exploring one's experience, keeping an open and investigating mind to all the facets of the experience (Baer, 2003; Hayes, 2002; Segal, Williams, & Teasdale, 2002).

In these two examples, specifying one's experience in detailing its many facets results in a better outcome than a general processing approach.

There are not only empirical reasons to doubt the naïve theory, there are also theoretical reasons to question the assumption that specifying a personal negative experience necessarily results in acuter distress. These reasons emanate from a theoretical rationale based on multilevel theories of emotion. In the next section, multilevel theories of emotion will be presented in order to develop a rationale about the relationship between specificity in processing emotional information and emotion regulation.

EMOTION REGULATION IN MULTILEVEL THEORIES

From a theoretical perspective, the key issues regarding the relationship between specificity and emotion regulation are to determine (a) what triggers emotional arousal during the evocation of an emotional experience, (b) what processes might increase or decrease such arousal, and (c) how specificity in processing interferes with (a) and (b). Multilevel theories of emotion (e.g., Brewin, 2001; Dalgleish, 2004; Leventhal, 1984; Philippot, Baeyens, Douilliez, & Francart, 2004; Teasdale & Barnard, 1993) offer a rich theoretical basis for answering this question. In this theoretical perspective, emotion is represented and processed at different levels of cognitive organization; these two notions, representation and process, being central to the understanding of emotion elicitation and regulation. We have recently attempted an integration of these models: the dual memory model of emotion (Philippot et al., 2004).

Emotion representation in multilevel theories

The basic characteristic of the dual memory model architecture is the distinction between the types of representation—the structure—involved in the elicitation and regulation of emotion, and the processes operating on these structures. At the structural level, two types of representation systems are postulated, a "schematic" or "associative" system and a "propositional" or "conceptual" system. These two types represent a distinction common to all multilevel models. The associative/schematic system refers to implicit representations that convey the immediate emotional meaning of a situation for a given individual. The conceptual/propositional system pertains to declarative, conceptual knowledge about an emotion or episodic and declarative knowledge about an emotional experience.

Associative/schematic representations are built as schemata: A schema is an abstract and implicit representation that integrates sensory, perceptual, and semantic information typical of a given category of emotional experiences, on the one hand, and their relations to the activation of specific body response systems, on the other hand. All authors do not agree on the specific nature of schemata: Some see them as purely associative representations, whereas others view them as analogical or metaphoric representations. Following the germinal work of Leventhal (1984), we propose that schemata can be conceptualized as the records of the individual's emotional classical conditioning. When perceptual elements are repeatedly activated at the same time as innate connections between perceptual features and body responses, they become integrated in an abstract representation that encodes high order reoccurrences between the activation of perceptual—and, later in ontogeny, semantic—elements and body responses. For example, touch and odor features of the mother's breast are perceptual features that automatically trigger an approach body response in the newborn. Repeated associations between experiences of activation of these basic innate features and the approach response, together with new features, such as auditory features of the mother's voice or the smell of her perfume, will become integrated in a schema.

In contrast, the conceptual/propositional system consists of declarative knowledge about emotion. It refers to semantic knowledge—what we know about emotion in general—but it also consists of episodic knowledge about our emotional experiences. Representation units of this system are discrete concepts and images about the different elements of emotional situations. These concepts are linked with one another through specific semantic or episodic relationships. Knowledge at the propositional level can be activated willfully and consciously. It constitutes the basis for conscious identification of emotion, for verbal communication about emotion, for the recollection of past emotional experiences, as well as for the imaginary projection in future experiences; therefore, it also allows for willful problem solving and coping in emotional situations.

Emotional processing in multilevel theories

As mentioned above, different types of processes operate on the information contained in the associative/schematic and conceptual/propositional systems. These processes differ in terms of automaticity/voluntariness, in terms of consciousness, and in terms of the output they produce. At the schematic level, processes are automatic and unconscious. The activation of any facet of a schema arouses the whole representation. An important aspect of these automatic processes is that activation is bi-directional. Indeed, as these representations are associative in nature, information can flow in one direction as well as in the other. For instance, a schema can activate a specific body response system. Conversely, the activation of a response system can trigger a related schema. At the neurological level, this circular activation has been described as an "as if" loop in the brain, in which central body makers can reactivate a "primary" emotion representation (Bechara, 2004). A large literature has demonstrated that the activation of a specific body state activates the other facets of the corresponding emotion responses, be it via the face (Matsumoto, 1987), the posture (Stepper & Strack, 1993) or respiration (Philippot, Chapelle, & Blairy, 2002).

Similarly, while perceptual indices automatically activate the related schema, the activation of a schema will automatically influence the perceptual system by lowering the perceptual threshold for indices that have been associated with the schema. There is ample evidence of this phenomenon in the clinical literature. For instance, trait social anxiety, that can be conceptualized as the chronic activation of a social fear schema, is characterized by a lowered perceptual threshold for threatening face, a very relevant stimulus for the social fear schema (e.g., Mogg & Bradley, 2004).

Finally, the activation of a schema will also automatically prime the conceptual/propositional representations, be it concepts or images, that have been associated with the schema. Conversely, the activation of a conceptual/propositional representation that has been associated with a schema will automatically arouse that schema. To illustrate this point, let's take the example of someone suffering from panic attacks. If that person, when panicking, thus when his panic schema is activated, repeatedly interprets his experience as a heart attack, the concepts and images related to heart attack will become associated with his panic schema. Consequently, the simple sight of the drawing of a heart, or reading the word heart, i.e. the mere activation of that concept, will be sufficient to automatically arouse the panic schema. For instance, this person might experience a panic attack when receiving a Valentine card depicting a heart. Conversely, the panic schema might be activated by the, even unconscious, perception of body sensations associated with panic. In turn, the activation of the panic schema will result in automatic priming of the associated images and concepts, such as those related to heart attack.

In sum, many positive feedback loops reinforce schema activation via automatic processes. These feedbacks are operating at the perceptual, body response, and conceptual levels. Thus, when a schema is activated, it tends to bias the processing of other cognitive systems toward information that has been associated with it. Such instances generate intense emotion activation. Clearly, in multilevel theories of emotion, the arousal of emotional states directly depends on the activation of a schema.

At the propositional level, information can be activated automatically, such as in priming, but it can also be accessed consciously. Networks of concepts and images and their relations are then sufficiently activated to be transferred into working memory and to become conscious. We can thus deliberately activate our knowledge about emotion, identify and label our emotional states, recollect past emotional experiences, talk about them, and make decisions about how to behave. It should be noted that when a network of conceptual information about an emotional experience is activated, it is likely that that network comprises some concepts or images that have been associated with a schema, and some that have not. For instance, the person suffering from panic attack evoked above might remember his last experience of panic attack. This memory will comprise elements that are unlikely to be related to the panic schema, such as when and where it happened, what the person was doing, etc., and elements that are likely to be associated with the panic schema, such as bodily sensations that have been felt, the fact that the person thought he was having a heart attack, etc., i.e. elements that have been repeatedly experienced during panics. The activation of these latter elements, during the recollection of the memory, will automatically trigger the panic schema, potentially resulting in an intense emotional arousal, including body responses.

This latter point is crucial for understanding the relationship between the processing of emotional information at a conceptual level, i.e. consciously thinking about emotion, and the seemingly automatic activation of emotion at the associative/schematic level that potentially generates states of intense arousal. The dual memory model proposes direct links between these two levels through the concept/images stored at the conceptual level, that have been associated with a schema. Through such associations, a schema may prime concepts and images at the conceptual level, and conversely, concepts and images can activate the associated schema.

Such associations bear important functions. Most importantly, they allow for the activation of an emotional state during the evocation of a past emotional experience, or during the imagination of a future possible experience. It is through such associations that emotion would actually be aroused during the activation of emotional information, allowing for "hot cognitions." The capacity to mentally instantiate an emotional event is central to many psychological processes related to self-regulation. It allows for the development of reflexive (autonoetic) consciousness (Wheeler,

Stuss, & Tulving, 1997), a state in which one is conscious of being the subject of an experience. Autonoetic consciousness is necessary for remembering specific episodes of our past experience, for imagining how we would feel in a hypothetical future experience. It is thus through such processes that we are able to benefit from each of our specific experiences for problem solving and decision making (e.g., Bechara, 2004; Damasio, 1994). This capacity for autonoetic consciousness would be proper to human adults (Belzung & Philippot, 2007; Wheeler et al., 1997).

However, as noticed by Conway and Pleydell-Pearce (2000), beyond allowing for autonoetic awareness, the capacity of arousing emotion when activating emotional information also bears a cost. If emotional arousal becomes too intense when thinking about emotions, it can interfere in several ways with ongoing emotional information processing. First, according to Yerkes–Dodson's (1908) law, cognitive performance drops when the level of optimal activation is exceeded. Emotional arousal would thus disrupt ongoing processes when reevoking an intense emotion. Second, as developed above, the activation of an emotional schema results in the priming, at the conceptual level, of the concepts and images that have been associated with the schema. Such priming biases information processing toward information that is congruent to the schema. Finally, schema activation also results in a lowered perceptual threshold for information relevant to the schema. This perceptual bias favors schema-congruent information. Each of these three mechanisms can in turn result in a vicious circle leading to increasing schema activation: body arousal, congruent concepts and images, and perceptual indices all feeding back into the emotional schema whose overactivation paralyzes the cognitive system. Obviously, the adaptive advantage of the ability to reinstantiate an emotional state when thinking about emotion might turn into a nightmare if it is not accompanied by the capacity to regulate the activation of these self-instantiate emotional states. What would happen to us, for instance, if each time we think about a past emotion, we would reexperience the emotional state originally felt with its full intensity?

Emotion regulation and specificity of processing in multilevel theories

From the model presented above, it follows that emotion regulation in multilevel theories is primarily a matter of regulating the activation of emotional schemata. As such activation rests on automatic processes, the regulation of the schema is indirect and operates through the down-regulation of the perceptual, bodily, and conceptual feedback loops that maintain or increase schema activation. When emotions are cognitively activated, i.e., when emotions are aroused by thinking about past or future emotional experiences, the main feedback loop to be regulated is the reciprocal links between the emotional schema and the concepts/images that have been associated with it.

How does this relate to the level of specificity in processing emotional information? Overgenerality in information processing mostly refers to the activation of generic categories of repeated experiences, for instance, "each time I am going to the swimming pool," while specificity refers to unique instances of experience. By definition, generic information is constituted by elements that are repeatedly activated during a given type of experience; they constitute its prototype. Because of the repeated nature of these generic elements, they are very likely to be associated with an emotional schema. To refer to a previous example, if most of the times that X experiences a panic attack, X thinks he is victim of a heart failure, the concepts and images related to heart failure will be part of the generic representation of the panic attack, and will become associated with the panic schema.

Our proposal is that in an overgeneral mode of processing, generic conceptual information is predominantly activated. As this information is likely to be associated with emotional schema, overgeneral processing will favor the establishment of feedback loops between generic concepts/images and the corresponding emotional schema, resulting in increasing emotion activation. In contrast, in a specific mode, a wide range of information needs to be activated, in particular, the unique information that defines the specificity of the event, and that is clearly contrasted with generic information. Thus, to mentally construct a specific emotional episode, one needs to activate the unique information that signs this episode, and to resist the natural tendency of favoring generic information. Indeed, because of its more general and repeated nature, generic information is cognitively more accessible than unique information. Foremost, because of feedback loops with the emotional schema, generic information is particularly primed during schema activation. As a consequence, the mental construction of a specific emotional episode requires important executive resources to maintain the attention on information relevant to the task: i.e. specific and unique information, while attention is automatically attracted to generic information related to the emotional schema. These executive resources might also comprise a functional inhibition of emotional structures as evidenced by neuroimaging research (Bush, Luu, & Posner, 2000; Drevets & Raichle, 1998). In contrast, overgeneral processing does not necessitate such important executive resources (e.g., Williams et al., 2006).

This theoretical proposal bears two implications. First, if executive resources are lacking, or are disturbed by too intense arousal, the mental construction of emotional episodes will mostly comprise generic information, resulting in an overgeneral mode of processing. This would explain the fact that clinical populations characterized by executive deficits (e.g., depression, schizophrenia) or intense physiological arousal (e.g., post-traumatic stress disorder and general anxiety disorder) are also characterized by an overgeneral mode of processing emotional information.

The second implication is that overgeneral processing of emotional information, because it mostly relies on generic information, favors the activation of emotional schema, and hence of emotional arousal. In contrast, specific processing implies the control of schema activation. It should be noted that this prediction is counter-intuitive and opposed to the naïve theory that we have presented above. It constitutes the tenet of our theoretical argument that the naïve theory is likely to be false. Disentangling what theory is correct, i.e. whether specifying emotion information results in the down or up regulation of emotion intensity, bears important implications for our understanding of the cognitive regulation of emotion. It would also offer a valuable cue for optimizing emotional processing in psychotherapy. The following sections are devoted to a research program from our laboratory that tested the naïve theory against the counter-intuitive prediction derived from multilevel theories of emotion.

THE EMOTIONAL CONSEQUENCES OF SPECIFYING EMOTION

In a first series of experiments, we directly investigated the emotional consequences of overgeneral versus specific mode of processing emotional episodes (Philippot, Schaefer, & Herbette, 2003). In a first experimental session, participants were invited to report personal memories related to particular emotions. These memories were categorized as general or specific according to Williams's (1996) definition. In a second experimental session, before undergoing an emotion induction procedure, participants were primed with two of these memories. According to the experimental condition, participants were primed with either overgeneral or specific memories in order to activate a general or specific mode of processing. In a control condition, participants had to find synonyms and antonyms of common neutral words. In the first study, emotion induction consisted of reliving a recent negative experience through a mental imagery procedure. Results showed that participants reported more intense emotion when primed with overgeneral memories than when primed with specific memories or when they completed the control task. A second study replicated these results with a different method of emotion induction (exposing participants to film excerpts) and different types of emotion: joy, anger, fear, and sadness. All emotion conditions displayed the same pattern of results, although it was statistically significant only for joy and anger. Overall, the results of these two studies suggest that people's naïve theory is incorrect and support the prediction of the dual memory model: Priming a general mode of processing emotional information resulted in more intense emotions than did priming a specific mode of processing.

One could object that emotional memories were primed at a specific or a general level *before* emotion induction. Participants were not explicitly instructed to process information at a general or a specific level *during* emotion induction. This procedure was chosen to ensure perfectly similar and comparable emotion induction conditions and to avoid biases due to different instructions during emotion induction. However, this conservative choice bears the limitation that one does not know whether the effect observed is due to the priming procedure itself or to the mode of information processing that has been primed and applied during the subsequent emotion induction procedure. To overcome this limitation, another study was designed (Schaefer et al., 2003). In that study, participants were trained to generate emotional mental imagery. In addition, during imagery trials, participants had to repeat sentences reflecting a particular way of appraising the scenario and to imagine that these sentences were their own thoughts occurring during the situation being imagined. The overgeneral or specific mode of processing was manipulated using one of two sets of sentences. For the overgeneral mode, metaphoric sentences reflecting a generic way of appraising the situation were used (e.g., "Everything collapses around me"). For the specific mode, explicit questions about specific emotional elements of the scenario were used ("Is this situation important for me?"). This procedure was used with scenarios of joy, anger, tenderness, sadness, and a neutral state. Heart rate and brain activity (recorded via a PET scanner) were recorded during baseline and imagery trials. Participants reported the intensity of their feeling state after each trial. The results of this study clearly showed that for all emotions, participants reported more intense feelings for the overgeneral condition than for the specific one. These subjective reports were corroborated by heart rate differences. Finally, brain activity clearly differentiated the two modes of processing: Specifically, the overgeneral mode of processing was associated with increased activity in the ventromedial prefrontal cortex, whereas the specific mode was associated with activation of the dorsolateral prefrontal cortex. These results were replicated in another study that did not use brain activity recording (Schaefer & Philippot, 2000). In sum, specific processing of emotional information during emotion induction via mental imagery results in less intense emotion, at the subjective and physiological levels, and in a differentiated brain activation pattern than overgeneral processing.

In further experiments (Neumann & Philippot, 2006), rather than manipulating general versus specific mode of processing, we directly attempted to activate either generic or unique information. In one of these studies, participants were invited to relive in imagery two negative and two positive personal memories. The imagery was guided by specific questions that manipulated the type of information that was elaborated, either generic or specific. Generic information concerned mostly the type of body sensations that are typical of the considered emotion; the specific information was about contextual details, such as where and when the episode occurred. In two consecutive studies, activating generic information resulted in a more intense emotional feeling state than activating specific information, the control condition (no instruction) falling in-between. This effect was observed for positive as well as for negative emotions. In a third study, participants recollected specific emotional experiences and were either constrained to identify and specify elements that they typically experience in that type of situation (generic condition), or elements that were uniquely experienced in that situation (unique condition). Again, the specification of unique elements yielded less intense reported emotion than the specification of generic elements.

Altogether, these results suggest that specifying emotional information reduces the emotional arousal generated by emotional information processing. However, this reduction only operates when the focus of attention is the information that is unique to the emotional episode considered. In other words, congruently with our theoretical model, it only operates when the elements activated are not related to an emotional schema.

If these results support our counter-intuitive hypothesis, it should be noted that, in none of the reported experimental situations were the participants attempting to rein in a negative emotional state. Rather, they were either trying to produce an emotional state (during mental imagery trials) or, at best, trying not to regulate their emotion (when exposed to film excerpts, or when recollecting past experiences). As most emotional disorders are characterized by a failure to keep negative emotions in check, one may wonder how well our results generalize to clinically relevant situations in which people tend to down regulate their emotion.

To address this question, we conducted another set of studies (Philippot et al., 2006) in which a state of anxious apprehension was induced: Participants were expecting to give an oral presentation and to be evaluated based on their presentation. Before the presentation, participants were proposed a mental training task to help them diminish their anxiety. According to the condition to which they were assigned, participants performed one of three tasks: a specific thinking task, a general thinking task, and a control task. In all three tasks, participants listened to a ten-minute audiotape of questions to which they were instructed to answer mentally. In the specific thinking task, questions required participants to specify in detail their worries about the speech. In the general thinking task, questions addressed general impressions and meanings evoked by their worries about the speech. In the control task, participants distracted themselves in finding antonyms of a series of nonemotional words. The three allegedly anxiety regulating tasks were judged equally effective by the participants. Participants reported the intensity of their anxiety before and after the manipulation. Confirming the counter-intuitive prediction, results showed that anxiety and fear diminished very significantly in the specific thinking condition ($\eta^2 = .52$), whereas these feelings tended to increase in the general thinking condition and to remain stable in the control condition.

However, one alternative explanation of the preceding findings is that the specific thinking instructions led participants to reappraise the emotional meaning of the situation. Indeed, anticipating fears of ridicule in situations of speech may often be exaggerated. Specifying one's experience in such a situation might have made more apparent the exaggerated aspect of these fears and led participants to reappraise the situation in a less threatening way, thereby reducing the intensity of their anxiety. To examine this possibility, another study (Philippot et al., 2006) using the same procedure was designed. In addition to the general thinking condition, a catastrophizing condition required participants to specify their worst fears and worries and a reappraisal situation constrained them to reevaluate the situation in a positive manner, specifying the beneficial aspects of that experience. Results revealed that while anxiety tended to increase in the general condition, it significantly diminished in the two specific (catastrophizing and reappraisal) conditions, suggesting that specific thinking has a direct effect on emotion regulation, without necessary mediation via reappraisal.

In a further study (Philippot, Muller, & Vrielynck, 2007), students had to actually perform a speech, and the recording of their performance was objectively evaluated by judges. Before the speech, they were proposed one of the three training tasks, inducing either specific processing, general processing, or distraction. The results show that the more participants specified their worries, the better their objective performance was, and the less anxious they were. Another interesting finding of this study is that those actual effects of specification were obtained in participants who had reported an opposite naïve theory in a previous session. Indeed, in that session, participants were interviewed about their belief regarding the emotional consequences of thinking specifically or overgenerally about an upcoming emotional experience. They had clearly reported that more emotion was to be expected as a result of specific thinking as compared to general thinking.

Taken as a whole, these results suggest that the down regulatory effect of specifying the unique aspects of emotional experience can be applied to the regulation of negative emotions in clinically relevant situations. It has effects not only upon feeling states, but also upon physiological arousal (e.g., Schaefer et al., 2003), and behavioral performance. We have also shown in further studies that specifying experiences, even of failure, has a positive effect on self-efficacy beliefs (van Lede, Neumann, Galland, Bourgeois, & Philippot, 2007), a variable of primary importance in clinical condition (Bandura, 1982). Still, these results have to be replicated in real clinical populations. We are presently conducting such experiments with highly socially anxious individuals.

SUMMARY AND CONCLUSIONS

The present chapter stems from the notion that the way people think about their emotions determines how they regulate them. More particularly, we focused on the level of specificity at which emotions are cognitively processed. Indeed, the clinical literature has evidenced that overgenerality in processing emotion characterizes many psychopathological conditions. For instance, it is associated with depression vulnerability and it characterizes anxious rumination.

Several authors (e.g., Borkovec, 2002; Williams, 1996) have proposed that overgenerality in processing emotion is an avoidant coping strategy: By remaining more general and more abstract, people would seek to avoid painful acute feeling states associated with specific experiences. This interpretation is partly corroborated by the naïve theory, shared by many individuals, that specifying emotional information increases emotional arousal, while thinking generally of an emotion, maintains arousal at a stable average intensity. Our research has shown that not only is such a naïve theory prevalent in the general population, but also it is even more discriminant in populations suffering from emotional disorders. Thus, although allegedly effective in the short run, this avoidant coping would bear a long term cost as it results in a failure in emotional processing: Too general and abstract emotional information would be impossible to disconfirm and modify.

However, a wealth of studies conducted in our laboratory, and replicated in other laboratories (Raes, Hermans, Williams, & Eelen, 2006), demonstrate that constraining people to process emotional information specifically yields beneficial outcomes, suggesting that the naïve theory is incorrect, at least under certain conditions. As compared to overgeneralizing, specifying emotional information results in less intense emotional feelings and physiological arousal, in increased sense of self-efficacy, and in more adapted behavior and performance. These effects seem to be similar, whether the specification process is applied to past, present or future experiences.

Our research suggests that certain conditions are necessary for the occurrence of these beneficial effects of specifying emotional information. First, the process of specification has to be voluntary. Indeed, according to the underling theoretical model, a key element rests in the mobilization of executive resources to fully explore the emotional experience. It has been suggested that such mobilization might have an inhibitory effect on the brain structures supporting schematic activation (Drevets & Raichle, 1998). In contrast, the automatic and direct activation of specific information, such as in flash-back, does not have this characteristic, and might result in intense emotional arousal.

Second, the type of information specified seems determinant. The relevant feature concerns whether the information activated is related to an emotional schema. Our basic proposal is that the activation of schema-related information will lead to emotion arousal. This information is constituted by the concepts and images that, because they were repeatedly activated at the same time as an emotional schema, became associated with it. Schema-related information thus consists of the prototypic and generic information about emotional experiences.

In contrast, the information that makes an event specific is the unique features that were present only during that precise experience. Because of their uniqueness, these features are unlikely to be associated with an emotional schema. Thus, their activation will not feed back into the schema. We propose that the regulatory effect of specifying emotion results from the fact that it implies the activation of information that does not feed back into the emotional schema, and thus prevents the instantiation of feedback loops that increase schema activation. However, maintaining attention on these unique elements requires important executive resources as schema-related generic elements are cognitively more accessible: they are more frequent, and foremost, they are primed by the schema.

An important aspect of our rationale is that emotional regulation is not achieved by a change in emotional information *content*, as it has been proposed by previous theories of emotional information processing (e.g., Foa & McNally, 1996). Rather, we propose that it is the change in *processing mode*, and more specifically in strategic attention allocation to unique features of emotional experience, that results in beneficial regulation. Indeed, not only does the specification process down regulate emotional arousal, but it also promotes a better knowledge of the self, by contributing to the building of a specific and detailed data bank about one's experiences. Such knowledge is necessary for effective interpersonal and personal problem solving, and for reducing the tension between the ideal and the real selves.

The gap between naïve theory and empirical evidence regarding the effect of specification on emotion regulation might constitute a maintenance factor for emotional disorders. Indeed, avoiding experiencing specific memories/predictions emotionally implies being deprived of an opportunity to learn how to regulate emotional arousal, how to maximize problem solving capacities, and ultimately how to be in touch with one's unique present experience. As proposed by Barlow et al. (2004), most emotional disorders result from an attempt to avoid emotions that are perceived as intolerable. In this perspective, general processing of emotion certainly constitutes an important mechanism of avoidance.

REFERENCES

Baer, R. A. (2003). Mindfulness training as a clinical intervention: A conceptual and empirical review. *Clinical Psychology: Science and Practice, 10*, 125–143.

Bandura, A. (1982). Self-efficacy mechanism in human agency. *American Psychologist, 37*, 122–147.

Barlow, D. H., Allen, L. B., & Choate, M. L. (2004). Towards a unified treatment for emotional disorders. *Behavior Therapy, 35*, 205–230.

Bechara, A. (2004). A neural view of the regulation of complex cognitive functions by emotion. In P. Philippot & R. S. Feldman (Eds.), *The regulation of emotion* (pp. 3–32). New York: Erlbaum.

Beck, A. T., Emery, G., & Greenberg, R. L. (1985). Cognitive structures and anxiogenic rules. In A. T. Beck, G. Emery, & R. L. Greenberg (Eds.), *Anxiety disorders and phobias* (pp. 54–66). New York: Basic Books.

Belzung, C., & Philippot, P. (2007). *Anxiety from a phylogenetic perspective: Is there a qualitative difference between human and animal anxiety?* Manuscript under review.

Borkovec, T. D. (2002). Life in the future versus life in the present. *Clinical Psychology: Science and Practice, 9*, 76–80.

Borkovec, T. D., & Hu, S. (1990). The effect of worry on cardiovascular response to phobic imagery. *Behaviour Research and Therapy, 28*, 69–73.

Borkovec, T. D., & Inz, J. (1990). The nature of worry in generalized anxiety disorder: A predominance of thought activity. *Behaviour Research and Therapy, 28*, 153–158.

Brewin, C. R. (2001). A cognitive neuroscience account of posttraumatic stress disorder and its treatment. *Behaviour Research and Therapy, 39*, 373–393.

Bush, G., Luu, P., & Posner, M. I. (2000). Cognitive and emotional influences in anterior cingulated cortex. *Trends in Cognitive Science, 4*, 215–222.

Conway, M. A., & Pleydell-Pearce, C. W. (2000). The construction of autobiographical memories in the self-memory system. *Psychological Review, 107*, 261–288.

Dalgleish, T. (2004). Cognitive approaches to posttraumatic stress disorder: The evolution of multirepresentational theorizing. *Psychological Bulletin, 130*, 228–260.

Damasio, A. R. (1994). *Descartes' error: emotion, reason and the human brain.* New York: Grosset/Putnam.

Drevets, W. C., & Raichle, M. E. (1998). Reciprocal suppression of regional cerebral blood flow during emotional versus higher cognitive processes: Implications for interactions between emotion and cognition. *Cognition & Emotion, 12*, 353–385.

Foa, E. B., & McNally, R. J. (1996). Mechanisms of change in exposure therapy. In R. M. Rapee (Ed.), *Current controversies in the anxiety disorders* (pp. 329–343). New York: Guilford.

Goddard, L., Dritschel, B., & Burton, A. (1996). Role of autobiographical memory in social problem solving and depression. *Journal of Abnormal Psychology, 105*, 609–616.

Harvey, A. G., Bryant, R. A., & Dang, S. T. (1998). Autobiographical memory in acute stress disorder. *Journal of Consulting and Clinical Psychology, 66*, 500–506.

Hayes, S. C. (2002). Acceptance, mindfulness, and science. *Clinical psychology: Science and practice, 9*, 55–68.

Leventhal, H. (1984). A perceptual motor theory of emotion. In K. Scherer and P. Ekman (Eds.), *Approaches to emotion* (pp. 271–291). Hillsdale, NJ: Erlbaum.

Matsumoto, D. (1987). The role of facial responses in the experience of emotion: More methodological problems and a meta-analysis. *Journal of Personality and Social Psychology, 52*, 769–774.

McNally, R. J., Lasko, N. B., Macklin, M. L., & Pitman, R. K. (1995). Autobiographical memory disturbance in combat-related posttraumatic stress disorder. *Behaviour Research and Therapy, 33*, 619–630.

Mogg, K., & Bradley, B. P. (2004). A cognitive-motivational perspective on the processing of threat information and anxiety. In J. Yiend (Ed.), *Cognition, emotion and psychopathology: Theoretical, empirical and clinical directions* (pp. 68–85). New York: Cambridge University Press.

Moses, E. B., & Barlow, D. H. (2006). A new unified treatment approach for emotional disorders based on emotion science. *Current Directions in Psychological Science, 15*, 146–150.

Neumann, A., & Philippot, P. (2006). *Emotional feeling intensity as a function of the type of information activated during the specification of an autobiographical memory.* Manuscript under review.

Philippot, P., Baeyens, C., & Douilliez, C. (2006). Specifying emotional information: Regulation of emotional intensity via executive processes. *Emotion, 6*, 560–571.

Philippot, P., Baeyens, C., Douilliez, C., & Francart, B. (2004). Cognitive regulation of emotion. In P. Philippot & R. S. Feldman (Eds.), *The regulation of emotion* (pp. 71–100). New York: Erlbaum.

Philippot, P., Chapelle, C., & Blairy, S. (2002). Respiratory feedback in the generation of emotion. *Cognition & Emotion, 16*, 605–627.

Philippot, P., Muller, V., & Vrielynck, N. (2007). *Emotional and behavioral consequences of specifying anxious apprehension in a public speech situation.* Manuscript in preparation.

Philippot, P., Schaefer, A., & Herbette, G. (2003). Consequences of specific processing of emotional information: Impact of general versus specific autobiographical memory priming on emotion elicitation. *Emotion, 3*, 270–283.

Raes, F., Hermans, D., Williams, J. M. G., & Eelen, P. (2006). Reduced autobiographical memory specificity and affect regulation. *Cognition & Emotion, 20*, 402–429.

Schaefer, A., & Philippot, P. (2000, August). *Schematic and reflexive processing during an emotion-inducing task.* XIth conference of the International Society for Research on Emotions, Québec City, Canada.

Schaefer, A., Collette, F., Philippot, P., van der Linden, M., Laureys, S., Delfiore, G., et al. (2003). Neural correlates of hot and cold emotions: A multilevel approach to the functional anatomy of emotion. *Neuroimage, 18*, 938–949.

Segal, Z. V., Williams, J. M. G., & Teasdale, J. D. (2002). *Mindfulness-based cognitive therapy for depression: A new approach to preventing relapse.* New York: Guilford.

Stepper, S., & Strack, F. (1993). Proprioceptive determinants of affective and nonaffective feelings. *Journal of Personality and Social Psychology, 64*, 211–220.

Stoeber, J., & Borkovec, T. D. (2002). Reduced concreteness of worry in GAD: Findings from a therapy study. *Cognitive Therapy and Research, 26*, 89–96.

Taylor, S. E., Pham, L. B., Rivkin, A. D., & Armot, D. A. (1998). Harnessing the imagination: Mental simulation, self-regulation, and coping. *American Psychologist, 53*, 429–439.

Teasdale, J. D., & Barnard P. J. (1993). *Affect, cognition and change: Remodelling depressive thought.* Hove, UK: Erlbaum.

van Lede, M., Neumann, A., Galland, B., Bourgeois, E., & Philippot, P. (2007). *Autobiographical memory specificity: Impact of state and trait specificity on academic self-efficacy beliefs.* Manuscript under review.

van Vreeswijk, M. F., & de Wilde, E. J. (2004). Autobiographical memory specificity, psychopathology, depressed mood and the use of the Autobiographical Memory Test: A meta-analysis. *Behaviour Research and Therapy, 42*, 731–743.

Wheeler, M. A., Stuss, D. A. T., & Tulving, E. (1997). Toward a theory of episodic memory: The frontal lobes and autonoetic consciousness. *Psychological Bulletin, 121*, 331–354.

Williams, J. M. G. (1996). Depression and the specificity of autobiographical memory. In D. C. Rubin (Ed.), *Remembering our past: Studies in autobiographical memory* (pp. 244–267). Cambridge: Cambridge University Press.

Williams, J. M. G., Chan, S., Crane, C., Barnhofer, T., Eade, J., & Healy, H.

(2006). Retrieval of autobiographical memories: The mechanisms and consequences of truncated search. *Cognition and Emotion, 20,* 351–382.

Williams, J. M. G., Ellis, N. C., Tyers, C., Healy, H., Rose, G., & MacLeod, A. K. (1996). The specificity of autobiographical memory and imageability of the future. *Memory and Cognition, 24,* 116–125.

Williams, J. M. G., Stiles, W. B., & Shapiro, D. A. (1999). Cognitive mechanisms in avoidance of painful and dangerous thoughts: Elaborating the assimilation model. *Cognitive Therapy and Research, 23,* 285–306.

Yerkes, R. M., & Dodson, J. D. (1908). The relation of strength of stimulus to rapidity of habit-formation. *Journal of Comparative Neurology and Psychology, 18,* 459–482.

9

Socio-Emotional Processing Competences: Assessment and Clinical Application

Martin Peper and Roland Vauth

Supported by grants of the Deutsche Forschungsgemeinschaft (Pe 499/3).

The different social factors and underlying neurobiological mechanisms that may influence and compromise an effective regulation of emotion have a direct relevance for many clinical fields of application. Severe mental disorders such as schizophrenia, for example, are typically associated with profound social and emotional information processing deficits (e.g., Hooker & Park, 2002; Lee, Farrow, Spence, & Woodruff, 2004). In these patients, disorders of socio-emotional information processing may predict those social skill deficits that also limit their personal functioning in everyday life. Subgroups of psychotic patients may show specific profiles of symptoms or deficits in this domain (Penn, Corrigan, Bentall, Racenstein, & Newman, 1997; Vauth, Rüsch, Wirtz, & Corrigan, 2004). Patients of the forensic services, to give another example, also tend to show more or less severe problems in emotion regulation, emotional behavior, and coping skills: depending on the individual disorder and comorbid conditions such as substance abuse, the deficit may emerge, for example, as an impaired control of emotional or motivational impulses (e.g., Bufkin & Luttrell, 2005; Myers, Husted, Safarik, & O'Toole, 2006). However, a reduced emotionality, such as poor comprehension of socio-emotional signals or victim empathy is also a common symptom in certain delinquents with personality disorders such as psychopathy (e.g., Sommer et al., 2006).

These examples illustrate the obvious fact that mental disorders are associated with quite heterogeneous profiles of socio-emotional functioning and indicate that emotion processing deficits are among the most promi- nent dysfunctions (Cohen, Forbes, Mann, & Blanchard, 2006; Stieglitz & Vauth, 2005; Vauth, 2004; Vauth et al., 2004). Common problems of these patients are related to perceptual and experiential aspects of emo- tion, deficits of recognition, and production of affective behaviors such as facial or vocal cues, as well as to the control and management of emotion and cognitive resources under stressful conditions.

Among the etiological determinants, neurobiological factors have been identified that suggest abnormalities of neurotransmission; dysfunction of limbic forebrain, amygdala, hippocampus, and basal ganglia; hyper- or hypoactivation of frontal lobe functioning, etc. (for reviews, see Blake- more & Frith, 2004; Harris, 2003; Phillips, Drevets, Rauch, & Lane, 2003a, b). In addition to hard-wired and genetically based determinants of schizophrenia, social or environmental factors have a considerable impact on the course of illness.

The individual patient as well as patient subgroups may show deficit patterns that are specific to the person or disorder and to the emotional or motivational stimulus condition. A detailed evaluation of the functional profile seems to be critical to differential diagnosis as well as for decisions on treatment and rehabilitation options. It is evident that the selection of a specific assessment approach has important implications for the patient and the involved mental health professionals.

In the field of legal expert assessments, for example, it is of interest whether some patients might be a cause of danger for the public (e.g., due to a lack of impulse control in certain patients with Cluster B personality disorders). Obviously, an appropriate decision depends on a qualified as- sessment of the specific disorder of emotional control in question. Never- theless, it is typical for the present state of assessment that procedures challenging the specific symptoms or disorders, and thus possessing a certain validity for everyday life functioning, are rarely available. Social- emotional processing competences appear to possess a particular predic- tive value that can be explored in the context of intervention programs.

Since the psychosocial outcome of (cognitive) rehabilitation programs appears to be limited, it is useful to explore the particular barriers to suc- cessful psychosocial treatment and rehabilitation (Vauth et al., 2004). Cog- nitive deficits (vigilance, memory, and executive functioning) and negative symptoms have clearly been shown to limit treatment and rehabilitation readiness, that is, the ability to benefit from interventions. Nevertheless, cognitive dysfunctions, that is, nonsocial information processing defi- cits, appear to have only a limited predictive value for social functioning (Barch, 2005; Hooker & Park, 2002). In contrast, appropriate processing of socio-emotional information has a greater external validity and provides an improved understanding of the patient's social competences and problems in everyday life (Penn et al., 1997; Vauth et al., 2004).

Thus, a first central purpose of psychometric assessments of socio-emotional functioning is a better discrimination of persons with mental disorders. Appropriate assessments provide an improved data base supporting the categorization of patients (i.e., a diagnostic aid). How can socio-emotional information processing best be assessed and how might this help in differential diagnosis? A second aim is to improve the assignment of persons to treatment procedures to maximize treatment success (i.e., an indication aid). Which measures will predict successful rehabilitation? How can successful treatment and relapse prevention be assessed? A third reason to inspect socio-emotional functions is that the intervention technology itself may be derived from the respective theories.

A scientific evaluation of these different aspects would require an in-depth analysis based on the pertinent theoretical and methodological considerations related to assessment and nosology, as well as to the formal principles of clinical decision making (Brune, 2001; Lenzenweger, 1999). Due to lack of space, we have to focus our review here on some important aspects that, in our view, appear to be central from a practical and clinical perspective. We emphasize here the association of neuropsychological findings pertaining to emotion regulation processes on one hand and their practical consequences for devising psychotherapy intervention programs on the other (Grawe, 1998).

The present chapter first reviews the basic constructs and functional components that form the building blocks of socio-emotional competences and behaviors. The hierarchically organized dimensional structure of socio-emotional abilities is scrutinized. Secondly, we provide a brief overview and taxonomy of available assessment procedures. Thirdly, we consider the relevance of socio-emotional constructs and their implications for the treatment of patients with psychiatric diseases. A rehabilitation program for patients with schizophrenia is briefly summarized that focuses on the training of high-level socio-emotional skills.

Finally, the different low- and high-level constructs are integrated into a neuropsychological working model of emotion regulation. We suggest an executive core processing system that contains the hierarchically organized connectional pattern of prefrontal brain areas on one side and the structure of socio-emotional and cognitive functioning on the other. Taken together, this review reflects the necessity to assess, evaluate, and treat emotional regulation processes in a much broader, systematic, and more ecologically valid way. Multivariate testing approaches (Eid & Diener, 2006) may help to improve assessment procedures, to test structure–function hypotheses, to guide the diagnostic process, and to devise new treatment programs that are differentially adapted to the individual profile of dysfunction.

 ## ORGANIZATION OF SOCIO-EMOTIONAL COMPETENCES

The domain of social cognition includes the abilities that originate from the necessity to appreciate and integrate the relatively subtle social and emotional cues of social situations, to acquire and recall social knowledge, to mediate social communication and interaction, to correctly interpret details of nonverbal behavior, and to control socially inadequate responses (Keysers & Gazzola, 2006). Emotions represent fast and flexible systems that provide basic response tendencies for adaptive action (Scherer, 1999) and comprise several subfunctions (for details see Kappas, this volume; Mauss, Bunge, & Gross, this volume; Scherer, 1984; Scherer & Peper, 2001). It is debated whether these component functions are activated in a sequential or a parallel mode during an emotional episode (Scherer, 1999).

Although current theoretical models focus on different components and phases of emotion, the suggested constructs are not entirely independent. Higher-order dimensions can be identified, in which the basic emotional processes can be located as lower-order factors. A hierarchical structure including primary and secondary emotions is well accepted today (Russell, 1994). For example, the basic emotions (Ekman, 1992) can be seen as higher-order factors with respect to the variable outcomes of appraisal processes. The concept of modal emotions (Scherer, 1994) accounts for the existence of a limited number of emotion families, which refer to frequently occurring patterns of appraisal of universally encountered events. The members of these emotion families share some but not all of the distinctive appraisal patterns.

On a lower level, individual emotion family members share common appraisal profiles (Scherer & Peper, 2001; see Table 9.1). The lowest level consists of the continuous adaptational changes that are produced by single appraisals. Examples are the simple defense and orienting responses which are a part of higher-order emotions such as surprise or fear. Thus, different levels can be identified where lower-order functions group together on a higher level. A representative assessment theory of socio-emotional functioning would identify the respective level of the construct, the component function, and the phase of the emotion episode that is addressed. This latent structure of subfunctions needs to be described more precisely to achieve a higher degree of integration and replication.

Table 9.1 Hierarchical organization of hypothetical emotional component functions (according to Scherer & Peper, 2001, modified).

Emotion concepts or domains of function	Basis for high-order grouping	Example
Continuous adaptational changes		Orienting reflex, defense reflex, startle, sympathetic arousal, etc.
Basic, fundamental, discrete, modal emotions or emotion families	Similarity of appraisal, motivational consequences, and response patterns; convenient label for appropriate description and communication	Anger, fear, sadness, joy, etc.
Dimensional concepts	Conceptual or meaning space for subjective experience and verbal labels	Valence (positive/negative emotions), approach/ withdrawal, activity (active/passive), control, etc.
Appraisal/response configurations for recurring events/ situations	Temporal coordination of different response systems for a limited period of time as produced by a specific appraisal pattern	Righteous anger, jealousy, mirth, fright, etc.

ASSESSMENT OF SOCIO-EMOTIONAL FUNCTIONS

Taxonomy of data sources

Similar to the domain of cognitive performance, socio-emotional competences and behaviors represent an extremely heterogeneous class of behaviors. Given the relative broad range of relevant functional components, mental operations, materials, and results or products involved, the structure of the "universe" of socio-emotional items needs to be scrutinized. Since a dimensional analysis is a costly endeavor, a starting point would be a description of available items, test materials, and behavioral technologies. A taxonomy of psychometric data (Cattell, 1957) can be applied to the socio-emotional domain in a first attempt to categorize assessment instruments (see Table 9.2).

Table 9.2 Taxonomy of data and error sources in the assessment of socio-emotional measures (cf. Cattell, 1957, modified).

Level	Self-descriptions	Behavior descriptions by observers		Medical data and physiological functions
	Self-report (Q), self-observation	Life data (L), behavior rating (BR)	Objective tests (L, T), behavior observation (BO)	Objective tests (T)
Data source	Subject	Observer	Observer / instrument	Observer / instrument
Data range	Reports on emotional experience, behavior; description of emotional perceptions, disorders or disease symptoms	Behavior or responses in natural situations or in the lab	Nonverbal behavior, abilities, communicative behavior, etc.	Physiological functions, biochemical data, medical findings, etc.
Typical methods	Rating scales or self-reports; personality questionnaires, mood state questionnaires. Other methods: narrative reports of present/past experiences, interview data, self-administered protocols of current behavior	Ratings by experts or other observers based on behavior observations, test data or behavior during interview, etc.; scoring of social, emotional, behavioral deviations in everyday life	Direct observation, behavior recordings by means of test apparatus, paper and pencil tests, apparative tests, specific tests of sensory, perceptual, or cognitive function, response bias scales	Symptoms of emotional disorders from chart, physiological registrations of central and peripheral measures, functional tests, patient history
Reactivity	yes	possible	possible	partially possible
Typical error sources	Implicit concepts of personality, acquiescent response bias, memory recall bias, other types of introspection and self-observation errors	Implicit concepts and theories of the observer, observation errors	Observation errors, erroneous interpretation of instructions, error sources of tests and instruments	Observation errors, errors of registration and measurement devices, influences of medication, metabolic activity, etc.

Whereas neuro-emotional research approaches typically use nonstandardized T data (physiological and behavioral functions), clinical assessment procedures prefer standardized Q, BR, and BO data. According to the triple response measurement strategy, the assessment of emotional behavior should include responses in the verbal, gross motor, and physiological (autonomic, cortical, neuromuscular) response systems (Lang, Rice, & Sternbach, 1972). However, the well-known response fractionation or inconsistency indicates a lack of covariation of the different data types.

Instrumentation and assessment methods

The socio-emotional domain has been labeled quite differently by psychometric handbooks or test archives: tests of emotional or adaptive emotional functions, emotional intelligence, or personality (Spies & Plake, 2006; Educational Testing Service, 2007). Textbooks of neuropsychological assessment subsume socio-emotional functions under the chapters on mood, personality, and adaptive function (Strauss, Sherman, & Spreen, 2006) or personal adjustment and emotional functioning (Lezak, Howieson, & Loring, 2004). It is an obvious fact that methods to assess emotional functioning occupy relatively little space in comparison to behavioral and cognitive tests—at least in neuropsychology handbooks. This might be attributed in part to a certain reluctance concerning subjective data, a lack of satisfaction with available behavioral procedures, or to the fact that—due to the multitude of relevant data sources—this is a particularly complex area.

The social necessity to assess emotion regulation behaviors in various contexts is reflected by a vast number of available instruments for different operational areas. The total number of relevant test publications available in English can be retrieved from the thousands of publication records documented, for example, by online test archives (e.g., Educational Testing Service, 2007) or the *Mental Measurements Yearbook,* which summarizes assessment instruments in the fields of psychology (Spies & Plake, 2006).

In an attempt to locate relevant English language tests, we inspected the Educational Testing Service (2007) records for the social and emotional domain (N = 838 tests since 1938) that are currently in use to assess socio-emotional function in adults. We limited this set of records to those published from 1990 to the present (N = 180). Regarding the above data categories, the self-report questionnaire is the most frequent method (93%, N = 167), followed by behavior ratings of experts or significant others (7%, N = 12) and by projective techniques (2%, N = 4). Some instruments use multiple data sources (2%). For the class of physiological methods, no standardized tests could be retrieved.

Self-descriptions

Rating scales, self-report measures, and personality questionnaires are the most frequently used instruments in contemporary clinical practice. With respect to operational areas, the largest group includes medical problems questionnaires which assess self-ratings of general well-being, perception of general health, mental functioning, emotional state or depression, and social performance in healthy persons or individual clinical populations of the physically and mentally ill (38%, N = 68). Here, emotional well-being is just one aspect of health-related quality of life. Another important area is the application of self-ratings to specific types of emotional behavior (e.g., aggression, expressive behavior, emotional needs) or of emotional disturbance conditions (24%, N = 43). Some of these inventories assess emotional experience and psychopathological symptoms (e.g., screening for depression) in accordance with the criteria of the Diagnostic and Statistical Manual of Mental Disorders, 4th ed.

Assessment of interindividual variations of relatively stable socio-emotional dispositions, and of related internal or observable symptoms of emotionality by questionnaire is a typical method. Investigations into individual differences have revealed several personality trait dimensions such as emotionality, extraversion, psychoticism, openness, agreeableness, and other related constructs that possess a certain stability and transsituational consistency. Inventories that focus on personality traits or stable behavioral disorders account for 17% (N = 30) of the test sample.

Another cluster of questionnaires includes scales to assess coping with emotional distress (10%, N = 18). Here, the subject may describe task-oriented, emotion-oriented, and avoidance-oriented coping behaviors or coping behaviors associated with the stressful effects of medical problems, health related behaviors, or diseases (see section below, "Assessment of emotional regulation competences"). Other instruments were constructed to evaluate mood regulation, such as self-regulation by withholding negative emotions, or generalized expectancies of negative mood regulation (12%, N = 21).

A number of recent inventories have been constructed to evaluate management of emotional and social affairs (N = 26, 14%). Some of these instruments have been constructed to assess relatively broad constructs ("emotional intelligence," EI), designed for vocational contexts (N = 3; see section "Assessment of emotional regulation competences"). Social support not only augments resilience to stress, but may also increase perceived pressures from the social network, as well as social and emotional dependencies that can be evaluated by means of self-perception scales (2%, N = 4). It is well known that the above Q data may be obscured by implicit concepts and folk psychology theories, acquiescent response bias, memory recall bias, and other types of introspective and self-observation errors (Table 9.2; Kerlinger & Lee, 2000).

Behavior descriptions by observers

Direct behavior observations obtained from experts, staff, relatives, friends, or coworkers can be used to assess, for example, aggressive behaviors, emotional expressiveness, communication style, or other problematic aspects. Emotional control behavior can be evaluated as one aspect among other executive functions. Other methods implement clinical multiaxial inventories for the measurement of psychiatric outcome. Overall, relatively few instruments are available to obtain behavior ratings of others (2%, N = 3).

Free response tasks such as the so called "projective tests" (Rorschach Test and similar techniques) represent a mixture of behavior observation and response ratings during an interview. However, projective tests typically suffer from poor validation, standardization, missing normative data, and observation or interpretation errors as summarized in Table 9.2. Despite the fact that the validity and reliability of "free response" data obtained from projective testing is controversially discussed, many practitioners continue to rely upon this type of data (Lezak et al., 2004).

An alternative approach to verify socio-emotional self-descriptions and personality trait ratings is to evaluate life data, for example, by means of data mining techniques. Here, data are compiled from different sources such as demographic data, public records, court records, property deeds, behavior history records, memberships in organizations, media, public and private databases, and other sources of statistical information. One example are the so-called actuarial instruments that are widely used in forensic psychiatry to aggregate information from various sources (Hilton & Simmons, 2001). These ratings and selection strategies may be flawed by implicit concepts and theories of the observer, by observation errors, and by the error sources of the respective tests or actuarial instruments. Moreover, the variable aggregation levels of the selected measures might induce further reliability problems.

Medical data and physiological function

The complexities and methodological problems associated with assessing and interpreting psychophysiological measures are discussed in Cacioppo,

Tassinary, and Berntson (2000). Physiological measurement is typically used to assess emotional activation (activation, arousal, strain, stress, etc.). Psychophysical reactivity or arousability denotes the dispositional or stimulated variability of activation under certain test conditions. Activation can be described with respect to aspects of valence (quality of emotional experience), directedness (motivational and orientating functions), intensity (global organismic changes), and selectivity (specific patterns of change) (Peper & Fahrenberg, 2007, in press). Objective tests can be used to obtain information pertaining to the level, scatter, and shape of activation variables. The activation patterns may be specific to a certain stimulus, to individual subjects or groups of subjects, and to certain motivational/emotional conditions or contexts (Stemmler, 1992).

It is increasingly accepted that single physiological measures may not be readily used as "objective indicators" of emotion. Selecting one or two "optimal" psychophysiological measures such as electrodermal activity (EDA), heart rate (HR), or startle electromyographic (EMG) activity, to name a few, may neglect other confounders or relevant dimensions of the stimulus situation. More recently, brain imaging technologies have instigated and revived the debate on objective personality tests (see the "lie detection" controversy; Spence et al., 2004). However, the hope for "objective" indicators or even standardized physiological tests of human emotionality has still not been fulfilled. In addition to the typical error sources and confounders summarized in Table 9.2, many technical and methodological limitations remain (Peper, 2006).

PERSPECTIVES OF APPLICATION

Assessment of emotional regulation competences

From the array of socio-emotional measures, one class of procedures is of particular relevance for the present volume as well as for several fields of application: those designed to assess emotional regulation capacities. On a low level of processing, the necessity to regulate emotional reactions is hardwired into the brain to enable such mechanisms as habituation, negative feedback, or protective inhibition. These processes all prevent the organism of excessive (emotional) stimulation (Peper, 2006). On a higher level, behavioral and cognitive regulation processes have been investigated (Gross, 1998; Ochsner & Gross, 2005; cf. Philippot, Neumann, & Vrielynck, this volume; Greenberg & Vandekerckhove, this volume).

For many decades, coping research (Folkman & Lazarus, 1990) has shown that emotional experiences are strongly influenced by cognitive activities that influence attention and alertness (avoidance and escape), vigilance processes (information search and problem solving), as well as cognitive activities. The latter modulate person–situation interactions and actions that change the person–environment relationship. Typical cognitive regulation strategies include rejection and accommodation strategies (Parkinson & Totterdell, 1999). Cognitive work subsumes engagement (reconceptualization, reevaluation strategies such as rationalization or reappraisal) and distraction techniques.

In general, the outcome of coping processes depends on the valence, ambiguity, controllability, and changeability of a stressor (Perrez & Reicherts, 1992). Input-related regulation, i.e. denial, distraction, defense, or cognitive restructuring (Folkman & Lazarus, 1990) or antecedent-focused regulation, i.e. selection, modification, or cognitive restructuring of situational antecedents (Gross, 1998) have been differentiated from response-focused regulation processes such as the suppression of expressive behavior and physiological arousal (Gross, 1998; Mauss et al., this volume). Lazarus (1999) has emphasized the processual character of emotional regulation with variable strategies applied during early and late stages of coping.

A special set of emotional coping functions has been subsumed under the EI construct (see Bar-On & Parker, 2000; Salovey & Mayer, 1990). EI has become popular following a publication by Goleman (1995), which refers to prior work by Salovey and Mayer (1990). It includes a general emotional processing "quotient" as well as specific socio-emotional skills. It represents the capacity to understand and use emotional information (Ciarrochi, Chan, Caputi, & Roberts, 2001), and includes personal, emotional, and social competencies and skills that influence the ability to cope with environmental demands and pressures (Bar-On, 2001). Current EI measurement typically aims at several domains of adaptive function with a variable emphasis on the self-awareness, social awareness, emotional coping and management skills, social skills, emotion–cognition interactions, and stable personality traits and mood dispositions (for an overview, see Table 9.3).

The suggested components of EI represent complex constructs on a high level of generality. The subfunctions are aggregated on a secondary level and involve emotional, motivational, cognitive, and behavioral aspects. Thus, EI emerges as a tertiary factor close to the level of "general personality." An example of how the concept of EI could be implemented in a clinical training program of socio-emotional function is presented in the subsequent section.

Table 9.3 Overview of subconstructs of current emotional intelligence tests.

Test	Self-awareness	Social awareness	Emotional coping skills	Social skills	Emotion–cognition interactions	Personality traits, mood dispositions
Mayer-Salovey-Caruso Emotional Intelligence Test (MSCEIT)	perceive emotions	emotional understanding	manage emotions for personal growth		emotions facilitate thought	
(1990–1999)	emotional self-awareness	emotional understanding	emotional self-management		integrating emotions	
Goleman (1995)	social awareness	emotional comprehension/ empathy	regulate distressing affects, inhibit emotional impulsivity	relationship management social skills	integration of emotion in thinking, emotional reasoning	
Emotional Competence Inventory (ECI)	self-awareness	social awareness	social awareness	relationship management		emotional self-control
Boyatzis & Goleman (2001)	emotional self-awareness/ assessment/ confidence	empathy, organizational awareness, service orientation	self-management	develop others, leadership influence, change catalyst, communication, conflict management, bonding, teamwork, collaboration		trustworthy, conscientious, adaptive, achievement orientation, initiative

Test	Self-awareness	Social awareness	Emotional coping skills	Social skills	Emotion–cognition interactions	Personality traits, mood dispositions
Emotional Intelligence Scale (1998)	alexithymia, attention to feelings, clarity of feelings		impulse control, mood repair			optimism
Emotional Intelligence Style Profile (EISP)	reflective / empathetic EI	conceptual EI	organized EI			
Bar-On Emotional Quotient Inventory (EQ-i) (1998)	intrapersonal components	interpersonal components	stress management components	interpersonal components	adaptability components	general mood
EQ-i:S Short form (2002)	emotional self-awareness	empathy	stress tolerance, impulse control	interpersonal relationship, responsibility	problem solving, reality testing, flexibility	intrapersonal components assertiveness, self-regard/- actualization, independence
Emotional Intelligence Questionnaire (EIQ) (1999, 2000)	self-awareness	interpersonal sensitivity	emotional resilience	influence	decisiveness (EIQ), intuitiveness (EIQ:G)	motivation, conscientiousness, integrity
Emotional Intelligence Instrument (EI) (2000)						maturity, morality, sociability, calm disposition, compassion

	intrapersonal / self-awareness	interpersonal / awareness of others	emotional/ behavioral coping	contact / social skills	categorical/esoteric/ personal superstitious thinking	optimism
Constructive Thinking Inventory (CTI) (2000)			emotional/ behavioral coping		categorical/esoteric/ personal superstitious thinking	optimism
Emotional SMARTS (1998–2002)	awareness skills emotional self-awareness, emotional management, assertiveness, self-actualization	empathy	behavioral skills independence, stress management, impulse control, conflict management	contact skills relationship building, social responsibility	decision-making skills problem identification, creativity, selecting solutions, reality testing	
Leader Emotional Quotient Survey (EQ-s) (2003)	intrapersonal emotional competency emotional self-awareness	interpersonal emotional competency empathy, interpersonal relationship, social responsibility, interdependence	stress management stress tolerance, impulse control, proactivity	conflict management, change management		affect motivation happiness, optimism self-assurance/ -regard/ -actualization
Emotional Judgment Inventory (EJI) (2003)	being aware of emotions, identifying own emotions	identifying others' emotions	managing own emotions, expressing emotions adaptively	managing others' emotions, impression management	emotions in problem solving	

Rehabilitation of socio-emotional disorders

Since the time of Eugen Bleuler, one of the pioneers of schizophrenia research, emotional processing deficits have been regarded as a core feature of schizophrenic dysfunction which is independent of cultural background. Deficits in facial affect recognition are well established (Sachs, Steger-Wuchse, Kryspin-Exner, Gur, & Katschnig, 2004). The relevance of emotion recognition as a predictor of functional outcome has been documented (Hall et al., 2004; Phillips, 2004). In the following, we illustrate the relevance and implications of socio-emotional competences for the treatment of patients with schizophrenia.

There are two main reasons to address socio-emotional information processing deficits in patients with schizophrenia. Firstly, emotional processing deficits may represent "rate-limiting factors" for psychosocial function and response-rate to psychosocial interventions (Vauth et al., 2004). Cognitive behavioral interventions may thus enhance the patient's readiness to rehabilitation and social functioning within the community. Secondly, since emotional information processing deficits play an important role in stress vulnerability, a reduction of such deficits may be an appropriate strategy for general relapse prevention (Horan & Blanchard, 2003).

In spite of the importance of social cognition and emotional processing in schizophrenia, less emphasis has been placed upon the improvement of socio-emotional abilities. Recently, however, training programs have been developed to address the issue of socio-emotional skills and behavior (Hogarty et al., 2004; Penn, Kohlmaier, & Corrigan, 2000; Vauth & Stieglitz, 2001). The "Integrated Psychological Treatment" (Hodel, Kern, & Brenner, 2004) emphasizes general cognitive capabilities, but also incorporates social skill training. Cognitive Enhancement Therapy (Eack, Hogarty, Greenwald, Hogarty, & Keshavan, 2007) is one of the few attempts to address both social processing and cognitive deficits.

Due to growing evidence suggesting that social cognition and emotional processing skills may influence role functioning (Penn et al., 1997; Vauth et al., 2004), some approaches directly focus on this set of functions. We have previously adapted an "Emotional Intelligence Training program" for schizophrenia (Vauth, Dreher-Rudolph, Ueber, & Olbrich, 1997; Vauth et al., 2001). This approach has been developed within the above-described EI framework of Salovey and coworkers (Mayer, Caruso, & Salovey, 2000; Mayer, Salovey, & Caruso, 2000). The first three factors (emotional perception, emotional understanding, and emotional management) constitute the basis of this training program because emotional self-perception, perception of others, and shifting to another perspective were found to compromise social problem-solving and empathy (Mueser, 1993).

The ability to understand emotional information was specifically impaired in schizophrenia. Problems in emotional perspective taking co-occurred with emotional comprehension and reasoning deficits (Greig, Bryson, & Bell, 2004). Emotional management also aims at mood regulation deficits in schizophrenia (Horan & Blanchard, 2003). It is well accepted that persons with schizophrenia tend to cope with negative emotions and stress in a relatively avoidant and ineffectual manner using passive avoidant strategies, reduced reliance on active problem solving, and poor social support seeking (Lysaker, Campbell, & Johannesen 2005; Lysaker, Lancaster, Davis, & Clements, 2003).

Emotional reactivity and subsequent higher stress responsiveness has been demonstrated to be more pronounced in schizophrenia (Cohen & Docherty, 2004). Because higher reactivity to emotional stress was found to be related to the disposition to experience intense aversive emotional states and to a lower tendency to experience positive or rewarding emotional states (Berenbaum & Williams, 1995), our program focuses on both coping with negative emotions as well as the ability to maintain positive emotional states.

Training of socio-emotional regulation competences

Our EI training for patients with schizophrenia is described here as an example of how a remediation of socio-emotional competences can be accomplished. This training schedule consists of 12 sessions during a 6-week period. Two 80-minute sessions per week are administered to patient groups with a mean size of 6–8 participants. In each session, three blocks (emotional perception, emotional understanding, and emotional management) are practiced. These target areas are mostly treated in parallel but with different focuses. Therapist and patient materials have been developed for each session. In the first part of the session, skills related to the perception and interpretation of emotional information are trained. The focus of the second part of each training session is emotional management, that is, to enhance the capacity to self-regulate emotions.

Perception and interpretation of emotions

Discrimination tasks. Patients are requested to distinguish different emotions (Ekman and Friesen series of facial affect expressions). Usually, two pictures are presented to show the difference between the emotional states of the depicted stimulus persons.

Matching tasks. (1) The patient is asked to compare facial affect recognition pictures with his inferences concerning the core emotions of the stimulus person in a written short story (e.g., situations of loss, threat, or enjoyment). (2) To improve self-perception of emotional states, affect recognition and shared feelings are addressed by asking patients to select one or two pictures or objects (e.g., different postcards, scarves, or small stones) presented on a table, which may reflect their current mood. The patient is requested to explain the picture to the group (training of emotional expression). Patients are further encouraged to explore whether other group members validate the emotional meaning, are aware of their own feelings, and are able to share these with others (training of emotional perspective taking). These perception tasks may also be regarded as activation exercises (motivation and promotion of cognitive receptiveness).

Training of social inferences and reasoning in affective social situations. This section focuses on emotional understanding. Here, written short stories describing situations of loss, threat, or enjoyment are given and questions are posed, such as "Describe what was going on," "Why do you think that . . .," "What is the evidence for supposing that . . .," "What do you think, would be the consequence of . . ."

Behavioral analyses. Behavioral analyses are intended to support the development and consolidation of emotional reasoning processes. Here, two patients are requested to interview each other ("reporter exercise") concerning internal or external stimuli that may elicit specific emotional responses.

Self-regulation of emotion

The strategies trained in the second part of each training session include coping with negative affective states such as depression (sessions 1–3) and anxiety (sessions 4–6). In the following sessions, specific strategies for maintaining positive emotional states (sessions 7–9) and developing interests and initiative (sessions 10–12) are elaborated.

The emotional management section starts with a *psychoeducational phase* that provides a rationale for enhancing coping skills for a particular target emotion which aims at both relapse prevention and everyday functioning. The importance of the specific target emotion is elaborated interactively for the participants (e.g., disengagement of therapy or rehabilitation and depression). The role of negative emotion as a destabilizing factor or as a prodromal symptom of an emerging relapse and of positive emotion as a protective factor is discussed. Situational models of individual "vicious circles" (emotion–perception–interpretation–action) are elaborated and "exit" strategies are discussed. Moreover, the neurobiological rationale of pharmacological treatment of negative emotions such as depression and anxiety is provided.

In the following two sessions on each target emotion, this knowledge is individually applied. Here, the aim is to improve coping with negative emotions in subjectively relevant social and job related situations. Personal triggers of negative feelings are elaborated.

Self-recording corresponding with the *ABC-Scheme* (i.e., recording of the activating event, of beliefs and automatic thoughts, and of the consequences) is applied to situations that are experienced as stressful by the individual. Exploring internal and external cues of the respective target emotion and identifying coping strategies is trained by role reversal in a *"reporter" exercise*: "You said that you are depressed after . . .," "What did you think about this?," "How did you try to feel better?" Results are presented to the group and the other participants are requested to make suggestions how to cope more efficiently with the situation.

This section aims at replacing dysfunctional coping strategies such as alcohol and drug consumption or social withdrawal with more efficient techniques. These techniques of appropriate self-management are enhanced by *modeling and rehearsal of additional coping strategies* (such as relaxation techniques, identification and challenge of dysfunctional thoughts, distracting and focusing strategies). Supported by the therapist, each patient chooses a maximum of three coping strategies and records them on "coping cards" that are kept in a pocket or posted in the patient's private environment. The patient is encouraged to read them regularly (e.g., three times a day). These cards may have several forms such as writing a central automatic thought or belief on one side and its adaptive response on the other, devising behavioral strategies for specific problem situations, or arranging activating self-instructions.

The session devoted to the *promotion of positive feelings* involves an elaboration of individual strategies for emotional self-control. The patient learns to apply various techniques to promote positive feelings, to systematically plan positive activities (pleasure-technique), to use self-reinforcement, or to plan periods of enjoyment. In sessions 10–12, strategies for an appropriate leisure-time planning are developed on the level of the individual. Already existing strategies and behaviors such as the identification of significant reinforcers and their contingent use are also promoted.

As an effect of "Cognitive Enhancement Therapy," an improved understanding and managing one's own and others' emotions could be demonstrated (Eack et al., 2007). Although deficits of social perception are typical concomitants of schizophrenia (Kerr & Neale, 1993), it remains a matter of ongoing debate whether impaired emotional perception may be regarded as a specific "trait marker" of schizophrenia (Gaebel & Wölwer, 1992) or not (Bellack & Mueser, 1994).

It also remains unclear whether these deficits represent a general deficit (Corrigan, Green, & Toomey, 1994) or a differential impairment (Archer, Hay, & Young, 1994). Moreover, it is controversial whether emotion perception impairments are limited to the domain of negative emotions (Morrison, Bellack, & Mueser, 1988). Nevertheless, given the close relationship between social processing and social functioning, additional efforts should be made to further develop these therapy approaches (Vauth et al., 2004).

DISCUSSION

There is an enormous demand for validated and standardized assessment of socio-emotional function in many areas of clinical and nonclinical service. Many current diagnostic routine procedures aim at an assessment of partially overlapping emotion regulation functions, symptoms, and deficits. A vast number of published questionnaires demonstrates an extensive reliance of clinicians on self-report data assessing higher-level socio-emotional processing. In contrast, neuropsychological research procedures typically focus on preattentive and automatic aspects of emotional function. Unfortunately, most psychophysiological procedures are not standardized or are less applicable in clinical practice.

Shortcomings of current assessment approaches

The methodological uncertainties associated with introspective methods have been identified ever since the beginnings of psychometric assessment: the operationalization of socio-emotional function by means of self-report and questionnaires remains problematic due to limitations of self-observation, memory, and response biases, etc. (Kerlinger & Lee, 2000). As discussed above, personality research has shown that self-descriptions are based upon personal constructs, that is, subjective representations that poorly converge with other data sources and may be biased by several factors (Myrtek, 1998). Questionnaires to assess regulation (coping) strategies typically fail to differentiate the time range, intensity, and effectiveness of adaptive efforts. Thus, it is not surprising that the predictive power of coping trait scales is relatively low (Mitmansgruber, 2003).

In the EI domain, the expected improvement by introducing a standardized battery of objective behavioral tests has not been achieved. Operationalization and measurement is limited here to a small number of constructs with an unsettled convergent, discriminant, and dimensional validity (e.g., Asendorpf, 2003). Are components that are supposed to belong to the same domain such as self-awareness and awareness of others actually correlated? Can emotional functioning be clearly distinguished from the well-known factors of psychometric intelligence? Obviously, many of the suggested subfunctions rest upon "cognitive" competences such as language, concept formation, perceptual object recognition, theory of mind, or other specific abilities. Thus, it remains uncertain to what extent socio-emotional functioning actually represents an independent dimension. Moreover, this type of assessment fails to considerably exceed what is already known from folk psychology. There is a lack of discriminant or incremental validity in relation to the well-known personality inventories that contain scales to assess, for example, emotionality, extraversion, psychoticism, conscientiousness, or agreeability. Many of these scales and items have been integrated into the above EQ instruments.

Although the EI concept may possess a certain face validity as a potential predictor of private and vocational success, this has not been clearly demonstrated empirically. Long-term studies suggest that personality characteristics may increase vocational success to a lesser degree than suggested (Asendorpf, 2003). Thus, the "capability to help individuals and organizations truly change" very much rests upon the competences of the motivational trainers. Similarly, therapists will have to face the fact that many "basic" socio-emotional component functions of personality are much more stable than expected. It should be kept in mind that habits or temperament traits may certainly not be acquired or changed in a fast and easy way. Thus, in terms of a scientific approach to socio-emotional functioning, the vague operational definitions, the lack of empirical data on dimensionality, convergent and discriminant validity, as well as reliability issues remain major obstacles on the way to a valid testing approach.

Need of objective socio-emotional tests

Mental diseases such as schizophrenia show a clear association with the inherited functional connectivity of brain systems and their structural dynamics (e.g., white matter abnormalities, Kubicki et al., 2007). In particular, the fronto-striatal systems are important target sites in patients with schizophrenia (e.g., Habel et al., 2000). This disease clearly shows the close relationship of brain abnormalities on the biological level and the dysfunction of socio-emotional and nonsocial processing capacities on the behavioral level. Current assessment and therapy approaches account for each system level.

As discussed above, the suggestion that verbalized personal constructs that have been acquired in response to the social necessities during development could be generalized to the activity of all dysfunctional cerebral response systems is highly questionable. In contrast to verbal approaches that cover only a limited set of left hemispheric functions, the basic emotional response systems are governed by different modes of functioning (e.g., autonomic responding, automatic behavior control, etc.). These relatively independent functions have stimulated different assessment approaches. However, although objective tests of emotion regulation and personality have a long tradition in psychological assessment (e.g., Cattell & Warburton, 1967), the basic difficulties have not yet been overcome and standardized tests are still not available. Much hope has been devoted to emotional brain imaging, but many of the inherited methodological issues that are associated with the assessment of emotional function in humans remain unresolved (Peper, 2006; Peper, Herpers, Spreer, Hennig, & Zentner, 2006).

A socio-emotional executive core processing system

A neuro-emotional model that accounts for the organizational principles of both the physiological substrate as well as of the related but ontologically different realm of socio-emotional data requires an integrating view. Firstly, it is well accepted that the connectional pattern of the brain provides the basis of its functional connectivity. This cerebral connectivity is hierarchically organized (Passingham, Stephan, & Kötter, 2002) and can be conceptualized as a multilevel system (Peper, 2005). Secondly, as described above, socio-emotional functioning can be conceived of as a hierarchy of component functions that are integrated on higher levels. In this sense, emotional regulation or EI can be interpreted as tertiary factors that include several lower (secondary and primary) levels.

Thirdly, with respect to structure–function relationships, it has been shown that tasks loading high on a "general intelligence" factor recruit working memory capacities of the fronto-lateral cortex of one or both hemispheres (Duncan et al., 2000). Cognitive working memory or attentional tasks typically activate the anterior cingulate cortex and the left inferior frontal gyrus (Osaka et al., 2004). Similar to these subfunctions of nonsocial intelligence, emotional tasks recruit specific component subfunctions of the central executive. Emotional working memory, for example, has been associated with subregions of the prefrontal cortex (Davidson, 2001; Paus, 2001); emotional regulation tasks activate several prefrontal regions (Ochsner & Gross, 2005).

Taken together, these propositions can be summarized by a neuro-psychological core working model of emotion regulation that might be represented by a Brunswik-type lense structure (Figure 9.1). The neuro-biological side of this model (left half of lense) is represented by the connectivity pattern of the prefrontal cortex (Passingham, Stephan, & Kötter, 2002), with additional connections to the temporal cortex and amygdale (not shown). On the psychological side (right half of lense), the cognitive structure has been borrowed from interindividual differences research (Oberauer, Süß, Wilhelm, & Wittmann, 2003) combined with hypothetical emotional subfunctions (Davidson, Jackson, & Kalin, 2000).

This type of neuro-lense is a hypothetical metamodel, which may have important methodological implications for convergent and divergent construct validation procedures (e.g., double dissociation strategies). The systematical assessment of neuro-data and their association with the other side of the lense may help to establish neuro- and breakdown-compatible models of socio-emotional functioning, which also account for typical reliability issues such as symmetry and the levels of generality problem. Lense approaches call for representative designs and enhance ecological validity and predictive power (Wittmann, 1988).

Problems and advantages in clinical fields of application

The disorders and symptoms of patients with mental disease clearly demonstrate the necessity of intact socio-emotional regulation capacities in everyday life. Disorders of socio-emotional function may severely impair the personal and vocational rehabilitation process. Independent of the question of whether the disorder has particular biological or social determinants, it is well accepted that socio-emotional functioning needs to be appropriately assessed (Larsen & Prizmic-Larsen, 2006). However, as discussed above, inconsistencies of self-report or questionnaire data, behavior observations, and behavioral or physiological responses in the lab illustrate the extremely heterogeneous nature of socio-emotional functioning. This renders the overwhelming reliance on questionnaire approaches to emotion regulation behavior problematic.

Many procedures or tests designed to elicit and assess EI and emotional behavior have promised an improved differential diagnosis or categorization of patients. However, validity and reliability issues are still critically

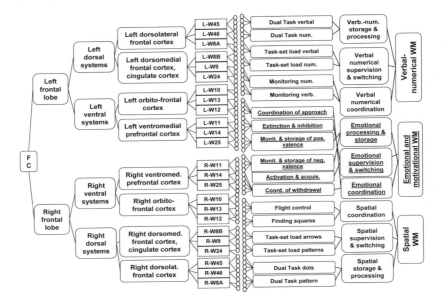

Figure 9.1 Neuropsychological lense model of emotional and nonemotional executive functioning. The neural connectivity information (left) was taken from Passingham, Stephan, and Kötter (2002). The structure of working memory function (right) and its operationalizations were adapted from interindividual differences research (Oberauer et al., 2003) and expanded with hypothetical emotional functions (Davidson et al., 2000).

discussed. Due to a lack of convergent validation, it remains difficult to relate such data to the official diagnostic criteria in a consistent way. Additional research is needed to evaluate the latent structure of this domain and to relate it to the pertinent diagnostic categories. A prognostic approach could be more promising than potential contributions to differential diagnosis. This would use emotional disorders, temperament traits, social context, and risk variables to predict the success of, for example, the assigned treatment. The decision making process could thus be empirically evaluated.

We have criticized here the relatively broad concepts that have a certain proximity to folk psychology concepts. However, this could also be an advantage in many practical and clinical settings. In these contexts, the practitioner is typically required to translate theoretical terms into a language that is comprehensible to the patient. General constructs such as EI possess a certain surplus meaning and a broad overlap with everyday language.

Taken together, assessment of socio-emotional function may help to improve assignment and indication of therapies. This process could be empirically optimized to fulfill certain predefined criteria of success (everyday life functioning, quality of life). Moreover, the organization and content of the therapy program itself could be stimulated by the pertinent dimensions of emotional regulation capacities. We have presented herein the outline of such a therapy program that focuses on central aspects of socio-emotional functioning in patients with schizophrenia. The benefits of this program (as measured by relapse prevention in patients with schizophrenia and other disorders) provide evidence for the practical usefulness of the discussed constructs.

In the long run, however, it seems necessary to revise and optimize the psychometric and conceptual basis of socio-emotional training programs. This could be accomplished, for example, by validating the model of emotion regulation by means of structural information available from differential psychology that could be further constrained by means of neuron-connectional data. Medical staff or expert witnesses involved in diagnosing or decisionmaking could be trained in the systematic assessment of the basic dimensions of neuron-emotional functioning. This type of information could directly be related to clinical presentation, differential diagnosis, course of illness, and treatment planning.

CONCLUSIONS

We have summarized herein the most important higher-order latent classes of socio-emotional function that constitute secondary or tertiary factors such as self-awareness, social awareness of others, emotional coping and management skills, or specific social skills. Many of these functions are assessed by means of self-report data. However, these approaches may overlook the vast neurobiological evidence of interindividual variations of affective infrastructures in the brain (Panksepp, 1998). In many instances, subcortical activities and autonomic reactions associated with emotional stimulation escape attention and subsequent verbal description (Peper, 2000). There is a growing need for instruments that are based on independent data sources such as systematic behavior ratings by experts or certain types of physiological data that permit a more objective assessment. Behavioral neuroscience provides new methods to assess social communication processes, beliefs, preferences, predispositions, high-level evaluation checks, and other kinds of socio-culturally modulated influences (Scherer & Peper, 2001).

The higher-level cognitive systems regulate emotional behavior, for example, by modulating the activity of fronto-striatal brain systems. New models are needed to systematically assess socio-emotional function and its interaction with executive brain function (Keysers & Gazzola, 2006). We presented herein an expansion of the general intelligence model that integrates the subfunctions of EI and IQ. It postulates a set of central executive functions (processing and storage, supervision and switching, coordination) for different content types of tasks (verbal-numerical, spatial, versus socio-emotional). Future research is needed to explore the relative independence of socio-emotional processing mechanisms and associate these with the appropriate levels of neural system variables. Expanding cognitive training programs into the adjacent socio-emotional domain may provide definite advantages for patients with mental diseases. Independent of the questions of whether emotion regulation or EI are reasonable constructs or how these are related to executive brain function, we may conclude that the evaluation of therapy effects in patients with schizophrenia documents the importance of multivariate testing and training of socio-emotional capacities in the area of clinical application and service.

REFERENCES

Archer, J., Hay, D. C., & Young, A. W. (1994). Movement, face processing and schizophrenia: Evidence of a differential deficit in expression analysis. *British Journal of Clinical Psychology, 33*, 517–528.

Asendorpf, J. (2003). *Psychologie der Persönlichkeit* (3rd ed.). Berlin: Springer.

Barch, D. M. (2005). The relationships among cognition, motivation, and emotion in schizophrenia: how much and how little we know. *Schizophrenia Bulletin, 31*, 875–881.

Bar-On, R. (2001). Emotional intelligence and self-actualization. In J. Ciarrochi, J. Forgas, & J. D. Mayer (Eds.), *Emotional intelligence in everyday life: A scientific inquiry* (pp. 82–97). New York: Psychology Press.

Bar-On, R., & Parker, J. D. (Eds.) (2000). *The handbook of emotional intelligence*. San Francisco, CA: Jossey-Bass.

Bellack, A. S., & Mueser, K. T. (1994). Schizophrenia. In L. W. Craighead, W. E. Craighead, A. E. Kazdin, & M. J. Mahoney (Eds.), *Cognitive and behavioral interventions: An empirical approach to mental health problems* (pp. 105–122). Boston, MA: Allyn & Bacon.

Berenbaum, H., & Williams, M. (1995). Personality and emotional reactivity. *Journal of Research in Personality, 29*, 24–34.

Blakemore, S. J., & Frith, U. (2004). How does the brain deal with the social world? *Neuroreport, 15*, 119–128.

Boyatzis, R. E., & Goleman, D. (2001). *Emotional competence inventory—university version. Self-assessment questionnaire, profile and interpretive notes.* London: Hay Resources Direct.

Brune, M. (2001). Social cognition and psychopathology in an evolutionary perspective. Current status and proposals for research. *Psychopathology*, *34*, 85–94.

Bufkin, J. L., & Luttrell, V. R. (2005). Neuroimaging studies of aggressive and violent behavior: current findings and implications for criminology and criminal justice. *Trauma, Violence, & Abuse*, *6*, 176–191.

Cacioppo, J. T., Tassinary, L. G., & Berntson, G. G. (Eds.) (2000). *Handbook of psychophysiology*. New York: Cambridge University Press.

Cattell, R. B. (1957). *Personality and motivation structure and measurement*. Yonkers-on-Hudson, NY: World Book.

Cattell, R. B., & Warburton, F. W. (1967). *Objective personality and motivation tests: A theoretical introduction and practical compendium*. Chicago: University of Illinois Press.

Ciarrochi, J., Chan, A., Caputi, P., & Roberts, R. (2001). Measuring emotional intelligence. In J. Ciarrochi, J. Forgas, & J. D. Mayer (Eds.), *Emotional intelligence in everyday life: A scientific inquiry* (pp. 25–45). New York: Psychology Press.

Cohen, A. S., & Docherty, N. M. (2004). Affective reactivity of speech and emotional experience in patients with schizophrenia. *Schizophrenia Research*, *69*, 7–14.

Cohen, A. S., Forbes, C. B., Mann, M. C., & Blanchard, J. J. (2006). Specific cognitive deficits and differential domains of social functioning impairment in schizophrenia. *Schizophrenia Research*, *81*, 227–238.

Corrigan, P. W., Green, M. F., & Toomey, R. (1994). Cognitive correlates to social cue perception in schizophrenia. *Psychiatry Research*, *53*, 141–151.

Davidson, R. J., 2001. Prefrontal and amygdala contributions to emotion and affective style. In G. Gainotti (Ed.), *Handbook of neuropsychology. Vol. 5. Emotional behavior and its disorders* (pp. 111–124). Amsterdam: Elsevier.

Davidson, R. J., Jackson, D. C., & Kalin, N. H. (2000). Emotion, plasticity, context, and regulation: Perspectives from affective neuroscience. *Psychological Bulletin*, *126*, 890–909.

Duncan, J., Seitz, R. J., Kolodny, J., Bor, D., Herzog, H., Ahmed, A., et al. (2000). A neural basis for general intelligence. *Science*, *289*, 457–460.

Eack, S. M., Hogarty, G. E., Greenwald, D. P., Hogarty, S., & Keshavan, M. S. (2007). Cognitive enhancement therapy improves emotional intelligence in early course schizophrenia: Preliminary effects. *Schizophrenia Research*, *89*, 308–311.

Educational Testing Service (ETS) (2007). *Educational Testing Service—Test Collection Database*. SydneyPLUS Knowledge Portal, http://sydneyplus.ets.org. Princeton, NJ: ETS.

Eid, M., & Diener, E. (Eds.) (2006). *Handbook of multimethod measurement in psychology*. Washington, DC: American Psychological Association.

Ekman, P. (1992). Facial expression of emotion: New findings, new questions. *Psychological Science*, *3*, 34–38.

Folkman, S., & Lazarus, R. S. (1990). Coping and emotion. In N. L. Stein, B. Leventhal, & T. Trabasso (Eds.), *Psychological and biological approaches to emotions* (pp. 313–332). Hillsdale, NJ: Erlbaum.

Gaebel, W., & Wölwer, W. (1992). Facial expression and emotional face recognition in schizophrenia and depression. *European Archives of Psychiatry & Clinical Neuroscience, 242*, 46–52.

Goleman, D. (1995). *Emotional intelligence.* New York: Bantam.

Grawe, K. (1998). *Psychologische Therapie.* Göttingen: Hogrefe.

Greig, T. C., Bryson, G. J., & Bell, M. D. (2004). Theory of mind performance in schizophrenia: diagnostic, symptom, and neuropsychological correlates. *Journal of Nervous and Mental Disease, 192*, 12–18.

Gross, J. J. (1998). The emerging field of emotion regulation: An integrative review. *Review of General Psychology, 2*, 271–299.

Habel, U., Gur, R. C., Mandal, M. K., Salloum, J. B., Gur, R. E., & Schneider, F. (2000). Emotional processing in schizophrenia across cultures: standardized measures of discrimination and experience. *Schizophrenia Research, 42*, 57–66.

Hall, J., Harris, J. M., Sprengelmeyer, R., Sprengelmeyer, A., Young, A. W., Santos, I. M., et al. (2004). Social cognition and face processing in schizophrenia. *British Journal of Psychiatry, 185*, 169–170.

Harris, J. C. (2003). Social neuroscience, empathy, brain integration, and neurodevelopmental disorders. *Physiology and Behavior, 79*, 525–531.

Hilton, N. Z., & Simmons, J. L. (2001). The influence of actuarial risk assessment in clinical judgments and tribunal decisions about mentally disordered offenders in maximum security. *Law & Human Behavior, 25*, 393–408.

Hodel, B., Kern, R. S., & Brenner, H. D. (2004). Emotion management training (EMT) in persons with treatment-resistant schizophrenia: First results. *Schizophrenia Research, 68*, 107–108.

Hogarty, G. E., Flesher, S., Ulrich, R., Carter, M., Greenwald, D., Pogue-Geile, M., et al. (2004). Cognitive enhancement therapy for schizophrenia: Effects of a 2-year randomized trial on cognition and behavior. *Archives of General Psychiatry, 61*, 866–876.

Hooker, C., & Park, S. (2002). Emotion processing and its relationship to social functioning in schizophrenia patients. *Psychiatry Research, 112*, 41–50.

Horan, W. P., & Blanchard, J. J. (2003). Neurocognitive, social, and emotional dysfunction in deficit syndrome schizophrenia. *Schizophrenia Research, 65*, 125–137.

Kerlinger, F. N., & Lee, H. B. (2000). *Foundations of behavioural research* (4th ed.). Orlando, FL: Harcourt.

Kerr, S. L., & Neale, J. M. (1993). Emotion perception in schizophrenia: Specific deficit or further evidence of generalized poor performance? *Journal of Abnormal Psychology, 102*, 312–318.

Keysers, C., & Gazzola, V. (2006). Towards a unifying neural theory of social cognition. *Progress in Brain Research, 156*, 379–401.

Kubicki, M., McCarley, R., Westin, C. F., Park, H. J., Maier, S., Kikinis, R., et al. (2007). A review of diffusion tensor imaging studies in schizophrenia. *Journal of Psychiatric Research, 41*, 15–30.

Lang, P., Rice, D. G., & Sternbach, R. A. (1972). The psychophysiology of emotion. In N. S. Greenfield & R. A. Sternbach (Eds.), *Handbook of psychophysiology* (pp. 623–643). New York: Holt.

Larsen, R. J., & Prizmic-Larsen, Z. (2006). Measuring emotions: Implications of a multimethod perspective. In M. Eid & E. Diener (Eds.), *Handbook of multimethod measurement in psychology* (pp. 337–352). Washington, DC: American Psychological Association.

Lazarus, R. S. (1999). *Stress and emotion: A new synthesis.* New York: Springer.

Lee, K. H., Farrow, T. F., Spence, S. A., & Woodruff, P. W. (2004). Social cognition, brain networks and schizophrenia. *Psychological Medicine, 34,* 391–400.

Lenzenweger, M. F. (1999). Schizophrenia: Refining the phenotype, resolving endophenotypes. *Behaviour Research and Therapy, 37,* 281–295.

Lezak, M. D., Howieson, D. B., & Loring, D. W. (2004). *Neuropsychological Assessment.* Oxford: Oxford University Press.

Lysaker, P. H., Campbell, K., & Johannesen, J. K. (2005). Hope, awareness of illness, and coping in schizophrenia spectrum disorders: Evidence of an interaction. *Journal of Nervous and Mental Disease, 193,* 287–292.

Lysaker, P. H., Lancaster, R. S., Davis, L. W., & Clements, C. A. (2003). Patterns of neurocognitive deficits and unawareness of illness in schizophrenia. *Journal of Nervous and Mental Disease, 191,* 38–44.

Mayer, J. D., Caruso, D. R., & Salovey, P. (2000). Emotional Intelligence meets traditional standards for an intelligence. *Intelligence, 27,* 267–298.

Mayer, J. D., Salovey, P., & Caruso, D. R. (2000). Competing models of Emotional Intelligence. In R. J. Sternberg (Ed.), *Handbook of human intelligence.* New York: Cambridge University Press.

Mitmansgruber, H. (2003). *Kognition und Emotion. Die Regulation von Gefühlen im Alltag und bei psychischen Störungen.* Göttingen: Hogrefe.

Morrison, R. L., Bellack, A. S., & Mueser, K. T. (1988). Deficits in facial-affect recognition and schizophrenia. *Schizophrenia Bulletin, 14,* 67–83.

Mueser, K. T. (1993). Schizophrenia. In A. S. Bellack & M. Hersen (Eds.), *Handbook of Behavior Therapy in the Psychiatric Setting* (pp. 260–291). New York: Plenum Press.

Myers, W. C., Husted, D. S., Safarik, M. E., & O'Toole, M. E. (2006). The motivation behind serial sexual homicide: Is it sex, power, and control, or anger? *Journal of Forensic Sciences, 51,* 900–907.

Myrtek, M. (1998). Metaanalysen zur psychophysiologischen Persönlichkeitsforschung. In F. Rösler (Ed.), *Enzyklopädie der Psychologie: Band CI5. Ergebnisse und Anwendungen der Psychophysiologie* (pp. 285–344). Göttingen: Hogrefe.

Oberauer, K., Süß, H.-M., Wilhelm, O., & Wittmann, W. W. (2003). The multiple faces of working memory: Storage, processing, supervision, and coordination. *Intelligence, 31,* 167–193.

Ochsner, K. N., & Gross, J. J. (2005). The cognitive control of emotion. *Trends in Cognitive Sciences, 9,* 242–249.

Osaka, N., Osaka, M., Kondo, H., Morishita, M., Fukuyama, H., & Shibasaki, H. (2004). The neural basis of executive function in working memory: An fMRI study based on individual differences. *Neuroimage, 21,* 623–631.

Panksepp, J. (1998). *Affective Neuroscience.* New York: Oxford University Press.

Parkinson, B., & Totterdell, P. (1999). Classifying affect-regulation strategies. *Cognition and Emotion, 13,* 277–303.

Passingham, R. E., Stephan, K. E., & Kötter, R. (2002). The anatomical basis of functional localization in the cortex. *Nature Reviews Neuroscience, 3,* 606–616.

Paus, T. (2001). Primate anterior cingulate cortex: Where motor control, drive and cognition interface. *Nature Reviews Neuroscience, 2,* 417–424.

Penn, D. L., Corrigan, P. W., Bentall, R. P., Racenstein, J. M., & Newman, L. (1997). Social cognition in schizophrenia. *Psychological Bulletin, 121,* 114–132.

Penn, D. L., Kohlmaier, J. R., & Corrigan, P. W. (2000). Interpersonal factors contributing to the stigma of schizophrenia: Social skills, perceived attractiveness, and symptoms. *Schizophrenia Research, 45,* 37–45.

Peper, M. (2000). Awareness of emotions: A neuropsychological perspective. *Advances in Consciousness Studies, 16,* 245–270.

Peper, M. (2005, August 31–September 4). *Neuropsychological assessment.* Paper presented at the 8th European Conference on Psychological Assessment (ECPA), Budapest, Hungary.

Peper, M. (2006). Imaging emotional brain functions: Conceptual and methodological issues. *Journal of Physiology Paris, 99,* 293–307.

Peper, M., & Fahrenberg, J. (in press). Psychophysiologie. In Sturm, W., Herrmann, M., & Münte, T. (Eds.), *Lehrbuch der klinischen Neuropsychologie* (2nd ed.). Heidelberg: Spektrum Akademischer Verlag.

Peper, M., Herpers, M., Spreer, J., Hennig, J., & Zentner, J. (2006). Functional neuroimaging of emotional learning and autonomic reactions. *Journal of Physiology Paris, 99,* 342–354.

Perrez, M., & Reicherts, M. (1992). *Stress, coping and health: A situation behavior approach.* Seattle, WA: Hogrefe & Huber.

Phillips, M. L. (2004). Facial processing deficits and social dysfunction: How are they related? *Brain, 127,* 1691–1692.

Phillips, M. L., Drevets, W. C., Rauch, S. L., & Lane, R. (2003a). Neurobiology of emotion perception I: The neural basis of normal emotion perception. *Biological Psychiatry, 54,* 504–14.

Phillips, M. L., Drevets, W. C., Rauch, S. L., & Lane, R. (2003b). Neurobiology of emotion perception II: Implications for major psychiatric disorders. *Biological Psychiatry, 54,* 515–528.

Russell, J. A. (1994). Is there universal recognition of emotion from facial expression? A review of the cross-cultural studies. *Psychological Bulletin, 115,* 102–141.

Sachs, G., Steger-Wuchse, D., Kryspin-Exner, I., Gur, R. C., & Katschnig, H. (2004). Facial recognition deficits and cognition in schizophrenia. *Schizophrenia Research, 68,* 27–35.

Salovey, P., & Mayer, J. D. (1990). Emotional intelligence. *Imagination, cognition, and personality, 9,* 185–211.

Scherer, K. R. (1984). On the nature and function of emotion: A component process approach. In K. R. Scherer & P. Ekman (Eds.), *Approaches to emotion* (pp. 293–318). Hillsdale, NJ: Erlbaum.

Scherer, K. R. (1994). Toward a concept of "modal emotions." In P. Ekman &

R. J. Davidson (Eds.), *The nature of emotion* (pp. 25–31). New York: Oxford University Press.

Scherer, K. R. (1999). Appraisal theory. In T. Dalgleish & M. Power (Eds.), *Handbook of cognition and emotion* (pp. 637–663). Chichester: Wiley.

Scherer K. R., & Peper, M. (2001). Psychological theories of emotion and neuropsychological research. In G. Gainotti (Ed.), *Handbook of neuropsychology. Vol. 5. Emotional behavior and its disorders* (pp. 17–48). Amsterdam: Elsevier.

Sommer, M., Hajak, G., Dohnel, K., Schwerdtner, J., Meinhardt, J., & Müller, J. L. (2006). Integration of emotion and cognition in patients with psychopathy. *Progress in Brain Research, 156*, 457–466.

Spence, S. A., Hunter, M. D., Farrow, T. F., Green, R. D., Leung, D. H., Hughes, C. J., et al. (2004). A cognitive neurobiological account of deception: Evidence from functional neuroimaging. *Philosophical Transactions of the Royal Society of London, Biological Sciences, 359*, 1755–1762.

Spies, R. A., & Plake, B. S. (Eds.) (2006). *The seventeenth mental measurements yearbook*. Lincoln, NE: Buros Institute of Mental Measurements.

Stemmler, G. (1992). *Differential psychophysiology: Persons in situations*. Heidelberg: Springer.

Stieglitz, R.-D., & Vauth, R. (2005). Verhaltenstheoretische Konzepte in der Ätiologie schizophrener Symptome. *Fortschritte der Neurologie und Psychiatrie, 73*, 60-65.

Strauss, E., Sherman, E., & Spreen, O. (2006). *A compendium of neuropsychological tests: Administration, norms, and commentary* (3rd ed.). New York: Oxford University Press.

Vauth, R. (2004). SAS - Die Social Adjustment Scale. In B. Strauss & J. Schumacher (Eds.), *Klinische Interviews und Rating-Skalen* (pp. 393–397). Göttingen: Hogrefe.

Vauth, R., Dreher-Rudolph, M., Ueber, R., & Olbrich, H. M. (1997). Das "Training Emotionaler Intelligenz." Ein neuer Therapieansatz in der Gruppenpsychotherapie schizophrener Patienten. In C. Mundt, M. Linden, & W. Barnett (Eds.), *Psychotherapie in der Psychiatrie* (pp. 87–91). New York: Springer.

Vauth, R., Joe, A., Seitz, M., Dreher-Rudolph, M., Olbrich, H., & Stieglitz, R. D. (2001). Differenzielle Kurz- und Langzeitwirkung eines "Trainings Emotionaler Intelligenz" und des "Integrierten Psychologischen Therapieprogramms" für schizophrene Patienten? *Fortschritte neurologischer Psychiatrie, 69*, 518–525.

Vauth, R., Rüsch, N., Wirtz, M., & Corrigan, P. W. (2004). Does social cognition influence the relation between neurocognitive deficits and vocational functioning in schizophrenia? *Psychiatry Research, 128*, 155–165.

Vauth, R., & Stieglitz, R.-D. (2001). Diagnostik schizophrener Störungen. In R.-D. Stieglitz, U. Baumann, & H.-J. Freyberger (Eds.), *Psychodiagnostik in der klinischen Psychologie, Psychiatrie, Psychotherapie* (2nd ed., pp. 405–417). Stuttgart: Thieme.

Wittmann, W. W. (1988). Multivariate reliability theory. Principles of symmetry and successful validation strategy. In J. R. Nesselroade & R. B. Cattell (Eds.), *Handbook of multivariate experimental psychology* (pp. 505–560). New York: Plenum.

10

Emotional Experience, Expression, and Regulation in the Psychotherapeutic Processes

Leslie Greenberg and Marie Vandekerckhove

The search for certain affects is an important motivator in people's lives (Greenberg, 2002). Most of what people think and do is motivated by their affective goals. People generally seek to feel calm, to feel joy, to feel pleasure, pride, excitement, and interest and equally seek to not feel pain, and shame, and fear. People thus organize to regulate their affects. People are motivated by their emotion states; they are motivated to do things because they feel better or in order to avoid feeling bad. People would not flee from danger unless they felt afraid and would not bond unless it made them feel good. Also people, from infancy, relate to others in order to help regulate their affect. They seek connection because it helps them feel secure and they seek understanding or empathic mirroring from others because it makes them feel special. The security and validation provided by others is a major source of affect regulation. Marriage and interpersonal connection is one of the major sources of human emotion, and is sought after because it makes people feel joyful, secure, excited, and proud and in this way is a primary regulator of affect.

Emotions are part of a complex process of reacting to the environment. They are signals produced by the affective system, which integrates information from diverse sources and provides important feedback about the adaptiveness of specific behaviors. Too much or too little emotion can disrupt effective responding to environmental challenges. In treatment contexts, however, emotion regulation often has come to mean regulating undercontrolled emotion such as anger, and doing this by the coordination of the emotions and cognitive systems. The question of how much people can control their emotions and how much this is done by constraining them has long been an issue in psychotherapy.

Two different views of emotion regulation reflecting a narrower view of regulation as the control of too much disruptive emotion or too much of the wrong type of emotion, versus a broader view of regulation as the having of desired emotion at adaptive levels at the right time, will be described below. In line with a broader view, the therapy we propose involves differential intervention with clients' emotions, helping them to have access to and integrate certain emotions by exploration, expression, soothing, and transformation and by regulating and transforming others. In this chapter, we propose the adoption of a one-factor, dynamic systems view of emotion regulation and distinguish between different types of emotion, such as primary and secondary emotions as well as adaptive and maladaptive emotions. As the reader will learn, secondary emotions, as responses to our primary emotional responses, often need to be explored in order to get access to more adaptive primary emotions. When primary emotions become maladaptive, they have a repetitive stereotypical character and often are based on unresolved responses from the past. Sometimes, in order to work with dysregulated emotional arousal, promotion of a working distance from the emotion is necessary rather than an activation or intensification of the emotion. More deliberate cognitive approaches and direct relaxing techniques such as, for instance, physiological relaxation, cognitive reappraisal, and meditation are then helpful in order to regulate arousal. Furthermore, maladaptive emotion can be transformed by activation of an opposing more adaptive emotion. The coactivation of the more adaptive emotion along with or in response to a maladaptive emotion helps synthesize a new response to the evoking situation. In this chapter we also describe the ingredients of a psychotherapeutic relationship that help promote emotion regulation. We suggest that therapeutic work with emotions requires the provision of a warm therapeutic climate to facilitate access to, and articulation of, primary emotions and underlying needs, and the acceptance of painful unresolved emotions to allow new meaning and healthier emotional reactions to emerge from them.

 ## A TWO-FACTOR VIEW OF EMOTION REGULATION

In the narrow sense, emotion regulation refers to the processes by which people influence which emotions they have, when they have them, and most importantly how they experience and express them (Gross, 1998). In this view cognitive appraisals are seen as resulting in emotion, suggesting that once we have emotions, we then need to regulate them. This view is the result of the current dominance of cognitive views in psychology. Regulation of negative, stressful emotion then occurs through rationally disputing or cognitively reappraising the given information or situation to change one's view (Gross, 1999; Hariri, Bookheimer, & Mazziotta, 2000; Mauss, Bunge, & Gross, this volume). One thus should change the way one thinks about a potentially emotion-eliciting situation in order to modify its emotional impact (Lazarus, 1966, 1993; Gross, 1999; Hariri et al., 2000).

The regulation of emotion is defined predominantly in terms of the conscious or volitional self-regulation of emotion. Emotion regulation refers here to the set of control processes by which people voluntarily control their experience of their emotions. In support of this view, several experimental studies (Gross & Levenson, 1993; Gross, 2002) have shown that reappraisal has a direct adaptive effect. It decreases both the experience and the behavioral expression of negative emotion without any increase in physiological activation. In this context, we assume that this decline in negative emotion after reappraisal processes also helps the recovery of painful events and therefore emotional health in the short run. It is clear that strategies to regulate emotion suggested by the two-factor view, such as reappraisal of an emotional situation as well as the selection of a situation and response modulation, involve higher levels of cognitive intervention.

In correspondence with this view, cognitive psychotherapy (Beck, 1979) has emphasized changing the way people feel by consciously changing the way they think. We refer to this control view of emotion regulation as the *narrow* sense, and indicate it with the term ER. The narrow view clearly is a two-factor view, in which one system is seen as generating emotion and another is seen as subsequently regulating emotion. Treatments such as anger management and how to control anger flow from this perspective. An emotion-focused approach involves accessing the primary emotions that often underlie secondary symptomatic emotions, and the awareness, tolerance, and experience of underlying emotions as a first step in the subsequent decrease in negative emotion in the longer run (Hunt, 1998).

 ## A ONE-FACTOR VIEW: EMOTION REGULATION AS AN INHERENTLY REGULATED AND REGULATORY PROCESS

Within the one-factor broader view, emotion regulation is seen as being intrinsic in the experience of generating emotion. Emotion regulation, rather than self-control, is seen as *an integral aspect of the generation of*

emotion and coterminous with it (Campos, Frankel, & Camras, 2004). Appraisal and emotion are seen as occurring simultaneously to generate emotional meanings and experience. Emotion in this broader view thus is both inherently regulated and regulatory. The cognitive system is seen as *receiving information* from the emotion system as well as influencing it, and as both *guided* by emotion, as well as making sense of emotion. Not only can emotion receive information from the cognitive system, but also the cognitive system has the ability to receive adaptive information and regulation from the emotion system. Emotion systems thus can be transformed or regulated by processes other than cognitive processes, such as by other emotions and by attachment (Greenberg, 2002). Essential affective self-regulatory processes are involved in self-maintenance, rather than self-control, and these occur largely below conscious awareness. These regulatory processes probably occur after being processed by the more subcortical areas such as the amygdala, and the orbitofrontal cortex which takes over amygdala and lower level right hemispheric functioning in more complex processing (Lane and Nadel, 2000; Schore, 2003).

Complementary to the narrow view, the broader view sees the first experience in the world and the information used to guide our reactions as being primarily affective in nature, rather than cognitive (LeDoux, 1995; Panksepp, 1998). This broadens the conception of emotion regulation. A view based on the primacy of affect in governing response necessarily has consequences for the way one conceptualizes the regulation of affect. If one considers information processing as primarily affective, we assume that the way to regulate or change an emotion and its processes of elicitation needs to be a primarily affective one. Emotion regulation not only has to be considered as involving higher-level cortical executive cognitive strategies but especially also as involving earlier subcortical affective levels of information processing. Regulation, too, will include many other aspects of emotion processing such as emotional awareness, its representation, utilization, and transformation. Thus the issue is how people synthesize adaptive responses to the world rather than how they control dysregulated responses.

In this view, in order to be able to change negative emotional distress and its associated meanings, it is necessary to activate underlying affective experience and to focus on its experiential meaning (Gendlin, 1964; Greenberg, Elliott, & Lietaer, 2003; Leijssen, 2004). Awareness and expression of self-related material, when accompanied by experiential meaning, is considered as more effective in facilitating emotional stress regulation than intellectual insight alone. Therefore, it should be important in the processing of affect to move from the theoretical-abstract or external narrative levels to the level of immediate lived experience, including emotional feelings. One needs to specify what type of emotions to access and increase and which to down-regulate, which to access and which to transform. Later in this chapter we will discuss different types of emotions and different types of processes of working with emotions in therapy. First, we will discuss some findings from affective neuroscience to support the broader, one-factor view of emotion regulation.

▨ AFFECTIVE NEUROSCIENCE

An affective neuroscience perspective appears to support the broader view of emotion regulation as integrated with emotion generation rather than a narrower two-factor, conscious control, view (Cozolino, 2002). Regarding the anatomical side of primary affect, affect is primarily dependent on the ascending reticular activating system in the upper brainstem midline and on intratalaminar nuclei of the thalamus, with extensions into the cerebral cortex providing feedback to the brainstem centers that play a role in arousal and alertness (Bogen, 1995; Frith, Perry, & Lumer, 1999; Young & Pigott, 1999).

According to LeDoux (1995), there appears to be a direct connection from the thalamus to the amygdala. The amygdala is a collection of nuclei in the anterior medial temporal lobe that receives highly processed sensory information. It links (1) information about external stimuli conveyed by sensory cortices on one hand and (2) somatic, visceral, and endocrine processes on the other hand. The amygdala plays an important role in assigning affective significance to experiential stimuli and in initiating emotional arousal (Panksepp, 2003). As part of the limbic area, the amygdala is central in emotionally arousing processes of implicit learning and explicit memory (Markowitsch, 1998; Siebert, Markowitsch, & Bartel, 2003). For instance, in confrontation with potentially dangerous stimuli, the amygdala becomes triggered, giving rise to fear and anxiety which lead the organism into a stage of alertness, getting ready for flight or fight in service of self-preservation. The activation of the amygdala occurs very quickly and can be achieved without the intervention of cortical areas, although only for a very short period: approximately 12 milliseconds (Markowitsch, 1998). An acoustic stimulus that reaches the amygdala via the thalamus needs much less time than the stimulus that reaches the amygdala via the cortical pathway. In other words, the direct thalamic input to the amygdala makes it possible for information to bypass the cortex and thus higher cognitive processing. This input cannot give sufficient details on the exact identification of the stimulus to the amygdala, but it can provide a fast signal. These thalamo-amygdala projections are particularly important in generating the primary, first un-conscious affective meaning of relatively simple affective sensory and per-ceptual information. Although the prefrontal cortex is connected to and can influence the amygdala, the amygdala is highly connected to many parts of the brain and to the prefrontal cortex and influences decisions (Damasio, 1999; LeDoux, 1995).

The activation of the amygdala in psychotherapy is necessary in order to reach the deeper affective imprints it contains and to be able to cor-rect them. To change primary affective processes one has to change the deep, limbically represented pieces or schemes of affective memory piece by piece by activating and allowing them first. When affective or limbic subcortical areas are not activated in the therapeutic process, the thera-peutic input remains at an almost purely cognitive level. Starting without real contact with affective layers does not change developmentally built, emotionally loaded, schemata or traumatic experiences. Talking "about" something activates more cognitively represented memory, without the deeper affective tone or meaning of it. This does not deliver meaningful affective information.

On the other hand, as we discuss in this chapter, overwhelming emotion, which is not represented on a cognitive level, may elicit behavior that is not constrained and informed by this higher-level cognitive prefrontal process-ing. Then, there is no way to cope with the situation and the person is in-capable of giving a meaning to his or her experience and cannot engage in healthy self-regulation, self-control, and planning. In such a lower-mode state, conscious perceptual and cognitive processing do not influence current affective experience. The individual is "stuck" in a behavioral pattern that is not responsive to the demands placed upon it by the envi-ronment. In the extreme, a deficit in distinguishing between actual mental representations of ongoing reality or perception and current emotions can also occur.

Lateralization

Functions such as emotional social self-regulation appear to require an enhanced activation of the right side of the brain (Tucker, 1981). Un-conscious quick processing is mediated more by the right hemisphere of the brain, and conscious, slower, and serial processing more by the left hemisphere (Markowitsch, 1998). Implicit affect regulation that occurs through right hemispheric processes, not verbally mediated is, as we assume, most directly affected by processes such as emotion and emotion regulation by relational and emotional communication, facial expression, vocal quality, and eye contact. The right hemisphere appears not only to be preferentially active under emotion but under stress conditions too (Tucker, 1981; Bremner, 2002; Driessen et al., 2004). In psychotherapy, working with emotional stress as a focus of attention involves high subcortical right hemispheric involvement. The relationship between right hemispheric involvement and stress has been shown by the findings that posttraumatic stress disorder may be paralleled by right hemispheric dysfunction (Driessen et al., 2004). Traumatized individuals may be unable to respond to stress in similar ways as normal individuals, possibly due to a dysfunction of right hemispheric brain processing (Wittling, 1997). Also, measurements of resting right frontal electroencephalographic (EEG) activity have been found to predict children's responses to stress (Davidson & Fox, 1989). Children of mothers who were depressed during pregnancy tend to exhibit a characteristic pattern of enhanced right frontal EEG activity even until the age of 3 years (Dawson & Ashman, 2000; Field, 1998). In accordance with these findings, we assume that enhanced right hemispheric laterality may be associated later in ontogenetic development with an enhanced vulnerability for negative emotional stress associated with reactive inhibition systems. Deficits in empathy and emotional connection between infants and their caretakers have been found to affect areas of right brain development involved in empathy and compassion (Schore, 2003). In order to work with unresolved emotional stress, we suggest that emotional stress has to become activated enhancing right hemispheric activation. In correspondence, in a remarkable study, Bergdahl, Larsson, Nilsson, Ahlstrom, and Nyberg (2005), applying an affect-focused intervention program on chronically stressed employees, found relatively increased activity in the left prefrontal cortex prior to their intervention, whereas they found that the right prefrontal cortex showed relatively enhanced activation after the intervention, probably due to a higher emotional state of awareness and more openness to emotion.

The orbitofrontal cortex

The orbitofrontal cortex (OFC) becomes involved as modulator and integrator between affective processes and cognitive processes. This part of the brain connects the cortex to the limbic system and is crucially involved in the more advanced regulation of emotions and in the selection of behavioral choices and situations (Eslinger, 1999; Rolls, 1999; Vandekerckhove, Markowitsch, Mertens, & Woermann, 2005). The OFC becomes gradually involved after the involvement of the amygdala, which, as indicated, is more active in the more unconscious affective levels of emotion regulation. Emotional awareness, as we will discuss later in the text, symbolizing the affective experience while finding the right words for it, is a process where unconscious and conscious affective and cognitive processes meet each other and become increasingly intertwined. The OFC becomes involved when affective and cognitive feedback loops interact with each other. The main difference between the two-factor and the one-factor view is that within the one-factor view we primarily work with unconscious emotions represented within the amygdala. It is only gradually that more cognitive processes enter the process of emotion regulation.

The orbitofrontal cortices on the basal surface of the frontal lobe have a polymodal processing capacity. They receive input from different sensory modalities, directly or indirectly. The OFC controls the sympathetic and parasympathetic branches of the autonomic nervous system and thus cardiac and respiratory responses in emotional and stressful situations. It has an important function in the transition to more conscious, voluntary, and regulated behavior such as social knowledge of how to behave, the selection of appropriate behavior, and social and interpersonal self-regulation (cf. Mauss et al., this volume; Hofer & Eisenberg, this volume; Poder, this volume; Trommsdorff & Rothbaum, this volume). In particular, the right orbitofrontal system is thought to act as the neural basis by which humans regulate their emotional responses through cognitive processes (Hariri et al., 2000), although this type of cognitive process does not rely on reason or deliberate effortful processing. For instance, emotional disturbances of posttraumatic stress disorder are supposed to have their origins in the inability of the right orbitofrontal cortex to modulate amygdala functions.

In a positron emission tomography (PET) study (Semple et al., 1992), regional cerebral blood flow during script-driven imagery in childhood sexual abuse-related posttraumatic stress disorder was investigated, showing right hemisphere and orbitofrontal dysfunction to modulate amygdala functions, in particular the right amygdala, known to process frightening faces and unseen fear (cf. Adolphs, Tranel, & Damasio, 2001; Koenen et al., 2001). Without emotion regulation by orbitofrontal feedback and representation of the fear within conscious awareness, the organism may remain in an amygdala-driven defensive response state longer than necessary and may activate an overwhelming stressful emotional response associated with enhanced levels of stress hormones. The orbitofrontal cortex is thus an important part of a complex system in which regulated affect is generated.

A dynamic systems view of emotion regulation

Seeing the complexity of brain functioning involved in affect, the regulation of emotion is best viewed as embedded in a rapid cascade of effects moving up and down the different subcortical and cortical areas. Instead of cognitive control of emotion we have massive feedback loops in which different parts of the brain discussed above, plus others, interact with each other leading to a synchronization coherence—which results in the self-organization of the entire brain. The more executive or controlled cognitive processes are involved, the more prefrontal involvement there is. The orbitofrontal area operates as a mediator between subcortical and cortical area and as an integrator of affective and cognitive emotion regulation processes. We will now move on to look at emotion regulation in psychotherapy, based on a broader, dynamic systems view of emotion regulation.

▣ EMOTION REGULATION IN PSYCHOTHERAPY

The therapeutic relationship

How the therapist joins and connects emotionally with a client is the very first experience in therapy that influences emotion regulation. How safe, received, and soothed the clients feel will affect what emotions they experience. An empathic relationship and a good working alliance involving a respectful, emotion-validating therapeutic bond is a crucial element of helping people calm down. In addition to providing a relationship, therapists also begin to influence clients' manner of processing emotion by selectively attending to primary adaptive emotions and thereby helping shift clients' focus of attention to their bodily felt experience.

In our view, the relationship serves a dual purpose in psychotherapy (Greenberg & Watson, 2005). First, the relationship is therapeutic in and of itself by serving an affect regulation function which is internalized over time. This function is accomplished by offering a soothing, affect attuned bond characterized by the therapist's presence and empathic attunement to affect as well as acceptance and congruence. Second, the relationship functions as a means to an end. The relationship offers the optimal environment for facilitating specific modes of emotional processing. Affect is much more likely to be approached, tolerated, and accepted in the context of a safe relationship.

This chapter will discuss elements such as pacing and facial, tonal, and postural communication of affect that create a therapeutic emotional climate. In addition to the climate's role in promoting enhanced affect regulation, its role in providing the optimal environment for facilitating emotional processing will also be discussed.

The nature of an emotion-regulating relationship

Therapists first thus create a warm, safe, and validating climate by their way of being with the client. The emotional climate has to do with the total attitude of the therapist, being perceptive and attuned to the client is communicated by means of therapists' verbal expressions as well as body posture, vocal, and facial expression. Clearly, the therapist's overall attitude, not only his/her techniques, influences the clients' responses and the way the clients' feelings are experienced and expressed in the therapeutic relationship. Buber (1958) wrote that a compassionate human face, when unadorned by pretense, role, or assumption of superiority, offers more hope to another than the most sophisticated psychological techniques.

In working with emotion, although the therapist may be an expert in the possible therapeutic steps that might be facilitative, it is made clear that the therapist is a compassionate human being who is a facilitator of client experience. The therapist who conveys genuine interest, acceptance, caring, compassion, and joy and no anger, contempt, disgust, and fear creates the environment for a secure emotional bond.

In a recent analysis of the classic film "Three Psychotherapies" by Rogers, Perls, and Ellis with patient "Gloria," Magai and Haviland-Jones (2002) studied the emotional climate created by the therapists. This analysis revealed that each of these therapists, in their behavior in the film, in their theories, and more generally in their personalities and personal lives, expressed and focused on very different emotions. Rogers showed interest, joy, and shame. Perls showed contempt and fear, and Ellis anger and fear. Anyone who has seen these films can see that they created very different therapeutic environments.

Facial communication

The therapists' facial, postural, and vocal expression of emotion clearly set very different emotional climates and are aspects of their ways of being. Facial expression thus is a central aspect of relational attunement. People have been shown to read facial affect automatically at incredibly high speed, especially those affects such as anger and fear that are crucial to survival. Clients thereby are helped to acknowledge that they themselves do experience and that they communicate their feelings. Put more simply a client feels "Oh, you get it, you get me, and I get that you get me too!"

For example, when clients are experiencing grief or sadness, therapists respond to clients' pain in different ways. Therapists' faces register pain, maybe their eyes even fill with a tear, they lean in, listen closely. Then to bring this experience into the room even further, and help solidify it with the client, therapists might ask clients what it is like to share these feelings with them, how they experience the therapist or what their sense of the therapist is in the moment. The therapist also might ask what the client sees in his or her face, and how this makes the client feel. Therapists may also share with their clients their own sense of feeling close to them as clients share their feelings. This validates the client's ability to be with these feelings, and also to let them into the experience. In this way therapists deepen the dyadic experience.

Therapist pacing

A slow pace for example is essential for working with sad emotions. The tone, energy, rhythm, and cadence need to be appropriate to the emotion being worked with. A slow soothing tone and manner is crucial in accessing core vulnerable emotions. An encouraging, more energetic tone is helpful in supporting the more boundary setting emotions of anger and disgust.

Reestablishment of attachment patterns

Like for newborns and older children, an intuitive, caring, and predictable environment is the primary basis for secure attachment patterns and a buffer against enhancing vulnerability for the client (cf. Shaver, Mikulincer, & Chun, this volume). In the chain of several possible emotion regulation strategies, the creation of a sense of reliable sameness for the client is as important as it is with infants to create a sense of security. Repeated experience of emotional stress-reduction is vital for inducing confidence in predictability and "basic trust," which forms the basis for working toward a more stable personal identity and future dependable patterns of attachment. Only within a secure therapist–client interaction can the neural basis be established for later resistance and protection against stress. As the newborn human, most clients have well-developed capacities for sympathy with the expressions of interest and affection in a therapist, and this sets up the process of mutual attachment that is essential for normal development of therapeutic process and corrections within established and disturbed attachment patterns.

Although the relationships with the first caregivers functions as an imprint for later attachment relationships and for coping with emotional stress within that relationship, correction of attachment patterns throughout life is possible through alternate intimate relationships. The relationship with the therapist can provide a powerful buffer or psychobiological coregulation for a client. Imitative and contingent caring responsiveness, focused on the client, supports the client's sense of efficacy and autonomy and stimulates neural and thus cognitive and emotional assimilation. If clients are intuitively "understood" and confirmed in their impulses by a consistent intimate caring therapeutic relationship, they learn to trust the specific relation with their therapist, and with the therapist behavior and associated affects. Furthermore, secure internal representations of relationship attachment and the related emotional regulation behaviors, such as soothing, appear to function as a buffer against emotional stress, enabling the client not to lose trust, when for instance the partner is not emotionally available.

Interpersonal soothing

As in early childhood, and also later in life, it is a relationship with an attuned other, such as the caregiver, the partner, the therapist that is essential in developing interpersonal soothing as emotion regulation. When an empathic connection is made with the therapist, affect processing centers in the brain are effected and new possibilities open up for the client. This creates an optimal therapeutic environment in which clients feel safe to fully engage in the process of self-exploration and new learning but also contribute to clients' affect regulation by providing interpersonal soothing. Over time this external interpersonal regulation of affect (as the prompt soothing by the mother of the crying infant) becomes internalized into self-soothing or the capacity to regulate inner states. Soothing mainly comes interpersonally in the form of empathic attunement and responsiveness to one's affect and through acceptance and validation by another person. The provision of a safe, validating, supportive, and empathic environment in therapy helps primarily to soothe automatically generated underregulated distress as well as the internalization of the soothing of the therapist which strengthens emotion regulation capacities such as self-soothing.

People with underregulated affect have been shown to benefit as much from interpersonal validation as from the learning of emotion regulation and distress tolerance skills (Linehan, 1993; Linehan et al., 2002). Problems in vulnerable personalities arise most from deficits in the more implicit forms of regulation of emotion and emotional intensity, although deliberate behavioral and cognitive forms of regulation—more left hemispheric process—are useful for people who feel out of control. Over time it is the building of implicit or automatic emotion regulation capacities that is important for highly fragile personality disordered clients. Implicit forms of regulation often cannot be trained or learned as a volitional skill. Directly experiencing an aroused affect being soothed by relational or nonverbal means—a more right hemispheric process—is one of the best ways to build the implicit capacity for self-soothing. Being able to soothe the self develops initially by internalization of the soothing functions of the protective other (Stern, 1985). Empathy from the other over time is internalized and becomes empathy for the self (Bohart & Greenberg, 1997). These optimal therapeutic relational qualities thus facilitate the dyadic regulation of emotion through provision of safety, security, and connection. This breaks the client's sense of isolation, confirms self-experience, and promotes both self-empathy and self-exploration.

EMOTIONAL CHANGE IN THERAPY

In this section we shift focus and articulate principles of emotion assessment and of emotional change in therapy consistent with a one-factor and dynamic systems view of emotion regulation. Although these principles of emotional change were derived specifically for Emotion-Focused Therapy (EFT) (Greenberg, 2002) they are as applicable and potentially useful to other established therapy approaches, particularly those that include emotional components in their treatment.

Types of emotion

Not all emotions are the same; hence, therapists don't simply help clients get in touch with feelings or encourage the expression of all emotions. Rather, they distinguish among different types of emotions to guide their interventions. Therapists intervene differentially with clients, helping them to accept and integrate certain emotions, to acknowledge but bypass others, to express those that will enhance the relationship and to contain and soothe, or explore and transform others. This approach to differential intervention is based on the premise that some emotional expressions are adaptive whereas others are maladaptive. For example, anger may be adaptive or maladaptive depending on the function it serves in a given interaction. Below, we briefly explain our typology of emotions (Greenberg, 2002).

Primary adaptive emotions are the person's most fundamental, original reactions to a situation and are productive. These include rapid emotional reactions that originate from limbic areas of the brain, such as the amygdala (LeDoux, 1995). These include sadness in relation to loss, anger in response to violation, and fear in response to threat.

Secondary emotions are those responses that are secondary to other more primary internal processes and may be defenses against these processes. Secondary emotions are our reactions to our own emotional responses to a stimulus rather than the responses to the situation itself. They involve more implicit and explicit processing than primary responses, are much more influenced by conscious processing, and involve the evaluation and sometimes the inhibition or distortion of primary responses. Examples include feeling angry in response to feeling hurt, feeling afraid about feeling angry, or feeling guilty about a traumatic event by attributing responsibility to oneself for the event. In couples' interactions, secondary emotions are generally the harder relationship-damaging emotions of anger, disgust, and contempt. Secondary emotions need to be explored in order to get at their more primary generators.

Maladaptive primary emotions involve repetitive negative feelings that resist change. In being the very first reaction these are primary emotions, but they are based on wounds and unresolved past experience rather than on adaptive responses to present circumstances. These are feelings such as a core sense of loneliness, abandonment, shame, worthlessness, or recurrent feelings of anxious inadequacy or the explosive anger or abusive contempt that destroys relationships. These are the emotions we want to help clients regulate and transform. Having distinguished between different types of emotions important at the clinical level in discriminating what emotions are more or less functional for adaptive living, it is important to have a set of principles to guide therapeutic intervention.

Principles of emotional change in therapy

A set of empirically grounded principles is described below (Greenberg, 2002; Greenberg & Watson, 2005). These relate to both emotional arousal and emotion regulation in the broad sense of these terms. Before discussing ways of emotion regulation, especially in the broader view, certain distinctions about emotions need to be made in order to work with emotion.

Emotional awareness and expression of primary emotions

This involves helping clients to symbolize emotions in words and express them to someone. Putting emotion into words can be curative in and of itself. In therapy this helps people reveal their inner worlds both to themselves and to the therapist in a manner that has not previously occurred. This type of emotional awareness is not just talking about feeling—it involves experiencing the feeling in awareness. Accessing and experiencing emotions also are important in that they involve overcoming avoidance. People learn that by facing and acknowledging their most dreaded feelings and painful emotions and surviving they are more able to cope (Greenberg & Bolger, 2001). Emotional awareness provides access to the information and to the action tendency in the emotion (Greenberg, 2002). It helps us to make meaning of our experience and facilitates the assimilation of this experience into our self.

When we pay attention to our bodily experiencing, we find that it has in it the complexity of how we are living with oneself and others. At first this is an unclear, whole sense in your body that does not yet have words or parts, but is felt quite distinctly. We will try to measure a *"bodily felt sense"* of our situations. Experiential awareness is a process within the emotional process and part of the chain of emotion regulation. By facing dreaded feeling and other negative emotions, clients become more able to handle them. It makes them also aware that they "can" handle them! Symbolizing emotion in awareness promotes new meaning and helps to unblock the process by developing new narratives. The symbolization of experiences helps to unfold the process of processing and helps to organize the experience into a coherent story.

Emotional expression

The ability to communicate negative emotions to others in order to work through these emotions is often helpful in alleviating depression. For older children and adults, expressing verbally the experience of positive and painful experiences helps to process and organize these experiences (Bremner, 1999). We will look at how the principle of emotional expression operates within the context of EFT couple therapy. First, helping individuals gain emotional awareness of underlying emotions such as adaptive anger or sadness or even maladaptive fear and shame underneath their anger or contempt is a key to interactional change. In couples, secondary emotions such as angry blaming responses tend to fuel conflict. They represent attempted solutions to the problem of not getting needs met for closeness and autonomy, but instead these solutions become the problem. These responses tend to focus on the other and involve attack and attempts to destroy.

In these states people use "you" language, i.e. "You are bad, wrong, to blame, etc." Expressing secondary anger that obscures hurt and vulnerability does not dissipate the anger or enhance communication, but rather just tends to lead couples into further negative cycles and the therapy process in circles. Expression of the more vulnerable emotions of fear and shame allows partners to draw closer. Thus, if a partner feels secondary rage, he or she needs to learn how to calm the rage and access what is at the bottom of it. If one often gets very angry, one needs not only to control one's anger but also learn to experience and express more vulnerable feelings beneath the anger. Usually this involves feelings of shame, powerlessness, vulnerability, helplessness or feeling sad, lonely, or feeling abandoned. Expressing underlying fear, shame, or hurt will have a very different impact on one's partner than expressing destructive rage. Hence, being aware and getting in touch with core feelings as they arise are key ways to prevent the development of destructive rage. Therapists need to help people develop the ability to soothe their own maladaptive emotional states and insecurities and also to soothe these states in their partner. One of the best antidotes to negative escalation is the ability to soothe vulnerability in the self and other.

Regulation of emotional intensity

Emotions that require regulation generally are either secondary emotions, such as despair and hopelessness, or primary maladaptive emotions such as the shame of being worthless, the anxiety of basic insecurity and/or panic. Emotion regulation skills involve such things as identifying and labeling emotions, allowing and tolerating emotions, establishing a working distance, increasing positive emotions, reducing vulnerability to negative emotions, self-soothing, breathing, and distraction. Regulation of under-regulated emotion thus involves getting some distance from overwhelming despair and hopelessness and/or developing self-soothing capacities to calm down and comfort core anxieties and humiliation. Rather than dwelling on these activities, positive experience and support are helpful. Maladaptive emotions of core shame and feelings of shaky vulnerability also benefit from regulation in order to create a working distance from these rather than become overwhelmed by them. At the more deliberate levels, promoting clients' abilities to both distract, reappraise, and receive and be compassionate to their emerging painful emotional experience can be an important first step toward helping them tolerate emotion and being able to self-soothe (see below). Deliberate behavioral and cognitive forms of regulation—more left hemispheric process—are useful for people who feel out of control. Helping find ways to consciously, purposively, cope with emotions is a therapeutic first step for people who are highly distressed.

Physiological relaxation

Within the range of possibilities, progressive relaxation techniques, breathing techniques, massaging of the person who is in stress or suffers from stress appears to be effective to decrease the stress. Taking a warm bath to calm down (sensory regulation) or learning to distract by counting to ten if angry (cognitive regulation) can improve coping.

Aside from the pure physiological effects of tactile stimulation and relaxation, active relaxation of oneself improves the ability to make effective attempts at self-relaxation to handle future incoming stress. At the more deliberate levels, promoting clients' abilities to both distract, reappraise, and receive and be compassionate to their emerging painful emotional experience can be an important first step toward helping them tolerate emotion and being able to self-soothe (see below).

Mindfulness

Forms of meditative practice and self-acceptance often are most helpful in achieving a working distance from overwhelming core emotions. The ability to regulate breathing, and to observe one's emotions and let them come and go are important processes to help regulate emotional distress. Mindfulness treatments have been shown to be effective in treating generalized anxiety disorders and panic (Kabat-Zinn et al., 1992), chronic pain (Kabat-Zinn, Lipworth, Burney, & Sellers, 1986), and prevention of relapse in depression (Teasdale et al., 2000). Mindful awareness of emotions coupled with awareness of breathing is helpful in regulating symptoms of depression and anxiety and enhances coping.

Reappraisal

Reappraisal also has been found to help regulate emotion better than suppression (Gross, 1998). The creation of new meaning can help one view things in a new way and this helps regulate emotion. Sometimes it should be effective to reappraise cognitively the given information or situation in order to self-regulate and decrease negative emotion (Gross, 1999; Hariri et al., 2000). As we discussed before, we assume that this decline in negative emotion after reappraisal processes also helps the recovery of painful events and therefore emotional health, especially in the short run, in comparison with an experiential mode of processing intensifying negative emotion at first, but probably decreasing negative emotion in the longer run.

Positive imagery

Accentuating pleasant experience as well as accessing suppressed, unpleasant emotional experience is important. For example, a depressed person who is feeling "numb" may listen to a sad piece of music to help activate sad feelings and thereby become "unstuck." Imagination is a means of bringing about an emotional response. With practice people can learn how to generate opposing emotions through imagery and use these as an antidote to negative emotions.

Toleration of emotion and self-soothing

Another important aspect of regulation is developing clients' abilities to tolerate emotion and to self-soothe. Emotion can be downregulated by developing tolerance and by soothing at a variety of different levels of processing. Physiological soothing involves activation of the parasympathetic nervous system to regulate heart rate, breathing, and other sympathetic functions that speed up under stress. Implicit soothing of distressing emotion can be developed.

At the more deliberate behavioral and cognitive levels, promoting clients' abilities to receive and be compassionate to their emerging painful emotional experience is the first step toward tolerating emotion and self-soothing. Amygdala-based emotional arousal needs to be approached, allowed, and accepted rather than avoided or controlled (Greenberg & Paivio, 1997). In this process people use their higher brain centers such as the prefrontal and orbitofrontal area (cf. section "Affective Neuroscience" above) to consciously recognize the emergency messages sent from the lower level and then act to calm the activation by using coping self-talk and other conscious strategies for self-calming.

It appears that simply acknowledging, allowing, and tolerating emotion is an important aspect of helping regulate it. This soothing of emotion can be provided by individuals themselves, reflexively, by an internal agency, or from another person. As we have seen, self-soothing involves among other things diaphragmatic breathing, relaxation, development of self-empathy and compassion, and self-talk. Soothing also comes inter-personally (repetition) by feeling that one exists in the mind and heart of the other and the security of being able to soothe the self developed by internalization of the soothing functions of the protective other (Sroufe, 1996; Stern, 1985). It is important to make a distinction in emotion work between intensity of emotion and the depth of processing of the emotion. It is the depth of experience that is crucial, and it is the regulation of in-tensity that overwhelms that is vital in promoting the required depth of processing of emotion. Finally, emotion regulation involves not only the restraint of emotion, but at times its maintenance and enhancement.

Reflection on emotion

In addition to recognizing emotions and symbolizing them in words, promoting further reflection on emotional experience allows partners to integrate their emotions into their own stories. This final principle of emotional change is related to the first, emotional awareness, in that it involves making meaning of emotion. Reflection helps to create new meaning and develop new narratives to explain experience (Greenberg & Pascual-Leone, 1995). Reflection also allows people to reframe emotions and take a new position vis-à-vis others thereby regulating their emotion. Thus in relationships rather than one feeling, "I can't survive. I need you," a person can say, "I need you but I see that you have needs too." Simi-larly, reflecting on anger may allow one to change one's position from, "I am angry. I hate you and it is all your fault that I feel so alone and aban-doned," to "Yes, I do feel angry at you but it is not all your fault. I realize some of my anger belongs to my mother."

In addition, symbolizing traumatic emotion memories in words helps promote their assimilation into a person's ongoing self-narrative (van der Kolk & Fisler, 1995). Pennebaker, Francis, and Booth (2001) have also shown the positive effects of writing about emotional experience on auto-nomic nervous system activity, immune functioning, and physical and emotional health (e.g., Pennebaker, 1993, 1997). Pennebaker (1993) con-cludes that through language, individuals are able to organize structure and ultimately assimilate both their emotional experiences and the events that may have provoked the emotions. In addition, once emotions are in words, people are able to reflect on what they are feeling, create new meanings, and evaluate their own emotional experience.

▓ EMOTION TRANSFORMATION ·

A most fundamental principle of emotional processing involves the transformation of one emotion into another. Although the more traditional ways of transforming emotion either through their experience, expression, and completion or through reflection on them to gain new understanding do occur, we have found another process to be more important. This is a process of *changing emotion with emotion*. This novel principle suggests that a maladaptive emotional state can be transformed best by undoing it with another more adaptive emotion. In time, the coactivation of the more adaptive emotion along with or in response to the maladaptive emotion helps transform the maladaptive emotion. Spinoza (1967) was the first to note that emotion is needed to change emotion. He proposed that "An emotion cannot be restrained nor removed unless by an opposed and stronger emotion" (p. 195). Reason clearly is seldom sufficient to change automatic emergency-based emotional responses. Darwin (1897) on jumping back from the strike of a glassed-in snake, noted that having approached it with the determination not to start back, his will and reason were powerless against the imagination of a danger which he had never even experienced. Rather than reason with emotion one can transform one emotion with another.

Empirical evidence is mounting to support the importance of a process of changing emotion with emotion. Parrott and Sabini (1990) early on found that mood repair occurs by people recalling events that counteract both sad and happy moods, and that this is done without awareness. In a further interesting line of investigation, positive emotions have been found to undo lingering negative emotions (Fredrickson, 1998; Fredrickson & Levenson, 1998). The basic observation is that key components of positive emotions are incompatible with negative emotions. These results suggest that positive emotions fuel psychological resilience. In a further study, Tugade and Fredrickson (2004) found that resilient individuals cope by recruiting positive emotions to regulate negative emotional experiences. They found that these individuals manifested a physiological bounce back that helped them to return to cardiovascular baseline more quickly. In a study dealing with self-criticism, Whelton and Greenberg (2000) found that people who were more vulnerable to depression showed more contempt but also less resilience in response to self-criticism than people less vulnerable to depression. The less vulnerable people were able to recruit positive emotional resources like pride and anger to combat the depressogenic contempt and negative cognitions. These studies together indicate that emotion can be used to change emotion.

Davidson (2000) also suggests that the right hemispheric, withdrawal related, negative affect system can be transformed by activation of the approach system in the left prefrontal cortex. He defines resilience as the maintenance of high levels of positive affect and well-being in the face of adversity and highlights that it is not that resilient people do not feel negative affect but that what characterizes resilience is that the negative affect does not persist. Levenson (1992) has also reviewed research that indicates that specific emotions are associated with specific patterns of autonomic nervous system activity providing evidence that different emotions change one's physiology differentially. Emotion also has been shown to be differentially transformed by people's differing capacity to self-generate imagery to replace unwanted, automatically generated emotions with more desirable imagery scripts (Derryberry & Reed, 1996), suggesting the importance of individual differences in this domain.

Bad feelings appear thus to be able to be replaced by happy feelings—not in a simple manner by trying to look on the bright side—but by the evocation of meaningfully embodied alternate experience to undo the negative feeling. For example in grief, laughter has been found to be a predictor of recovery. Thus being able to remember the happy times, to experience joy, helps as an antidote to sadness (Bonanno & Keltner, 1997). Warmth and affection similarly often are an antidote to anxiety. In depression, a protest-filled, submissive sense of worthlessness can be transformed therapeutically by guiding people to the desire that drives their protest—a desire to be free of their entrapment. Isen (1999) notes that it has been hypothesized that at least some of the positive effect of happy feelings depends on the effects of joy on specific parts of the brain that influence purposive thinking. Mild positive affect has been found to facilitate problem solving (Isen, 1999). There is growing evidence that positive affect enhances flexibility, problem solving, and sociability (Isen, 1999). In addition, research on mood congruent judgment has shown that moods affect thinking and types of reasoning (Palfia & Salovey, 1993).

In a different line of research on the effect of motor expressions on experience, Berkowitz (2000) reports a study on the effect of muscular action on mood. Subjects who had talked about an angering incident while making a tightly clenched fist reported having stronger angry feelings, whereas fist clenching led to a reduction in sadness when talking about a saddening incident. This indicates both the effects of motor expression on intensifying congruent emotions and on dampening other emotions. Thus it appears that the expression of even the muscular expressions of one emotion can change another emotion. In addition and in line with the James–Lange theory of emotions, Flack, Laird, and Cavallaro (1999) have demonstrated that adopting the facial, postural, and vocal expression of an emotion increases the experience of the emotion whether or not the subject is aware of what emotion he/she is expressing. The experience of an emotion to some degree can thus be induced or intensified by putting one's body into its expression. It is interesting to note that there are individual differences in this capacity, with those who are more body sensitive showing this tendency to a greater degree. A more general line of research in social psychology on the effects of role-playing on attitude change also supports the idea that performing actions in a role brings people's experience and attitudes in line with the role (Zimbardo, Ebbesen, & Malasch, 1997). Role-playing can transform what is at first not real into something real, as saying something can lead to believing it (Myers, 1996). Thus, a possible way to evoke another emotion is to have people role-play its expression. As they express an emotion it will change their experience toward the expression.

In psychotherapy research, it has been found that music is helpful in evoking alternate emotions and even more helpful than imagery for changing emotion (Kerr, Walsh, & Marshall, 2001). Right frontal EEG activation normally associated with sad affect was shifted toward symmetry by both massage and music (Field, 2000). Shifts to more positive mood or at least to symmetry between sad and happy affect were accompanied by shifts from right to left frontal EEG activation, in both mothers and children (Field, 2000).

Finally, results of our single case investigations of therapies of depression combined with the larger groups studies, relating emotional arousal to outcome (Greenberg, 2002), supported the principle that emotional arousal and the attendant replacement of emotion with emotion occurred significantly more in cases with recovery of their depression than in poor outcome cases with no recovery of their depression. In a number of intensive analyses of good outcomes we found reductions in shame and fear and increases in anger, sadness, contentment, and joy. The patterns of emotional transformation however were idiosyncratic. However, which emotions replaced which were idiosyncratic to each case. It is important to note that the process of changing emotion with emotion goes beyond ideas of catharsis or completion, exposure or habituation, in that the maladaptive feeling is not purged, nor does it simply attenuate by the person feeling it. Rather, another feeling is used to transform or undo it. Although exposure to emotion at times may be helpful to overcome affect phobia in many situations in therapy, change occurs because one emotion transforms into or is replaced by another emotion rather than simply attenuating. In these instances emotional change occurs by the activation of an incompatible, more adaptive experience that undoes or transforms the old response. Clinical observation and our descriptive research suggest that emotional transformation often occurs by a process of dialectical synthesis of opposing schemes. When opposing schemes are coactivated they synthesize compatible elements from the coactivated schemes to form new higher-level schemes, just as in development when schemes for standing and falling, in a toddler, are dynamically synthesized into a higher-level scheme for walking (Greenberg & Pascual-Leone, 1995; Pascual-Leone, 1991). Schemes of different emotional states similarly are synthesized to form new integrations. Thus in therapy, maladaptive fear, once aroused, can be transformed into security by the more boundary-establishing emotions of adaptive anger or disgust, or by evoking the softer feelings of compassion or forgiveness. Similarly, maladaptive anger can be undone by adaptive sadness resulting in acceptance. Maladaptive shame can be transformed into acceptance by accessing both anger at violation, self-comforting compassion, and by accessing pride and self-worth. Thus the tendency to shrink into the ground in shame is transformed by the thrusting forward tendency in newly accessed anger at violation to produce confidence. Withdrawal emotions from one side of the brain are transformed by approach emotions from another part of the brain or vice-versa (Davidson, 2000).

How then are new emotions accessed? How does a therapist help people in the midst of their maladaptive experience to access emotions that will help them transform their maladaptive feelings and beliefs? A number of ways are listed below (see Greenberg, 2002, for a fuller description of methods of accessing new emotions).

Shift attention. Shifting people's focus of attention to pay attention to a background or subdominant feeling is a key method of helping them change their states. The subdominant emotion is often present in the room nonverbally in tone of voice or manner of expression.

Access needs/goals. Ask clients, when they are in their maladaptive state, what they *need* to resolve their pain. Raising a need or a goal to a conscious self-organizing system opens a problem space to search for a solution. At the affective level it conjures up a feeling of what it is like to reach the goal and opens up neural pathways to both the feeling and the goal.

Expressive enactment of the emotion. Ask people to adopt certain emotional stances and help them deliberately assume the expressive posture of that feeling and then intensify it. Thus you might use psychodramatic enactments and instruct your client "Try telling him I'm angry. Say it again, yes louder. Can you put your feet on the floor and sit up straight?" Coach the person in expressing until the emotion is experienced.

Remember another emotion. Remembering a situation in which an emotion occurred can bring the memory alive in the present.

Cognitively create a new meaning. Changing how one views a situation or talking about the meaning of an emotional episode often helps people experience new feelings.

The therapist expresses the emotion for the client. The therapist might express outrage, pain, or sadness the client is unable to express.

Utilizing the therapy relationship to generate new emotion. A new emotion is evoked in response to new interactions with the therapist.

■ CONCLUSION

Based on findings from affective neuroscience that the first experience in the world and the initial information we use to guide our reactions, is processed mentally primarily in an affective, subcortical, automatic, rather than in a cognitive, cortical, executive way, a complementary broader approach to emotion regulation has been proposed. In a broader sense, emotional regulation refers to all aspects of emotional processing, to its awareness, utilization, and transformation. In order to be able to change negative emotional distress and its associated meanings it is necessary to activate underlying affective experience and make it accessible to new experience. Awareness and expression of experiential self-related material and emotion is considered as more effective in facilitating emotional stress regulation than intellectual insight or cognitive change in itself. In this framework therapists work to enhance emotion-focused coping by helping people to become aware of, accept, make sense of, and transform their emotional experience. A necessary condition in psychotherapy is the relationship which is therapeutic, in and of itself, by serving an affect regulatory function which becomes internalized over time. This function is accomplished by offering a soothing, affect attuned, bond characterized by the therapist's presence and empathic attunement to affect as well as by acceptance and congruence. This type of relationship creates an optimal therapeutic environment in which clients feel safe to fully engage in the process of self-exploration and new learning, but also contributes to clients' affect regulation by providing interpersonal soothing. Within emotion-focused psychotherapy, three of the major empirically-supported principles are: (a) emotion awareness, (b) emotion regulation, and (c) emotion transformation.

(a) Emotional awareness and expression in psychotherapy involves the symbolization of emotions in words and the expression of them to someone. In therapy this helps people reveal their inner worlds in a manner that has not previously occurred, experiencing the feeling in awareness.

(b) Emotion regulation involves labeling, allowing, and tolerating emotions, establishing a working distance, increasing positive emotions, reducing vulnerability to negative emotions, self-soothing, breathing, and distraction. Regulation of underregulated emotion thus involves getting some distance from overwhelming emotion and/or developing self-soothing capacities to calm down and comfort these negative emotions. For people who feel out of control, deliberate, more left-hemispheric and prefrontal cognitive forms of regulation are useful. Helping people to find ways to consciously, purposively, cope with dysregulated emotions is a therapeutic first step for people who are highly distressed. Reflection on emotion to make sense of feelings and to create new narratives to explain experience. These narratives influence how we see the world and react to it.

(c) The last and probably most fundamental principle of emotional processing involves the transformation of one emotion by another. Although the more traditional ways of transforming emotions either through their experience, expression, and completion or through reflection on them to gain new understanding do occur, we have found the process of *changing emotion with emotion* as especially effective. This principle suggests that a maladaptive emotional state can be transformed best by undoing it with another more adaptive emotion.

REFERENCES

Adolphs, R., Tranel, D., & Damasio, H. (2001). Emotion recognition from faces and prosody following temporal lobectomy. *Neuropsychology, 15*, 396–404.

Beck, A. T. (1979). *Cognitive therapy and the emotional disorders.* New York: Meridian.

Bergdahl, J., Larsson, A., Nilsson, L. G., Ahlstrom, K. R., & Nyberg L. (2005). Treatment of chronic stress in employees: Subjective, cognitive and neural correlates. *Scandinavian Journal of Psychology, 46*, 395–402.

Berkowitz, C. D. (2000). *Pediatrics: A primary care approach* (2nd ed.). Philadelphia, PA: Saunders.

Bogen, J. E. (1995). On the neurophysiology of consciousness: I. An overview. *Consciousness and Cognition, 4*, 52–62.

Bohart, A. C., & Greenberg, L. S. (1997). *Empathy reconsidered: New directions in psychotherapy.* Washington, DC: American Psychological Association.

Bonanno, G. A., & Keltner, D. (1997). Facial expressions of emotion and the course of conjugal bereavement. *Journal of Abnormal Psychology, 106*, 126–137.

Bremner, J. D. (1999). Does stress damage the brain? *Biological Psychiatry, 45*, 797–805.

Bremner, J. D. (2002). *Does stress damage the brain?* New York: Norton.

Buber, M. (1958). *For the sake of heaven.* New York: Meridian.

Campos, J. J., Frankel, C. B., & Camras, L. (2004). On the nature of emotion regulation. *Child Development, 74*, 377–394.

Cozolino, L. (2002). *The neuroscience of psychotherapy.* New York: Norton.

Damasio, A. R. (1999). *The feeling of what happens.* New York: Harcourt Brace.

Darwin, C. (1897). *The formation of vegetable mould, through the action of worms with observations on their habits.* New York: Appleton.

Davidson, R. J. (2000). Affective style, psychopathology, and resilience: Brain mechanisms and plasticity. *American Psychologist, 55,* 1196–1214.

Davidson, R. J., & Fox, N. A. (1989). Frontal brain asymmetry predicts infants' response to maternal separation. *Journal of Abnormal Psychology, 98,* 127–131.

Dawson, G., & Ashman, S. B. (2000). On the origins of a vulnerability to depression: The influence of the early social environment on the development of psychobiological systems related to risk of affective disorder. In C. A. Nelson (Ed.), *The Minnesota Symposia on Child Psychology: The effects of early adversity on neurobehavioral development* (Vol. 31, pp. 245–279). Mahwah, NJ: Erlbaum.

Derryberry, D., & Reed, M. A. (1996). Regulatory processes and the development of cognitive representations. *Development and Psychopathology, 8,* 215–234.

Driessen, M., Beblo, T., Mertens, M., Piefke, M., Rullkoetter, N., Silva-Saavedra, A., et al. (2004). Posttraumatic stress disorder and fMRI activation patterns of traumatic memory in patients with borderline personality disorder. *Biological Psychiatry, 15, 55,* 603–611.

Eslinger, P. J. (1999). Orbital frontal cortex: Historical and contemporary views about its behavioral and physiological significance. An introduction to special topic papers: Part I. *Neurocase, 5,* 225–229.

Field, T. M. (1998). Maternal depression effects on infants and early interventions. *Preventive Medicine, 27,* 200–203.

Field, T. M. (2000). Infants of depressed mothers. In S. L. Johnson, A. M. Hayes, T. M. Field, N. Schneiderman, & P. M. McCabe (Eds.), *Stress, coping, and depression* (pp. 7–22). Mahwah, NJ: Erlbaum.

Flack, W. F., Laird, J. D., & Cavallaro, L. A. (1999). Emotional expression and feeling in schizophrenia: Effects of specific expressive behaviors on emotional experiences. *Journal of Clinical Psychology, 55,* 1–20.

Fredrickson, B. L. (1998).What good are positive emotions? *Review of General Psychology, 2,* 300–319.

Fredrickson, B. L., & Levenson, R. W. (1998). Positive emotions speed recovery from cardiovascular sequelae of negative emotions. *Cognitions & Emotion, 12,* 191–220.

Frith, C., Perry, R., & Lumer, E. (1999). The neural correlates of conscious experience: An experimental framework. *Trends in Cognitive Sciences, 3,* 105–114.

Gendlin, E. (1964). A Theory of Personality Change. In P. Worchel & D. Byrne (Eds.), *Personality change* (pp. 100–148). New York: Wiley.

Greenberg, L. S. (2002). *Emotion-focused therapy: Coaching clients to work through feelings.* Washington, DC: American Psychological Association.

Greenberg, L. S., & Bolger, E. (2001). An emotion-focused approach to the overregulation of emotion and emotional pain. *Journal of Clinical Psychology, 57,* 197–211.

Greenberg, L. S., Elliot, R., & Lietaer, G. (2003). Humanistic-experiential psycho-therapy. In G. Stricker & T. A. Widiger (Eds.), *Handbook of psychology. Vol. 8. Clinical psychology* (pp. 301–326). Hoboken, NJ: Wiley.

Greenberg, L. S., & Pascual-Leone, J. (1995). A dialectical constructivist approach to experiential change. In R. Neimeyer & M. Mahoney (Eds.), *Constructivism in psychotherapy* (pp. 169–194). Washington, DC: American Psychological Association.

Greenberg, L. S., & Paivio, S. C. (1997). *Working with emotions in psychotherapy*. New York: Guilford.

Greenberg, L. S., & Watson, J. C. (2005). *Emotion-focused therapy for depression*. Washington, DC: American Psychological Association.

Gross, J. J. (1998). The emerging field of emotion regulation: An integrative review. *Review of General Psychology, 2*, 271–299.

Gross, J. J. (1999). Emotion regulation: Past, present, future. *Cognition & Emotion, 13*, 551–573.

Gross, J. J. (2002). Emotion regulation: Affective, cognitive and social consequences. *Psychophysiology, 39*, 281–291.

Gross, J. J., & Levenson, R. W. (1993). Emotional suppression: Physiology, self-report, and expressive behavior. *Journal of Personality and Social Psychology, 64*, 970–986.

Hariri, A. R., Bookheimer, S. Y., & Mazziotta, J. C. (2000). Modulating emotional responses: Effects of a neocortical network on the limbic system. *Neuro-Report, 11*, 43–48.

Hunt, M. G. (1998). The only way out is through: Emotional processing and recovery after a depressing life event. *Behaviour Research and Therapy, 36*, 361–384.

Isen, A. M. (1999). Positive affect. In T. Dalgleish & M. J. Power (Eds.), *Handbook of cognition and emotion* (pp. 521–539). Chichester: Wiley.

Kabat-Zinn, J., Lipworth, L., Burney, R., & Sellers, W. (1986). Four-year follow-up of a meditation-based program for the self-regulation of chronic pain: Treatment outcomes and compliance. *Clinical Journal of Pain, 2*, 159–173.

Kabat-Zinn, J., Massion, A. O., Kristeller, J., Peterson, L. G., Fletcher, K. E., Pbert, L., et al. (1992). Effectiveness of a meditation-based stress reduction program in the treatment of anxiety disorders. *American Journal of Psychiatry, 149*, 936–943.

Kerr, T., Walsh, J., & Marshall, A. (2001). Emotional change processes in music-assisted reframing. *Journal of Music Therapy, 38*, 193–211.

Koenen, K. C., Driver, K. L., Oscar-Berman, M., Wolfe, J., Folsom, S., Huang, M. T., et al. (2001). Measures of prefrontal system dysfunction in posttraumatic stress disorder. *Brain and Cognition, 45*, 64–78.

Lane, R. D., & Nadel, L. (2000) (Eds.). *Cognitive neuroscience of emotion*. New York: Oxford University Press.

Lazarus, R. S. (1966). *Psychological stress and the coping process*. New York: McGraw-Hill.

Lazarus, R. S. (1993). Coping theory and research: Past, present, and future. *Psychosomatic Medicine, 55*, 234–247.

LeDoux, J. E. (1995). Emotion: Clues from the brain. *Annual Review of Psychology, 46*, 209–235.

Leijssen, M. (2004). Empathie als instrument voor effectieve geneeskunde. In M. Leijssen & N. Stinckens (Eds.), *Wijsheid in gesprekstherapie* (pp. 313–332). Leuven: Universitaire Pers Leuven.

Levenson, R. W. (1992). Autonomic nervous system differences among emotions. *Psychological Science, 3*, 23–27.

Linehan, M. M. (1993). *Cognitive-behavioral treatment of borderline personality disorder*. New York: Guilford.

Linehan, M. M., Dimeff, L. A., Reynolds, S. K., Comtois, K. A., Welch, S. S., Heagerty, P., et al. (2002). Dialectical behavior therapy versus comprehensive validation therapy plus 12-step for the treatment of opioid dependent women meeting criteria for borderline personality disorder. *Drug and Alcohol Dependence, 67*, 13–26.

Magai, C., & Haviland-Jones, J. (2002). *The hidden genius of emotions: Lifespan transformations of personality*. Cambridge: Cambridge University Press.

Markowitsch, H. J. (1998). Differential contribution of right and left amygdala to affective information processing. *Behavioural Neurology, 11*, 233–244.

Myers, J. M. (1996). *Cures by psychotherapy: What effects change?* New York: Praeger.

Palfia, T. P., & Salovey, P. (1993). The influence of depressed and elated mood on deductive and inductive reasoning. *Imagination, Cognition, and Personality, 13*, 57–71.

Panksepp, J. (1998). *Affective neuroscience*. New York: Oxford University Press.

Panksepp, J. (2003). Can anthropomorphic analyses of separation cries in other animals inform us about the emotional nature of social loss in humans? Comment on Blumberg and Sokoloff (2001). *Psychological Review, 110*, 376–388.

Parrott, W. R., & Sabini, J. (1990). Mood and memory under natural conditions: Evidence for mood-incongruent recall. *Journal of Personality and Social Psychology, 59*, 321–336.

Pascual-Leone, J. (1991). Emotions, development and psychotherapy: A dialectical constructivist perspective. In J. Safran & L. Greenberg (Eds.), *Emotion, psychotherapy and change* (pp. 302–335). New York: Guilford.

Pennebaker, J. W. (1993). Overcoming inhibition. Rethinking the roles of personality, cognition and social behavior. In J. W. Pennebaker (Ed.), *Emotion, inhibition and health* (pp. 100–115). Seattle, WA: Hogrefe & Huber.

Pennebaker, J. W. (1997). *Opening up: The healing power of expressing emotion*. New York: Guilford.

Pennebaker, J. W., Francis, M. E., & Booth, R. J. (2001). *Linguistic inquiry and word count*. Mahwah, NJ: Erlbaum.

Rolls, E. T. (1999). The functions of the orbitofrontal cortex. *Neurocase, 5*, 301–312.

Rolls, E. T. (2000). The orbitofrontal cortex and reward. *Cerebral Cortex, 10*, 284–294.

Schore, A. N. (2003). Early relational trauma, disorganized attachment, and the development of a predisposition to violence. In M. F. Solomon & D. J. Siegel

(Eds.), *Healing trauma: Attachment, mind, body, and brain* (pp. 107–167). New York: Norton.

Semple, W. E., Goyer, P., McCormick, R., Morris, E., Compton, B., Donvan, B., et al. (1992). Increased orbital frontal cortex blood flow and hippocampal abnormality in PTSD: a pilot PET study. *Biological Psychiatry*, 31, 129.

Siebert, M., Markowitsch, H. J., & Bartel, P. (2003). Amygdala, affect, and cognition: Evidence from ten patients with Urbach–Wiethe disease. *Brain*, 126, 2627–2637.

Spinoza, B. de (1967). *Opera–Werke*. (Latin and German, K. Blumenstock, Ed.). Darmstadt: Wissenschaftliche Buchgesellschaft.

Sroufe, L. A. (1996). *Emotional development: The organization of emotional life in the early years*. New York: Cambridge University Press.

Stern, D. (1985). *The interpersonal world of the infant: A view from psychoanalysis and developmental psychology*. New York: Basic Books.

Teasdale, J. D., Segal, Z. V., Williams, J. M., Ridgeway, V. A., Soulsby, J. M., & Lau, M. A. (2000). Prevention of relapse/recurrence in major depression by mindfulness-based cognitive therapy. *Journal of Consulting and Clinical Psychology*, 68, 615–23.

Tucker, D. M. (1981). Lateral brain function, emotion, and conceptualization. *Psychological Bulletin*, 89, 19–46.

Tugade, M. M., & Frederickson, B. L. (2004). Resilient individuals use positive emotions to bounce back from negative emotional arousal. *Journal of Personality and Social Psychology*, 86, 320–333.

van der Kolk, B. A., & Fisler, R. (1995). Dissociation and the fragmentary nature of traumatic memories: Review and experimental confirmation. *Journal of Traumatic Stress*, 8, 505–525.

Vandekerckhove, M. M. P., Markowitsch, H. J., Mertens, M., & Woermann, F. (2005). Bi-hemispheric engagement in the retrieval of autobiographical episodes. *Behavioural Neurology*, 16, 203–10.

Whelton, W., & Greenberg, L. (2000). The self as a singular multiplicity: A process experiential perspective. In J. Muran (Ed.), *Self-relations in the psychotherapy process* (pp. 87–106). Washington, DC: American Psychological Association.

Wittling, W. (1997). The right hemisphere and the human stress response. *Acta Physiologica Scandinavica*, 640(Suppl.), 55–59.

Young, G. B., & Pigott, S. E. (1999). Neurobiological basis of consciousness. *Archives of Neurology*, 56, 153–157.

Zimbardo, P., Ebbesen, E., & Malasch, C. (1997). *Influencing attitudes and changing behavior*. Reading, MA: Addison-Wesley.

PART IV

Setting the Stage: Culture and Society as Emotionally Regulated and Regulating Arenas

11

Passions as Cognitive and Moral Mistakes: The Case of Honor Killings in Europe

Unni Wikan

The verdict that was passed in Østre Landsret (Court of Appeal, Copenhagen on June 28, 2006) sent shock waves through the Pakistani community in Denmark—and beyond. Nine people were sentenced to a total of 120 years in prison for the murder of 18-year-old Ghazala, and attempted murder of her husband, Emal Khan. Six of the nine were family members, three were acquaintances or friends. All played their part in what the prosecutor called a mission carried out with military precision: to track the couple down—so that the family honor could be restored.

They made a mistake. And this is what occasioned the shock waves. "It's not right" protested some Danish-Pakistani boys with whom I talked right after the verdict, "to sentence the others, only the father and the brother!" True, the father had ordered the murder and the brother had carried it out—in broad daylight, at Slagelse train station, Denmark, where the couple were fleeing from their would-be assassin. "My brother, what are you doing?" Ghazala managed to emit, before she fell to the ground, shot three times. That's how Emal came to know that the murderer was her brother. Emal was badly wounded, but survived. They had been married for two days, and had been on the run for 18 days. An illicit love affair between two young people who should have had all the right in the world to fall in love and marry, had reached its "logical" conclusion. Ghazala had been in no doubt that her father would have her murdered.

The mistake of the operation destined to take Ghazala and Emal's lives was to think that the accomplices would go free; indeed, the plan seemed to have been that only the brother would be sentenced, if found guilty (he would argue that he had acted in self-defense as Emal attacked him). It would be hard on him, a young man, 30 years old, whose wife had borne him a son two days before he took his sister's life. He was a hard-working taxi driver with a clean record. But he was a Danish citizen, unlike his elder brother, hence the cost to the family of *him* landing in jail would be moderate; he could not be evicted from Denmark.

Not so with three of the "gang of nine" who, with stoic calm, received their sentences in Østre Landsret. Two were sentenced to eviction on completion of their time in jail. One was the only woman in the group, Ghazala's beloved aunt, Perveen, who was used to trick the couple out of their hiding place.

Utterly convinced that her father would have her murdered, Ghazala and Emal had sought protection from the police on two occasions during their 18 days in hiding; the police could not fathom what was at stake, and the couple was left to fend for themselves, realizing more and more what an impossible ordeal they faced. Indications were that the taxi milieu in Copenhagen (Ghazala's father was a powerful taxi company owner) was all on the lookout for them, so Ghazala and Emal fled far away, to Jylland, northern Denmark, where there are few Pakistanis. Here social workers understood their plight, and they were promised lodging shortly. It was in Jylland that they married, in a civil ceremony; a social worker bought Ghazala a bouquet of flowers. It was from Jylland that they traveled some three hours on the train to meet with Ghazala's aunt Perveen at a location outside of Copenhagen. It was to have been a secret meeting. Perveen had convinced them that she wanted to arrange a reconciliation between them and the father, and that her husband, Ghazala's mother's brother, was agreed; her daughter, Imran, was a close friend whom Ghazala had kept secret contact with, by email, since she ran away.

But Perveen was part of the operation—*the* crucial part. No one else could have lured Ghazala out from her hiding place. And so, as the tears flowed in the happy reunion where Perveen's 3-year-old son, whom Ghazala adored, also took part, Perveen's mobile phone was set so that her husband and his accomplices could hear their every word. Two hours after the reunion began, Ghazala lay dead. Mission completed. Emal's life was saved only thanks to the speed with which he received intensive care. He was now in a hospital that "the deadly operation" did their utmost to discover. For the mission *was not* completed. It was short of one life—the life of the one who would tell the full story of the meeting with Perveen and the many other sordid details of a story, set in a civilized country, that is reminiscent of the Middle Ages.

I should add that Emal did not say a bad word against Perveen during his testimony in court. He spoke of Ghazala's love for her, and her trust in her. Was the truth, also for him, too much to bear?

A civilized country, modern times. Ghazala's father is a dignified man,

30 years' resident of Denmark and fluent in Danish. He is very wealthy and highly respected. He was sentenced to life imprisonment whereas his son, the murderer, only got 16 years in jail. A 16-year sentence was also imposed on Ghazala's two uncles who had bought the pistol and urged the brother, against his instinctive protests, to kill Ghazala. Perveen got 14 years in jail; the one who drove the car to the place of execution got the lowest punishment, 8 years. He was employed in Ghazala's father's company and insisted that he had no clue as to what the party he drove was up to, which the court did not believe. Another driver who had been assigned the job before him ran away, suspecting full well what was going on.[1]

AN HISTORIC VERDICT

The verdict in the Ghazala case stands out as being the first in European history where the accomplices in an honor killing were sentenced, and not just the perpetrator(s).[2] In Sweden, the day before, the verdict fell in a case where a 17-year-old Afghan boy and his parents were charged with the murder of their sister/daughter's boyfriend. Only the boy was sentenced. In Germany, shortly before, three Kurdish-Turkish brothers were charged with the murder of 23-year-old Hatun Sürücü. But only the youngest, 17 years old, has been sentenced so far.

It is common in cases of honor killing to choose a minor to do the job, due to the mild sentence he will receive. (Four and nine years respectively in a youth institution, in the cases mentioned above.) Ghazala had no little brother and so it fell on her 30-year-old brother, father of two small children, to carry out the deed.

Honor killing

An honor killing is an extreme form of honor-related violence; it is violence carried to extremes—or what Fadime Sahindal's father, after murdering her, called "the final solution" (Wikan, 2003, in press a). "The final solution" is the end point, a last resort. It is used to restore honor for a collective, not just an individual. At stake is the honor of a clan, caste, tribe, family, or minority group. The murder is met with acclaim—it confers glory—which is why and how it is "honorable." The stain of dishonor is cleansed away. An honor killing is no impulsive act, but generally well planned, often long in advance, and carried out with meticulous "care." The perpetrator rarely acts under the influence of drugs or alcohol. An honor killing is murder executed in cold blood, which is not to say that the culprit is cold-hearted. He does what he has to do, whatever the complex of emotions in his heart.

Honor-related violence

Honor-related violence is a more humdrum, quotidian phenomenon. It does not draw attention to itself but parades as "the way things are." When Ghazala had confided in her mother her love for Emal, hoping for her mother's support, she was beaten by her brother and isolated in her room, left to eat all meals by herself. She was so distraught that she threatened to kill herself unless Emal helped her escape. At the airport in Islamabad, Pakistan, as Ghazala and her sister were taking leave with their mother, the mother embraced the sister, but not Ghazala. It was like slapping her in the face. Ghazala, already the outcast, was made distinctly aware that she was outside the bounds of natural, normal affections.

In the early hours of the morning after she arrived back in Copenhagen, she eloped. The police was told to tell her family that she had left by her own will, and was well. The family says they wanted to assure themselves, that's why they undertook to find her. Love and protection were the driving forces.

Love and protection *are* part and parcel of a system based on honor. That is why, time and again, girls who try to break out, find their way back. It is also why it is not given that finding one's way back will have dire consequences. Forgiveness and reconciliation can occur. But violence is usually just around the corner. Honor-related violence is part of a *system* of oppression. In day-to-day matters, it may not be so obvious. It enters as the way things are. But everyone knows full well their place within a hierarchy of powers and the consequences of disrespecting rules and regulations. They also know that minding one's own business is the rule in regard to the outside world. Reprisals, and the fear of reprisals, constitute part of an honor code.

Complicity of silence

It has been established without doubt that much if not all of the Pakistani milieu in Copenhagen knew in advance that Gholam Abbas's daughter was to be murdered because she had ruined the family honor by running away with an Afghan, a Pashtun. The Abbas family were high-ranking Gujers from Punjab who regarded Pashtuns as the bottom of the heap. Also in Oslo, Norway, many people knew. There had been a meeting comprising some 40 persons, several of them from Norway, at the Abbas family home in Copenhagen shortly after Ghazala eloped. The judgment of her father was unequivocal: his honor had been disgraced. It took no imagination to intuit what that meant.

So the question that haunts me is this: why did no one go to the police with what they knew? Why would a whole milieu sit back and let things happen? Let things move to their inexorable end? Some of those who "knew" would be people who were completely against honor killings, who would find it inhumane and utterly condemnable for a father to order his daughter's murder because she had simply fallen in love with a man—or for any other reason. We have to face these questions: Why the silence? What is at stake? What is it about honor that gives it such a hold over people's lives? What norms, values, and rules are implied?

And what emotions and feelings correspond to a concept of honor?

▨ HONOR KILLINGS

I shall try to take you part of the way to understand, based on my long-term research on honor, shame, and dishonor (Wikan, 1984, 1991, 2003). I say "part of the way" for I cannot claim ever to be able to understand, far less make others able to understand, what's honorable about murdering one's own daughter or sister. Ghazala's death haunts me continuously. But I can understand, and help others understand, the particular frame of reference, *the logic*, that lies behind, and that eventuates in some 5,000 honor killings yearly on a worldwide basis, according to Amnesty International. In Pakistan alone honor killings claim at least 1,000 lives annually, a third of which are men (Warraich, 2005). Males, however, are not killed by their own families, but by the enemy party in blood feuds, or by a lover's or wife's family. We do not find a pattern of families killing their own sons or brothers. We do find a pattern in several parts of the world of females being killed by their own brother, father, cousin, or spouse (who is often also a relative) (Ginat, 1997; Kressel, 1981; Mojab, 2004; Welchman & Hossain, 2005; Wikan, in press a). Put differently, what happened to Ghazala was not something that came as a surprise to people of the Pakistani community in Copenhagen. It made sense, also to those who deplored the murder. This "sense" is what we as analysts need to explore.

We do not know what is the frequency of honor killings in Europe. We have no reliable statistics. An honor killing can be defined as "an act of violence with the purported reason or intention to redeem the family's or clan's honor. This is achieved by killing the person who has shown disloyalty to his or her own group and thereby damaged the family's good repute. The family and its leaders are then exposed to the contempt and vilification or ridicule of others within the same social network or community" (Hjärpe, 2003, trans. mine).

The concept of honor killing is a newcomer to the European scene and it is only very recently that the police, in some countries, have been making an effort to assess the magnitude of the problem.[3] They are faced with a multitude of difficulties as honor killings may be covered up as suicides or accidents, or the victim may be taken abroad to be killed. What we can say with certainty, however, is that honor killings have "come West." We do not ever find in European history a pattern of daughters being killed by their own families (Johansson, 2005; Sandmo, 2005). Honor-related violence we find, and feuding, duels, and vendettas in which males were killed for honor-related reasons. In special cases, so called "bad feuds" (Elster, 1999, pp. 233–234), women and children might also be killed, but then always by *the other party*. What is particular and new to modern Europe is another phenomenon—of which Ghazala may stand to remind us.

▮ TO THINE OWN SELF BE TRUE

She did not leave behind many personal traces in the country of her birth, Denmark. She grew up in Pakistan and could not even speak Danish. She fell in love on a flight between Islamabad and Copenhagen to which she traveled yearly to renew her resident permit in Pakistan. We know that her family called her "Baby," which I take as a sign that she was a beloved girl. Even Perveen spoke of her as Baby in court, until she caught on to her interpreter's insistent reference to Ghazala. So we lost a little touch of intimacy—in a court case where the persons charged carried themselves with utter calm and control. But Ghazala's name is inscribed in Scandinavian history now as a person who stood true to her own self. "She chose the short-term happiness above no happiness at all," said the prosecutor, Jeanette Vincents Andersen. True to one's own self: it is a concept of honor that is highly regarded among many people, both East and West. It is also a concept that stands deadly opposed to the one that ruled Ghazala's life.

The communal rules

Honor here *is* a matter of rules. Said Fadime Sahindal in reference to her family's response to the murder of 15-year-old Sara in 1996: "My family thought it was right what happened. Sara got what she deserved. She knew the rules, she had broken the rules. The culprits were like martyrs to them [her family]" (SVT1, 1998). Sara, of Kurdish-Iraqi origin, had been murdered by her brother and cousin, 16 and 17 years old.

Sara is an interim person in the history of honor killings in Sweden. Sara's murder was the first to catch public attention and cause a debate as to whether honor killings existed or not. Was it right to charge "culture" with a role in condoning murder, or was this racist (cf. Demirbag-Sten, 2004; Elden, 2004; Wikan, 2002)? But the one to close the debate was Fadime. And so we will turn to her to give us some help in understanding what is at stake for many girls of immigrant background *and* for their parents. What is singular about Fadime's story is that she speaks to us from beyond the grave. She left traces, stamps, footprints engraved on Swedish soil; she left testimonies preserved for posterity in word, text, and picture. She was a public persona for the last four years of her life; she has become an icon after her death. In brief, this is the story of Fadime. (For two documentaries, see SVT1, 1998, 2002; for an in-depth account, see Wikan, 2003, in press a.)

Fadime

Fadime Sahindal was born in Eastern Turkey and came to Sweden when she was 7 years old. She had four sisters and one brother. She describes their life in Turkey as happy despite harsh material circumstance. They had clear-cut roles. Everyone knew what to do and what was expected of her or him. They were a close and tight-knit family. Things changed in Sweden. She was warned not to have Swedish friends and was not allowed to take part in outings at school. In her family's view "Kurdish girl" could not be reconciled with a "Swedish girl." The one was pure, the other not. Neither was education for a girl something her family valued. A girl should marry early a cousin from Turkey to help him get entry into Sweden. Education could give a girl ideas. Her future role was as housewife and mother. To be a virgin on marriage was also required. All of this entailed that the honor of the family was upheld.

At the age of 21, Fadime fell in love with Patrik, a Swedish-Iranian boy. When her family found out, Fadime realized that she had reached a crossroads. It was either Patrik or her family. She also knew what was in store when she chose Patrik: "I know I must live with death threats till their breath expires, it is the only way they can regain their pride, their honor" (SVT1, 1998). The family was further disgraced when Fadime, on receiving no help from the police, went to the media. "Maybe if I become publicly known, they will not dare to kill me," she said (ibid.). She was wrong. Publicity aggravates dishonor, it "is" dishonor. Honor resides not in acts or deeds, but in what becomes known or reputed about acts or deeds in the public domain.

Fadime next took her father and brother to court, and they were convicted for violence and death threats against her. She participated in a television documentary on her life in order to awaken the Swedish public and politicians to what they had not wanted to hear: that "honor" holds many girls in a tyrannical grip and that breaking the code of honor can mean death. But Fadime made it plain that her parents and her brother were victims too. They were controlled by the same system that celebrated the collective interest over and above the individual good. About her mother she said that she would be blamed, and would blame herself, for having failed to bring up a decent, well-behaved daughter. She believed her mother hated her. And when the journalist said it was not possible, a mother's love cannot just die, Fadime answered: "You don't understand; I have trampled on their honor; their honor is all they have. Now no one will want to marry girls of my clan. After what I have done, they will think that all are whores" (SVT1).

A month later, Patrik died in a car accident. A week afterwards, Fadime's brother tried to kill her on the street. She gathered together the shreds of her life and devoted herself to her studies in social work at a college in Östersund. She avoided the media after her brother was sentenced in August 1998. She felt that she had done her part, and wanted to be left at peace. Her family had extended her a lease on life: exile. She was warned to stay away from Uppsala or she would be killed. Fadime was killed in Uppsala on a secret meeting with her mother and two younger sisters. She lived to be 26 years old. "My father fired the shots, but others were behind," said her sister Songül in court. Sonül had been admonished by the mother to keep quiet and appeared in court with police escort.

BRINGING THE MATTER BACK HOME

My purpose in recounting parts of the cases of Ghazala and Fadime is to provide some concrete details with which to ponder analytical questions. It is also to bring the matter of honor killings "home." That Ghazala was a Danish citizen and Fadime a Swedish citizen grounds the problem in Scandinavia. That their families were long-time residents and not among the impoverished or ghettoized, bears mention. That in both cases there was *some* support within a community of people for taking a daughter's life, is significant. So is the fact that some of those who condemned the murder, said of the murderer: He had no choice, no alternative. Two cases only; we could mention others. But they suffice to highlight some common themes.

What emotions underpin the (particular) idea of honor that legitimates honor killings? How can honor killings be prevented? Or can they? Is it possible to regulate the drives, the motivations, or the mind-set that furnish support for honor killings? This latter question is essential, for as honor resides in the public gaze or "in the eye of the beholder," withdrawing support unmakes honor. I may be moving too swiftly here. Let us pause to clarify the concept of honor itself. Next we will move to an analysis of the emotions entwined with a concept of honor and of its relation to beliefs, judgments, and reason or rationality.

Clarifying the concept of honor

When Fadime said, "I have trampled on their honor, their honor is all they have," what is at stake? Who are "they"? And how can honor be "all"?

The "honor" Fadime refers to is one that is not easily conveyed in an Anglo-Saxon language where a single word "honor" confuses two distinct phenomena that in languages like Kurdish, Turkish, Arabic, Persian, Dari, Urdu, and Punjabi have different references. One is the honor you receive by virtue of your good deeds and material standing; it can be increased and decreased. The other is a matter of all or none. It can be lost and regained, but not diminished or added to. It is contingent on the moral/sexual conduct of females in the family, clan, caste, or tribe.

This honor is your due as an equal among equals. It is what Stewart (1994) labels a horizontal form of honor, in contradistinction to the vertical one mentioned above. It is collective and belongs to you as a member of a group; if besmirched, the *dis*honor will afflict all members jointly. "Now no one will want to marry girls of my clan, all are whores," said Fadime. Her clan had 1,000 members, 300 in Sweden alone. What Fadime did spelt disgrace for all; and it undermined their material position as well as their ability to forge political and social alliances through marriage.

Honor has to do with self-esteem and social recognition. They are two sides of the same coin (Pitt-Rivers, 1966). But in some societies the collective response, or reputation is *the* anchor point for honor—it *is* "honor." Hence there is little leeway for standing apart from the crowd, especially as a female. Socially regulated conventions control behavior, especially in regard to female sexuality and decency. Khader (2002) uses the word "sex-honor," but as he points out, behavior seen in the West as "social" may come under the label "sexual" in some immigrant communities.

The opposite of this concept of honor is not shame, which is too weak a word, but dishonor—honor's absence (Stewart, 1994). Shame can come in degrees. Dishonor is absolute, a matter of all or nothing. Not all honor "regimes" accept or exonerate honor killings. I have worked in Muslim societies where the mere thought of ordering a daughter's death would be inconceivable and abhorrent, even though "honor" is a salient value also there (Wikan, 1990, 1991, 1996). Observations of the complexities of real life are necessary to gauge the value of honor as a yardstick for practical life (Wikan, 1984).

What feelings pertain to honor

The feeling part of honor is pride. The feeling part of dishonor is humiliation and shame. It was vividly brought out in the court cases against Fadime's father. He cried his heart out that she had exposed him to world opinion (värdsopinionen). Ridicule was heaped on him, he sank into despair. It is the community response he refers to, or what he perceives as the community response. Fadime pestered and tormented the family, he contended. She painted them as a monster family. *She* was the aggressor, not the family. There is no doubt that the family was mortified, and had reason to feel mortified, by the picture of them that did appear in the media.[4]

Honor then, and its counterpart dishonor or no-honor, is a fact of the world, a public thing, as well as a state of mind. It is easier to understand *this* concept of honor as fact than as feeling and motivation. The task I set myself in researching the Fadime case was to understand the motivating force behind the murder: it meant trying to empathize with the perpetrator(s) without in any way condoning the abhorrent act. I was helped by having access to many different kinds of materials, sources, and viewpoints, and by attending the court case both at the municipal and the appeal level (Wikan, 2003, in press a). I gained an insight that eluded me at the Ghazala case, but stood me in good stead even here. The accused in the Ghazala case seemed cut in stone except for the aunt who cried when she was interrogated. Otherwise, she too kept a stoic face.

Throughout the 20 plus days in court, the males carried themselves with utter calm and control as if they did not have any feelings—with one exception. As Emal in his testimony comes to the point where he (badly wounded) gets on his knees and gazes down, only to see Ghazala dead beside him, the mother's brother starts wiping his eyes. He struggles to gain control but then leaves the room, and returns after a while, red-eyed. Had I not been sitting right next to him, I would not have noticed.

Had I not been provoked by his and his wife's joking and laughing until this point, as Emal spoke, I might have taken my eyes from him. Now I gained a glimpse of a heart hidden from view. I would not call it an enlightened moment—the phrase seems preposterous (though I have used "enlightened moment" elsewhere precisely to connote incidents or moments like this when parts of a puzzle suddenly come together) (Wikan, 1991, p. 238, 1990, pp. 139ff). But it helped me to see that here was a man—whether he was crying for Ghazala or for himself and his family (he had four children), or both, we cannot know.

The laughter and joking in court I now see as the couple's desperate attempt to keep themselves from falling apart publicly. It is a well-known formula that I know from research elsewhere (Wikan, 1990). And yet I was utterly judgmental, until the moment when the uncle started to cry.

An absence of emotion displayed does not mean that people do not feel. Social conventions regulate emotional expressions, also in times of trauma. The fact of an audience filters emotions by affecting self-presentation. The nine accused in the Ghazala case constituted a forum within the court hall. They held each other up the way a uniform can. The mother's brother breaking out in tears does not undermine this interpretation. He sat at the very back on this special occasion when Emal gave testimony and we had all been removed to a hall above the courtroom for reasons of top security. His coaccused, but for his wife, did not see him, they sat in front. The point here is the obvious one of the context affecting people's ability to keep up appearances.

Compare with the Fadime case, which was a very emotional affair. Emotions were strongly enacted and expressed both by the accused and his family in the audience. It was much easier to gauge the human dramas, indeed to conclude that "they" were human. The problematic facing me and others in the Ghazala case was the seemingly inhumane adversaries she had faced.

Now "honor" does require a man to be composed and contained. The accused in the Ghazala case stood true to form. But emotional expression is also strategic. Feelings do not just flow, they can be manipulated. An accused, like Fadime's father, whose only hope for a lenient sentence lies in being accorded psychosocial care, can well afford to be emotional in a way not befitting, or benefiting, an accused whose whole defense rests on his having wanted to rescue his sister out of the grip of a wild Afghan, when the latter attacked him, and the pistol misfired.

The accused in the Ghazala case all acted dignified—in line with their defense of being simply good people. Internal family dynamics also play a role. Ghazala's family presented a common front. But in the Fadime case, the sister Songül testified against the father. So an internal family drama was enacted in full view of the public, and with me sitting in the audience right among the family, I experienced in the flesh, so to speak, the full force of their emotional expressions. (I had been assigned a seat in the middle of the two rows in the back reserved for the family which afforded me a privileged viewpoint.) Add that Ghazala is reported to have said she hated her father, whereas Fadime loved hers.[5] Ghazala was convinced that her father would have her murdered whereas Fadime did not think that her father would kill her; it was her brother she feared. "Poor Daddy," she said three times on the evening when she was killed, according to her sister Songül.

BEYOND RESONANCE

As analysts, these snippets of information constitute part of the picture we try to piece together when at pains to understand the emotions—and feelings—of persons who elude understanding. I cannot for the life of me understand the nine accomplices who would have Ghazala murdered (and Emal, too). I understand the logic of the operation and the belief system that motivate people to play their part in an inhumane endeavor like this. I know what was at stake in terms of social and material costs. And yet *because* the persons elude me as full-fledged human beings, in a way that was not the case in the Fadime affair, I cannot extend them my empathy. I feel for Perveen who opposed her defense lawyer's staking his claim to a lenient sentence for her on the only option he had: culture. She was culturally obliged, he argued (referring to anthropological sources), to be submissive to her husband, hence she had no choice. Perveen did not agree. I feel for Ghazala's brother, who did not have much of a choice either, and for some of the others. But "feeling with" is not enough. There is an absence of my being able to enter into the feeling-mind, the emotional complex and deliberations of a community of people who reaped honor, or thought they would reap honor, by killing an 18-year-old girl whom they used to call Baby, a term of endearment, I believe, and her beloved husband.

Perhaps what is missing for me, most of all, is a glimpse of the *dilemmas* the persons faced. In all my previous research on the emotions, including the Fadime case, what has stood me in good stead has been to gain a glimpse of the complexities of the human heart, and the often insurmountable dilemmas and perplexities people faced. *Going beyond the words* is one way of phrasing it, *resonance* another (Wikan, 1992). We are helped in our understanding of honor killings (and failed honor killings) by having some accounts by near-victims (e.g., Güvercile, 2005;

Karim, 1996; Souad, 2003) or bystanders (Ginat, 1997; Swanberg, 2002). What they bear out is the disbelief even of persons who are reared in traditions where honor killings are well known, that *their* father or brother or uncle could will his honor above all else. Norwegian-Pakistani Nasim Karim, who barely escaped an honor killing, describes her shocking realization that her beloved father actually put his honor above her life (Karim, 1996); Swedish-Iraqi-Kurdish Breen Atrushi criticizes her father for "not being a man" in that, when *he* didn't have the guts to kill her sister Pela, he let his brothers do it. Nor can she fathom how her uncles, whom she and Pela loved and respected, could do what they did (Swanberg, 2002). In other words, the enigmatic nature of love turned into a demon that haunts family members as well.

Pela's mother divorced her husband after Pela's murder and her whole family was devastated. I assume that Ghazala's murder must also have been a traumatic affair to many of those who loved her, perhaps even to her father or brother. But we must further be prepared to find that honor killing is not "one thing." Cultural specificities can both ameliorate the "shame" and "disgrace" and aggravate the risks of "the only solution" being executed. Moreover, if it is true, as Tolstoy said, that all happy families are alike, but every unhappy family is unhappy in its own way, then surely this must apply prima facie to families tormented to the point where killing a family member seems the only way out.

Despite the differences between the Fadime case and the Ghazala case, I conclude that the *social* regulation of honor is similar in the two cases. It is the public that holds the key to honor or disgrace. It is gossip, ridicule, defamation, and disdain—or what is perceived to be so—that carry the day. How to effect change within such a system? How to move on to a *different* conceptualization of honor that is life-preserving and welfare-conducive— one that Ghazala and Fadime personified? Both attempted to do things the right way, to stay true to their parents' cultural traditions while opting for personal happiness and freedom that should have been their lot.

The need for rights

In his article "When justice replaces affection: the need for rights" Waldron (1988) poses the question: "Why do individuals need rights?" (p. 625). His argument is that "the structure of rights is not constitutive of social life, but instead to be understood as a position of fall-back and security in case other constituent elements of social relations ever come apart" (p. 629). What is especially relevant for the cases we have considered is a second point Waldron makes: that the structure of rights "also furnishes a

basis on which people can act to initiate *new* relations with other people."
Indeed:

> [t]hat may be the job of legal rules and legal rights: to constitute a non-
> affective framework for actions that are novel from a communal point of
> view. Without some such impersonal framework, the creative human desire
> for new initiatives faces a terrifying vacuum: If it is not to be stifled by ex-
> isting community, it must take its chances beyond community. But that
> would be a world unstructured by *any* basis for security and expectation.
> (pp. 631–632)

Romeo and Juliet provides an example:

> At a superficial level, Shakespeare's *Romeo and Juliet* is a noble and lamen-
> table tragedy of star-crossed 'death-marked' love . . . But *Romeo and Juliet*
> can also be read as a deeper text about the dangers that beset a new and
> unforeseen social initiative—in this case a romantic initiative—in circum-
> stances where the only available structures for social action are those embed-
> ded in the affections and disaffections of the existing community. (p. 632)

Rights as fall-backs give people the vantage point from which to proceed
when faced with "the tragedy of the broken bond":

> The point is not simply the liberal one about the importance of individuals
> autonomously shaping their lives. It is also that these processes of individ-
> ual thought, reflection, and change are source of many of the new begin-
> nings in the world, including new communal beginnings. (p. 645)

▊ NEW COMMUNAL BEGINNINGS

Ghazala and Emal could be seen as people who tried to forge new beginnings in a world cemented by ethnic and clan rivalries. They met on
an airplane, as people do nowadays. Paradoxically, it was her father's
doing that Ghazala moved back and forth between two continents. He
wanted her to grow up as a Pakistani girl while keeping her Danish citi-
zenship which vastly increased her value as a future bride. In Pakistan,
as the daughter of a rich man, Ghazala has access to email and SMS. She
strikes up a connection. She makes a new beginning. She tries to mobilize
her mother's support; how could she ever believe she would succeed? But
in the world today "death-marked" love happens at times without meeting with "the final solution." Things are moving, changing. Ghazala had
a foot in each culture. In Denmark, Emal may have seemed quite akin to

herself. He was a Muslim, like her, and spoke Urdu, like her. She knew she should marry a cousin, but also that she had the right to choose her own spouse—according to the Quran, Pakistani law, and Danish law. So where was the need for a "new" beginning?

Ethnic, clan, and caste rivalries are being reinforced in present-day Europe, as in much of the world. Communal bonds are being strengthened as the children and grandchildren of non-Western immigrants marry a fetched spouse to a higher degree than their forebears did (Charsley, 2005). The material value of marriage to a citizen or resident of Europe has increased. Family reunification through marriage provides a visa and other welfare benefits. Ghazala's murder was a warning to other girls to forgo "new communal beginnings." The attempted murder of Emal was a warning to men not to challenge hard-core boundaries and cleavages.

Öhman (2006) observes that from an evolutionary perspective, "an important priority for any culture is to domesticate emotions that are likely to generate conflicts and threaten group cohesion. An essential component of socialization, therefore, is to acquire the ability to regulate emotion" (p. 38). An important priority for any culture is also to reproduce. Progeny belongs among Muslims to the father's patrilineage. That Ghazala should bear a Pashtun child would seem outrageous to her caste. If other girls followed suit and bore "wrong children," the caste would diminish and be demeaned.

Ghazala and Emal valued their communal identities. Emal mobilized a mediator, a well-reputed Pakistani-Dane, who tried to contact Ghazala's father, unsuccessfully. But he stood by when they eloped and gave them lodging until it was too risky, whereupon he found them another helper. In other words, there *were* people there trying to forge new beginnings, not just Ghazala and Emal. There were people from the Pakistani-Danish community who went out of their way, at great personal risk, to help the young couple. They felt that love should be able to triumph over hatred and contempt; that in the modern world one has the right to create new bonds and new connections. Our Romeo and Juliet, Emal and Ghazala, did have a legal fall-back position. The problem is that the honor code is a law unto itself. But the law can help to regulate the emotions. One of the (non-family) convicts in the Ghazala case said: "Please tell everyone never to get involved in a thing like this. It's not worth it!" (Møller, 2006).

REGULATING THE EMOTIONS

A cost-benefit analysis can help regulate emotions, not just at the individual but at the societal level. Communities can decide that the cost of sacrificing a member is too much to bear—not just because of human affection or the prospect of punishment for the perpetrator(s), but also identity-wise: "honor killing" is linked with culture or tradition (Akkoc, 2004; Mojab, 2004). For a minority to be associated with honor killing is to be demeaned in the eyes of the majority. The general stance in cases of honor-related crimes in Scandinavia is for the accused to deny that honor was a motivating force. "Honor" has become a deeply compromised idea in the larger society as honor-related violence has become a human rights issue. Norway and Belgium have criminalized forced marriage in an attempt to provide support not just for youngsters but even their parents who can be under extreme pressure from relatives back home to provide "a human visa" through marriage (Storhaug, 2003).

Law can underscore human attachments which are there, but subject to societal pressure. Fadime's mother violated the honor code when she was reconciled with Fadime behind the menfolk's back and met secretly with her. Pela's mother divorced her husband after Pela's murder and her kin broke entirely with his kin. That Kurdish Iraq, where Pela had been brought to be murdered, passed a law just afterwards criminalizing honor killings, can support those affective bonds that value human life above all. There is no short-cut, however: a countereffect of the law is an upsurge of purported suicides among young women that are suspected to be covered-up honor killings (Begikhani, 2005). But significant changes in public consciousness are taking place thanks to the work of human rights activists, nongovernment and international organizations. But with what effect on the emotions?

Emotions are commonly regarded as evaluative judgments relating to questions of particular personal importance. Whether emotions can be chosen or not is debated. Solomon (1983) argues that they can; since emotions are judgments, then they are things that we choose and for which we can be held responsible. Others (e.g., Neu, 2004) contend that "it is not clear that judgments, any more than feelings, are generally things that we choose. Many of our judgments, emotional or otherwise, are no more the product of rational deliberation than are such things as . . . the career we follow, or the place we live" (Dixon, 2004, p. 3). Dixon (2004, pp. 3–4) further notes: "A second problem with the idea that we are responsible for our emotions is that, at the more primitive end of the spectrum, emotions are physical reactions that are virtually impossible to control." He suggests that "emotions" is "an unhelpfully broad category . . . and that we need to differentiate between primitive passions and cognitive sentiments, and to illuminate the ways in which each can be implicated in failures as well as successes of reason and virtue."

"The way we normally know emotions is through feelings, which are elusive, capricious and probably changed by the very act of observing them," notes Öhman (2006, p. 34). But emotions *are* observable as objects of research through verbal statements, body language, physiological changes, and action: "Actions are another good indicator of emotion, since an important function of emotion is to prime and add urgency to action" (p. 34). Damasio (1994) has argued that feeling is essential to reasonable judgment by helping to establish priorities for action. However, "[k]nowing about the relevance of feelings in the processes of reason does not suggest that reason is less important than feelings . . . On the contrary, taking stock of the pervasive role of feelings may give us a chance of enhancing their positive effects and reducing their potential harm" (p. 246).

■ CONCLUDING REMARKS

Damasio's insights can be applied to the problem of honor killing, I believe. It is feelings—feelings of shame, humiliation, despair, anguish, fear, anger, hatred, pride, contempt, resentment, and self-respect—that propel honor killings. Envy might also apply, as the public, which has a crucial role in inflicting dishonor through ridicule and gossip, can be motivated by envy and not just by having a common cause with the family of the victim by sharing a common tradition. The problem we face, however, is that from a certain moral viewpoint, killing for honor's sake *is* reasonable. It is rational. Feeling and reason interact to support one another. I believe, however, that when "reason" takes precedence it is because of the suppression of life-promoting feelings that could interfere with "reason"—feelings like love, pity, compassion, and respect. I assume that at some level there is a blockage between body and mind or emotion; that the mind becomes disembodied and detached from its basic feelings.

This is a point I cannot substantiate for lack of empirical evidence. We are still in infancy regarding research on this crime against humanity that has only recently been internationally defined as a human rights issue (Connor, 2005; Wikan, in press b). I have written above that honor killings are carried out in cold blood which is not to say that the person is cold-hearted. Fadime's father was unanimously described as a kind and mild-mannered man. Ghazala's brother was apparently a good person until tragedy struck. Heshu Yones's father tried to commit suicide after murdering her in London in 2002; family tragedies often follow in the wake of compliance with social pressure to kill.

Damasio (1994) quotes William Faulkner who told his fellow writers to leave no room in their workshops "for anything but the old verities and truths of the heart, the old universal truths lacking which any story is ephemeral and doomed—love and honor and pity and pride and compassion and sacrifice" (p. 254). Honor killings has it all, in superhuman proportions. We are just beginning to understand these terrible tragedies of the human heart and human lives. The legacies of Fadime and Ghazala are to enjoin us to muster all the understanding we can to help change a code that claimed their lives and ravaged their families. Condemning honor killings is not enough.

NOTES

1 Møller, 2006, provides a detailed account of the Ghazala case.
2 Among the fortuitous circumstances were (a) Emal surviving and being able to testify, (b) 6,000 telephone transcripts that revealed the coordination of the culprits, and (c) compromising evidence from two of the accused that undercut the coherent story of the six family members.
3 For example, the Swedish police estimate that there has been one to two honor killings yearly since the 1980s (Älgamo, 2004).
4 A poignant account is provided by Fadime's little sister, 13 years old, in Wikan, in press a.
5 The statement regarding Ghazala came from Emal and the woman who lodged the couple.

REFERENCES

Akkoc, N. (2004). The cultural basis of violence in the name of honour. In S. Mojab & N. Abdo (Eds.), *Violence in the name of honour: Theoretical and political challenges* (pp. 113–126). Istanbul: Bilgi University Press.

Älgamo, K. A. (2004). Confronting honour violence: The Swedish police at work. In S. Mojab & N. Abdo (Eds.), *Violence in the name of honour: Theoretical and political challenges* (pp. 203–210). Istanbul: Bilgi University Press.

Begikhani, N. (2005). Honor-based violence among the Kurds: The case of Iraqi Kurdistan. In L. Welchman & S. Hossein (Eds.), *"Honor": Crimes, paradigms and violence against women* (pp. 209–229). London: Zed Books.

Charsley, K. (2005). Unhappy husbands: Masculinity and migration in transnational Pakistani marriages. *The Journal of the Royal Anthropological Institute, 11,* 85–106.

Connor, J. (2005). United Nations approaches to "crimes of honor." In L. Welchman & S. Hossein (Eds.), *"Honor": Crimes, paradigms and violence against women* (pp. 22–41). London: Zed Books.

Damasio, A. R. (1994). *Descartes' error: Emotion, reason, and the human brain.* New York: Grosset/Putnam.

Demirbag-Sten, D. (2004). Gendering multiculturalism. In S. Mojab & N. Abdo (Eds.), *Violence in the name of honour: Theoretical and political challenges* (pp. 143–148). Istanbul: Bilgi University Press.

Dixon, T. (2004). Why I am angry: The return to ancient links between reason and emotion. *Times Literary Supplement,* October 1, 3–4.

Elden, A. (2004). Life-and-death honour: Young women's violent stories about reputation, virginity and honor—in a Swedish context. In S. Mojab & N. Abdo (Eds.), *Violence in the name of honour. Theoretical and political challenges* (pp. 91–100). Istanbul: Bilgi University Press.

Elster, J. (1999). *Alchemies of the mind: Rationality and the emotions.* New York: Cambridge University Press.

Ginat, J. (1997). *Blood revenge: Family honor, mediation, and outcasting.* Brighton: Sussex Academic Press. (Original work published 1987.)

Güvercile, S. (2005). *Æresdrab.* Copenhagen: Aschehoug.

Hjärpe, J. (2003). *Hedersmord.* Nationalencyklopedin. Retrieved Jan. 15, 2007 from http://www.ne.se.

Johansson, K. (Ed.) (2005). *Hedersmord: Tusen år av hederskulturer.* Lund: Lagerbringbiblioteket.

Karim, N. (1996). *Izzat: for ærens skyld.* Oslo: Cappelen.

Khader, N. (2002). *Ære og skam: Det islamske familie- oglivsmønster i Danmark og Mellemøsten.* København: Borgen.

Kressel, G. M. (1981). Sororicide/filiacide: Homicide for family honor. *Current Anthropology, 22,* 141–58.

Mojab, S. (2004). The particularity of "honour" and the universality of "killing." In S. Mojab & N. Abdo (Eds.), *Violence in the name of honour. Theoretical and political challenges* (pp. 15–38). Istanbul: Bilgi University Press.

Møller, A. S. (2006). *Ghazala—et æresdrab i Danmark.* Århus, Denmark: Siesta.

Neu, J. (2004). Emotions and freedom. In R. C. Solomon (Ed.), *Thinking about feeling* (pp. 163–182). New York: Oxford University Press.

Öhman, A. (2006). Making sense of emotion: Evolution, reason & the brain. *Dædalus, 135,* 33–45.

Pitt-Rivers, J. (1966). Honour and social status. In J. G. Peristiany (Ed.), *Honour and shame: The values of Mediterranean society* (pp. 19–77). London: Weidenfeld & Nicolson.

Sandmo, E. (2005). Hvorfor ikke? In K. Johansson (Ed.), *Hedersmord: Tusen år av hederskulturer* (pp. 3–7). Lund: Lagerbringbiblioteket.

Solomon, R. C. (1983). *The passions: The myth and nature of human emotion.* Notre Dame, IN: University of Notre Dame Press. (Original work published 1976.)

Souad. (2003). *Brûlée vive.* Paris: Oh! Editions.

Stewart, F. H. (1994). *Honor.* Chicago: University of Chicago Press.

Storhaug, H. (2003). *Human visas: A report from the front lines of Europe's integration crisis.* Oslo: Kolofon.

SVT1 (1998). *Striptease.* Samhällsmagasin. Reporter M. Spanner. First featured May 6, 1998.

SVT1 (2002). *Fadime—Frihetens Pris.* Dokument Inifrån. First featured October 17, 2002.

SVT4 (2002). *Hederns pris.* Reporter J. Åsard. First featured October 16, 2002.

Swanberg, L. K. (2002). *Hedersmordet på Pela: Lillasystern berättar.* Stockholm: Bokförlaget.

Waldron, J. (1988). When justice replaces affection: The need for rights. *Harvard Journal of Law and Public Policy, 11*, 625–647.

Warraich, S. A. (2005). "Honor killings" and the law in Pakistan. In L. Welchman & S. Hossein (Eds.), *"Honor": Crimes, paradigms and violence against women* (pp. 78–110). London: Zed Books.

Welchman, L., & Hossein, S. (Eds.) (2005). *"Honor": Crimes, paradigms and violence against women*. London: Zed Books.

Wikan, U. (1984). Shame and honour: A contestable pair. *Man, 19*, 635–652.

Wikan, U. (1990). *Managing turbulent hearts: A Balinese formula for living*. Chicago: University of Chicago Press.

Wikan, U. (1991). *Behind the veil in Arabia: Women in Oman*. Chicago: University of Chicago Press. (Original work published 1982.)

Wikan, U. (1992). Beyond the words: The power of resonance. *American Ethnologist, 19*, 460–482.

Wikan, U. (1996). *Tomorrow, God willing: Self-made destinies in Cairo*. Chicago: University of Chicago Press.

Wikan, U. (2002). *Generous betrayal: Politics of culture in the new Europe*. Chicago: University of Chicago Press.

Wikan, U. (2003). *For ærens skyld: Fadime til ettertanke*. Oslo: Universitetsforlaget.

Wikan, U. (in press a). *In honor of Fadime: Murder and shame*. Chicago: University of Chicago Press.

Wikan, U. (in press b). Honor, truth, and justice. In C. Wainryb, J. Smetana, & E. Turiel (Eds.), *Social development, social inequalities, and social justice*. Hillsdale, NJ: Erlbaum.

12 The Political Regulation of Anger in Organizations

Poul Poder

In this chapter I analyze how regulation of anger involves organizational processes of interpretation of feelings. Regulation as interpretation is either about dismissing or acknowledging personally experienced feelings in such a way as to give them a wider social significance. I draw on Campbell's (1997) concept of the politics of emotional expression, which refers to the fact that certain types of emotional experience are silenced rather than welcomed. On the basis of a case study of how employees and managers handled emotions during an organizational restructuring, I will describe how anger was not acknowledged in the relationship between management and employees in the case organization. The organizational members held on to an idea of "not being negative"; this had the effect of preventing them from getting the full informational value out of feelings, because they were anxious about expressing what they felt. Since anger is a feeling associated with perceived harm, a more acknowledging form of regulation of anger could therefore help facilitate better problem solving and thus reduce demoralization among employees. The studied organization exhibits structural and cultural features that can be found in many late-modern and hierarchical organizations, and some of the findings are supported by others' research. Consequently, this study can shed light on how anger is regulated in organizations generally.

I show how the interpretation of feeling is a political process influenced by organizational culture and structural regulation of anger, and I will argue that organizational reform is particularly pertinent, because of anger's exceptional function of restoring social order (Oatley, Keltner, & Jenkins, 2006, pp. 52–53).

From a psychological perspective, emotion regulation "refers to the process by which individuals influence which emotions they have, when they have them, and how they experience and express these emotions"

(Gross, 1998, p. 275). On the individual level, individuals might fear their own anger for reasons that have to do with how they were brought up (Greenberg & Vandekerckhove, this volume). Many studies view anger from a psychological perspective, describing the extent of anger and explaining its regulation through reference to psychological characteristics and individual differences (see, for example, Mauss, Bunge, & Gross, this volume; Greenberg & Vandekerckhove, this volume). This chapter emphasizes social forces that influence emotion regulation, and it thereby supplements much of the psychological research on how individuals self-regulate anger.

Anger is a frequent emotion in organizations (Barsade & Gibson, 1999; Bolton, 2005; Booth & Mann, 2005; Gibson, 1995; Gibson & Tulgan, 2002; Harlos & Pinder, 2000; Lazarus & Cohen-Charash, 2001). However, anger is a somewhat forbidden emotion. In a commonsense understanding, anger is believed to be destructive—anger as a vice. Consequently, anger is often considered to be in need of regulation. Anger requires emotional work: it needs to be carefully managed, regulated, and controlled (Lupton, 1998, pp. 49–50). The idea of anger as a "negative emotion" can also be found in psychological theory (Lazarus & Cohen-Charash, 2001, p. 55), which posits anger as a negative experience and destructive in its social consequences. Not surprisingly, many people also believe that the expression of anger should be severely regulated, and that ill-tempered persons should learn to manage their anger better. The publication of endless numbers of self-help books on how individuals can apparently learn to moderate their anger proves this point. But anger may actually make individuals feel more in command of their situation; in that they are doing something to overcome or avenge the offense they have suffered (Collins, 2004, p. 127; Lazarus & Cohen-Charash, 2001, p. 56). But the preconception of anger as undesirable can be problematic: perceiving anger as exclusively negative could legitimize an overregulation of anger that ignores how anger can facilitate social order (Shields, 2002, p. 142).

In response to this problem, I emphasize that anger is linked to morality understood as individuals' perceptions of how they deserve to be treated in, for example, respectful ways. From the perspective of interpersonal relationships, anger therefore has a functional role to play in articulating how certain individuals feel they and their rights have been violated. I outline this argument before analyzing examples of how anger was regulated in a case study of an organization (Poder, 2004), as the 'moral' approach to anger is important in order to understand how the actual regulation—acknowledgment or dismissing—of anger is linked to issues of demoralization and cynicism.

Firstly, I explain how anger can be viewed as integral to morality and how this approach is an alternative to predominant research into the regulation of anger. Secondly, I outline how regulation can be understood as influenced by a politics of expression. Regulation of anger is linked to issues of culture and social structure, and is thus not simply a question of particularly ill-tempered personalities. Thirdly, I exemplify how the expression of anger was segmented and privatized and interpreted dismissively in the interaction between manager and employees. Fourthly, I discuss the significance of my findings for organizations generally and for the theory of emotion regulation or management. I also discuss the practical implications of the dismissive and segmented regulation of anger.

In the following section I discuss how anger can be seen as linked to issues of identity and morality and therefore implied in strategies employed by individuals when establishing and reestablishing the moral order of their interaction with others.

 ## ANGER AS FUNCTIONAL IN HOW INDIVIDUALS RESTORE MORALLY IMPAIRED RELATIONSHIPS

The way in which anger is conceptualized has implications for the understanding of how anger should be regulated. If anger is conceived as unpleasant and destructive to social relationships, it would be obvious to suggest that, for example, managers should "diffuse employee anger, placate angry customers and control their own angry impulses" (Ramsey, 2004, p. 8). This preconception can therefore legitimize the idea that the expression of anger is unwanted per se.

If anger is seen as integral to morality, then its expression can be crucial in the establishing and reestablishing of social relationships. Anger in a social context basically suggests that some action by another person or agency is construed as a demeaning offense with respect to the kind of person one is or perceives oneself to be. Getting angry can be seen as implicitly claiming that one is a certain kind of person who in certain ways makes claims upon respect (Shields, 2002, p. 139). For example, as a member (employee) of an organization that claims to be interested in dialogue and empowerment of employees, one can rightly feel rejected if the manager does not answer one's questions at a meeting (see below). Individuals feel angry when they think that they have been denied something to which they believe they are entitled, or when they believe they have been treated unfairly (Shields, 2002, p. 140). Moreover, for anger to be directed toward someone, the object of anger must necessarily be held responsible for the loss or insult in some way (Shields, 2002, p. 143). Cropanzano and colleagues found that anger and resentment occur only when things would/could have been better and someone should have be-haved differently (Cropanzano, Weiss, Suckow, & Grady, 2000, p. 57).

Anger cannot merely be explained in terms of frustration as such. Frustration also leads to the generation of anxiety, guilt, shame, envy, or jealousy; consequently, it is too broad a category to explain anger. The goal that fuels anger is preservation and enhancement of our personal or social identity (Lazarus & Cohen-Charash, 2001, p. 62). Seen from the perspective of interpersonal relationships, anger can be described as aiming to facilitate social order (Shields, 2002, p. 142). One of the functions of anger is to motivate others to repair harm done as consequence of transgressions. Anger motivates the punishment of individuals who have transgressed rules of reciprocity (Oatley et al., p. 52–53). But, I will argue, it also motivates the punishment or at least criticism of individuals who are perceived to have harmed others' identities.

The function of anger is to signal that the angry person may not be sufficiently acknowledged as a person. If anger is not expressed, the involved parties do not become aware that the conflict entails perceived harm to central issues of identity in one of the parties. The expression of anger can be the first step in trying to repair relationships that have been damaged through perceived wrongdoing.

If feelings of anger are socially acknowledged, different possibilities emerge. One possibility is that the harm is recognized and the wrongdoer takes responsibility for it and seeks to compensate by way of apology. Another possibility is that the person being accused of having inflicted harm listens to the person feeling hurt in order to understand her interpretation of what has happened in the situation that she sees as causing the anger. The accused person may not agree with that interpretation, and may therefore not feel obliged to take any form of compensatory action. In such a situation, however, there will still be recognition of the other person in the sense that the accused person will now know what the other person feels and how this person has interpreted their previous interaction that triggered the anger. This recognition of different understanding of what has happened does not lead to a full restoration of the relationship, but it is still closer to such than a situation in which the anger of the person is merely dismissed.

I suggest that anger should not be seen as short-lived or episodic, which is a common feature of emotions according to much of the literature on emotion (Oatley et al., p. 29; Harlos & Pinder, 2000, p. 262). Emotions can have a short-lived or a longer existence depending on the durability of social context which is a constitutive part of emotion. The stability of the social context that forms an emotion determines whether the emotional experience is long or short-lived (Barbalet, 1998, p. 80). Moreover, it also depends on the interpretation and remembrance. If one's interpretation of the situation remains the same, then it can invoke the same emotions even after a long period of time.

Believing anger to be episodic ignores the way in which recalling the circumstances that caused the feelings can be sufficient to generate the same feelings. Consequently, instead of realizing the potential function of anger as facilitating social order (Shields, 2002, p. 142) one evades it, clinging to the illusion that the passage of time—rather than reconciliatory forms of action—will heal all wounds.

On the basis of this approach, which points up the moral significance of anger, it is important to see how feelings of anger are recognized as such in the social interaction between individuals; this will be the focus in the following analysis of anger regulation.

 ## THE POLITICS OF EMOTIONAL EXPRESSION REGULATE FEELINGS

In this section, I emphasize how to interpret feelings according to a politics of emotional expression in order to highlight the interactive interpretive processes that are also crucial in understanding regulation of emotion sociologically. To further understand regulation of emotion it is important to grasp how emotional experience is regulated by the way in which actors interpret others' experiences. Regulation also works through interpretive strategies that ensure the belittlement of the emotional experience of others.

Other people have considerable power over the feeling individual through their acts of interpretation (Campbell, 1997, p. 147). Campbell emphasizes how individuals or groups that already occupy positions of social power will interpret feelings through emotion categories that serve their needs and interests (Campbell, 1997, p. 147). Campbell argues that one has to acknowledge these two facts rather than being mystified by the ideological promise of privacy and authority about what to feel. Individuals are not sovereign beings determining their own feelings and how they can express themselves. They are dependent on either sympathetic or antipathetic interpreters in order to express their social, common, and also most intimate, local, idiosyncratic, and personal feelings (Campbell, 1997).

Renouncing the idea that feelings are (or ought to be) personal in an allegedly independent (private) sense, it is possible to appreciate the political option of seeking control over "the categories through which we are interpreted and to change the meaning of certain emotion concepts through our revisionary participation in practices associated with these categories"

(Campbell, 1997, pp. 147–148). The consequence of Campbell's argument is that regulation of emotion is not just a neutral regulation of something already given. Emotional experience is dependent on the ruling forms of "politics of emotional expression" (Campbell, 1997, p. 165).

Personal feelings may be private or they may be made public—that is, expressed and acknowledged by others in sympathetic ways. Personal feelings are not to be understood as representative of a pregiven authentic self—but as a significant possibility of personal significance. This possibility is dependent on how others serve as an either supportive or dismissive audience. Regulation is therefore a constructive process entailing differing degrees of ways in which not yet articulated emotional experiences (feelings) might be externalized and constructed as a particular emotion with a particular social significance. It is through other people's interpretations that one becomes aware of one's more or less unarticulated feelings as socially recognizable and recognized emotions.

Campbell's focus on the interpretive politics of emotional expression supplements the structural and cultural approach for the reason that emotion regulation is not automatically executed by structures or rules of feeling or display. Sometimes people draw on such rules in their interpretation and sometimes not. However, it is important in every respect to assess this level of interpretation. Not all areas of emotional life are heavily circumscribed by rules, and in such situation the focus on interpretive practices is particularly essential.

 ## CASE STORY: REGULATING ANGER IN DISMISSIVE WAYS

In the following I analyze the organizational regulation of anger among employees and managers during an organizational restructuring of the overall Human Resources (HR) organization within a large international pharmaceutical company based in Denmark (Poder, 2004). During a five-month period I interviewed 15 persons (1 director, 2 managers, 7 administrative employees, 2 office trainees, and 3 internal consultants) and also observed meetings and talked more informally with employees. The management wanted to professionalize by reallocating some of the HR-employees to new departments. The study focuses on the setting up of a new Staffing department and an internal service/help-desk department with about 10–12 people each, and is based on interviews and observation. It is a qualitative study of how emotion was handled in different ways during a period of change, and is a contribution to the understanding of emotion in organizations (Poder, 2004).

In the following analysis I draw on the perspective which emphasizes how emotion regulation is about the way in which feelings were interpreted. In conclusion I shall also consider how certain organizational ideals and organizational structure influenced the regulation of anger.

Angry or bitter employee

The first example concerns a male employee who contested the top management's claim that the aforementioned restructuring measures would engender more "professionalism." In his view, this justification by the management implied that the current group of employees had not been working professionally or professionally enough. He felt that this was wrong because he was of the opinion that a recent company survey had shown customers to be very satisfied with the quality of the services provided by his former department. At a meeting during the preparation of the restructuring, he had asked for clarification of what he saw as implicit and unfair criticism of his and his colleagues' work. But the responsible director had not bothered to respond to the question at all, which had made the employee even more furious.

This employee tried to make sure that he never expressed his anger and dissatisfaction to others outside the department. To outsiders, the employee would only emphasize good aspects of the restructuring measures. He dealt with his anger and dissatisfaction in private, working through his anger, disappointment, and sadness by talking about them with his partner and with one particularly trusted colleague. He adjusted to the new situation, trying to get as much out of it as possible. He emphasized that he did not normatively accept it, even though he accommodated the new situation. As long as he thought they were not being treated fairly, he could feel anger. Recalling the circumstances that caused the feelings can be sufficient to generate the same feelings (Barbalet, 1998). In other words, his display of anger was regulated in a strategic rather than a personal manner.

Furthermore, I want to emphasize that the employee was apparently unsure of his feeling of anger. When reflecting on his own emotional responses to the change process, he said: "All this grumbling and a little bellyaching of mine is just because the change has been running contrary to what could have been expected, what I had expected." This self-description can be seen as weakening the agency of the employee himself, as it takes out the potential moral justification underlying his emotion. It raises doubts as to whether he was feeling justifiably angry because he and his colleagues were being treated unfairly. Describing his feelings of anger and dissatisfaction as signs of bellyaching suggests that he might feel bitter, or that he thinks this is how others might regard him. This way of understanding himself implies a degree of self-blame, as it describes an emotionality that is considered problematic, if not destructive.

Whereas anger is due to something specific, and can in principle be justified, bitterness is less easy to justify. To be seen as a bitter person can have fatal consequences. Telling a person that he or she is "bitter" is meant to be silencing rather than challenging (Campbell, 1997, p. 169). According to Campbell, this interpretive strategy or charge implies that the person is being dismissed, which refers to a situation "when what we do or say, as assessed by what we have described as our intentions in that situation, is either not taken seriously or not regarded at all in the context in which it is meant to have its effect . . . Put more simply, if no one takes my anger seriously by making any attempt to account for his or her behavior or to change it, but, instead characterizes me as upset and oversensitive, I may be unsure, in retrospect, of how best to describe my behavior" (Campbell, 1997, p. 166). Such uncertainty seems to be what is going on with the abovementioned employee who begins by describing his anger but ends up questioning this anger.

It seemed that this employee was to some extent destined not to be taken seriously. The manager and some colleagues had categorized him as a grumbler whose attitude could have a negative effect on others and should therefore be kept in check. Such interactive processes can be seen as an example of how power operates not only through tangible repression of emotions but also through interpretive strategies that bring about that others' emotional experience is dismissed, in the sense of not being taking seriously.

Summing up, the account of the angry male employee reveals that feelings of anger were alive but were not expressed directly to those who were seen to be the offending parties. Anger was restricted to the closed private circle of the employee, and the employee stressed that he was not accepting the structural changes in a normative sense. Moreover, the self-blaming description removes the moral justification for the employee's emotion of anger as caused by the insensitive actions of others.

Angry or frustrated employee

Employees could state their preferences as regards the new departments to which they would be assigned. Many of them discussed this with their managers first. However, one administrative employee felt very disappointed that she had not been given her preferred position, even though the managers had dropped promising hints.

Employee: I remember I reacted strongly because I thought they [the managers] had changed the guidelines. And I thought they should have informed us. That would have made it fairer.

Interviewer: How did your manager respond?

Employee: Well, at that time he didn't respond because he was busy. He had to get on, and I . . . well I did need to talk to him. I didn't want to take up his time as he had to go round and tell everyone what decisions had been made, and not everybody was going to get a nice and happy message. I wasn't the only one whose needs were not satisfied . . . But he came into my office after a couple of days and asked if I was feeling better. "Certainly not," I told him. I was still as upset—and angry and disappointed and sad about the situation. And then I asked him if the complaints procedure, which he had given such a good press, was worth anything? Well, he thought that it was. And so I asked him what I was supposed to do, and then he explained how I should proceed. I told him that I knew what to write, I just wanted to know if I would get anything out of it. Would I actually get anything out of it? No, he didn't think so. So then I thought "I don't give a damn."

The employee was angry about how the managers conducted the allocation process. She was angry about what she considered to be a change in the guidelines concerning which jobs would be assigned to which new departments. All she wanted was a more honest message from the management. However, her anger was overlooked rather than taken seriously. The manager emphasized that she had a right to be frustrated, disappointed, and to take these feelings out on him. She was welcome to "kick" him and take out her frustrations on him as he had been responsible for the final decision concerning the job assignments which had caused her dissatisfaction and anger. He did not try to convince her that they had not altered the guidelines and could therefore not be blamed for any perceived wrongdoing. Alternatively, he could have offered a grudging admission of responsibility: you are right, and we are sorry about it. Moreover, the employee herself also played down her anger, as she excused her "angry" behavior as being "unfair." The employee thereby contributed to the definition of the situation in terms of sadness and disappointment, and less in terms of anger.

This example shows how the employee was construed as being (primarily or entirely) cross and frustrated. The manager focused on the employee's feeling of disappointment rather than on her anger. He construed the employee's emotionality along the lines of a "container" metaphor, according to which emotions are located inside the body (Planalp, 1999, pp. 107–108). As emotions become more intense, pressure builds up in the body (container) and the emotions have to be released before the container explodes or overflows. This ventilationist, safety-valve or cath-arsis view reflects the widespread belief that emotions must be expressed or they will cause damage, either by being suppressed or by exploding. This metaphor does not entail any understanding of emotion as depend-ent on the presence of a meaningful context for its expression (Planalp, 1999, pp. 107–108). The manager was thus drawing on a metaphor that invites no further exploration of the potential meaning of emotions. That the manager does not see anger in the subordinate employee can be understood from the structural perspective which predicts that anger is more legitimate when expressed by superiors.

In sum, focusing on broad categories for emotional reactions, such as "frustration," rather than on the potential moral message of anger, re-duces the possibility of repairing social relationships. When anger is not acknowledged, then the disposition to act restoratively with respect to the (perceived) cause of anger does not materialize.

Taking into account that the regulation of feeling or emotional experi-ence is also interpretation of feelings that assist the formation of emo-tion, I suggest that the employee's feeling of anger is not recognized by the manager. Thus, the employee experiences a double form of violation. First, she suffers the harm of feeling unjustly treated, and then she experi-ences that this is not recognized. Gabriel (1998) suggests that regulatory practice can result in shame:

> . . . an unanswered insult then marks a breach in justice which goes unpun-ished. It is highly effective in reaffirming power relations and laying bare relations of domination and subordination. The insulted party internalizes his/her anger into shame, an inability to restore justice by doing what is seen as the honourable thing, hence he/she is dishonoured in addition to being humiliated. (p. 1346)

The employee's feeling of anger is dismissed, which is also a way in which emotions can be regulated. The manner in which one's feelings become socially recognized emotions is dependent on how receptive others are to one's experiences. As the feeling of anger is not objectified, it does not become a message the manager has to take seriously and then reject, accept, or seek to modify.

No point in expressing anger

An administrative employee explained that she thought the management of the company did not know what harm they were inflicting on their personnel, and that the personnel of her department were exhausted by this particular restructuring measure. I asked the employee about how she raised the issue of the exhausted personnel with her manager:

Interviewer: Earlier you said something about "exhaustion of the personnel." So don't you get angry when you ask yourself why this suffering takes place?

Employee: You can get angry, yes . . . But does it lead to anything? . . . Well, I have some hobbies that help me relax and that's . . . good.

Interviewer: Do you think it's not that important for someone to express his or her anger? That you can't really do anything with that feeling?

Employee: Who could you get angry at? The company? Then you could write a hundred times "I'm angry with the company"? I don't know . . . I unwind by doing other things. The anger? You can shrug your shoulders and wonder why they [management] bother to act like that. Well, then it's good that retirement isn't that far away [laughs].

Interviewer: Do you try to make allowances for them [management]—is that what you mean?

Employee: I don't know if it's making allowances for them [management] . . . it's more just shaking your head in wonder. As I said before, why don't they [management] for once let some of the restructuring run for a couple of years to see if it really works? Instead of just letting it proceed for six months, which isn't long enough to judge if it really works. Sometimes things have just started functioning when it all gets bombed back again with some new restructuring.

Interviewer: It's my impression that it's difficult to express anger because, as employees, in some ways you're also in the same boat as the managers. It's been a new setup for the manager of your department too . . . And so it's more difficult to blame someone. And that makes it difficult to be angry with anyone in the departmental group, doesn't it?

Employee: Yes . . . Well, you can be mad at those who thought up this restructuring concept. You can be angry with them because they don't realize what they're doing to their personnel.

Interviewer: Then you might get in touch with the managing director, for instance. He's centrally placed in this restructuring, isn't he?

Employee: Yes.

Interviewer: Haven't you thought about that—sending him an email?

Employee: [Laughing loudly] Ha, ha. No.

Interviewer: But is that a possibility you've discussed with any of your colleagues?

Employee: No.

Interviewer: Have you at any point talked about protesting against the change or saying that you want better explanations for the rationale behind this change?

Employee: No, well, then people would think "How long will I keep my job?" That's something people think about more generally.

Interviewer: Does that mean there's an underlying fear?

Employee: Yes, I think so.

Interviewer: And not just you—but everybody?

Employee: It's a general fear, I think.

In this example, anger seemed a very distant possibility. Thinking about the situation, the experienced administrative employee could feel angry with "those who thought up this restructuring concept," but she found it pointless to express such anger. Should she "write a hundred times 'I'm angry with the company'?" she asked ironically. Her laughter when asked about getting in touch with the top management and explaining her thoughts on the restructuring measures brought this point home very effectively. "You have to laugh. If you cannot laugh about what is going on at work, you will have a tough time."

In sum, she was able to feel angry with the management as regards their responsibility for introducing ongoing organizational restructuring, but it seemed pointless to think about the situation in terms of voicing anger. There seemed to be no available audience that would make it meaningful for her to express her feeling of anger, and therefore her anger was not articulated in a forum where it could be socially recognized.

Drawing on Hochschild's theory, I argue that certain cultural ideas functioned as feeling and display rules and thereby influenced how the organizational members regulated their anger. Hochschild's (1983) classic theory of emotion management posits that emotion is a complex response partly determined by our "emotion management" rather than an automatic reaction. Emotion management is defined as "the management of feeling to create publicly observable facial or bodily display" (p. 7) and to create feelings other than those we have momentarily (p. 219). Like Gross's concept of emotion regulation, Hochschild's concept of emotion management includes efforts to excite, intensify, weaken, and form emotion rather than merely controlling or suppressing emotion. It is directed toward altering an emotion in terms of its quality, extent, and strength. Feeling emotions is an experience that is partly constituted by relating to socially defined and distributed "feeling rules." Such rules suggest what to feel and how to display emotions in particular situations. Emotion work is directed toward bringing emotion in line with the feeling norms of the situation. Emotion management is influenced by the emotion culture composed of existing ideas about how to recognize a feeling, how to label, appraise, and express a feeling. Given that ideology and class shape feeling rules, Hochschild emphasizes a sociological understanding of emotional experience.

Feeling rules can be seen as one way in which culture directs the action disposition that is intrinsic to emotion. Such rules guide who is entitled to receive and who is obliged to contribute in social exchanges. Feeling rules are ideal expectations entertained by groups of people, and they reflect forms of social membership. They are social guidelines telling how we wish to feel in particular situations. The existence of such rules is indicated in our concept of rights and duties linked to certain emotions; for example, in certain situations we explain to each other that "we have a right to be angry at someone."

One example of the corporate culture relevant to this discussion was the fact that the departmental members had promised each other that they would not reveal possible mistakes or problems to colleagues outside their department. They established a consensus not to communicate to other departments what could be perceived as negative messages about how things were operating in their own department. Mistakes are more likely during organizational restructuring processes, and thus the risk of losing face and being ridiculed is heightened. It is therefore not surprising that a department agrees to protect itself against potential loss of departmental honor. It was important for each department to do well in order to minimize the risk of being closed down when the company implemented a new round of restructuring. One experienced employee recommended that the manager should make sure that the name of their department was written on every piece of work to which they contributed in collaboration with other departments. This employee knew that the acknowledgment of contribution was important to attaining a position of respect. If one's contributions were not known and acknowledged within the company, there was a risk that other managers/departments would receive all the credit.

Managers and employees shared the ideal of not appearing as "being negative." This ideal can be seen as an example of the "have a nice day" syndrome of contemporary Western culture, a scripted culture character-ized by tight smiles, forced bonhomie, and other prescribed "positive" emotion displays (Mann, 1999, p. 21). Alleged "negative" emotions were assumed to be dynamic phenomena, able to spread and to sustain through colleagues talking and telling stories about the organization and the man-agement. "Negative" emotions were considered contagious, and the manager saw it as his task to try to restrict negative contagion. Managers categorized certain employees as "complainers," which testifies to the management's ongoing readiness to try and contain the potential spread of "negative energy."

The idea of "being negative" was used in an indeterminate sense. It seemed to be a shorthand expression covering a wide range of emotions. It could apply to censoring emotions as diverse as anger, sadness, fear, shame, guilt, disappointment, bitterness, disillusion, etc. It is therefore easily ap-plied as an all-encompassing standard in evaluating others' and one's own emotions. One can never be sure what others might regard as "being nega-tive." The strength of this regulative ideal lies in its vagueness. The ideal of not being or appearing to be "negative" can work as a very rigorously demanding ideal ensuring neutralization of the expression of a range of emotions.

The emotion management perspective is useful in order to grasp how organizational ideas of keeping troubles inside a department and not ap-pearing to be "negative" regulated how people dealt with their anger. I have shown how feelings of anger were regulated by managers by being interpreted as frustration or disappointment rather than as anger. This regulation by interpretation results in the feeling of anger being priva-tized rather than socially recognized. Consequently, the case analysis demonstrates how the regulation of emotion also involves processes of interpretation that ensure personal feelings do not gain an objectified social existence.

Another sociological perspective which can inform the context of the in-terpretation going on between individuals is the theory of how social struc-ture influences emotion regulation. One of the main findings of my study was that employees regulated their anger vis-à-vis management in strategic ways (Poder, 2004; Mann, 1999). The observed strategic character of the regulation of anger can be explained with reference to the unequal distribution of power characteristic of most contemporary organizations.

One research study concludes that "subordinates are less likely than superiors to directly confront offenders and/or try to constructively resolve the situation; thus, superiors may be unaware that subordinates are experiencing ongoing feelings of distress and distrust in the aftermath of an angry workplace interaction" (Fitness, 2000, p. 159). Tiedens and associates found that high status is associated with anger and pride, whereas low status is associated with stereotyped views of sadness, guilt, and appreciation (Tiedens, Ellsworth, & Mesquita, 2000, p. 568). A subordinate who expresses anger can easily be perceived as assuming a level of competence not formally ascribed to her position. Social stereotypes concerning emotion and status cause subordinates to expect that their superiors will express far more anger than those with lower social status.

Social structure not only influences emotional experience but also how individuals can express their emotion. The postulate of a productive link between power position and display freedom is supported by Pugh's research, which concludes that power differentials in dyads influence emotion regulation so that powerful parties have more freedom to express their felt emotions, while less powerful parties are expected to keep their emotions in check and thereby engage in greater emotion regulation (Pugh, 2002, p. 176). On the basis of their study of the interplay between status and emotion in work groups, Lovaglia and Houser (1996) conclude that "high-status members are freer to express negative emotion than are low-status members" (p. 869). Furthermore, a low-status employee risks encountering resistance from high-status coworkers if she or he does not mask feelings of resentment, anger, and frustration associated with her position. The low-status worker should also make efforts to induce positive emotions in high-status coworkers in order to gain influence in the work group (Lovaglia & Houser, 1996, p. 881). In sum, the key point of the structural perspective is the idea that socio-structural factors influence emotional experience and expression. Both the cultural and structural perspectives describe how the social context of interaction influences what is going on in interaction.

In conclusion, the organization segmented the expression of anger, which implies that the distribution of emotional expression operates on the basis of distinctions between being inside or outside the department (group identity), between intimacy and non-intimacy, between being "a colleague" or "a trusted colleague." The concept of segmentation of expression of emotions depicts the way in which individuals handled expressions according to principles of appropriateness, strategic shrewdness, or mutual trust (Poder, 2004). Certain organizational ideals and agreements contributed to make the expression of anger segmented: that is, relegated to specific audiences. This meant that the agents held responsible for grievances that triggered the angers were not part of the audience. In other words, the moral signal function of anger was not confronted directly in the interaction between employees and managers, and thereby possibilities of restorative work on the relationships were bypassed.

■ DISCUSSION

Application of findings to organizations in general

Since generalization is primarily linked to quantitative research aimed at documenting numbers and distribution of defined factors, extrapolation has been suggested as a more useful concept for the aim of generalization concerning qualitative research. Extrapolation refers to researchers' possibility of showing how the qualitative analysis relates more general processes beyond the data at hand (Silverman, 2000, p. 111).

As a way of extrapolating, I suggest that the observed segmenting and dismissive form of regulation of anger can shed light on how anger might be regulated in organizations in general. The studied organization was not idiosyncratic with respect to the studied phenomena. The case is about how people handle emotions influenced by hierarchical social structure and a culture that is critical of so-called negative emotions (Mann, 1999). These two features are not unusual but can be found in a lot of other organizations in late-modern societies. That being said, I also want to stress that organizational culture can vary a lot, and there can therefore be different ways of regulating anger and emotion more broadly between two organizations that are very similar in structural terms. With this reservation in mind, I believe that there are viable reasons to assume that the observed form of segmented and dismissive regulation of anger can also be found in other and similar organizational settings.

What is the significance of this study for theory and research of regulation or management of emotion?

One general finding is that anger was not repressed but, rather, segmented and privatized. In other words, anger is not easily managed away. It surfaces in one way or the other. In terms of theory of regulation or management of emotion, this suggests that anger might be a particularly forceful emotion. This can be explained in terms of the moral significance associated with anger. In a democratic and egalitarian culture many individuals do not want to give up on what they perceive as legitimate claims to personal respect.

In terms of theoretical approach, I have broadened the sociological perspective on emotion regulation by understanding regulation as interpretative strategies enacted in interaction among individuals. Regulation also works as either dismissing or acknowledging personally experienced feelings in such a way as to give them a wider social significance. Sociologically speaking, regulation is not merely defined by cultural rules and social positions in hierarchies.

Approaching anger as being linked to morality rather than to frustration opens up a perspective that sees anger as intrinsic to how individuals might restore relationships that have become impaired in a moral sense. From this perspective it becomes possible to discuss if regulation of anger can be overregulation in terms of individuals' possibility of restoring tensions in relationships. Seen from such a perspective one can, at least, give up the dogmatic ideas of anger being an immoral emotion as such.

Practical implications of segmentation and dismissive regulation of anger

In this chapter, the organizational level is treated as a level of analysis in its own right because regulation of emotion can vary significantly depending on the local, organizational, and cultural circumstances (Meyerson, 2000). The social forms of regulation can be different, and there is therefore reason to consider and possibly reform how existing organizational practices favor certain forms of regulation.

Not voicing, for strategic reasons, one's anger to the assumed offending party is also a self-weakening act, in the sense of abandoning the possibility of fighting for one's interests and working out a solution. This practical implication concerns an increased inequality of social relationships, which runs counter to the studied organizations' aim of employee empowerment (Poder, 2004, ch. 5). This is because "people who cannot get angry or cannot do so effectively are at a disadvantage because they lose the possibility of equal relationships and may not meet certain needs" (Reiser, 1999, p. 24). When people do not stand up for their legitimate identity interests and needs, they end up in submissive and subordinate positions.

Moreover, not voicing anger directly to the assumed offender will lead to a reduced understanding of this particular relationship. When employees' emotions are not expressed as clearly as they are felt, the management's (or others') chances of sensing what employees think and feel is diminished, leading to a reduced understanding of employees' actual situations and their organizational potential.

Since feelings of anger do not necessarily disappear of their own accord, it becomes vital to consider what is needed at the organizational level to achieve a more acknowledging regulation of anger. Renouncing the idea of "negative emotion" can stimulate an increased sharing of emotions since a focus on "negative emotion" prevents an understanding of the full range of emotional expressions. We need to confront all emotions in order to understand their background and possible informational value. Evaluating the behavior of others in a more refined way—rather than simply categorizing it as "negative" versus "positive" or "destructive" versus "constructive"—requires that people confront their emotions more directly. Such accepting appreciation of emotion probably requires sustained training, because it is easier to differentiate positive emotions such as joy or happiness from negative emotions such as sadness, anger, fear, and disgust, than it is to distinguish the negative emotions from one another (Planalp, 1999, p. 45).

CONCLUSION

Anger can be active in a double sense. Anger is cognitively evaluative of perceived transgressions and it is dispositional by preparing actions to the harmful situation in which the subject is located: "anger can serve as a warning, energize us for action, motivate us to understand others' feelings, and work towards justice" (Reiser, 1999, p. 28). I have emphasized anger as linked with morality in order to demonstrate the potential restorative function of anger in social interaction. Through this approach, and by understanding how regulation is also about interpreting (acknowledging or dismissing) feelings, one can appreciate the way in which dismissive interpretations of feelings can restrict the reparative function of anger and subsequently foster tensions in relationships (Mastenbroek, 2000, p. 35). If some kind of resolution or mutual reciprocity is not restored, the tensions are likely to be aggravated (Kast, 2001, p. 118).

However, the restorative function of anger is not necessarily realized— as is shown in the analysis. Anger was overregulated in the sense of limiting its potential for contributing to resolution of tensions in relationships. Consequently, the manner in which anger can be regulated more constructively is predominantly a matter of organizational reform, given that organizational culture and structure contributed to a segmenting and dismissive form of regulation of anger.

This chapter prompts a research question relating to ways in which organizations could acknowledge anger to a higher degree than the studied organization. Research has shown that: "Expressed pain is an invitation to connect. Expressed compassion is a response that affirms the human connection. While these expressions are often exchanged between two or a few people, they are facilitated or hindered by the organizations where people study and work" (Frost, Dutton, Worline, & Wilson, 2000, p. 35). The possibility of emotional expression is crucial for the constructive handling of pain, because expression affords both the suffering person and others a possibility to respond to the pain. Consequently, the questions of which organizational circumstances contribute to an emotional ecology cultivating compassion and courage to confront anger, and how anger can be expressed in constructive ways are relevant for further research.

In this chapter I have assumed that anger does not necessarily entail destructive aggression, given that individuals, in principle, can manage anger without being hostile or aggressive (Reiser, 1999). I do not thereby assume that managing anger in ways that restore impaired relationships is an easy task—on the contrary (Scheff, 1997). But that is a different story than this chapter's argument about the need to acknowledge how anger can be functional to ways in which individuals can reestablish the morality of their relationships.

REFERENCES

Barbalet, J. M. (1998). *Emotion, social theory, and social structure.* Cambridge: Cambridge University Press.

Barsade, S., & Gibson, D. (1999, August 11). *The experience of anger at work: Lessons from the chronically angry.* Paper presented at the Academy of Management, Chicago, IL.

Bolton, S. C. (2005). *Emotion management in the workplace.* London: Palgrave.

Booth, J., & Mann, S. (2005). The experience of workplace anger. *Leadership & Organization Development Journal, 26,* 250–262.

Campbell, S. (1997). *Interpreting the personal: Expression and the formation of feelings.* Ithaca, NY: Cornell University Press.

Collins, R. (2004). *Interaction ritual chains.* Princeton, NJ: Princeton University Press.

Cropanzano, R., Weiss, H., Suckow, K., & Grady, A. (2000). Doing justice to workplace emotion. In N. Ashkanasy, C. Härtel, & W. Zerbe (Eds.), *Emotions in the workplace: Theory, research and practice* (pp. 49–62). Westport, CT: Quorum.

Fitness, J. (2000). Anger in the workplace: An emotion script approach to anger episodes between workers and their superiors, co-workers and subordinates. *Journal of Organizational Behavior, 21,* 147–162.

Frost, P., Dutton, J., Worline., M., & Wilson, A. (2000). Narratives of compassion in organizations. In S. Fineman (Ed.), *Emotion in organizations* (2nd ed., pp. 25–45). London: Sage.

Gabriel, Y. (1998). An introduction to the social psychology of insults in organizations. *Human Relations, 51*, 1329–1354.

Gibson, D. (1995). Emotional scripts and change in organizations. In F. Massarik (Ed.), *Advances in organizational development* (Vol. 3, pp. 32–63). Norwood, NJ: Ablex.

Gibson, D., & Tulgan, B. (2002). *Managing anger in the workplace.* Amherst, MA: HRD Press.

Gross, J. J. (1998). The emerging field of emotion regulation: An integrative review. *Review of General Psychology, 2*, 271–299.

Harlos, K., & Pinder, C. (2000). Emotion and injustice in the workplace. In S. Fineman (Ed.), *Emotion in organizations* (2nd ed., pp. 255–276). London: Sage.

Hochschild, A. R. (1983). *The Managed Heart.* Berkeley, CA: University of California Press.

Kast, V. (2001). *Vredens Kraft [The force of anger].* Copenhagen: Gyldendal Uddannelse.

Lazarus, R., & Cohen-Charash, Y. (2001). Discrete emotions in organizational life. In R. Payne & G. Cooper (Eds.), *Emotions at work: Theory, research and applications for management* (pp. 45–81). Chichester: Wiley.

Lovaglia, M., & Houser, J. (1996). Emotional reactions and status in groups. *American Sociological Review, 61*, 867–883.

Lupton, D. (1998). *The emotional self.* London: Sage.

Mann, S. (1999). *Hiding what we feel, faking what we don't: Understanding the role of your emotions at work.* Shaftesbury: Element.

Mastenbroek, W. (2000). Organizational behaviour as emotion management. In N. Ashkanasy, C. Härtel, & W. Zerbe (Eds.), *Emotions in the workplace: Theory, research and practice* (pp. 19–35). Westport, CT: Quorum.

Meyerson, D. (2000). If emotions were honoured: A cultural analysis. In S. Fineman (Ed.), *Emotion in organizations* (2nd ed., pp. 167–183). London: Sage.

Oatley, K., Keltner, D., & Jenkins, J. (2006). *Understanding emotions* (2nd ed.). Oxford: Blackwell.

Planalp, S. (1999). *Communicating emotion: Social, moral and cultural processes.* New York: Cambridge University Press.

Poder, P. (2004). *Feelings of power and the power of feelings: Handling emotion in organisational change.* Ph.D. thesis, Copenhagen University.

Pugh, D. (2002). Emotional regulation in individuals and dyads: Causes, costs and consequences. In R. Lord, R. Klimoski, & R. Kanfer (Eds.), *Emotions in the workplace—Understanding the structure and role of emotions in organizational behavior* (pp. 147–182). San Francisco, CA: Jossey-Bass.

Ramsey, R. D. (2004). Managing workplace anger: your employees', your customers' and your own. *Supervision, 65*, 8–10.

Reiser, C. (1999). *Reflections on anger: Women and men in a changing society.* London: Praeger.

Scheff, T. (1997). *Emotions, the social bond, and human reality.* New York: Cambridge University Press.

Shields, S. (2002). *Speaking from the heart: Gender and the social meaning of emotion.* New York: Cambridge University Press.

Silverman, D. (2000). *Doing qualitative research—A practical handbook.* London: Sage.

Tiedens, L. Z., Ellsworth, P. C., & Mesquita, B. (2000). Stereotypes about sentiments and status: Emotional expectations for high- and low-status group members. *Personality and Social Psychology Bulletin, 26,* 560–574.

Moods and Emotional Cultures: A Study of Flow and Stress in Everyday Life

Charlotte Bloch

We are always emotional. Human emotionality is an ongoing stream pervading every aspect of our lives. This stream is delimited and labeled in different terms such as emotions, feelings, moods, affects, and sentiments. In the research literature, moods are usually characterized in comparison with emotions. Moods are conceived as long-term phenomena as opposed to short-term emotions; emotions are directed toward an object, whereas moods are objectless; in emotions there is a direct relationship between a specific cause and the emotion as an effect, whereas there is no obvious relationship between a specific cause and mood as an effect; moods are on the level of bodily meanings, thus they are not reducible to cognitive meanings or discourse. Thus, compared to emotions, moods, as such, are seen as being nondelimited, diffuse, and transitory phenomena. They are a mostly unnoticed emotional background of our being in the world and, by the same token, social science has somewhat overlooked moods as a research object.

Within one approach, that of existential phenomenology, however, moods are considered as fundamental to our being in the world; as the "bearing underground of life" (Bollnow, 1974, p. 36), and the primary source of our experience of self, other persons, and the world. According to this tradition, the human being may be in one mood or another, but she/he is always in some kind of mood (Bollnow, 1974; Heidegger, 1927). Our moods arise from the inner relationship between us and our life-space; they mediate between us and the social world into which we are born (Bollnow, 1974).

This chapter addresses the issue of how moods become regulated by emotional cultures. To this end, I present the results of a qualitative study of "flow" and "stress" experiences in different contexts of everyday life (work, family, and leisure). The study contains a phenomenological analysis of flow and stress and a cultural analysis of the interpretation and handling of flow and stress in different cultural contexts, whereby with "cultural" I herein refer to different cultures or spheres of everyday life that are found in many modern Western societies. Firstly, I show how flow and stress as experiences may be categorized as moods. Secondly, I outline how the interpretations and regulations of flow and stress are conditioned by different emotional cultures within the various spheres of everyday life. The objective of the presentation is to demonstrate the manner in which our emotional culture plays an active, but overlooked role in our interpretation and evaluation of pleasant and unpleasant moods.

I provide a brief outline of research on flow and stress, followed by an account of the results obtained from the phenomenological and cultural analyses. The relationship between flow and stress as lived experiences and the cultural interpretations of these moods are discussed subsequently. Emotional cultures work as interpretive filters which not only shape and mediate, but also disturb or ignore our moods. Thus, in the conclusion of this chapter, I suggest that emotional culture as an analytical dimension should be integrated into our understanding of the socio-cultural regulation of our moods.

▪ RESEARCH ON FLOW AND STRESS

Both flow and stress are categories of experience identified in the 20th century to delimit and give meaning to aspects of the stream of experiences encountered in modern everyday life. The concept of "flow" was developed in the 1970s by the humanistic psychologist Csikszentmihalyi (1975) on the basis of empirical studies of the experiences of a variety of groups of people, for example artists, athletes, surgeons, etc. One striking characteristic of these groups was that their activities appeared to be principally motivated by sheer enjoyment of the activity *itself* rather than by its results or external reward. Csikszentmihalyi (1975) therefore turned his attention to the analysis of the actual experience of these activities, to the way the processes were *felt*. Against this background, he identified a unique experience which he termed "flow." These experiences were operationalized in a flow-questionnaire consisting of three experience quotations referring to the experience of (a) being completely absorbed, (b) forgetting time, space, and everyday life, and (c) unity and oneness with the activity. Since then Csikszentmihalyi (1990) has developed the flow theory in order to specify the psychological conditions for the origins of flow experiences. A number of researchers (Allison & Duncan, 1988; Carli, Fave, & Massimini, 1988; Mitchell, 1983) have studied flow and the incidence of flow in different social groups, and work continues on developing methods for the study of this phenomenon (Vitterso, 2003).

The concept of "stress" was first introduced by Cannon (1935) as a term for specific physiological processes in order to maintain the homeostasis of the body (Lovallo, 1997). Later, in Selye's (1956) theory, stress refers to physiological reactions to environmental strains. This physiological understanding of stress has since been replaced by an interactional understanding of stress as psychological and physiological responses to what the individual experiences as a strain. This interactional understanding has given rise to different models with different degrees of complexity (Eckenrode & Gore, 1990; Karasek, Gardell, & Lindell, 1987; Lazarus & Folkman, 1984). Among recent theories of stress, the appraisal theories should be mentioned. According to appraisal theories, stress depends on a person's evaluation of the given situation and on the possibilities of coping experienced in relation to this situation. Appraisal theory is primarily a cognitive theory. According to Thoits (1990) and Lazarus (1991, 1999), there is, however, a growing awareness of the emotional aspects involved in stress experiences.

But what makes flow and stress interesting phenomena? In a historical perspective, flow and stress are both relatively new terms for subjective experiences. Furthermore, people experience flow in their everyday lives, but these experiences go mostly unnoticed (Csikszentmihalyi & Csikszentmihalyi, 1988); and a number of studies show that stress is a common experience in modern everyday life (Netterstrøm, 1997). Thus flow and stress experiences might indicate new structures of experiences occurring in contemporary daily life. In addition, flow and stress also appear as contradictory experiences: flow connotes qualities such as effortlessness and fluidity, whereas stress connotes qualities such as strain and resistance. However, while stress has become a highly integrated term in our language of everyday life, flow as a term lives in the shadows. The literature on flow and, in particular, stress is vast. However, in spite of a number of investigations, phenomenological studies of flow and stress, along with studies of the cultural regulation of these phenomena in daily life, are quite limited. In view of the specific contemporary grounding of flow and stress, their contradictory experiential qualities, and the particular differences in cultural attention paid to the two phenomena, I have decided to conduct a qualitative study of these experiences which is outlined in the following sections.

▨ DESIGN OF THE STUDY

In order to explore flow and stress in the everyday lives of "ordinary" people, data was collected by means of interviews with 36 ethnic Danes employed at a public service organization located in Denmark. The interviewees were selected to fulfill criteria regarding distribution by gender (equal number of women and men), age (in their thirties), estimated degree of autonomy in the work situation (secretarial training and academic education), and family conditions (nuclear families with children over 3 years of age). The interviewees were "ordinary" in the sense that they lived relatively regular and stable lives, were long-term employed, and had families with children mostly of school age.

The interviewees were asked to describe in as much detail as possible one experience of flow and one experience of stress within the sphere of work and in some setting other than their place of work, respectively.

Whereas stress is a well-known term that the interviewees immediately recognized, a phenomenological investigation of flow experiences presents some difficulties since everyday language does not include a specific and exclusive term referring to this experience. Thus, in order to introduce the phenomenon, the three experiential quotations found in Csikszentmihalyi's (1975) flow-questionnaire were presented to the interviewees for brief perusal, and thereafter put aside. All interviews were audio-recorded and transcribed.

This method of data collection yielded a total of 69 accounts of specific episodes of the experience of flow and 66 accounts of specific episodes of stress, transcripts of which were subjected to subsequent phenomenological analysis. The phenomenological analytical procedure was inspired by Giorgi's method of analyzing phenomenological data (Eckartsberg, 1986; Giorgi, Fischer, & Murray, 1975). Each account was thus subjected to a condensation of the transcribed text, followed by a reflective articulation of its meaning-configuration in order to formulate the situated structure of the particular description. Following this, the general structures were inferred by means of a reflective deduction of coherent structures embedded in the situated structures. Besides the phenomenological analysis, the transcribed interviews were also subjected to a hermeneutic interpretive analysis in order to identify norms, evaluations, and tacit assumptions surrounding flow and stress experiences in different contexts. This analysis was based on the collected narratives of flow and stress, on prompting questions concerning the interviewees' evaluations and interpretations of flow and stress, and on their interpretations of how they were perceived and evaluated by others when they were in stress and in flow episodes. This analysis also took into account verbal and nonverbal markers of shame (long pauses, hesitations, low voice, etc.) in the verbal utterances as indicators of the interviewees' emotional relationship to the issues in question (see Bloch, 1996; Retzinger, 1991; Scheff, 1990, 1994).

The detailed results of the phenomenological and cultural hermeneutical analyses are explicated in Bloch (2001, 2002). Within the scope of the present chapter, the general results and some illustrative examples from the interviews are employed. In the following section, the results of the phenomenological analysis of flow and stress are outlined and interpreted in the light of Bollnow's theory of moods.

 ## RESULTS: THE PHENOMENOLOGY OF FLOW AND STRESS

Most of the interviewees (22 persons) immediately recognized the type of experience described in Csikszentmihalyi's flow-questionnaire (Csikszentmihalyi & Csikszentmihalyi, 1988). According to the interviewees, these experiences were well-known occurrences in everyday life and in many different contexts. Some of these experiences were related to tasks at work. Others were far removed from the work sphere: do-it-yourself activities, games, various types of physical activity, etc. These experiences of flow can be illustrated by the following two situated descriptions, which are constructed versions of the account given by the interviewee; in order to make this clear, the third person singular is used rather than the first person.

In the first description, a female graduate employee describes a flow experience in connection with a work assignment:

> She has a task to perform and in that connection must become conversant with a professional universe with which she is not very familiar. She becomes caught up in the problem and it takes her most of a day. She has to write an assignment, and she experiences that she is dismissive of people who come into the office. She dismisses them by answering without raising her gaze from the computer screen. She searches for and considers several solutions to the assignment. The flow experience comes when she senses a solution to the task. When she experiences that she now has the right structure, she closes herself completely to her surroundings, and when she writes she must have total concentration. She becomes quite lost in the world of the assignment. She feels at ease, experiences her work as meaningful and important. She experiences that it is fun to have completed a difficult assignment in a simple way. She experiences satisfaction in becoming totally engrossed, and therefore experiences telephone calls as stressful because her thoughts are deep in the assignment. She remains completely concentrated

until she has finished. Afterwards, she is satisfied and proud at having performed a necessary task in relation to her workplace and in relation to herself as a professional.

The narrative shows that the interviewee becomes engaged in a problem that takes on the quality of a challenge; when this challenge is transformed into a tangible process, her concentration on the assignment is all-embracing and the interviewee becomes totally absorbed, feeling wellbeing, pleasure, competence, comfort, and pride, and afterwards an increase in self-esteem.

The second description is about flow when making music together. A male IT- employee describes this experience:

> He plays keyboard in a rock band which rehearses twice a week. He went to one of these practice sessions yesterday, and it was fantastic. He had not felt at all in the right mood when he was on his way to the session because the band had not sounded very good the last time they rehearsed. The band spent the first hour tuning their instruments; they then played a number he is not very keen on and for which their new singer had written the lyrics. The number surprised them. Their impression was that it had the makings of a hit—which gave them a lift. After that, they played four of their favorite numbers. They felt inspired and gave all they had to the music, these numbers being familiar ones. "The sound simply jumped off the ground." His experience of flow was one of playing new chords at just the right point in the movement of the music. They stopped after that, because rehearsal time was up and they felt exalted and happy. There was a lot of joking around—he thinks of this as waves of energy. The feeling was shared by all the members of the band and everyone felt it had been a fantastic session. His reflection on this sequence of events is that it is only after rehearsal, when a number has been given form, that it is possible to "speak the music. It's pure joy all the way through."

The situated description shows how a positive surprise creates an atmosphere in which playing together generates the kind of music that floats above the ground. They play faultlessly and with ease and are completely absorbed in the music.

The two examples illustrate different kinds of flow experiences. Although the assembled data of 69 accounts of flow demonstrated variations of the phenomenon, shared features also emerged. Common to all the accounts of flow was an experience of total involvement, of the activity flowing, a feeling of optimal presence where chronological time and everyday problems faded into the background, existing within the time of the activity, or an experience of time as a "stehendes jetzt" (nunc stans; "an abiding now," cf. Bollnow, 1974, p. 88), well-being, pleasure, excitement, pride, etc.

In contrast, experiences of stress in this study were mostly related to time constraints at work, unforeseen tasks, overload etc. In family life, stress was mostly related to demanding episodes with too many household chores: for example, when fetching children, doing the shopping, and getting to the post office at one and the same time, or when simultaneously cooking, relaxing after work, and enjoying time with the children.

Since stress, in contrast to flow, is a commonly recognized experience, I will only present one example of the situated descriptions. In the following example, a female clerical worker describes her stress experience in connection with a work assignment:

> She experienced stress a month ago. The computer system was working very slowly and the piles of cases grew. This caused her stress and she lost her overview. She experienced her work as unmanageable. She could not organize her tasks and what she did manage to get done was scattered and random. She felt bad, powerless, and experienced enormous dissatisfaction at not being able to get going. She just sat staring into thin air. Waiting ten minutes for a response from the new computer system was stressful because she knew that there were many other things awaiting her attention. What she had planned from the start was thwarted, and so the cases just lay there until the next day. Finally she experienced a form of giving up. She did not want to be there; she was in a bad mood because she was not getting anywhere. This lasted for almost a week, and it was so terrible that she was on the verge of handing in her notice. She felt that she simply could not deal with it. Every day she had a severe headache when she got home from work, because she was thinking about how much she might be able to get done tomorrow, what her superior would say (would he be very angry), if it would be taken out on her. She says that so many thoughts run through your mind on one of those days when, no matter what you touch, everything just goes wrong. She speculates about not letting it affect the family, and about everything that has to be done in relation to the family after work, and this adds to the feeling of stress. She realized that she was stressed because her family was experiencing her as someone who was totally unlike her true self: they saw her as aggressive and snappy, and as someone who felt that she had to do everything.

Common to the instances of stress was an experience of one's "subjective time" being contested. The concept of subjective time is inspired by the theory of temporality devised by Merleau-Ponty (1962) and Heidegger (1927). Merleau-Ponty distinguishes between objective (chronological) time, which is a succession of identical "nows," and subjective time, which is a qualitative experience of the future that becomes the past by being realized in the present, i.e., an experience in which past and future are united in the now (Merleau-Ponty, 1962, p. 420). In the present study, the interviewee might be fixated in the "subjective future," which is illustrated in the above description of the interviewee constantly thinking "about everything that has to be done in relation to the family after work" instead of concentrating on the job at hand. Or, conversely, the interviewee might be fixated in the "subjective past" in the sense that he or she experienced being mentally blocked, not knowing how to finish or to start, illustrated by the interviewee's "staring into thin air." Apart from the common feature of contesting the sense of subjective time, other common features of stress experiences were an experience of "reality" being a resistance, an experience of other people as barriers, a contestation of the embodied self, and feelings such as irritation, anger, shame, guilt, and helplessness.

The common phenomenological structures emerging from the analysis will now be discussed and interpreted in the light of Bollnow's (1974) existential phenomenological approach to moods. According to Bollnow, moods are not directed toward an object, but are pervasive, all-embracing states that color our world of actions, feelings, and thoughts. Likewise, flow and stress experiences do not have a specific focus, but are diffuse pervasive states of being. Bollnow sees each mood as characterized by a special experience of reality, the self, and time. Flow and stress are similarly characterized by specific experiences of reality. In flow, the interviewees experience reality as easy, clear, and supportive, whereas in stress they experience reality as threatening, as a resistance, as a burden, or as chaos. Furthermore, flow and stress were characterized by specific experiences of subjective time. In flow, the interviewees experienced an amalgamation of the time of the activity and their subjectivity, or an experience of time as a "stehendes jetzt," whereas in stress, they experienced a contestation of their sense of subjective time. According to Bollnow, emotional feelings build upon specific moods in the sense that moods constitute the framework for possible emotions. States of flow and stress also appear to work as frameworks for a number of specific feelings: in the case of flow, emotions such as pleasure, joy, ecstasy, happiness, excitement, and pride; and in the case of stress, emotions such as anger, guilt, helplessness, depression, powerlessness, hopelessness, etc.

In the psychological research literature, moods are quite often categorized according to basic continuums, e.g. pleasantness–unpleasantness, aroused–calm (Ben-Ze'ev, 2000, p. 87), and continuums between calm–tense and energy–tiredness (Thayer, 1996). Phenomenological approaches also categorize moods in polarities. Bollnow (1974), for instance, suggests a polarity between uplifted and depressive moods, and Buytendijk

(1950) suggests a polarity between nourishing and draining emotional states. Flow and stress also have polar characteristics on the experiential level (Donner & Csikszentmihalyi, 1992), in the sense that flow connotes an optimal state of being whereas stress connotes strains and resistance. Several of the interviewees described spontaneously how their flow, under time pressure, was transformed into stress, and vice-versa. Objective time and subjective time are not the same, but the objective conditions of time are significant for the subjective experience of time. Flow and stress thus fluctuate, to a certain extent, along the subjective time as a common axis. Besides the above-mentioned features, the emergence and decline of flow and stress also seem to follow the dynamics of moods in everyday life.

We are always "tuned" so that our experience of a certain mood usually means that our prevalent mood has shifted. According to Isen (1984), these shifts of moods are often rather unnoticed responses to apparently minor events in everyday life. This dynamic was also found in the analysis of flow and stress in everyday life. Very often, the interviewees were unsure as to how their experience of flow and stress came about, and they were frequently not even aware of these states. Several of the interviewees said, for example, that it was often other people who told them that they seemed stressed, thus making them aware of their state of stress. The cycle of everyday life delivers conditions for the emergence and decline of flow and stress experiences. Some of the interviewees reported that work stress "spilled over" and/or was reinforced by the demands of home and family life, whereas others reported that work stress gradually dissolved at home. As a male IT-employee says: "When I come home from work after a stressful day during which I've shouted at people, I sit down in my chair and I take off my shoes and socks. Then I feel the stress sinking downwards and leaving my body through my feet."

Furthermore, moods can be generated in a cumulative fashion over the course of time. Brief notions of negative interactions might collectively produce a negative mood as time progresses (Ben-Ze'ev, 2000). Correspondingly, several of the interviewees reported that minor obstacles contesting their sense of subjective time could contribute to their development of stress: "You know public transport—they don't stick to their timetable. Then you can't catch your bus. You arrive too late at work; the program crashes, etcetera, etcetera. All these small things play a big role in how your day goes."

The phenomenological analysis of flow and stress experiences provides a qualitative understanding of the two phenomena in everyday life. However, in order to understand how these experiences are actually lived out and negotiated in the different contexts of everyday life, it is also necessary to explore the values and norms of feelings by which they are regulated in these different contexts. This was the objective in the second phase of this investigation.

 ## REGULATION OF MOODS BY EMOTIONAL CULTURES

Beginning with an introduction to Hochschild's theory of emotional culture, the following section will present the analysis of interpretation and handling of flow and stress in work, family, and leisure time.

According to Hochschild (1983, 2003), different institutions, organizations, and contexts operate with different feeling rules and expression rules, as well as varied assumptions about feelings. Feeling rules refer to what we imagine we should and should not feel; expression rules refer to how we express feelings; and assumptions about feelings refer to notions found interwoven in the narrative of, for example, proverbs, romantic fiction, self-help books, and popular magazines. Individuals work on their emotions according to these cultural guidelines. In this context, Hochschild introduces the term "emotion work" in reference to different techniques used to transform our emotions in accordance with prevailing feeling rules.

Different spheres of everyday life, such as work, family, and leisure time also have emotional cultures in terms of the vocabulary of feelings, feeling rules, expression rules, and assumptions about feelings. In the following, I will show how these emotional cultures provide frameworks for our interpretations, evaluations, and handling of flow and stress.

Flow and emotional culture at work

As already mentioned, the workplace I studied was a public service institution. The employees were involved in casework on different levels. To a certain extent their work was routine and characterized by ongoing interruptions. However, under some work conditions, for example, involvement in more comprehensive tasks or absence of interruptions, the interviewees described experiences of flow. It appeared from the interviewees' presentations that the current behavioral and emotional norms of the studied workplace were norms of attendance, social accessibility, sociability, service-mindedness, as well as norms of nondeviation in any respect from the others.

According to Ben-Ze'ev, moods, in contradiction to emotions, have no particular facial expressions—at least, none that are universal and none that have signal value (Ben-Ze'ev, 2000). However, when the interviewees experienced flow, they were absorbed in their activity and lost to the world around them, i.e., they involuntarily displayed a particular outer appearance. Flow is neither integrated in our common vocabulary of emotions nor was it part of the emotional culture of the present workplace. As flow and its outer appearances were not part of the emotional culture, this behavior was interpreted through the prevailing feeling rules. Flow was thus generally regarded as breaking the norms of attendance, sociability, and service-mindedness. This prerogative evaluation was expressed in the interviewees' descriptions of themselves in flow and in their evaluation of how others experienced them. Taking the role of the other, they described themselves with negative expressions such as "absent-minded" or "abnormal"; when it came to their interpretations of how others evaluated them, they used prerogative terms such as "nonserious," "strange" or as one of the interviewees said: "I think they regard me as a bit ridiculous." They felt obliged to excuse their behavior.

According to the interviewees' descriptions, flow at work means a certain experience of ease and well-being in the work process, but it may also mean an experience of competence and pride. Within the working culture in question, the clerical staff as well as graduate employees interpreted such experiences as an expression of superiority, which were evaluated as breaking the norms. People therefore kept such experiences to themselves. As one interviewee said: "It's my general impression that one should not, well, provoke others by saying that everything is going very well." The expressions of specific feelings of self-esteem and pride linked to flow thus collided with this specific working culture. However, the interviewees experienced both pleasure and pride in connection with their work but, when they spoke about these feelings, they simultaneously expressed discomfort in doing so by means of nonverbal markers of shame, such as pauses and hesitations, and verbal markers of shame, such as mitigations and use of the third person as the narrative form, just as they stated directly that open acknowledgements of pride were regarded as a breach of etiquette.

To summarize: On the basis of the emotional culture of this workplace, behavioral and emotional aspects of flow were regarded as breaches of the workplace's rules of feelings and expression. The interviewees interpreted outward appearances of flow as being an expression of deviation in relation to the workplace's etiquette concerning social accessibility; feelings linked to flow, such as self-esteem and pride, were regarded as an expression of a disloyal distinction in relation to colleagues. Public expression of these experiences was looked upon as boasting and self-assertion. Flow as an experience was thus indirectly and on a nonconscious level associated with embarrassment and emotion work.

Flow and emotional culture in the family

Feeling rules within the family as expressed by the interviewees were norms of attendance, solidarity, intimacy, but also of authenticity and self-determination. While the interviewees spontaneously presented flow activities as a breach of the family's rules concerning attendance and solidarity in relation to children, spouses, and practical chores, at the same time the family's feeling norms with regard to authenticity and self-determination also allowed for pleasurable activities. However, the family's feeling norms of solidarity and attendance seemed to dominate, and therefore the interviewees had to manage their pleasure/flow activities with care and ingenuity by means of agreements and maneuvering in relation to the pockets of time in family life. Several of the male interviewees also described how they could experience flow while taking on large-scale, practical, but limited tasks in the home, such as building a carport, laying a floor, tiling the bathroom, building a terrace, etc. By taking on tasks that were beneficial to the family, the person was granted undisturbed time and space. In addition, pride in the work performed was regarded as a legitimate feeling. In the interview situation, the interviewees categorized these episodes as flow experiences, but in their immediate everyday interpretation it had merely been a matter of hard work. Apart from flow experiences in tasks that would benefit the family, interviewees reported flow experiences between family members in the shape of experiences of being in wholehearted attendance, emotional proximity, and letting oneself go. These experiences took place between couples, between parents and children, and between close family members, and displayed a form of "tacit knowledge."

To summarize: On the basis of the family's feeling rules pertaining to attendance and solidarity, flow was interpreted and evaluated as an expression of egoism, antisocial behavior, and lack of solidarity. However, the family was also associated with ideas of self-determination and authenticity. The interviewees presented these two groups of feeling norms as contrasts, and it was this contrast that was handled in a private and individualized management of flow. In addition, at times these feeling norms also provided a scope for flow between family members.

Flow in leisure time

Leisure time is a difficult sphere to delimit and in this study, leisure activities were limited to organized activities characterized by people assembled at a specific time and place around a chosen activity, such as playing football, rehearsing music in an orchestra, participating in art classes, etc.

Organized leisure activities permit devotion to and absorption in a given activity, and correspondingly the interviewees seldomly expressed any sense of collision between flow and the feeling norms of the organized leisure activities. This did not mean that flow was a discursive concept within the emotional culture, but rather that flow was tacitly recognized as an experience and was either described by use of expressions such as "uplifted," "levitating", or "feeling like a joint orgasm," or merely presented as legitimate "tacit knowledge" between the persons involved. As one interviewee said, during a description of flow in connection with the orchestra he plays in: "We don't go into much detail about whether this is flow, we just say: 'Cool, it really worked today.' We don't have to say very much to each other to experience that it's cool."

Besides these feelings, flow (in sports) is also associated with achievements that give rise to self-esteem and pride; for example, completing a run, performing a beautiful jump, etc. According to the interviewees, this feeling was openly expressed through cheering, shouting, or making victory signs, even though some indicated that these feelings should be expressed with a certain amount of restraint. The analysis showed, moreover, that the legitimacy of these experiences was limited to the social space of the activity being undertaken. It would not be acceptable to tell colleagues at work about flow experiences in connection with, for instance, yoga or parachuting. As one interviewee said: "They would think I was daft." Thus, in spite of the fact that flow existed under cover of other terms, the analysis of the organized leisure activities shows that the feeling rules of this sphere of everyday life have scope for flow. However, the feeling rules of leisure activities are not to be transferred to other contexts. This is shown in the following narrative, in which a female interviewee talks about how she became excited and focused during a table tennis match at a garden party:

> The game just flowed, I felt good, I became highly focused, I was really involved, but then my partner said: "Hello, relax, it's just fun." And she was right. At a garden party you are relaxed, easygoing, and you chat while you're playing. So I tried to discipline my excitement and commitment—but it was difficult.

The interviewee experienced flow in a sports game. This experience is permitted in the context of sport. However, in the context of a garden party she was rebuked.

To summarize: Within the framework of the feeling rules and expression rules in leisure activities, flow experiences were tacitly recognized and accepted as legitimate and valuable experiences. Flow was not part of the emotional vocabulary in the emotional culture of leisure time, but emotional culture seemed able to contain the experiences of flow and its manifestations.

Stress and emotional culture at work

Stress, unlike flow, is a well-known term, and therefore we have a common notion of stress which forms part of our interpretation of our own stress and that of others. According to Newton, Handy, and Fineman (1995), the popular scientific and academic perception of stress is characterized by:

Individualizing, i.e. stress is seen as conditioned on the individual's experience and manner of relation to his or her experience, for which reason it is up to the individual to handle her/his stress.

Naturalizing, i.e. the stress reaction is seen as an inappropriately phylogenetically conditioned physiological mode and reaction.

Normalizing, i.e. stress is understood as a normal and inevitable side of modern life.

Pathologizing, i.e. stress is related to physical and mental health and should therefore be handled with a view to avoiding illness (Newton et al., 1995, pp. 4–5).

Some of these principles were interwoven in the interviewees' interpretations of their own stress and that of others. However, at the same time, the interviewees' interpretations were also influenced by the prevailing feeling rules within work and family.

In the analysis of the interpretation of stress, a number of different interpretive perspectives on stress in work and in the family were identified. As any given interviewee could switch between different perspectives in his or her interpretations of stress, however, these particular interpretive perspectives were not linked to individuals.

Stress at work was a familiar experience to the interviewees at the present workplace. These experiences were mostly related to time constraints, unforeseen tasks, interruptions, new work demands, and work overload. On the basis of the interviewees' descriptions and evaluations of their own stress and that of others, I have identified three different interpretive perspectives of stress at work in close connection to Newton's framework: stigmatizing, normalizing, and critical interpretation.

The *stigmatizing interpretation* meant that stress at work was perceived as a sign of a personal problem involving both family and worklife. The interviewees presented the stressed person as a discursive figure with features such as slowness, inefficiency, anxiety, confusion, and helplessness, and as displaying nervous movements and a lack of overview and orientation skills. These traits were presented as being incompatible with the feeling rules of the job in relation to friendliness, courtesy, seriousness, and service-mindedness. Such characteristics also function as a stigma, in the sense that persons who exhibited some of them were interpreted by their colleagues as being generally emotionally disturbed, and thus not a viable employee in the long run. It could be imagined that the stigmatizing interpretation was a contributory factor in many of the interviewees' concealment of the stress they experienced. As one interviewee said: "It's probably more the pressure of work as such [that we talk about], but stress isn't mentioned. It's as if, I don't really know, people are ashamed. I think it's something people repress. They don't want to talk about it. Perhaps they're a bit ashamed of having a bad time with stress." For this reason, stress had to be concealed and handled by means of various types of emotion work.

The *normalizing interpretation* found expression in an assumption of stress under control as a normal state and in the assumption that a certain amount of stress was a sign of being active and productive at work. The normalizing interpretation was expressed through the interviewees' descriptions of how others or they themselves rejected, ridiculed, or made light of their own or others' complaints about stress by using remarks such as "But I'm stressed too" or "Oh do stop moaning—just because you've got a bit of work to do" or "Pull yourself together." By means of these remarks, stress is categorized as a normal feeling on the basis of the maxim "you shouldn't think you're having a worse time than anyone else." On the other hand, those who did not participate in confirming the maxim "we're all stressed" felt that they were regarded as deviants and were looked upon with suspicion. As one of the interviewees said a little ironically: "It [saying that you are busy] is a guarantee of quality."

While stress in the normalizing and stigmatizing interpretation was localized inside the individual, in the *critical interpretation* stress is seen as being caused externally, e.g., by the workplace, by superiors, the personnel policy, or the working conditions. Seen from this perspective, stress was interpreted as a legitimate feeling and one that could be explained. The critical interpretation was expressed in the interviewees' reflections about certain periods of stress, and in their descriptions of collective emotion work, i.e. situations in which the employees together complained about stressful working conditions and could thus give vent to their feelings.

The above-mentioned three interpretations draw on both Newton's interpretive principles and the feeling rules and values of the workplace. The stigmatizing principle can be interpreted as a radicalized version of the individualizing principle. The individual is responsible for her/his stress.

However, because stressed behavior is highly nonfunctional in a service institution, the stressed person becomes stigmatized as an unreliable employee. Similarly, the normalizing interpretation corresponds to Newton's equivalent principle, but it is also highly functional in the workplace as a means to get the employees to accept their conditions of work. The third interpretation, the "critical" perspective, goes beyond Newton's interpretive principles. This interpretation would seem to be rooted in employees' ideological stances at their place of work. At the workplace that was studied, however, the stigmatizing and normalizing interpretations were dominant. These two principles mutually justified one another, in the sense that contesting the normalizing principle was punished by stigmatization and, on the other hand, stigmatization was justified through normalization. Persons who could not control their stress in a normal way must be "abnormal," i.e. deviant. Taken together, these two interpretations created the basis for sustained emotion work, i.e. for working on feelings with a view to adapting these to the current feeling rules.

To summarize: In the present study, three interpretive perspectives on stress experiences were identified. These perspectives were based both on common interpretive principles (cf. Newton et al., 1995) and on the emotional culture of the workplace; they gave rise to an interpretation of stress as an individual problem that the individual has to conceal. Such interpretations necessitate recurrent emotion work.

Stress and emotional culture in the family

Stress in family life was related to overloads of demands from the family, to certain periods of time with too many household chores. On the basis of the interviewees' descriptions and evaluations, it was possible to distinguish between three interpretations of stress in the family: individualizing, normalizing, and what I have called a "backstage" interpretation.

In the *normalizing interpretation*, the above-mentioned forms of stress were interpreted as an inevitable and normal aspect of the modern family and everyday life, which was expressed in statements such as: "That's just the way it is and there's not much you can do about it," "It's difficult to avoid, but it's a pest," "Yes, and then you think that a time will come when they [the children] are of an age where they can look after themselves, and then perhaps you'll get some time to yourself," or "There's not much you can do about it—there are only so many hours in a day."

In contrast, the *individualizing interpretation* regarded stress as a feeling that was not permitted in the family and as a sign of individual inadequacy. Stress was perceived as a breach of the family's feeling norms pertaining to attendance, security, and intimacy, with the stressed person as a self-reproached sinner. The interviewees criticized themselves for being bad at planning, for not prioritizing properly, e.g., doing housework rather than having time for the children, and for taking stress from the workplace back home to the family. The individualizing interpretation opened up spirals of feelings such as stress-shame-guilt-stress etc. (cf. Lewis, 1971; Scheff, 1994). They are indicated, for example, in the following statement made by a female interviewee: "The family at home also expects something of me, and there are some days when you simply can't stretch to it all, and you get very stressed because you'd really like to be able to satisfy the family too. And that's not always possible." The individualizing interpretation of stress created a basis for a number of different techniques aimed at minimizing stress in the family; for example, cognitive techniques to evaluate and distinguish between important and less important activities. As one interviewee said: "Yes, but practical things are not all; if you can't manage to get the laundry done today, then you can do it tomorrow. I've started working on that." And as expressed by another interviewee: "I recognize the prelude to stress, and so then at least I can ease up on some of it [tasks she is in the process of performing] and then concentrate on the rest." Moreover, some interviewees emphasized behavioral stress reduction techniques, such as saying no to assignments at work that would involve overtime and thus create the preconditions for stress in family life.

The term "*backstage interpretation*" draws on Goffman's (1990) work. The "backstage" is defined in relation to the "front stage," in which we control the presentation of self in contradistinction to the "backstage," in which we may relax and suspend our controlled presentation of self. The starting point for this interpretation was a perception of the family as a free space, i.e. a space for self-determination and for being oneself, a space for one's own feelings. On the basis of this interpretation, it was regarded as legitimate to vent one's stress within the family framework. As one interviewee said: "I probably demand more from people who know me better and know why I react like I do."

The above-mentioned three interpretation perspectives draw on the common principles as described by Newton and also on the family's values and feeling norms. On the basis of the feeling norms of the family pertaining to attendance, security, and intimacy, stress in the individualized interpretation was perceived as a forbidden feeling and as an expression of personal inadequacy in relation to the needs of the family. In extension of this interpretation, the interviewees described various techniques for limiting their stress within the family. On the basis of the normalizing interpretation, stress was seen as an inevitable but not desirable feeling in family life. In itself, this perception can be interpreted as a cognitive defense against the individualized interpretation of stress. Finally, the family's feeling norms pertaining to authenticity opened the way for the "backstage" interpretation, in terms of which it was permitted to show one's stress within the family.

These interpretations interacted in the interviewees' presentations. Some of the interviewees said that they allowed their stress to emerge in the family, i.e. they followed the "backstage" interpretation, but simultaneously their statements could be full of nonverbal signs of shame, indicating that the individualizing interpretation was also active. Correspondingly, some were able to emphasize the normalizing interpretation while, at the same time, expressing guilt and discomfort concerning their stress.

To summarize: In the present study, three interpretive perspectives on stress in family life were identified. The individualizing and the normalizing perspectives form part of the common principles of interpretations of stress as described by Newton and colleagues (1995), but the individualizing and the backstage principles are also rooted in the feeling rules of family life. Stressed behavior contests the value and feeling rules of the family, thus stress experiences are interpreted as signs of individual inadequacy or as an inevitable aspect of normal family life. These interpretations also necessitate recurrent emotion work.

Summary of the phenomenological and the cultural analyses

Flow is an optimal experience for the self. In flow, we forget ourselves, are in the time of the activity or in a "stehendes jetzt," and we are united with the world in an active, harmonious, and giving relationship. Flow thus signals an optimal relationship between our world and us. In contrast to this, stress is a condition in which the world appears to be a resistance, a lack of clarity, and chaos; a state in which our sense of subjective time momentarily breaks down. Stress thus signals a destructive and burdened relationship between the world and us. The cultural analysis of flow and stress showed how the two phenomena were tagged by different emotional cultures within the institutions of everyday life. In the present working and family culture, the spontaneous externalization of flow was culturally split up into separate aspects which, on the basis of the dominant norms of feeling and expression, were evaluated as breaches of the current norms in work and family life. By means of this, on the nonconscious level, flow became a cause of embarrassment. This does not mean that the interviewees did not experience flow at work; they did experience flow but, to the extent that this was interpreted as a breach of the current feeling norms, flow as experience was overshadowed by demands for emotion work with a view to adapting flow to the dominant feeling norms. In the family, however, flow could be supported by means of undertaking measures that benefit the family's needs and values. In contrast to the dominant interpretations of flow at work and in the family, the analysis showed that the sphere of leisure time had feeling norms that could allow flow as "tacit knowledge."

As regards stress, the analysis showed that at the workplace interviewees were caught in interplay between stigmatization and normalization, which implies that receptivity to one's own experiences of stress is punished by stigmatization. Instead, stress is interpreted as normal and as something one must deal with on an ongoing basis. In family life, stress is interpreted as normal, but also as something that is an individual and personal problem to be dealt with. The analysis also showed how these cultural interpretations necessitate recurrent emotion work in order to conceal and to reduce stress.

▇ CONCLUSION AND DISCUSSION

The present chapter has aimed to throw light on the relationship between moods and emotional cultures. Based on a study of flow and stress, I have illustrated how these two phenomena are regulated by different emotional cultures. Emotional cultures may support, disturb, ignore, or displace the bodily meanings of flow and stress experiences. Emotional cultures not only regulate emotions, they also regulate moods. Thus, I would suggest that emotional cultures may be viewed as interpretive filters to our interpretations and handling of our moods. The main objective has been to illustrate the dynamic relationship between moods and emotional cultures; thus the results of the present study are not to be substantially generalized. Different workplaces, for instance, may have different emotional cultures, including cultures that allow flow at work.

In psychological research, moods are regarded as subjective states which inform individuals about the current states of affairs (Schwarz & Bless, 1991; Schwarz & Clore, 2003). It is assumed that positive moods tell us that the world is safe and that personal goals are not threatened. Furthermore, negative moods are supposed to signal that something is wrong, problematic, or unsafe (Västfjäll, Gaerling, & Kleiner, 2001). When the current mood is negative, i.e. unwanted or inadequate, the individual will be motivated to change or do something about the mood or the situation. When it is positive, i.e. welcome, this signals that the individual is doing well and does not need to direct attention to the situation (Västfjäll et al., 2001). The individual thus generally aims at maintaining positive emotional states and eliminating negative emotional states (Ben-Ze'ev, 2000). The present chapter illustrates, however, that we do not only maintain positive moods and eliminate negative moods; our regulation of moods is also conditioned by the interpretive filter yielded by different emotional cultures.

Moods arise from our immediate inner relationship to our life space, thus we can not freely choose our moods. In so far as those emotional cultures ignore, disturb, or displace our moods as a bodily experienced inner relationship to our life space, recurrent emotional frictions arise. These emotional frictions necessitate emotion work. Emotion work may help us to reduce the intensity of a given emotional experience; however, it is less effective in preventing the occurrence of a given mood. There is nothing wrong with emotion work to the extent that we are able to find a place for, and integrate our feelings in, a personal and culturally fertile way. Emotion work, however, is not necessarily without cost (cf. Greenberg & Vandekerckhove, this volume; Peper & Vauth, this volume). According to Hochschild (1983), continued emotion work can short-circuit the signals about people and places given by feelings. In addition, Freund operates with the concept of "dramaturgical stress" and "false emotional consciousness." Dramaturgical stress is the stress created by handling and processing one's own feelings with a view to playing the role demanded (Freund, 1998, p. 267). Freund also points out, like Hochschild, that continued regulation of our feelings can lead to us losing our original embodied feeling signals, i.e. we develop "a false emotional consciousness" (Freund, 1990, pp. 466–468).

Moods have hitherto been given rather limited attention in the mainstream of social science. In the present chapter, I argue that moods are important to our understanding of human social life and that moods are influenced and regulated by emotional cultures. Emotional cultures, however, are not static social constructions. Emotional culture is to be viewed as a field of tensions between dominant cultures and subordinate cultures and discourses that contest the dominant culture. Continuous frictions between moods and their interpretations call both for reflections on the conditions that give rise to particular moods and for reflections on the interpretations delivered by the prevailing emotional culture. In so far as frictions between moods and emotional culture imply recurrent emotion work, these frictions call for negations of emotional culture. The relationship between moods and emotional culture still remains an unexplored issue. I expect that future research regarding the contextual frame of moods in diverse institutional settings will contribute to new dimensions in our understanding of social life.

REFERENCES

Allison, M. T., & Duncan, M. C. (1988). Women, work and flow. In M. Csikszent-mihalyi & I. S. Csikszentmihalyi (Eds.), *Optimal experience: Psychological studies of flow in consciousness* (pp. 118–138). New York: Cambridge University Press.

Ben-Ze'ev, A. (2000). *The subtlety of emotions.* Cambridge, MA: MIT Press.

Bloch, C. (1996). Emotions and discourse. *Text, 16,* 323–341.

Bloch, C. (2001). *Flow og Stress.* Copenhagen: Samfundslitteratur.

Bloch, C. (2002). Moods and quality of life. *Journal of Happiness Studies, 3,* 101–128.

Bollnow, O. F. (1974). *Das Wesen der Stimmungen.* Frankfurt: Klostermann.

Buytendijk, F. J. (1950). The phenomenological approach to the problem of feelings and emotions. In M. C. Reymert (Ed.), *Feelings and emotions: The Mooseheart Symposium* (pp. 127–142). New York: McGraw-Hill.

Cannon, W. B. (1935). Stresses and strains of homeostasis. *American Journal of Medical Sciences, 189,* 1–14.

Carli, M., Fave, A. D., & Massimini, F. (1988). The quality of experience in the flow channels: Comparison of Italian and U. S. students. In M. Csikszentmihalyi & I. S. Csikszentmihalyi (Eds.), *Optimal experience: Psychological studies of flow in consciousness* (pp. 228–307). New York: Cambridge University Press.

Csikszentmihalyi, M. (1975). *Beyond boredom and anxiety.* San Francisco, CA: Jossey-Bass.

Csikszentmihalyi, M. (1990). *Flow: The psychology of optimal experience.* New York: Harper & Row.

Csikszentmihalyi, M., & Csikszentmihalyi, I. S. (Eds.) (1988). *Optimal experience: Psychological studies of flow in consciousness.* New York: Cambridge University Press.

Donner, E. J., & Csikszentmihalyi, M. (1992). Transforming stress to flow. *Executive Excellence, 9,* 16–17.

Eckartsberg, R. von (1986). *Life-world experience: Existential-phenomenological research approaches in psychology.* Lanham, MD: University Press of America.

Eckenrode, J., & Gore, S. (Eds.) (1990). *Stress between work and family.* New York: Plenum Press.

Freund, P. E. (1990). The expressive body: A common ground for the sociology of emotions and health and illness. *Sociology of Health & Illness, 12,* 452–477.

Freund, P. E. (1998). Social performances and their discontents: The biopsychosocial aspects of dramaturgical stress. In G. Bendelow & S. J. Williams (Eds.), *Emotions in social life* (pp. 268–295). London: Routledge.

Giorgi, A., Fischer, C. T., & Murray, E. L. (Eds.) (1975). *Duquesne studies in phenomenological psychology* (Vol. 1). Pittsburgh, PA: Duquesne University Press.

Goffman, E. (1990/1959). *The presentation of self in everyday life.* New York: Doubleday.

Heidegger, M. (1927). *Sein und Zeit* (Jahrbuch für Philosophie und phänomenologische Forschung, Bd. VIII). Halle: Niemeyer.

Hochschild, A. R. (1983). *The managed heart.* Berkeley, CA: University of California Press.

Hochschild, A. R. (2003). *The commercialization of intimate life. Notes from home and work*. Berkeley, CA: University of California Press.

Isen, A. M. (1984). Toward understanding the role of affect in cognition. In R. S. Wyer & T. K. Srull (Eds.), *Handbook of social cognition* (Vol. 3, pp. 179–236). Hillsdale, NJ: Erlbaum.

Karasek, R. A., Gardell, B., & Lindell, J. (1987). Work and non-work correlates of illness and behavior in male and female Swedish white collar workers. *Journal of Occupational Behavior, 8*, 187–207.

Lazarus, R. S. (1991). *Emotion and adaptation*. New York: Oxford University Press.

Lazarus, R. S. (1999). *Stress and emotion: A new synthesis*. New York: Springer.

Lazarus, R. S., & Folkman, S. (1984). *Stress, appraisal, and coping*. New York: Springer.

Lewis, H. B. (1971). *Shame and guilt in neurosis*. New York: International University Press.

Lovallo, W. R. (1997). *Stress and health: Biological and psychological interactions*. Thousand Oaks, CA: Sage.

Merleau-Ponty, M. (1962/1945). *Phenomenology of perception* (C. Smith, Transl.). London: Routledge.

Mitchell, R. C. (1983). *Mountain experience: The psychology and sociology of adventure*. Chicago: University of Chicago Press.

Netterstrøm, B. (1997). *Klar besked om stress*. Copenhagen: Aschehoug.

Newton, T., Handy, J., & Fineman, S. (1995). *Managing stress: Emotion and power at work*. London: Sage.

Retzinger, S. M. (1991). *Violent emotions: Shame and rage in marital quarrels*. Newbury Park, CA: Sage.

Scheff, T. J. (1990). *Microsociology: Discourse, emotion and social structure*. Chicago: University of Chicago Press.

Scheff, T. J. (1994). *Bloody revenge: Emotions, nationalism, and war*. Boulder, CO: Westview Press.

Schwarz, N., & Bless, H. (1991). Happy and mindless, but sad and smart? The impact of affective states on analytic reasoning. In J. P. Forgas (Ed.), *Emotion and social judgements* (pp. 55–71). Oxford: Pergamon Press.

Schwarz, N., & Clore, G. L. (2003). Mood as information: 20 years later. *Psychological Inquiry, 14*, 296–303.

Selye, H. (1956). *The stress of life*. New York: McGraw-Hill.

Thayer, R. E. (1996). *The origin of everyday moods: Managing energy, tension, and stress*. New York: Oxford University Press.

Thoits, P. A. (1990). Emotional deviance: Research agendas. In T. D. Kemper (Ed.), *Research agendas in the sociology of emotions* (pp. 180–203). Albany, NY: State University of New York Press.

Västfjäll, D., Gaerling, T., & Kleiner, M. (2001). Does it make you happy feeling this way? A core affect account of preference for current mood. *Journal of Happiness Studies, 2*, 337–354.

Vittersø, J. (2003). Flow versus life satisfaction: A projective use of cartoons to illustrate the difference between the evaluation approach and the intrinsic motivation approach to subjective quality of life. *Journal of Happiness Studies, 4*, 141–167.

INDEX